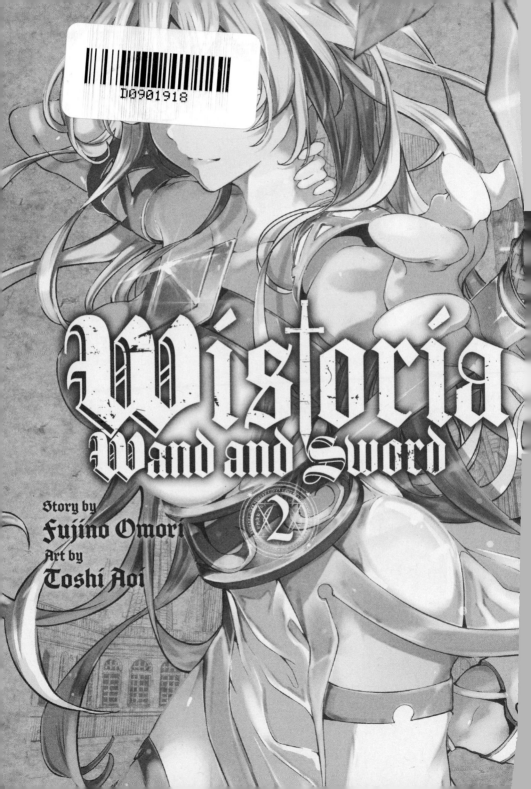

Wistoria
Wand and Sword

2

Story by
Fujino Omori

Art by
Toshi Aoi

Fujino Omori Toshi Aoi

Wistoria Wand and Sword 2

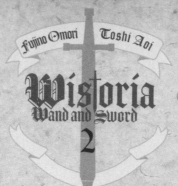

contents

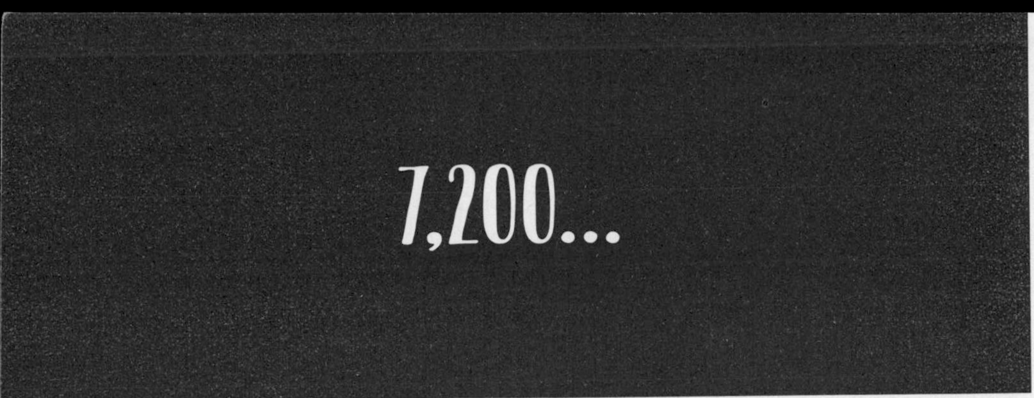
7,200...

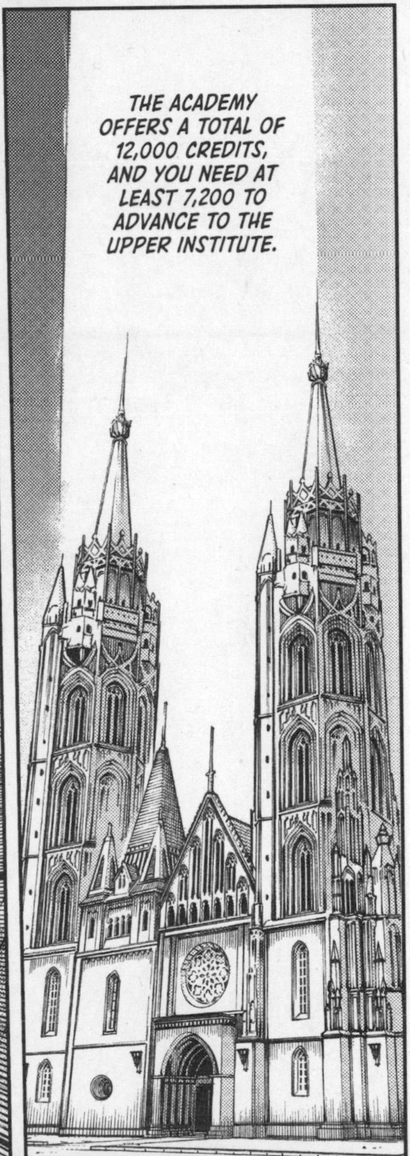
THE ACADEMY OFFERS A TOTAL OF 12,000 CREDITS, AND YOU NEED AT LEAST 7,200 TO ADVANCE TO THE UPPER INSTITUTE.

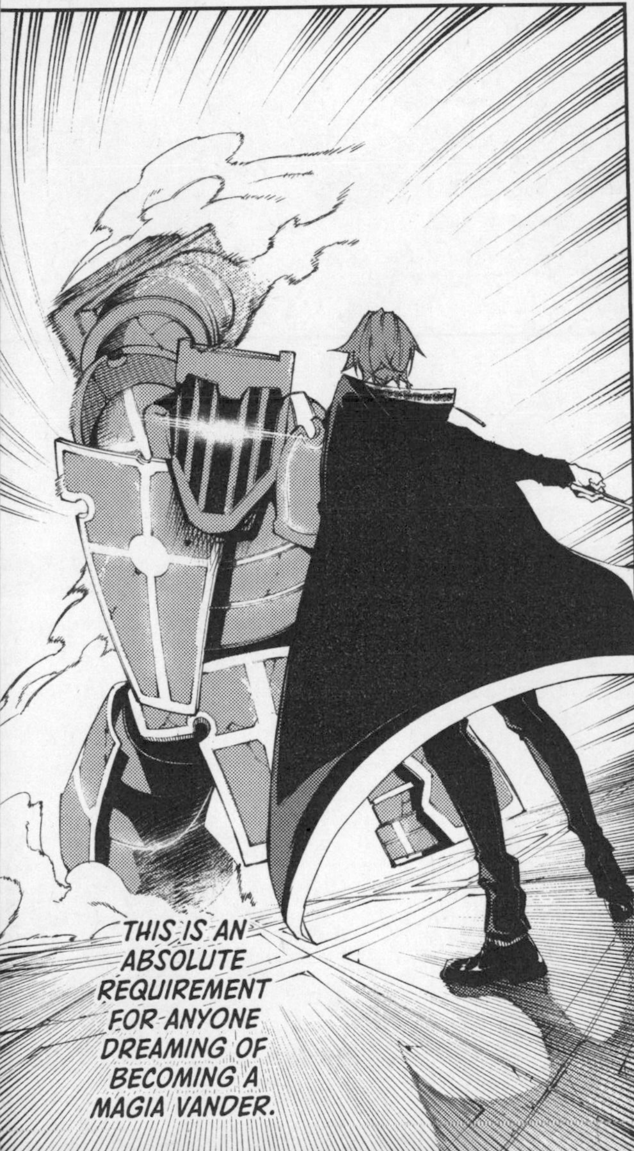
THIS IS AN ABSOLUTE REQUIREMENT FOR ANYONE DREAMING OF BECOMING A MAGIA VANDER.

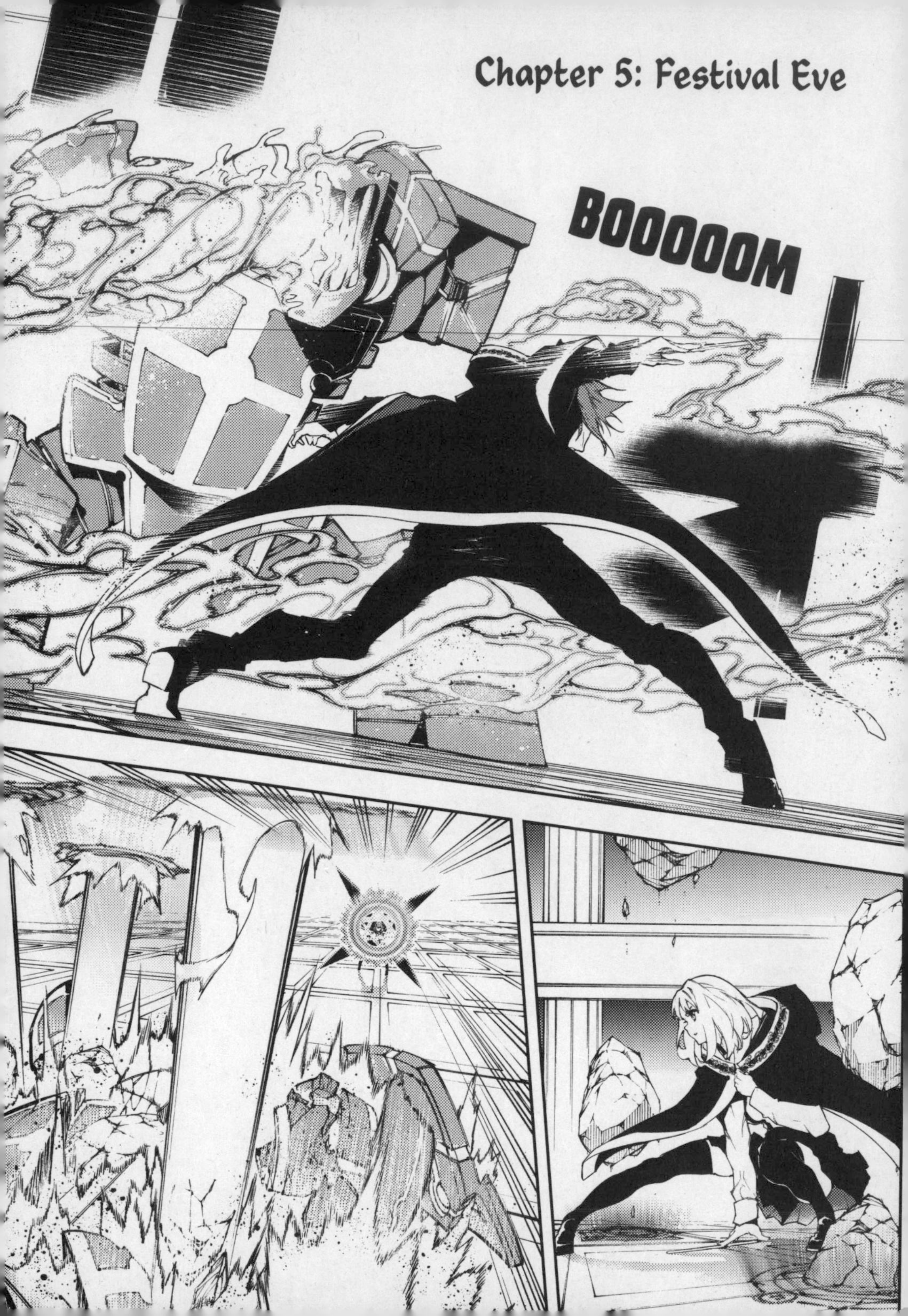
Chapter 5: Festival Eve
BOOOOOM

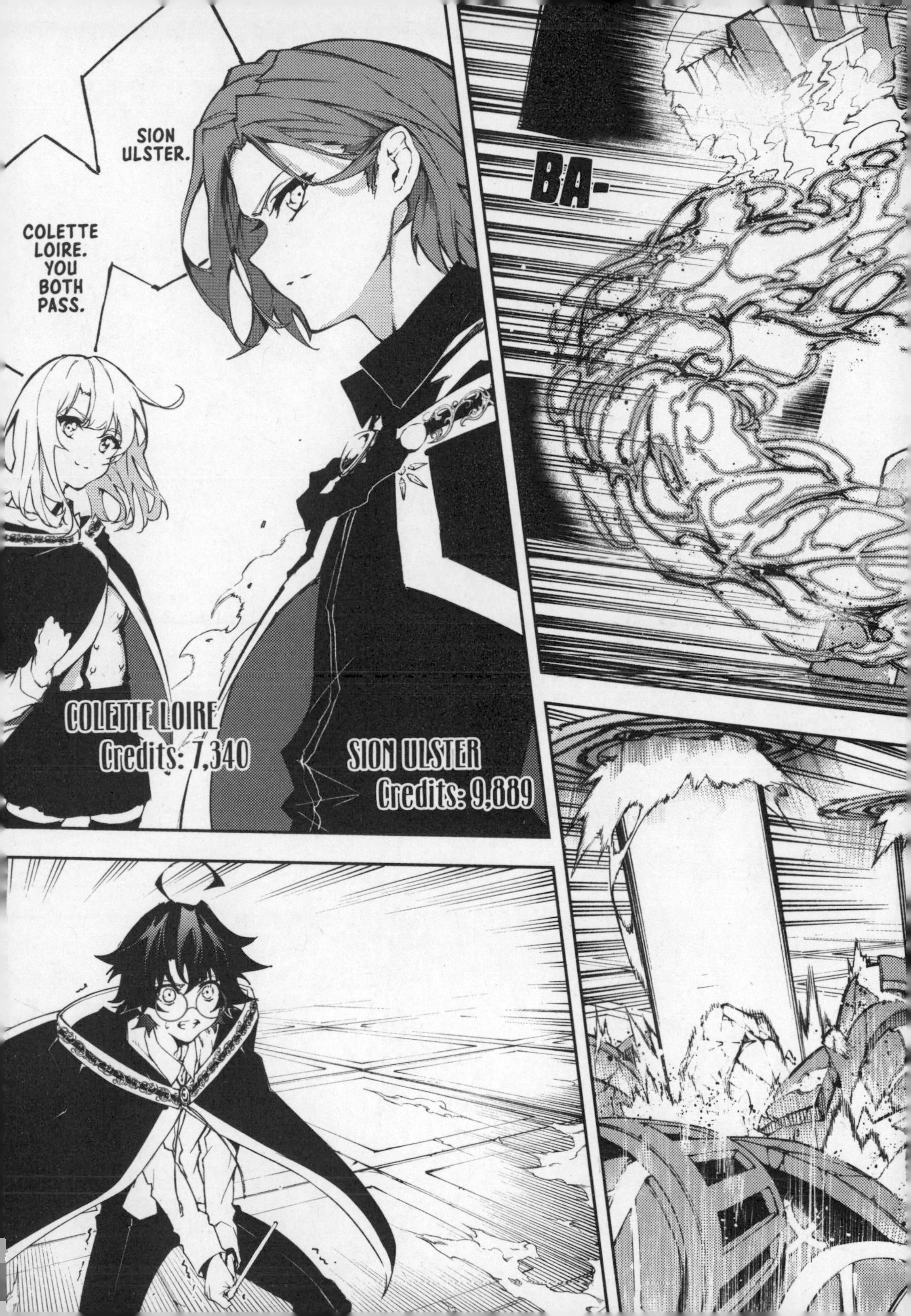
BA-
SION ULSTER.
COLETTE LOIRE. YOU BOTH PASS.
SION ULSTER
Credits: 9,889
COLETTE LOIRE
Credits: 7,340

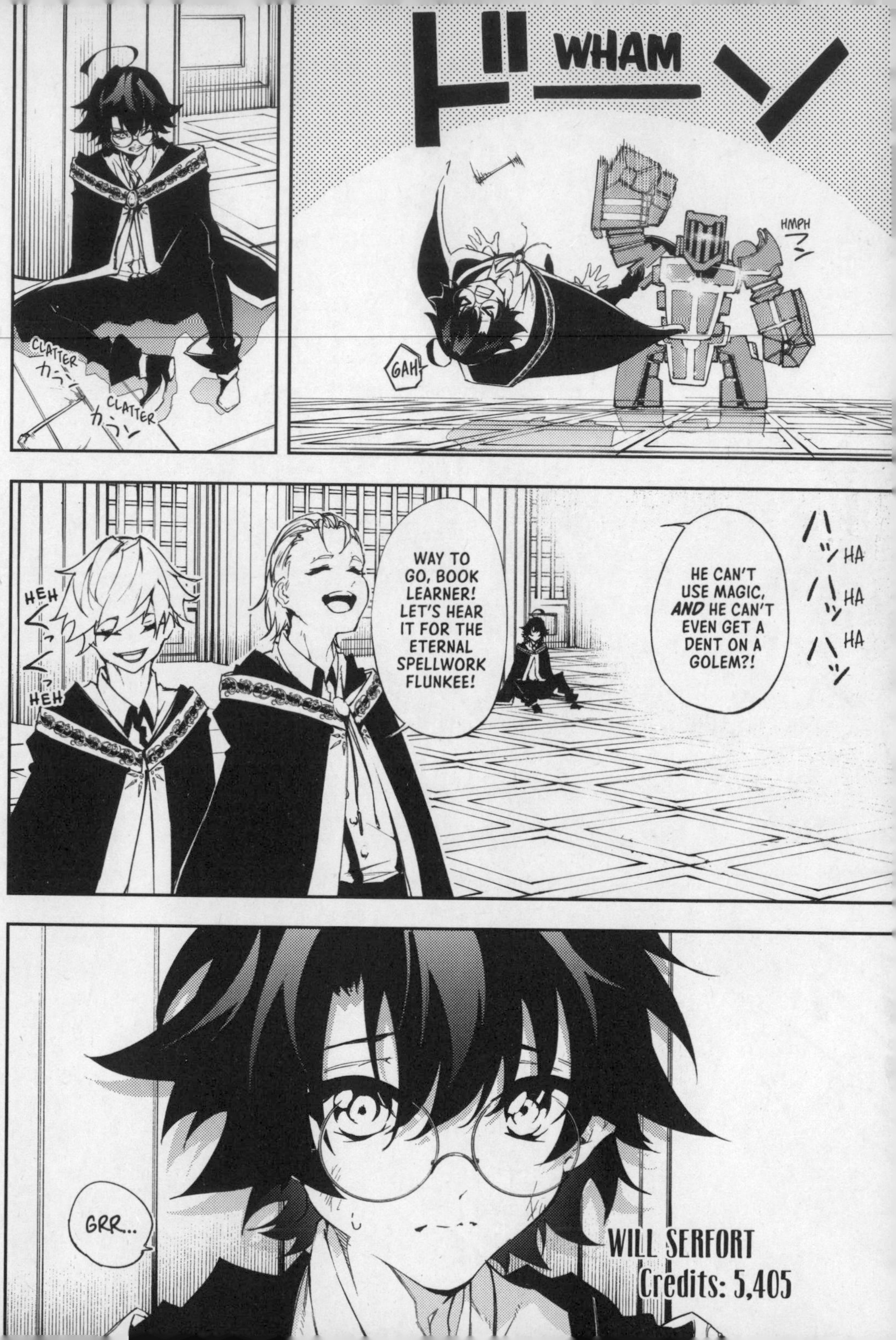
トーン WHAM
HMPH フン
GAH
CLATTER カラン
CLATTER カラン
ハッ HA ハッ HA ハッ HA
HE CAN'T USE MAGIC, ***AND*** HE CAN'T EVEN GET A DENT ON A GOLEM?!
WAY TO GO, BOOK LEARNER! LET'S HEAR IT FOR THE ETERNAL SPELLWORK FLUNKEE!
HEH くっ HEH くっ
WILL SERFORT
Credits: 5,405
GRR...

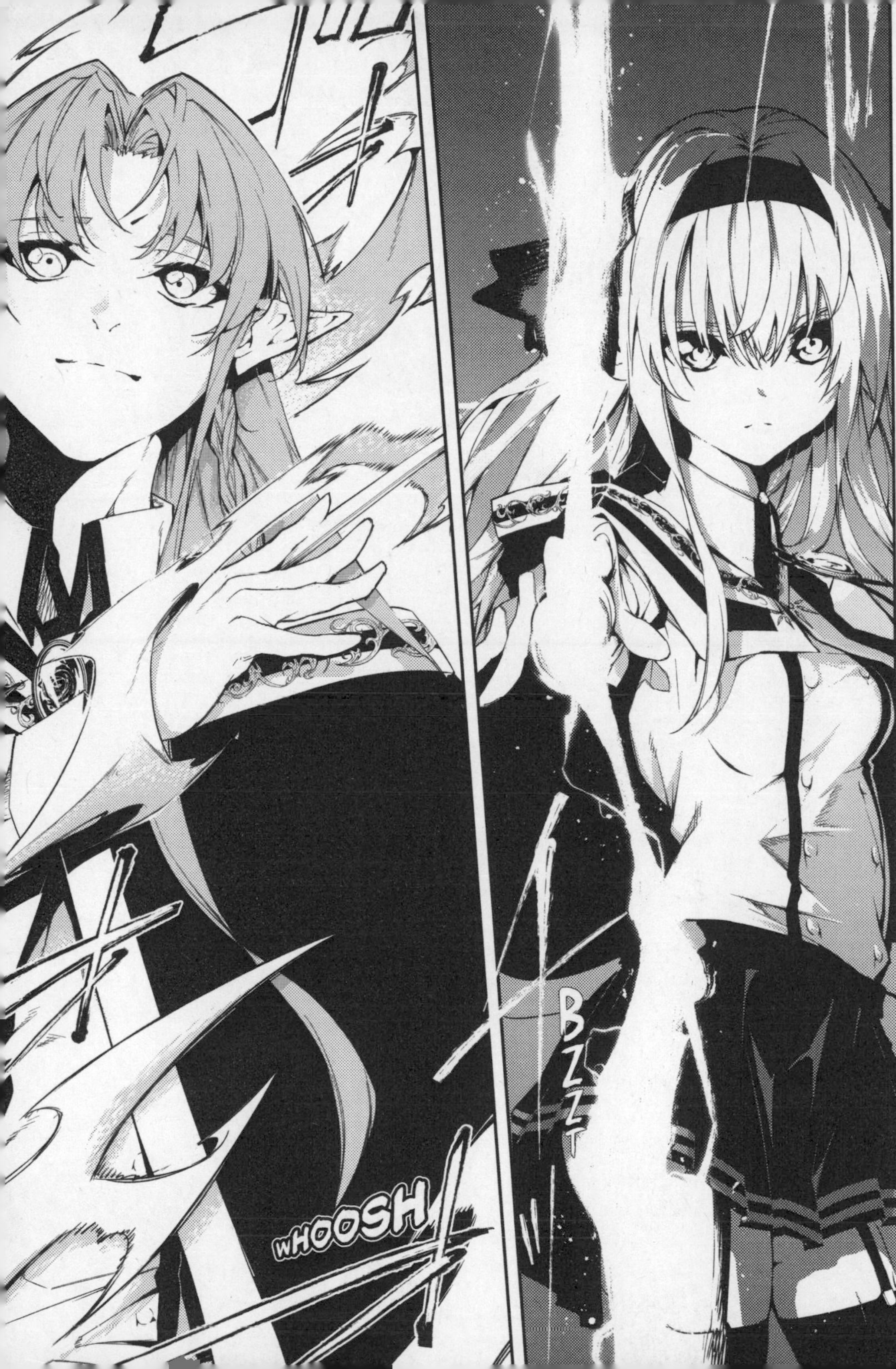
BZZT
WHOOSH

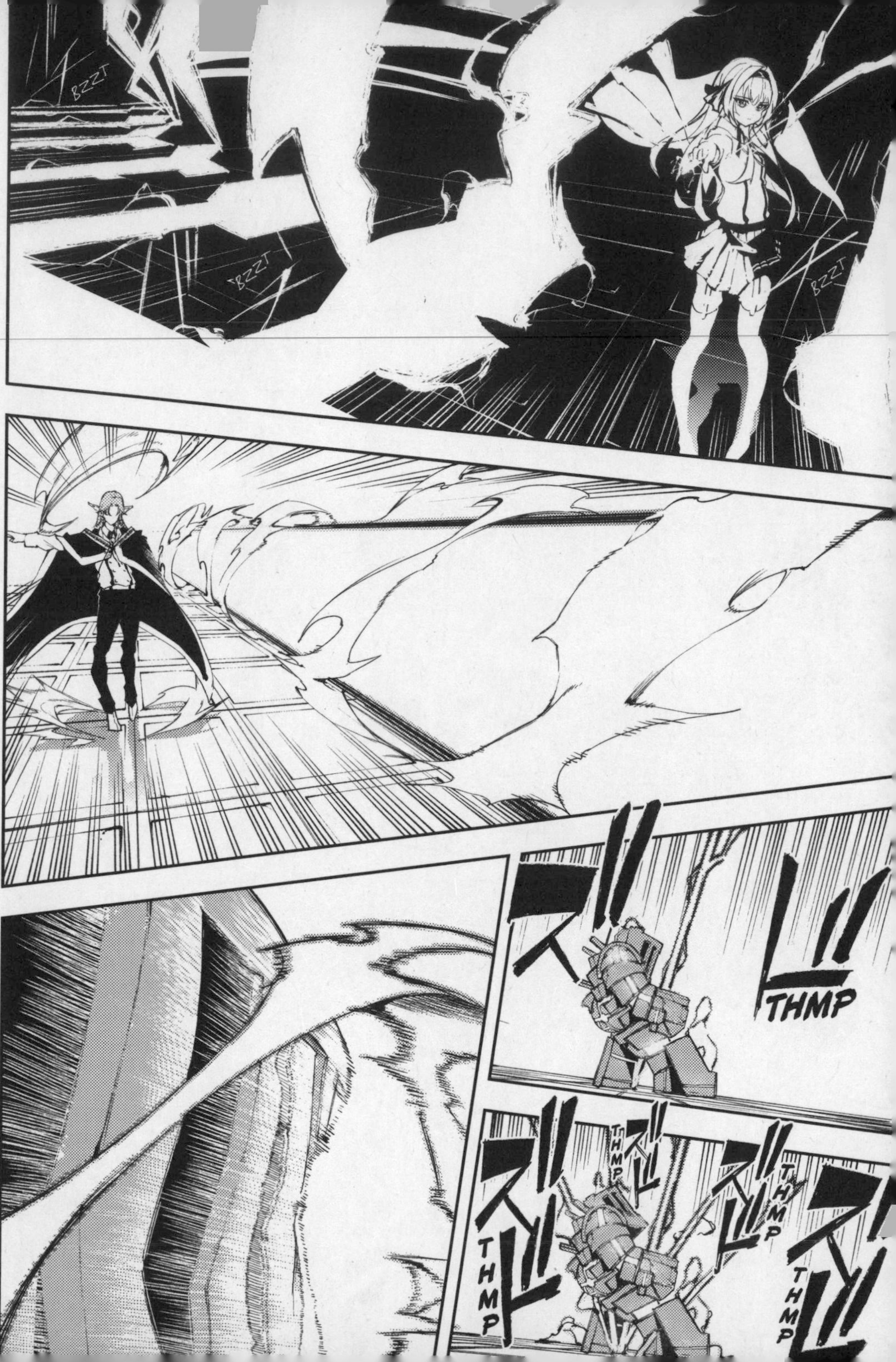
BZZT
BZZT
BZZT
THMP
THMP
THMP
THMP
THMP

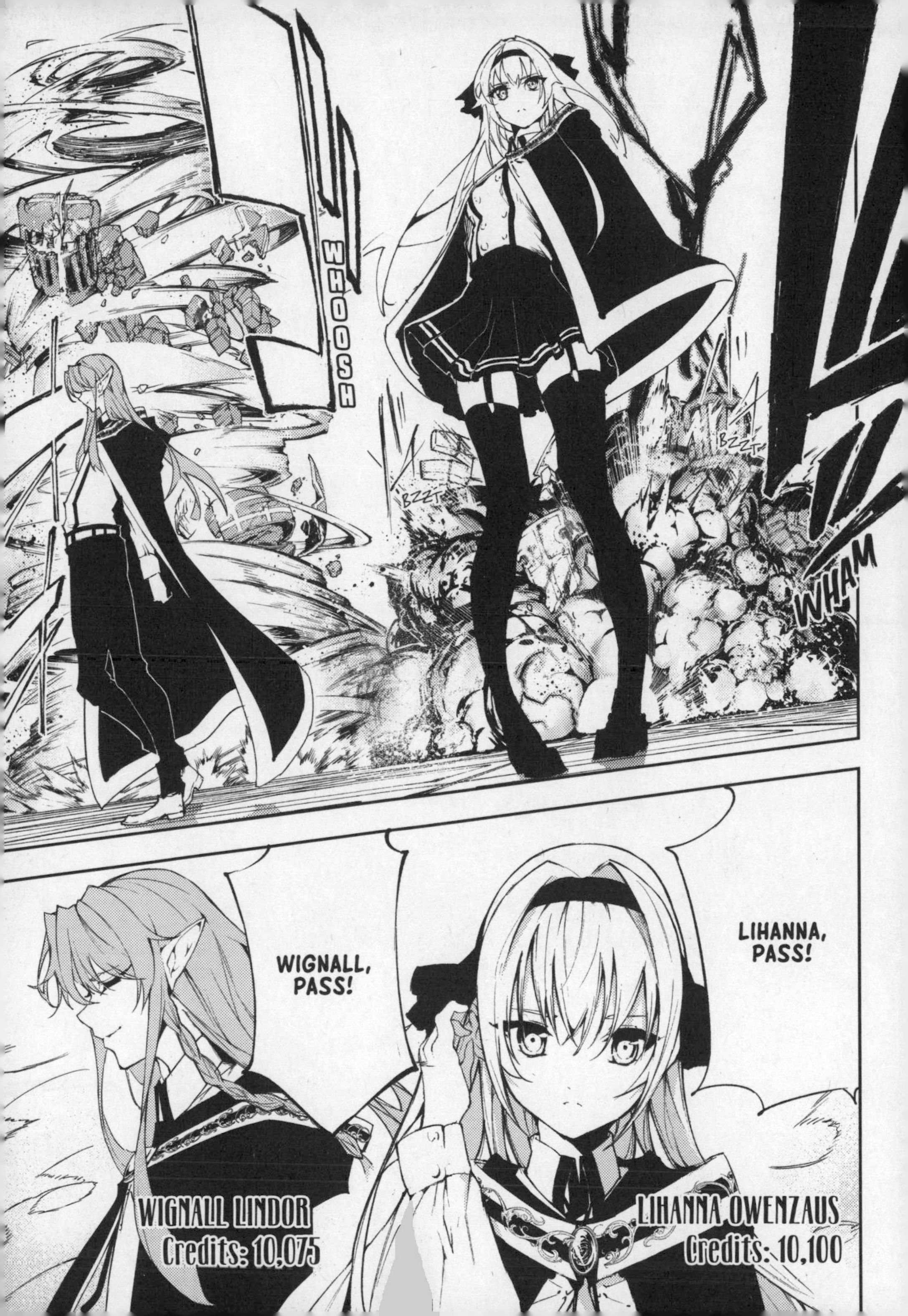
WHOOSH
BZZT
WHAM
BZZT
LIHANNA, PASS!
WIGNALL, PASS!
LIHANNA OWENZAUS
Credits: 10,100
WIGNALL LINDOR
Credits: 10,075

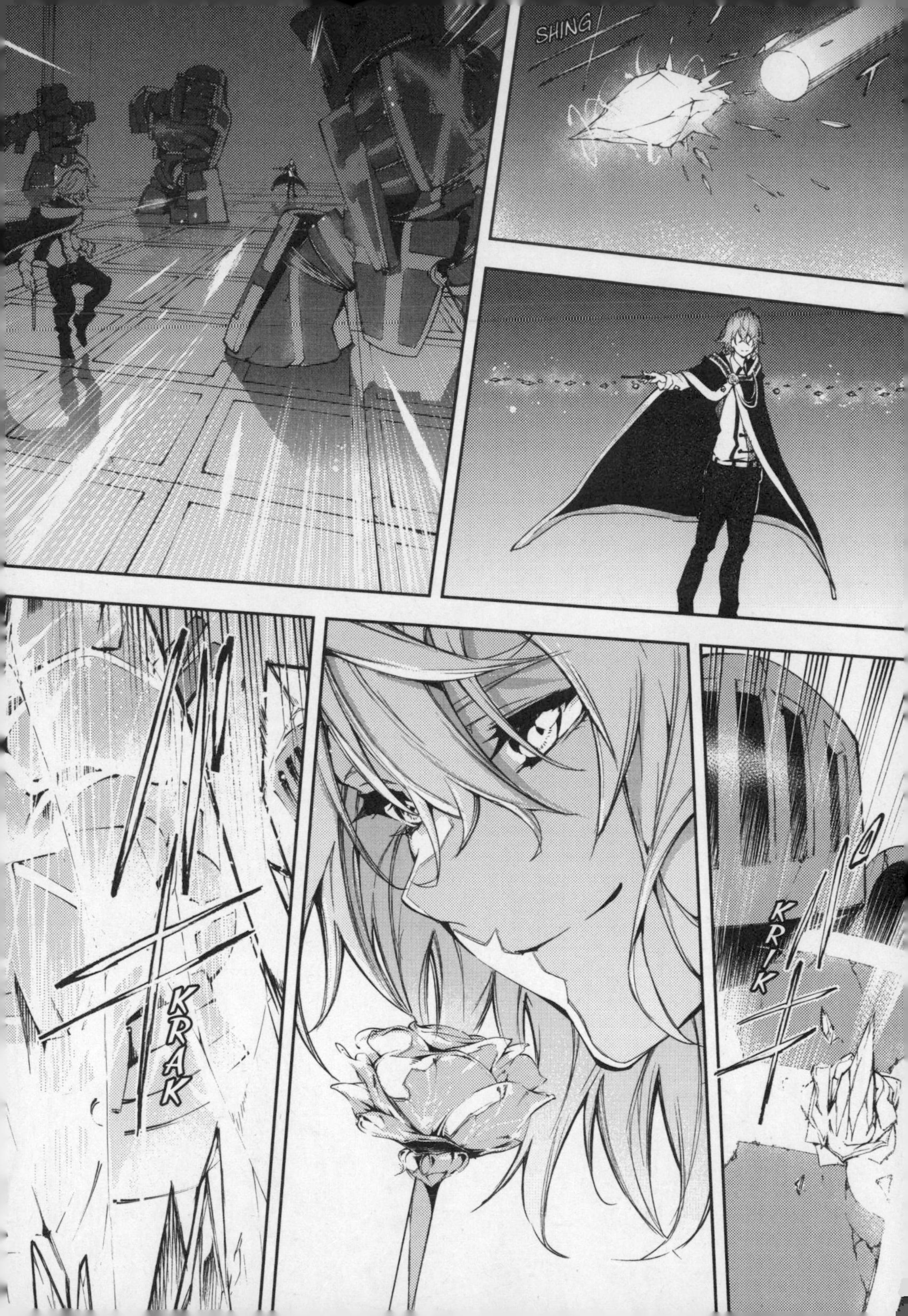
SHING
KRIK
KRAK

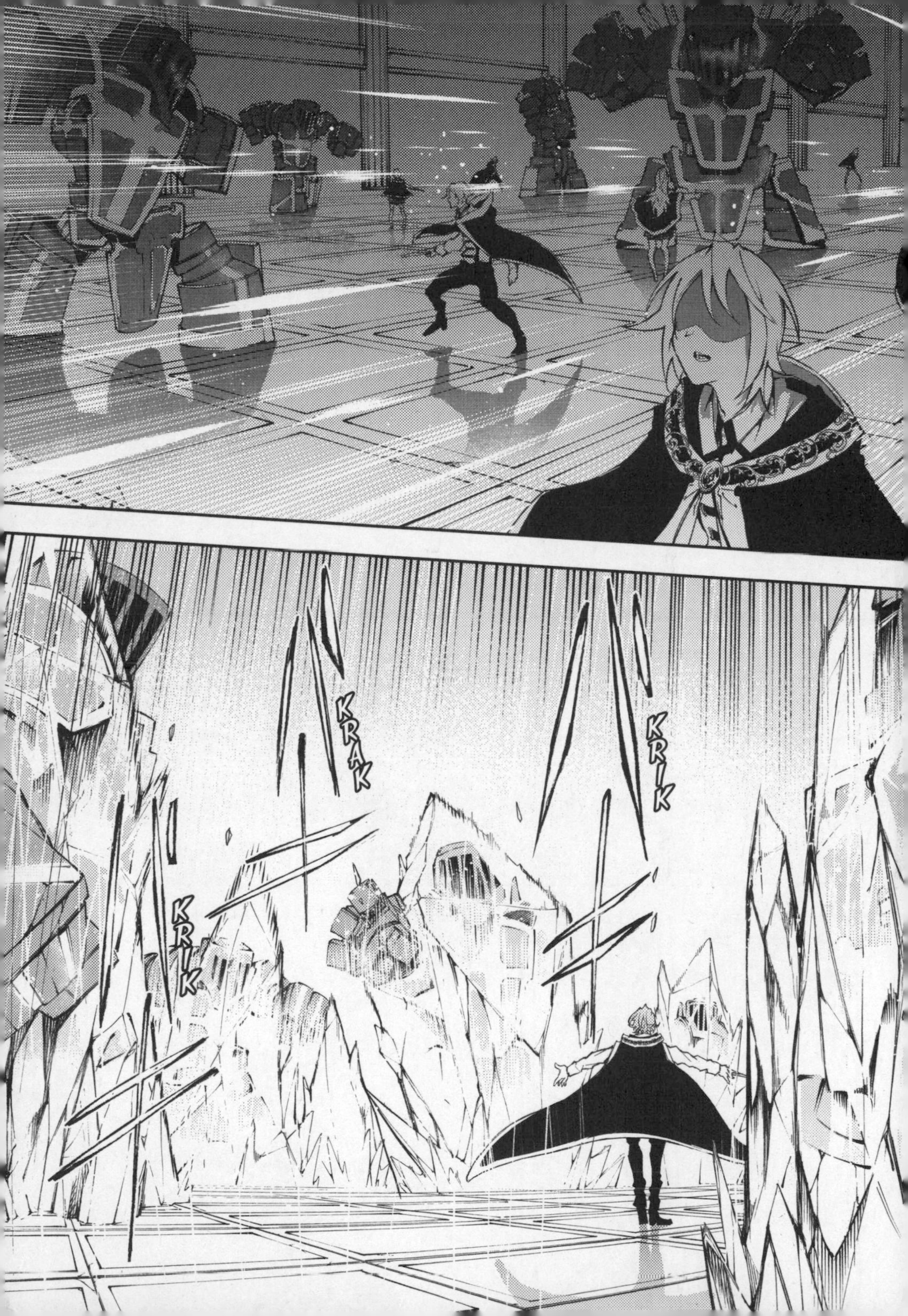
KRIK
KRAK
KRIK

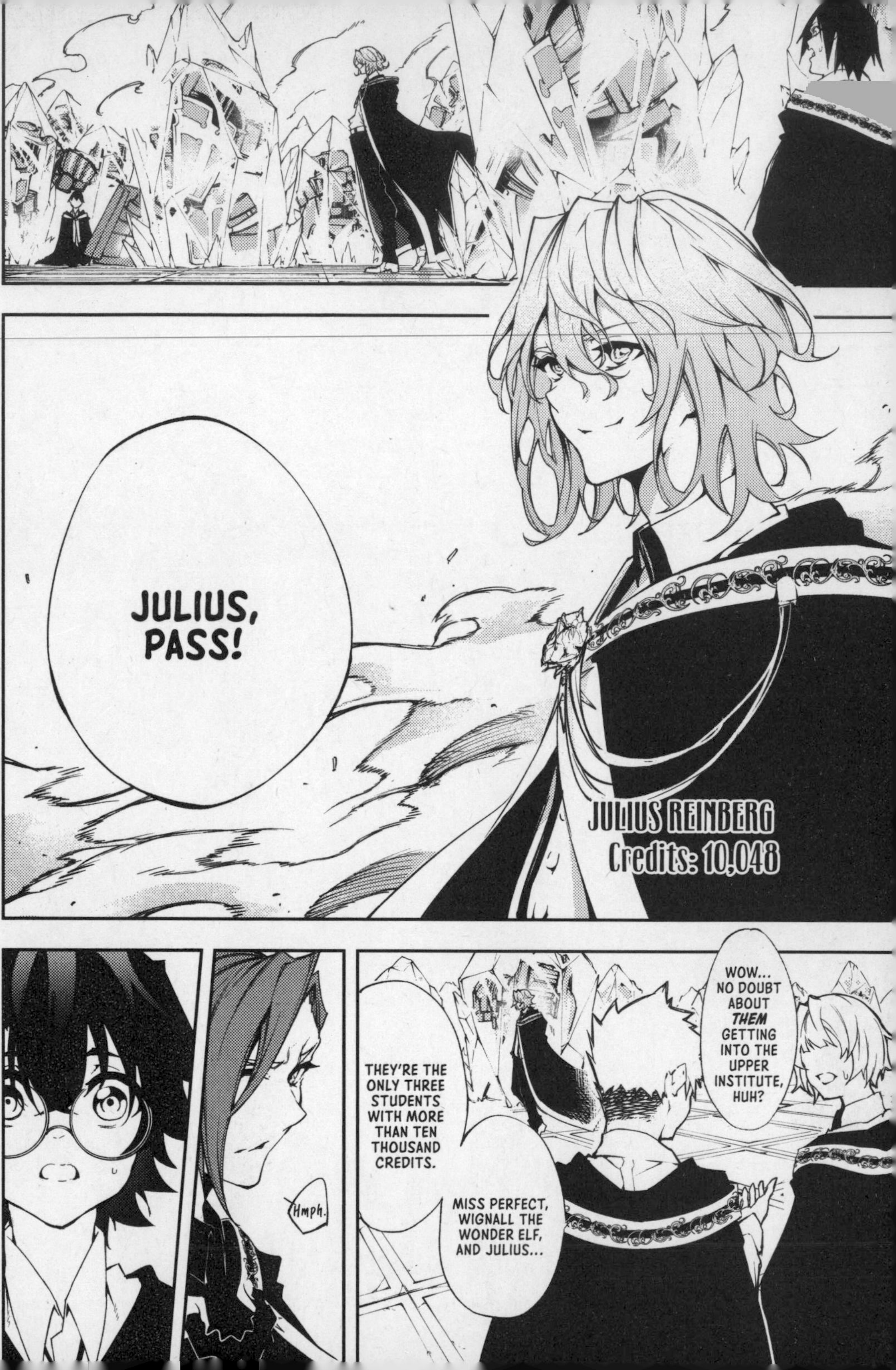
JULIUS, PASS!
JULIUS REINBERG
Credits: 10,048
WOW... NO DOUBT ABOUT *THEM* GETTING INTO THE UPPER INSTITUTE, HUH?
THEY'RE THE ONLY THREE STUDENTS WITH MORE THAN TEN THOUSAND CREDITS.
MISS PERFECT, WIGNALL THE WONDER ELF, AND JULIUS...
Hmph.

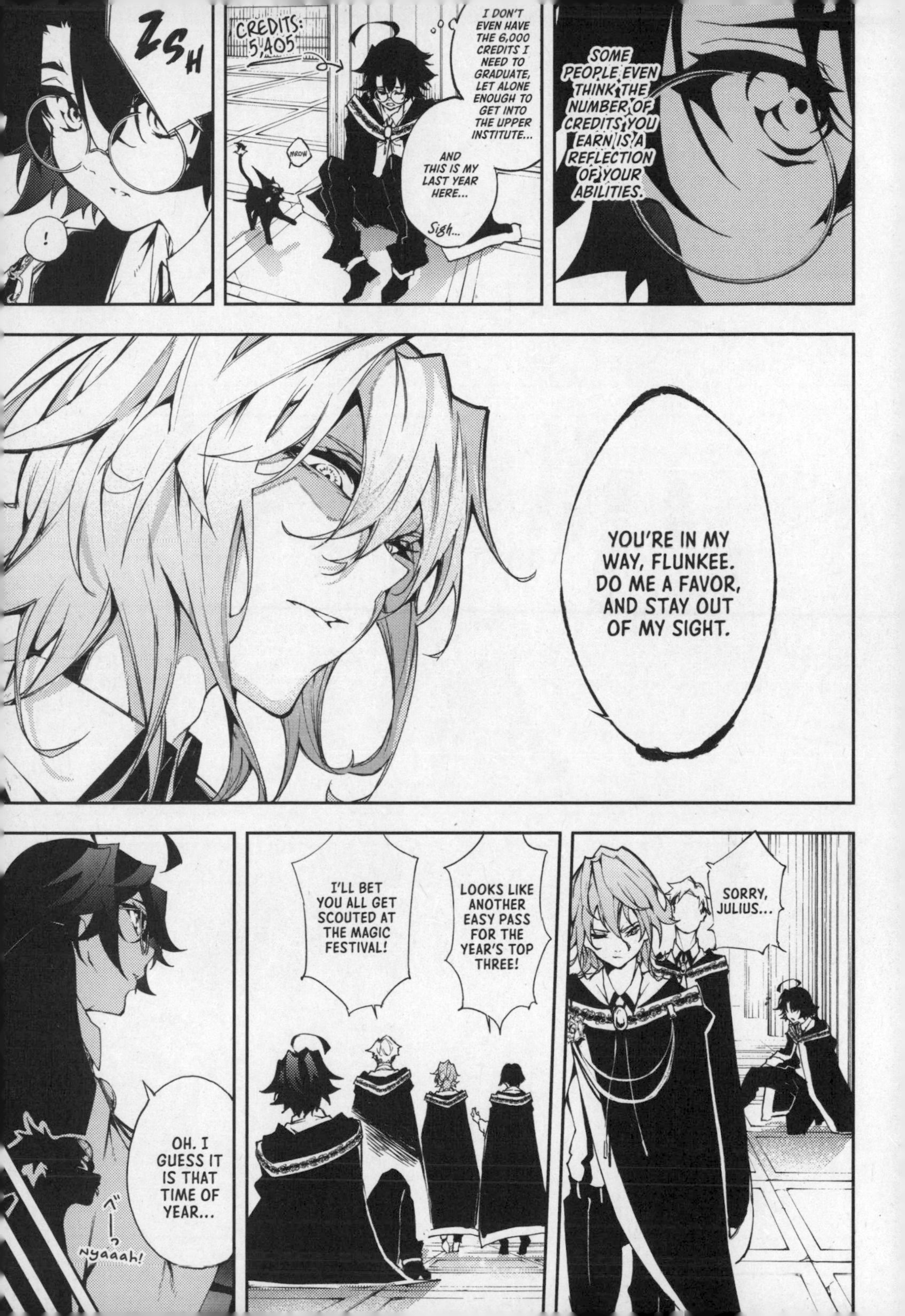
SOME PEOPLE EVEN THINK THE NUMBER OF CREDITS YOU EARN IS A REFLECTION OF YOUR ABILITIES.
I DON'T EVEN HAVE THE 6,000 CREDITS I NEED TO GRADUATE, LET ALONE ENOUGH TO GET INTO THE UPPER INSTITUTE...
CREDITS: 5,405
AND THIS IS MY LAST YEAR HERE...
MROW
Sigh...
ZSH
!
YOU'RE IN MY WAY, FLUNKEE. DO ME A FAVOR, AND STAY OUT OF MY SIGHT.
SORRY, JULIUS...
LOOKS LIKE ANOTHER EASY PASS FOR THE YEAR'S TOP THREE!
I'LL BET YOU ALL GET SCOUTED AT THE MAGIC FESTIVAL!
OH. I GUESS IT IS THAT TIME OF YEAR...
べーっ
Nyaaah!

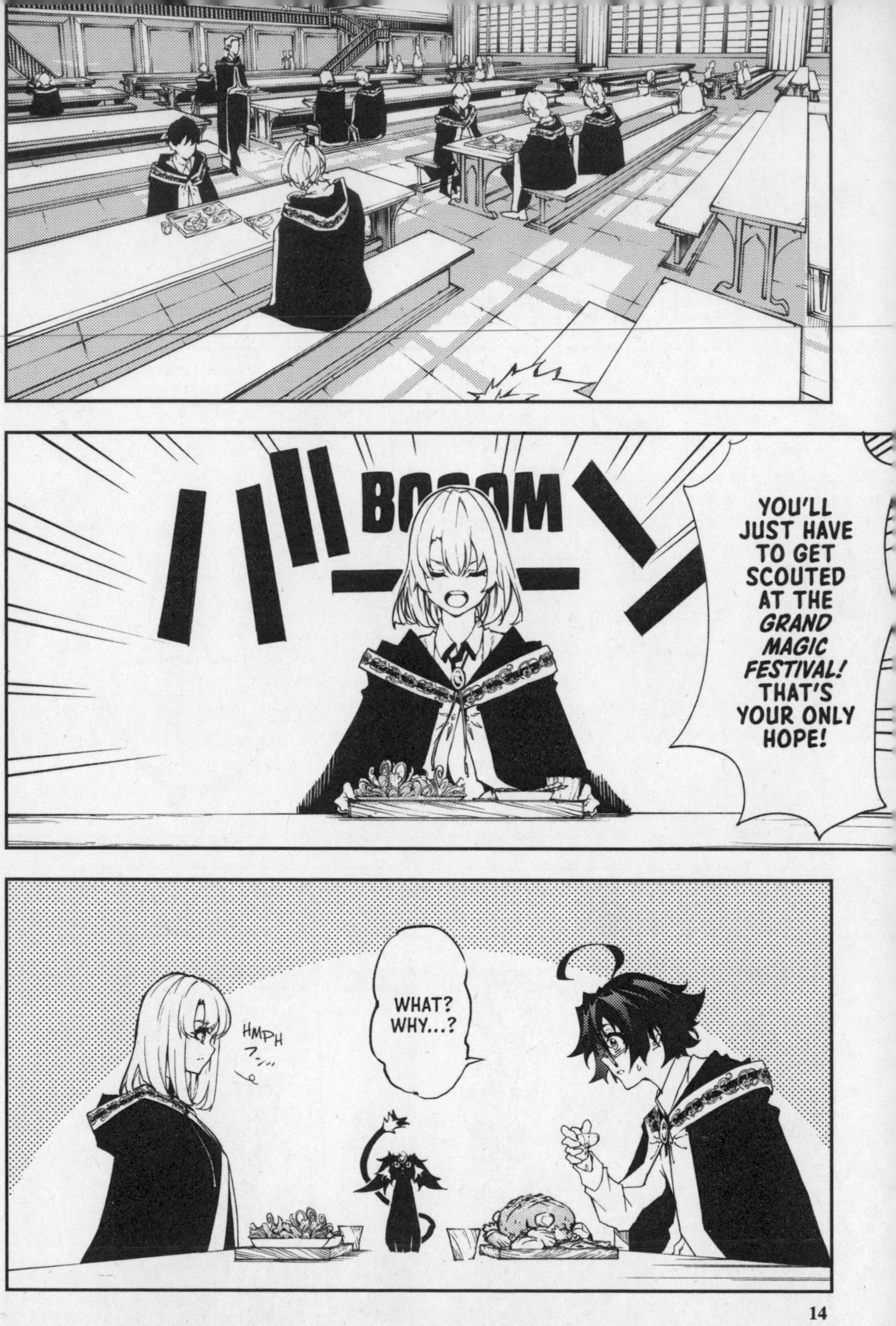
BOOOM
YOU'LL JUST HAVE TO GET SCOUTED AT THE *GRAND MAGIC FESTIVAL!* THAT'S YOUR ONLY HOPE!
WHAT? WHY...?
HMPH

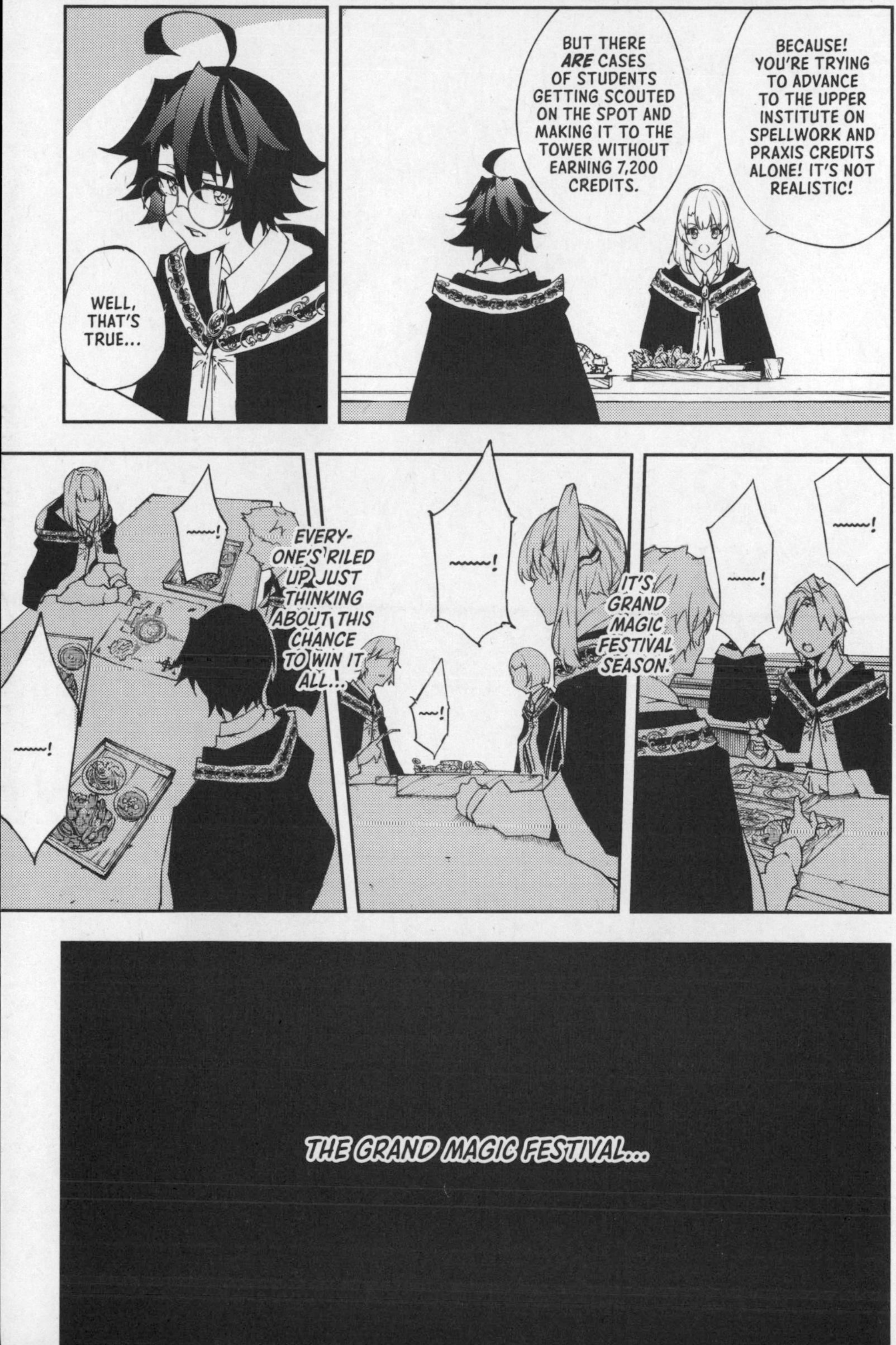
BECAUSE! YOU'RE TRYING TO ADVANCE TO THE UPPER INSTITUTE ON SPELLWORK AND PRAXIS CREDITS ALONE! IT'S NOT REALISTIC!
BUT THERE ARE CASES OF STUDENTS GETTING SCOUTED ON THE SPOT AND MAKING IT TO THE TOWER WITHOUT EARNING 7,200 CREDITS.
WELL, THAT'S TRUE...
~~~!
~~~!
IT'S GRAND MAGIC FESTIVAL SEASON.
~~~!
~~!
EVERY-ONE'S RILED UP JUST THINKING ABOUT THIS CHANCE TO WIN IT ALL...
~~~!
~~~!
THE GRAND MAGIC FESTIVAL...
~~~

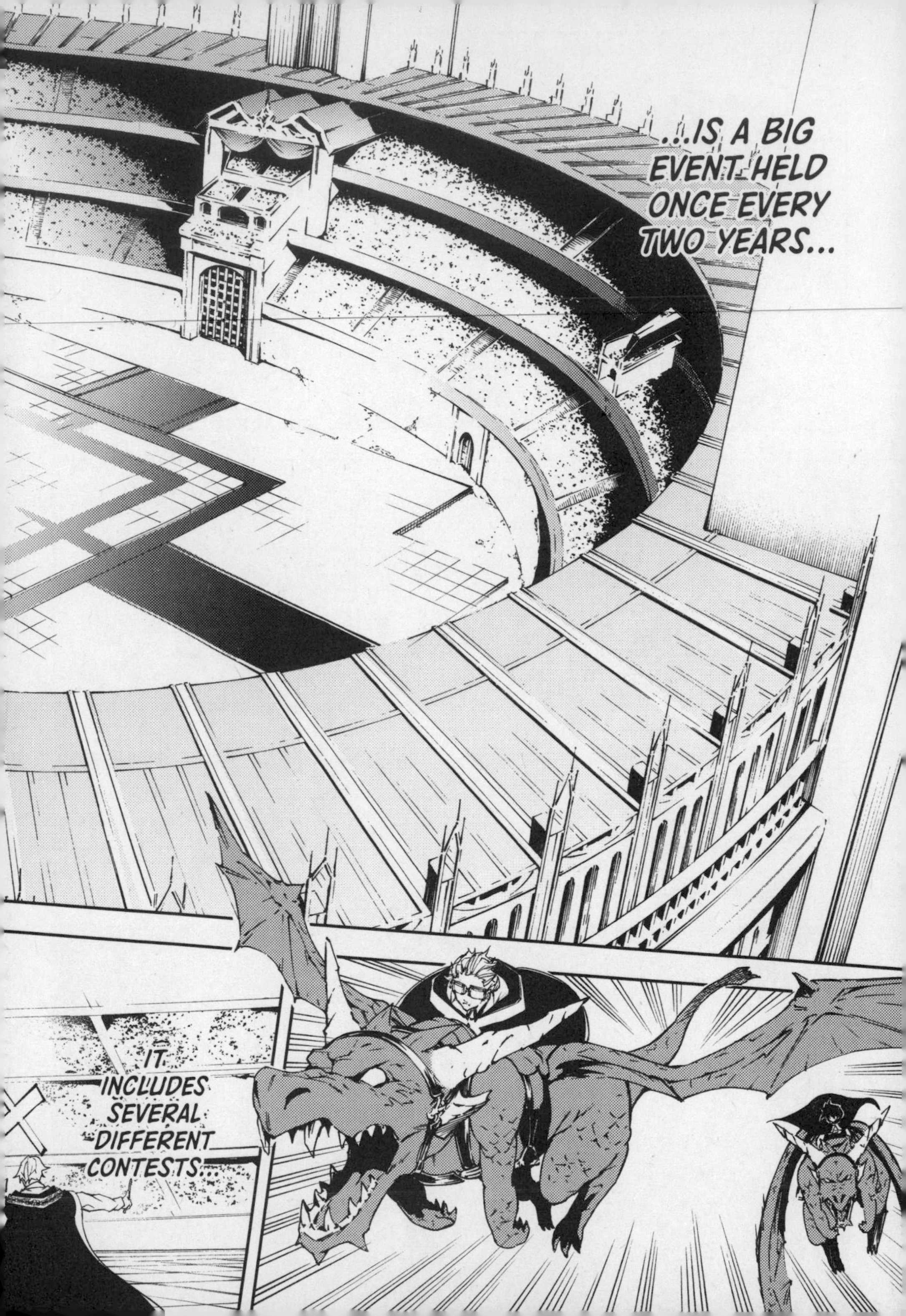
...IS A BIG EVENT HELD ONCE EVERY TWO YEARS...
IT INCLUDES SEVERAL DIFFERENT CONTESTS...

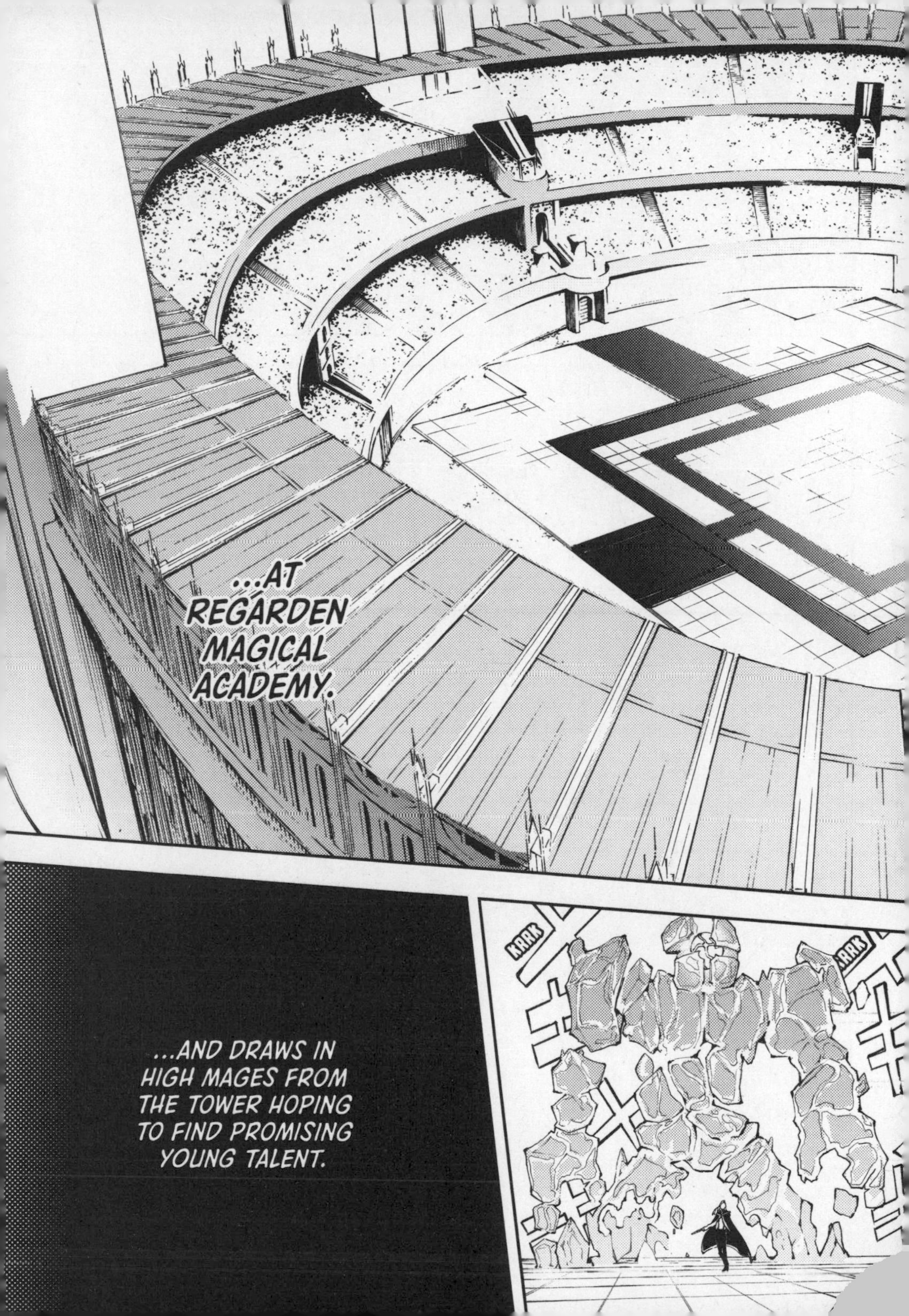
...AT REGARDEN MAGICAL ACADEMY.
KRRK
KRRK
...AND DRAWS IN HIGH MAGES FROM THE TOWER HOPING TO FIND PROMISING YOUNG TALENT.

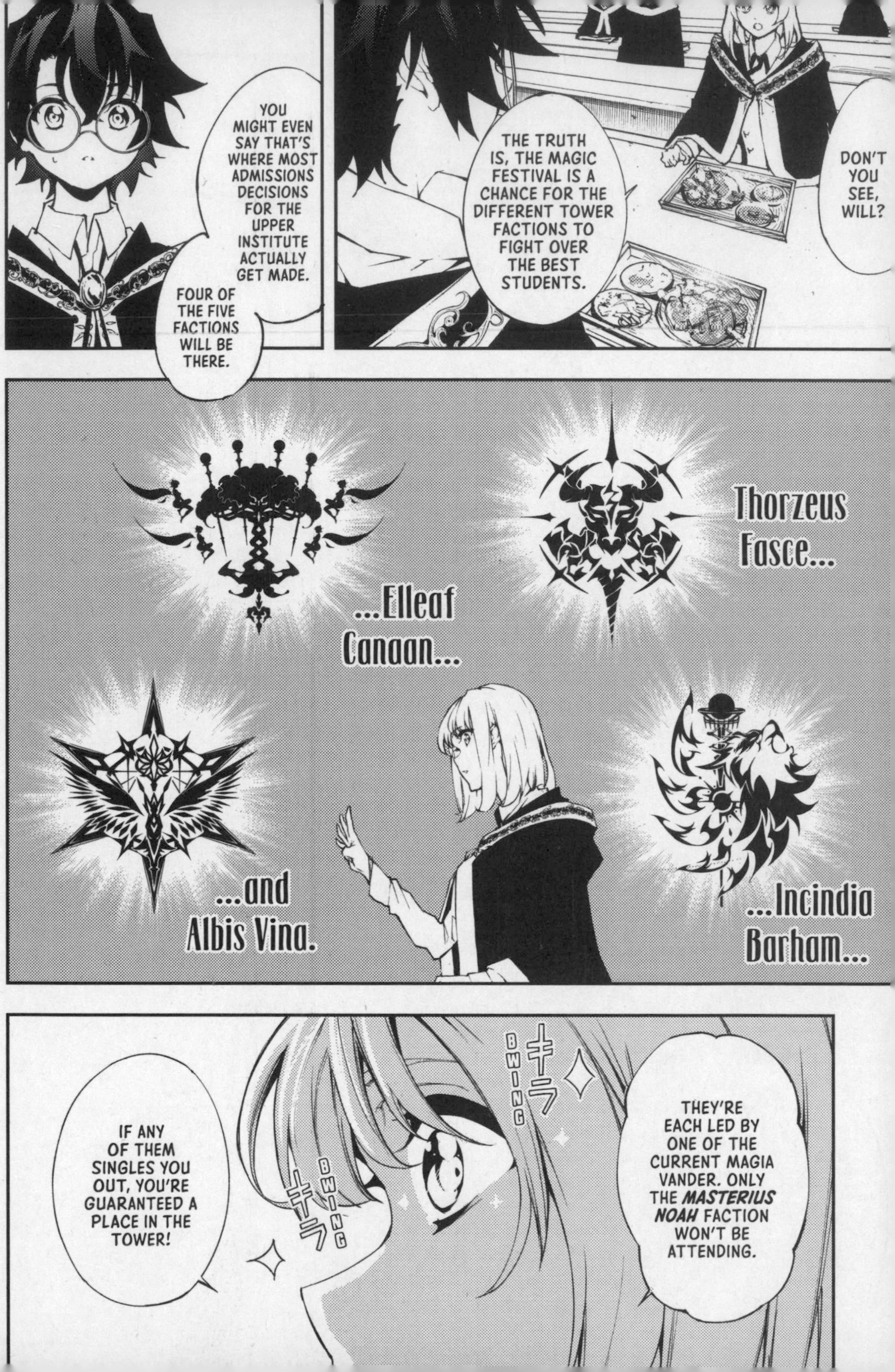
DON'T YOU SEE, WILL?
THE TRUTH IS, THE MAGIC FESTIVAL IS A CHANCE FOR THE DIFFERENT TOWER FACTIONS TO FIGHT OVER THE BEST STUDENTS.
YOU MIGHT EVEN SAY THAT'S WHERE MOST ADMISSIONS DECISIONS FOR THE UPPER INSTITUTE ACTUALLY GET MADE.
FOUR OF THE FIVE FACTIONS WILL BE THERE.
Thorzeus Fasce...
...Elleaf Canaan...
...Incindia Barham...
...and Albis Vina.
THEY'RE EACH LED BY ONE OF THE CURRENT MAGIA VANDER. ONLY THE ***MASTERIUS NOAH*** FACTION WON'T BE ATTENDING.
キラ
BWING
キラ
BWING
IF ANY OF THEM SINGLES YOU OUT, YOU'RE GUARANTEED A PLACE IN THE TOWER!

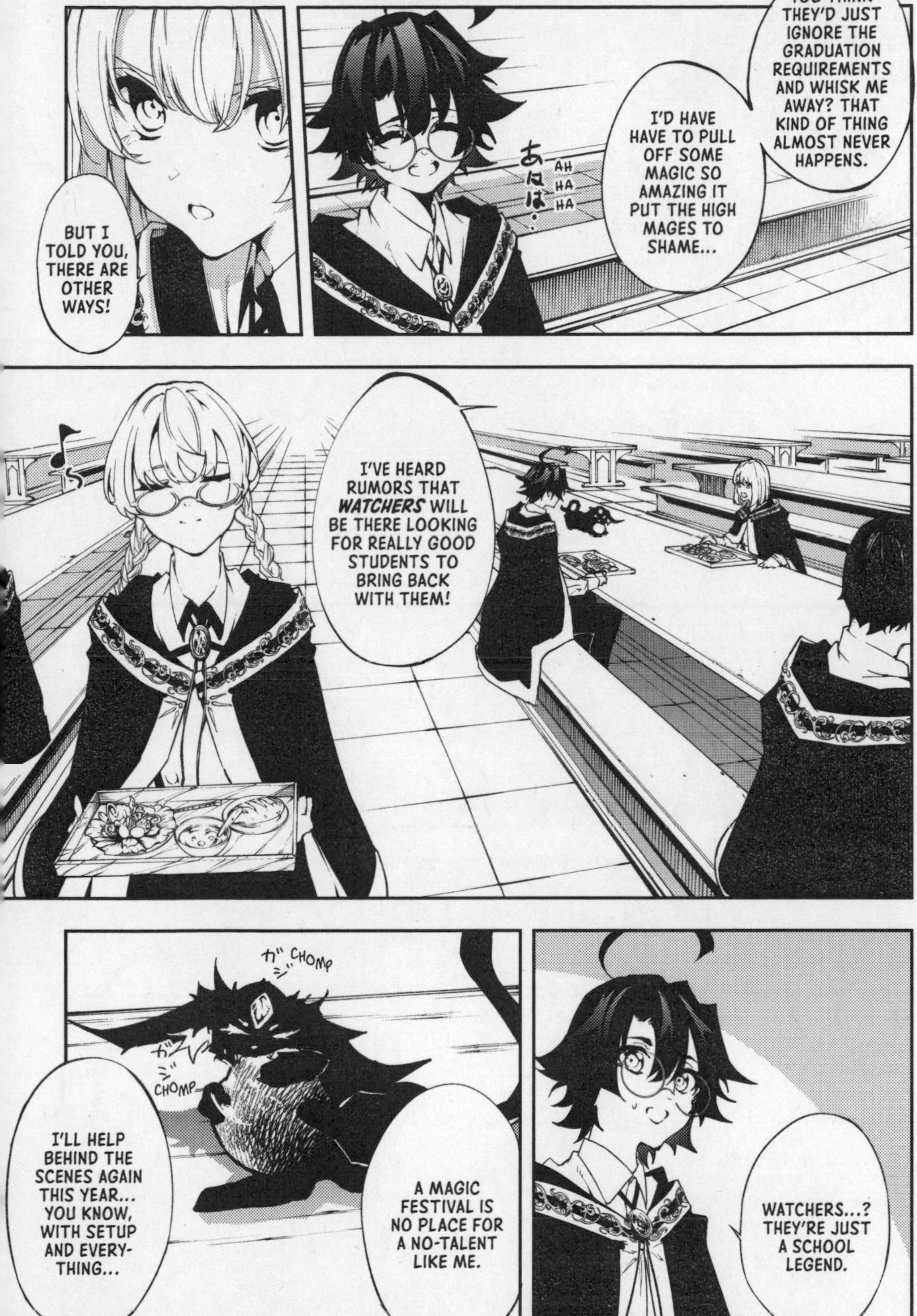
YOU THINK THEY'D JUST IGNORE THE GRADUATION REQUIREMENTS AND WHISK ME AWAY? THAT KIND OF THING ALMOST NEVER HAPPENS.
I'D HAVE HAVE TO PULL OFF SOME MAGIC SO AMAZING IT PUT THE HIGH MAGES TO SHAME...
あはは・・ AH HA HA
BUT I TOLD YOU, THERE ARE OTHER WAYS!
I'VE HEARD RUMORS THAT WATCHERS WILL BE THERE LOOKING FOR REALLY GOOD STUDENTS TO BRING BACK WITH THEM!
WATCHERS...? THEY'RE JUST A SCHOOL LEGEND.
ガジ CHOMP
ガジ CHOMP
A MAGIC FESTIVAL IS NO PLACE FOR A NO-TALENT LIKE ME.
I'LL HELP BEHIND THE SCENES AGAIN THIS YEAR... YOU KNOW, WITH SETUP AND EVERY-THING...

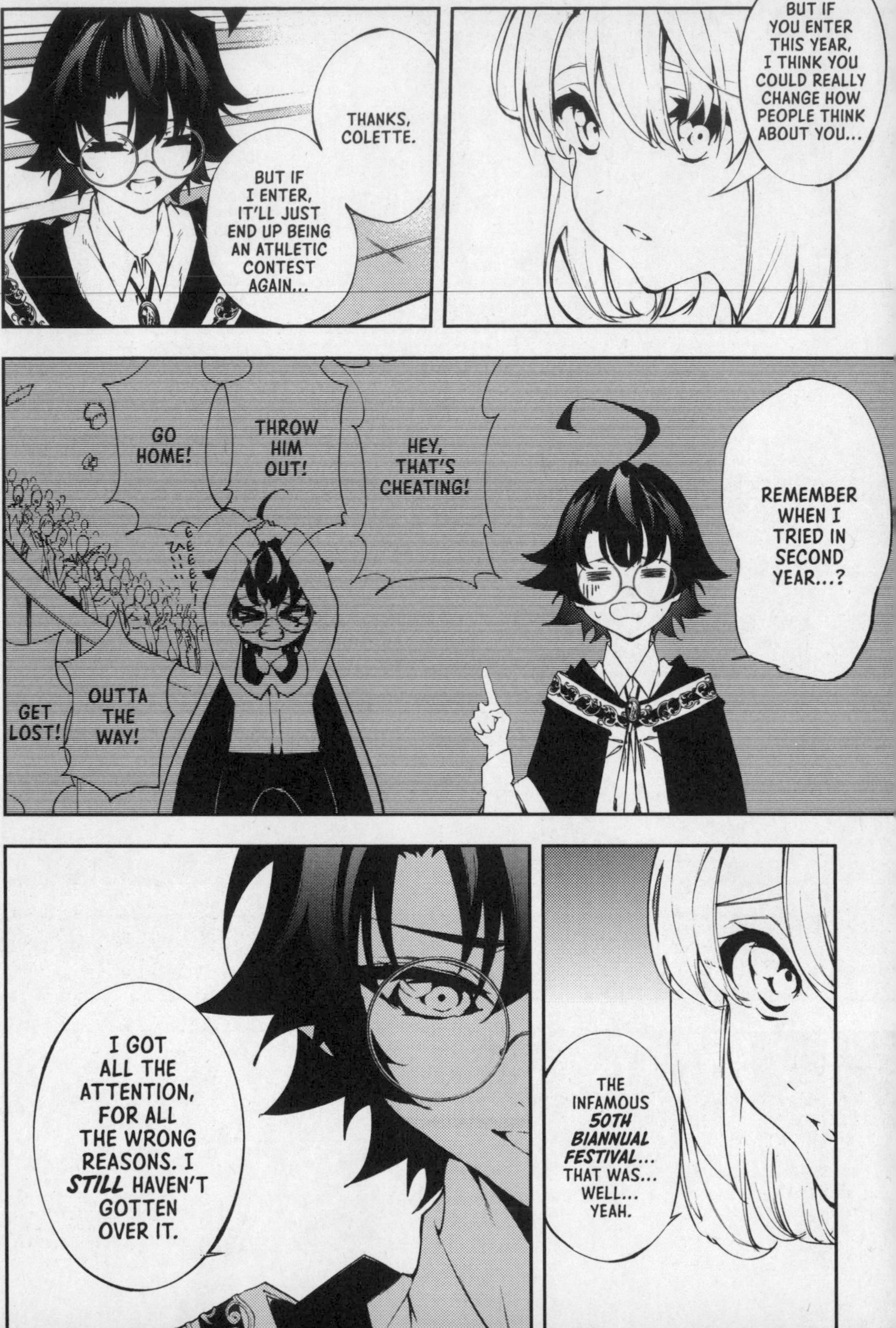
BUT IF YOU ENTER THIS YEAR, I THINK YOU COULD REALLY CHANGE HOW PEOPLE THINK ABOUT YOU...
THANKS, COLETTE.
BUT IF I ENTER, IT'LL JUST END UP BEING AN ATHLETIC CONTEST AGAIN...
REMEMBER WHEN I TRIED IN SECOND YEAR...?
HEY, THAT'S CHEATING!
THROW HIM OUT!
GO HOME!
OUTTA THE WAY!
GET LOST!
THE INFAMOUS *50TH BIANNUAL FESTIVAL*... THAT WAS... WELL... YEAH.
I GOT ALL THE ATTENTION, FOR ALL THE WRONG REASONS. I *STILL* HAVEN'T GOTTEN OVER IT.

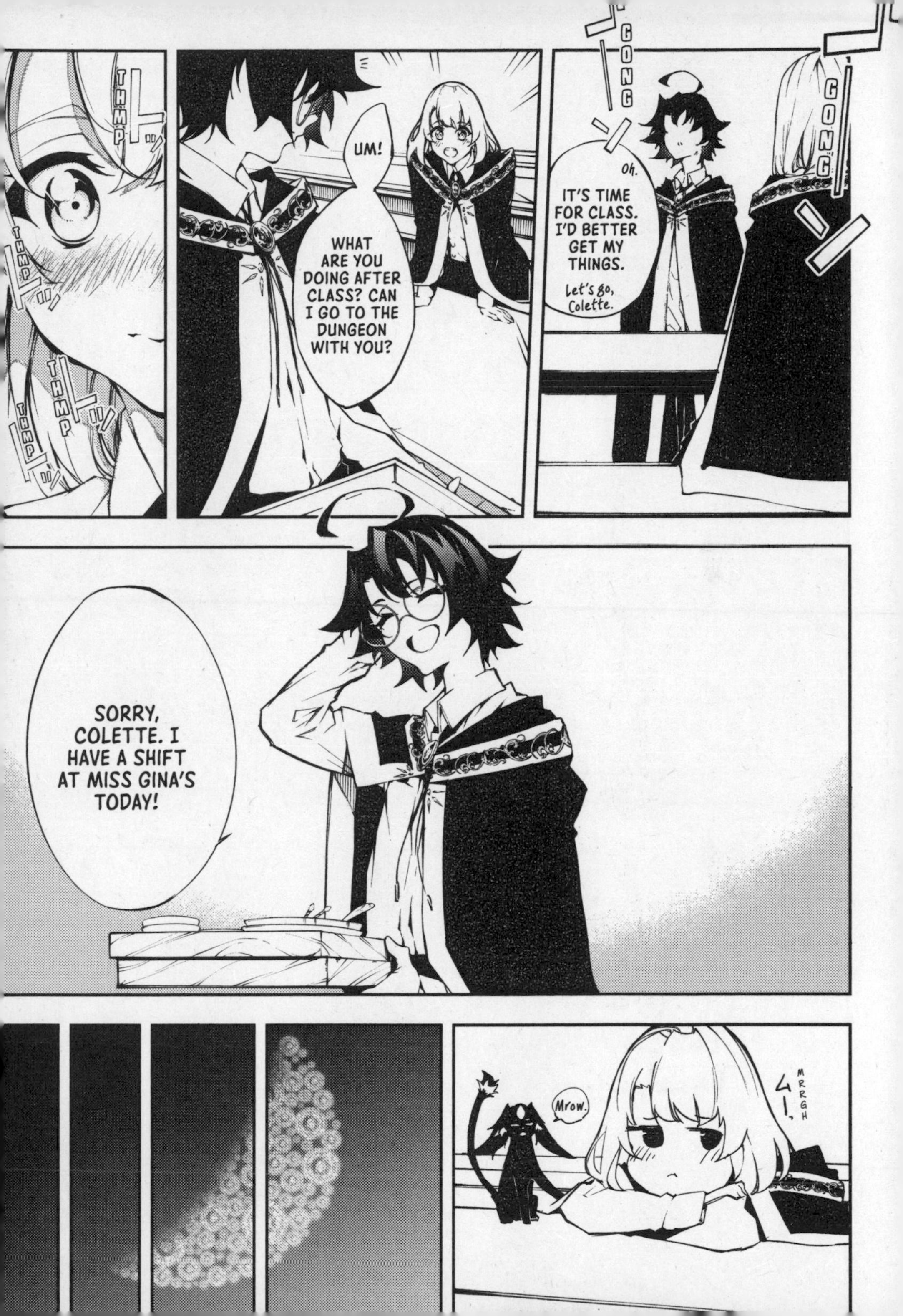
GONG
GONG
Oh.
IT'S TIME FOR CLASS. I'D BETTER GET MY THINGS.
Let's go, Colette.
UM!
WHAT ARE YOU DOING AFTER CLASS? CAN I GO TO THE DUNGEON WITH YOU?
THMP
THMP
THMP
THMP
SORRY, COLETTE. I HAVE A SHIFT AT MISS GINA'S TODAY!
MRRGH
Mrow.

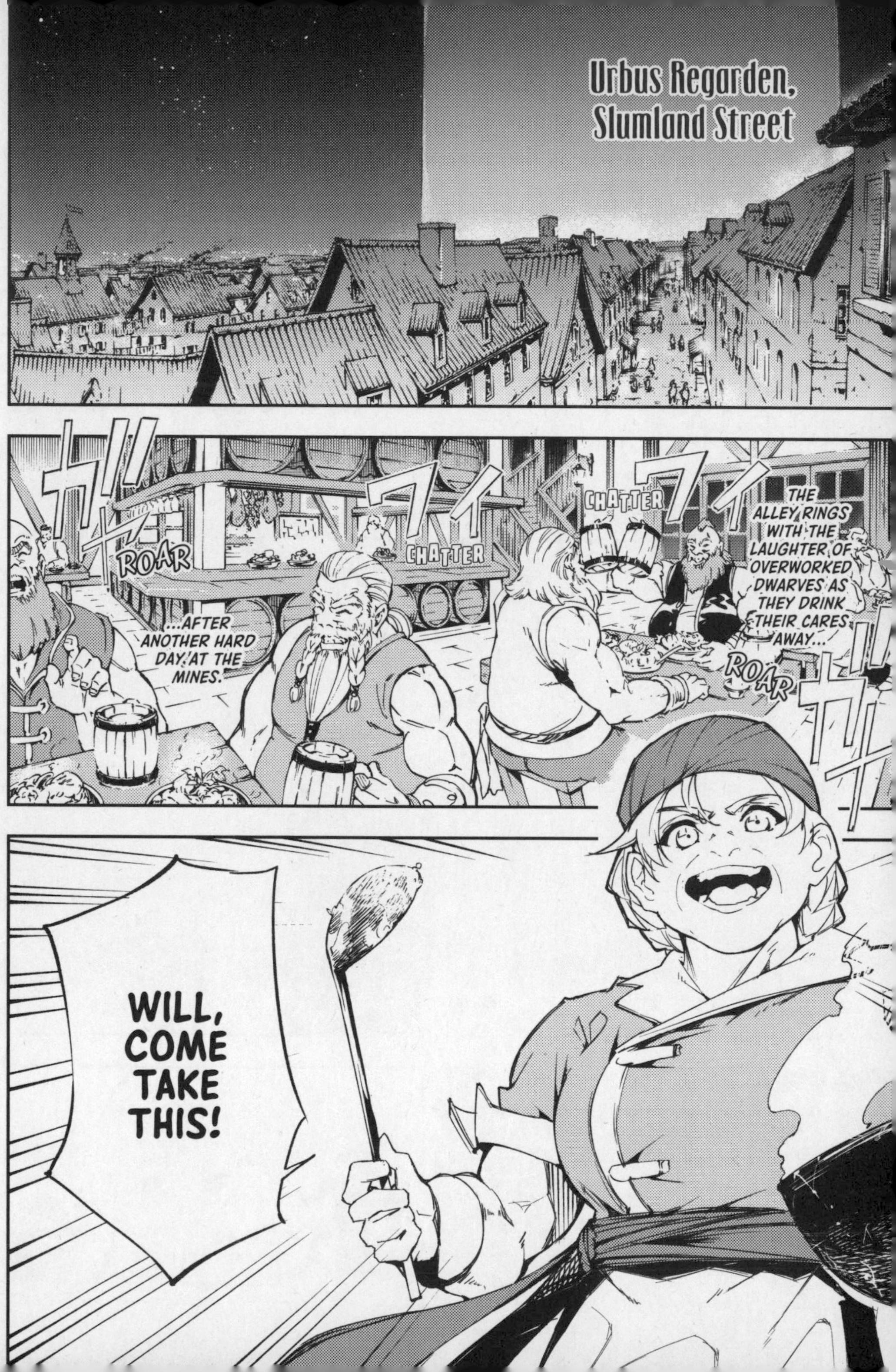
Urbus Regarden, Slumland Street
THE ALLEY RINGS WITH THE LAUGHTER OF OVERWORKED DWARVES AS THEY DRINK THEIR CARES AWAY...
ROAR
CHATTER
CHATTER
...AFTER ANOTHER HARD DAY AT THE MINES.
ROAR
WILL, COME TAKE THIS!

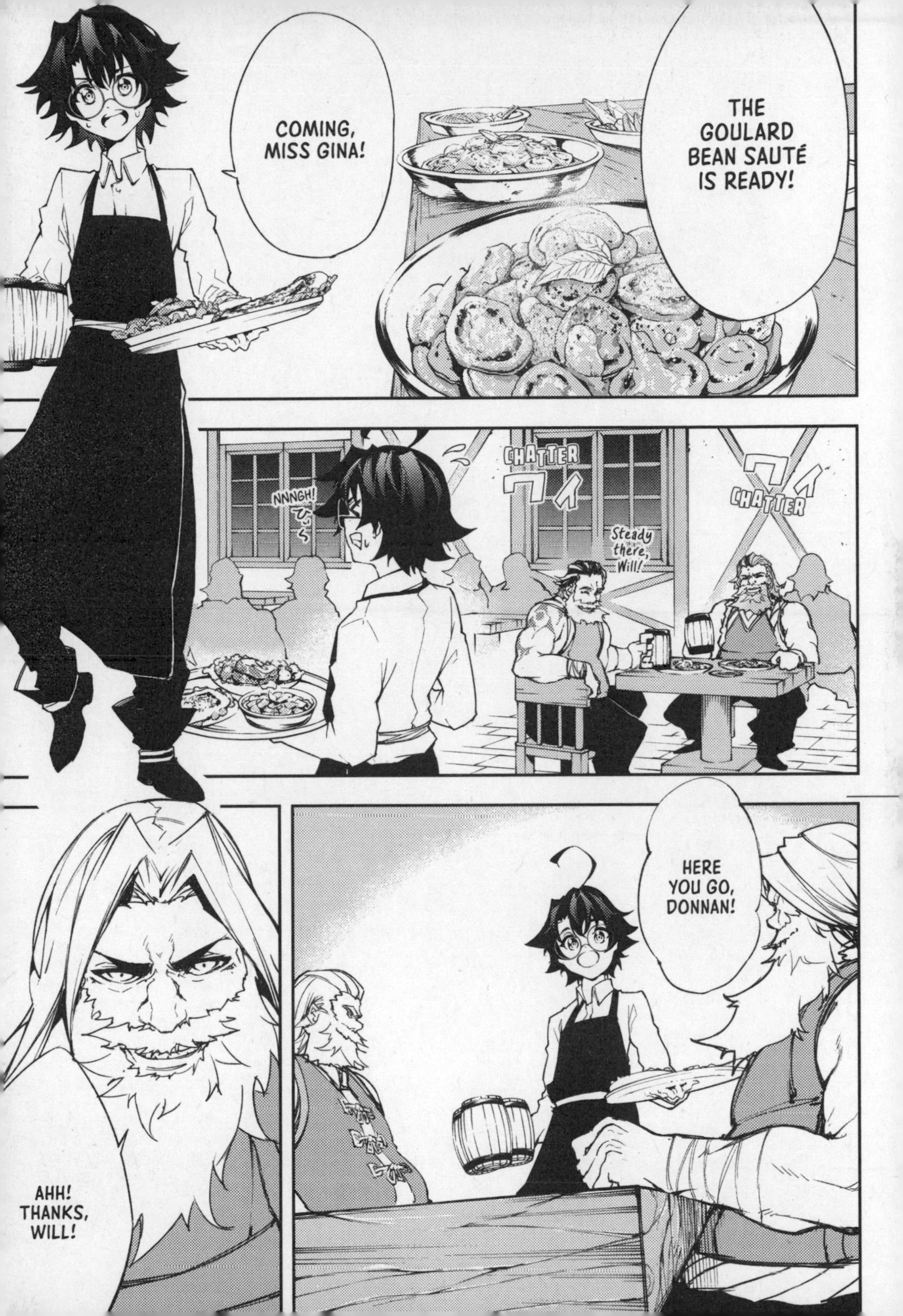
THE GOULARD BEAN SAUTÉ IS READY!
COMING, MISS GINA!
CHATTER
CHATTER
Steady there, Will!
NNNGH!
HERE YOU GO, DONNAN!
AHH! THANKS, WILL!

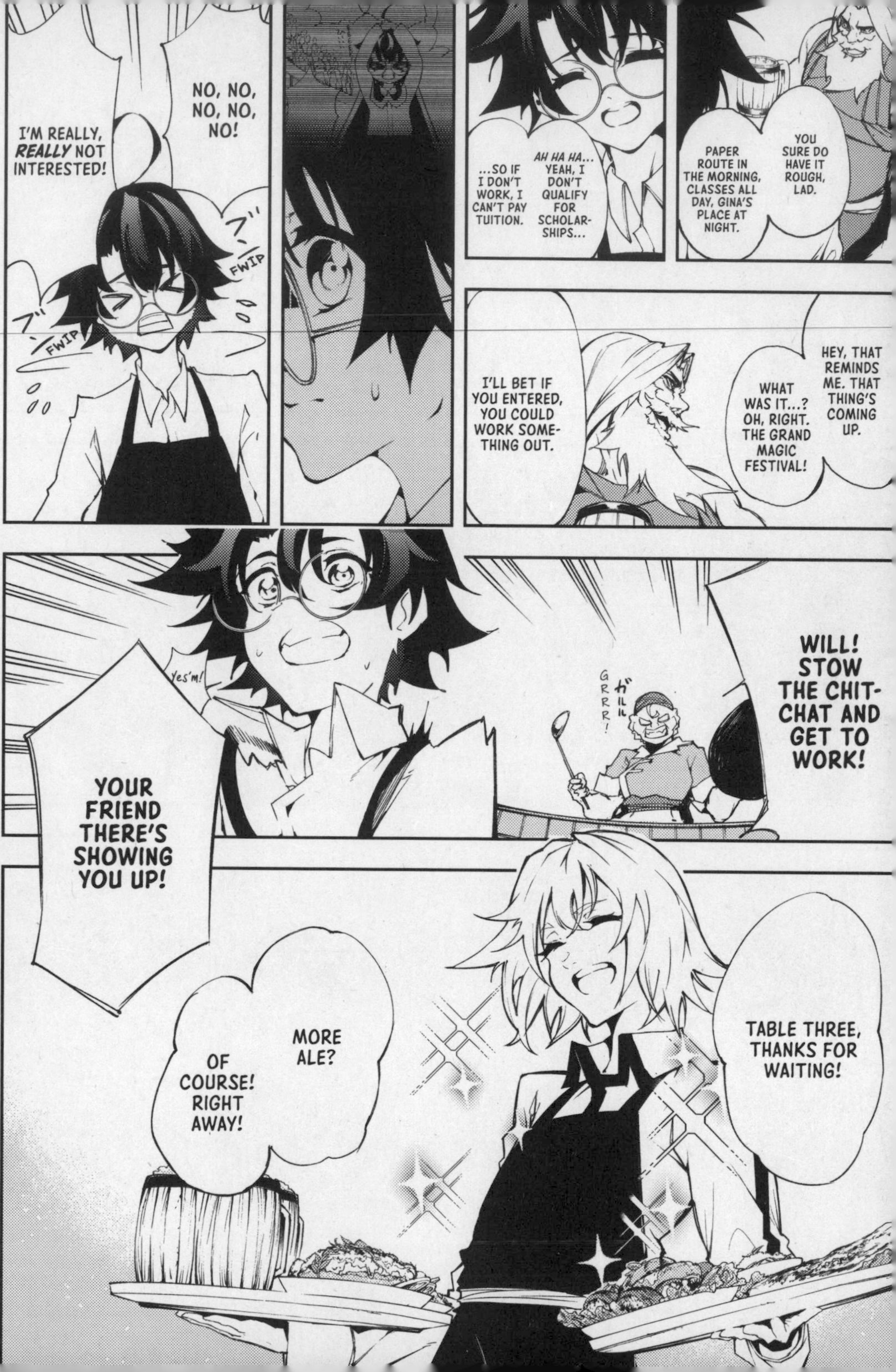
YOU SURE DO HAVE IT ROUGH, LAD.
PAPER ROUTE IN THE MORNING, CLASSES ALL DAY, GINA'S PLACE AT NIGHT.
AH HA HA... YEAH, I DON'T QUALIFY FOR SCHOLARSHIPS...
...SO IF I DON'T WORK, I CAN'T PAY TUITION.
HEY, THAT REMINDS ME. THAT THING'S COMING UP.
WHAT WAS IT...? OH, RIGHT. THE GRAND MAGIC FESTIVAL!
I'LL BET IF YOU ENTERED, YOU COULD WORK SOMETHING OUT.
NO, NO, NO, NO, NO!
I'M REALLY, REALLY NOT INTERESTED!
FWIP
FWIP
WILL! STOW THE CHIT-CHAT AND GET TO WORK!
GRRR!
Yes'm!
YOUR FRIEND THERE'S SHOWING YOU UP!
TABLE THREE, THANKS FOR WAITING!
MORE ALE?
OF COURSE! RIGHT AWAY!

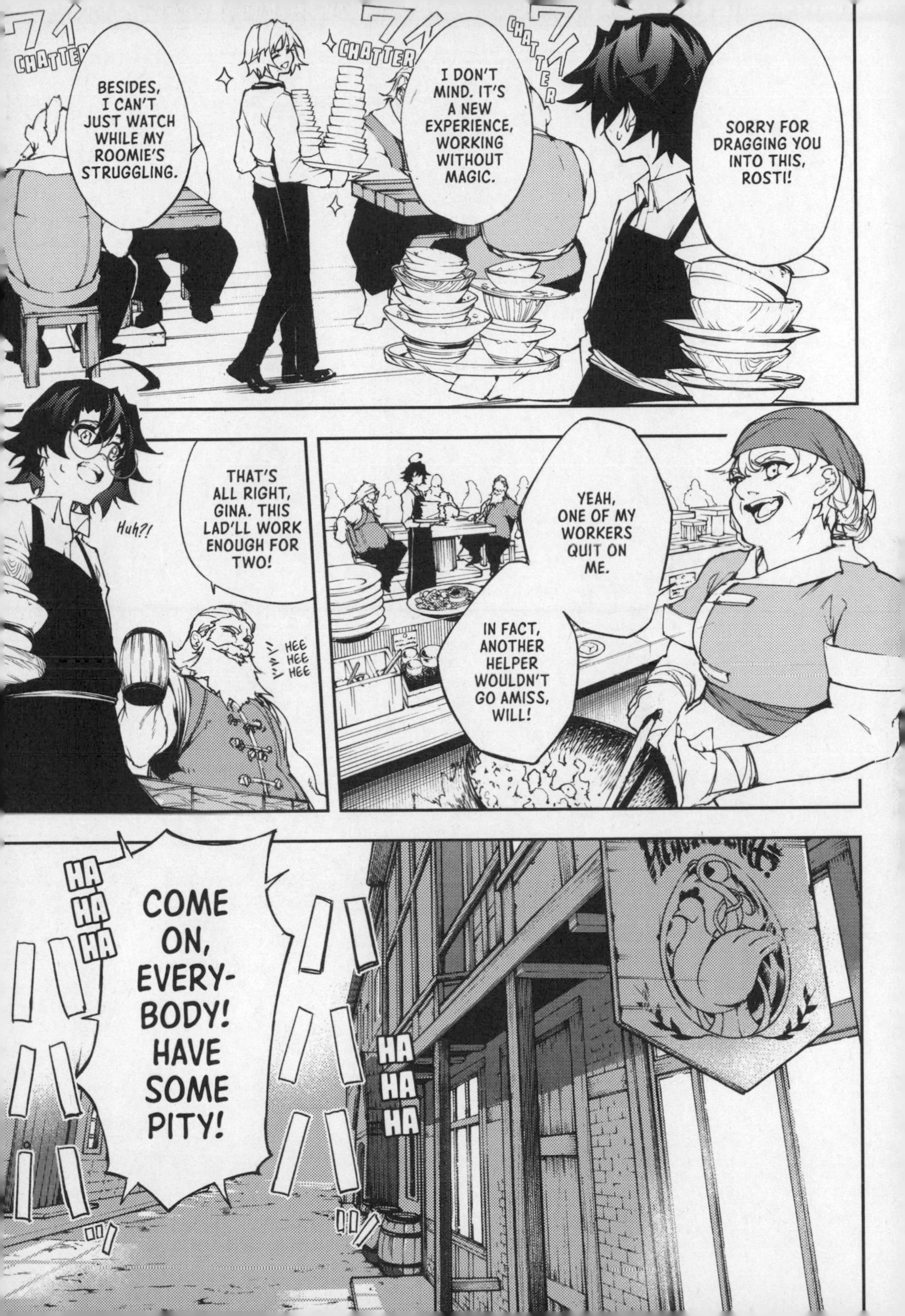
CHATTER
SORRY FOR DRAGGING YOU INTO THIS, ROSTI!
CHATTER
I DON'T MIND. IT'S A NEW EXPERIENCE, WORKING WITHOUT MAGIC.
CHATTER
BESIDES, I CAN'T JUST WATCH WHILE MY ROOMIE'S STRUGGLING.
YEAH, ONE OF MY WORKERS QUIT ON ME.
IN FACT, ANOTHER HELPER WOULDN'T GO AMISS, WILL!
THAT'S ALL RIGHT, GINA. THIS LAD'LL WORK ENOUGH FOR TWO!
Huh?!
HEE HEE HEE
HA HA HA
COME ON, EVERY-BODY! HAVE SOME PITY!
HA HA HA

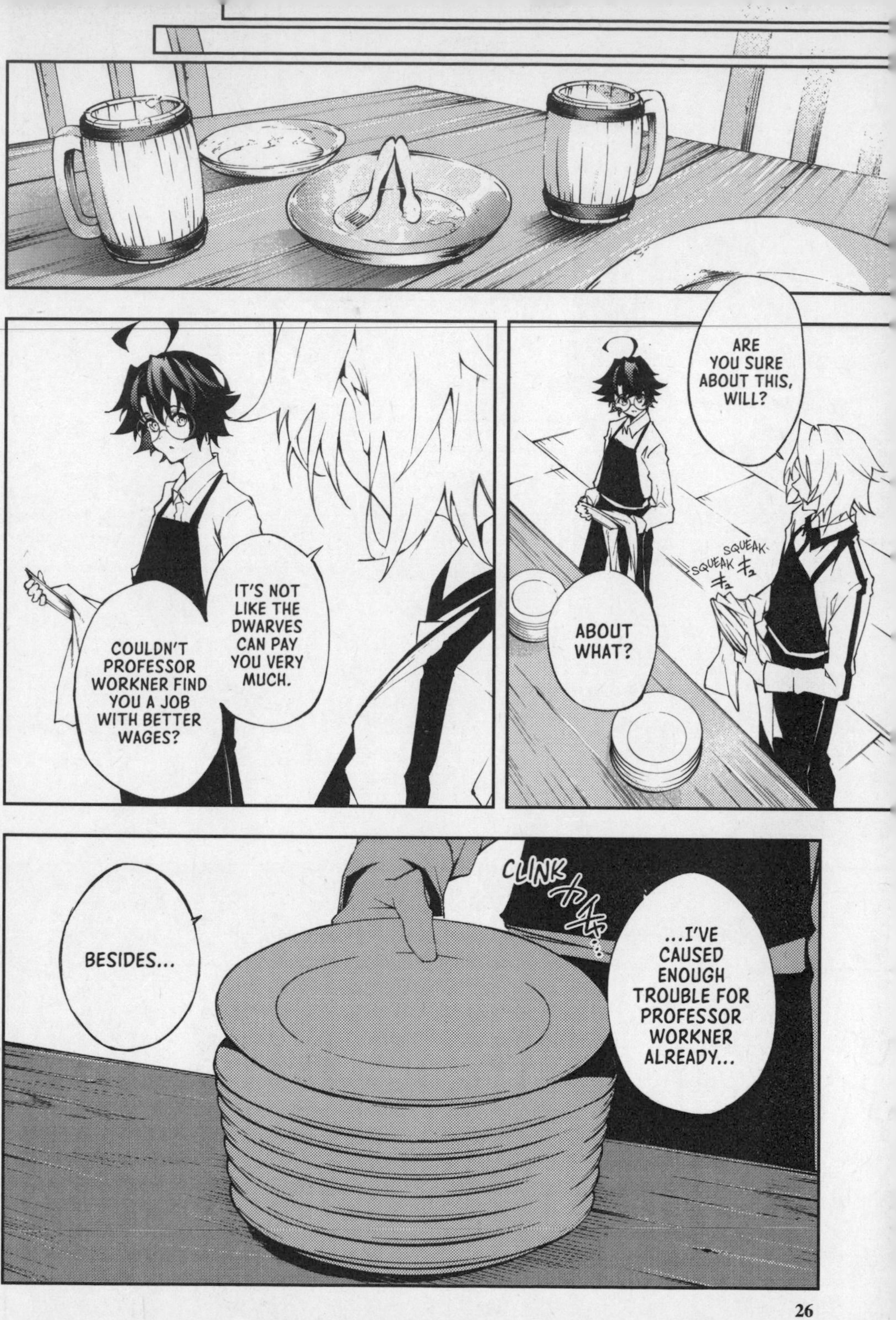

ARE YOU SURE ABOUT THIS, WILL?
SQUEAK
SQUEAK
キュ
キュ
ABOUT WHAT?
IT'S NOT LIKE THE DWARVES CAN PAY YOU VERY MUCH.
COULDN'T PROFESSOR WORKNER FIND YOU A JOB WITH BETTER WAGES?
CLINK
BESIDES...
...I'VE CAUSED ENOUGH TROUBLE FOR PROFESSOR WORKNER ALREADY...

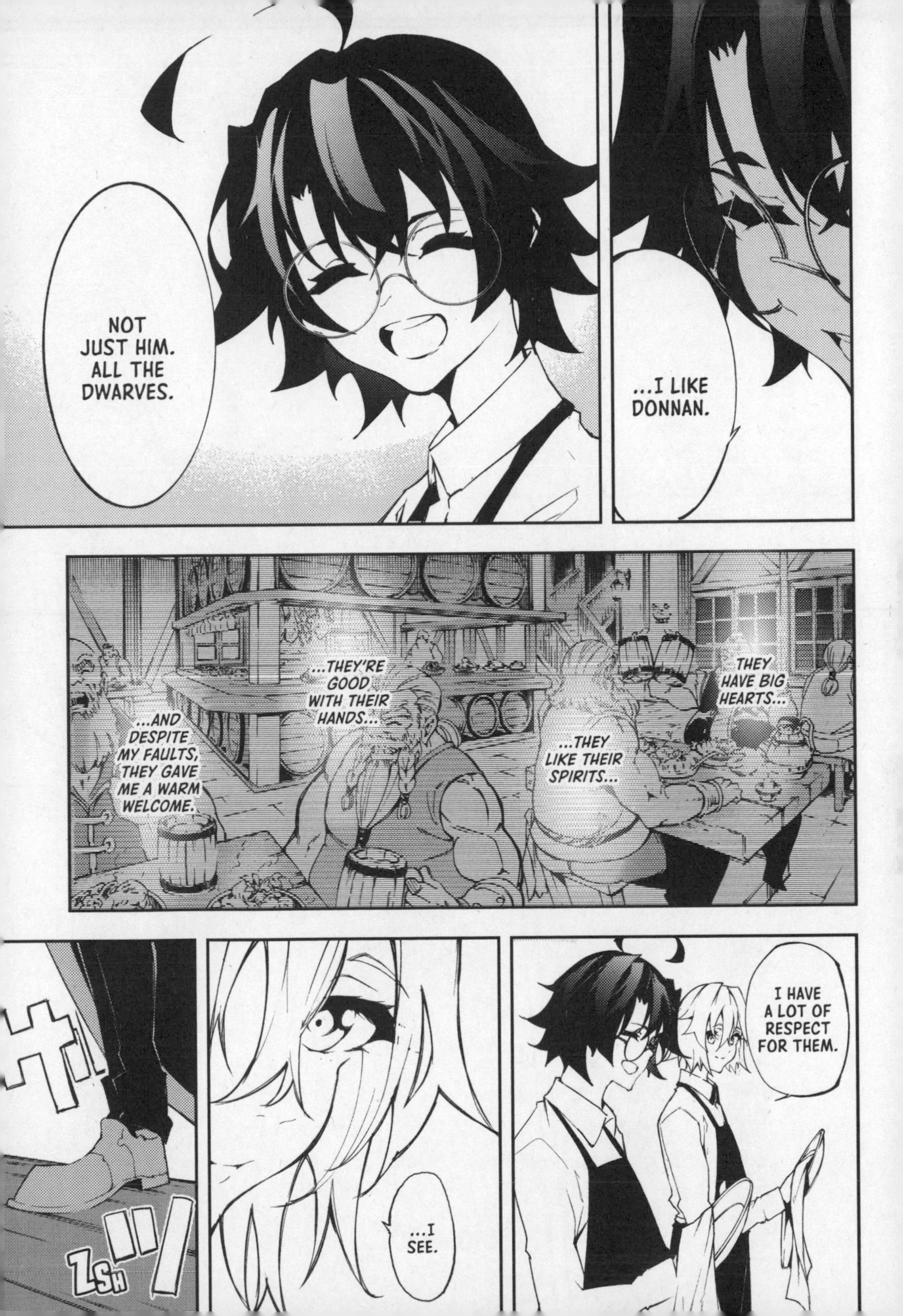
...I LIKE DONNAN.
NOT JUST HIM. ALL THE DWARVES.
THEY HAVE BIG HEARTS...
...THEY'RE GOOD WITH THEIR HANDS...
...THEY LIKE THEIR SPIRITS...
...AND DESPITE MY FAULTS, THEY GAVE ME A WARM WELCOME.
I HAVE A LOT OF RESPECT FOR THEM.
...I SEE.
ZSH

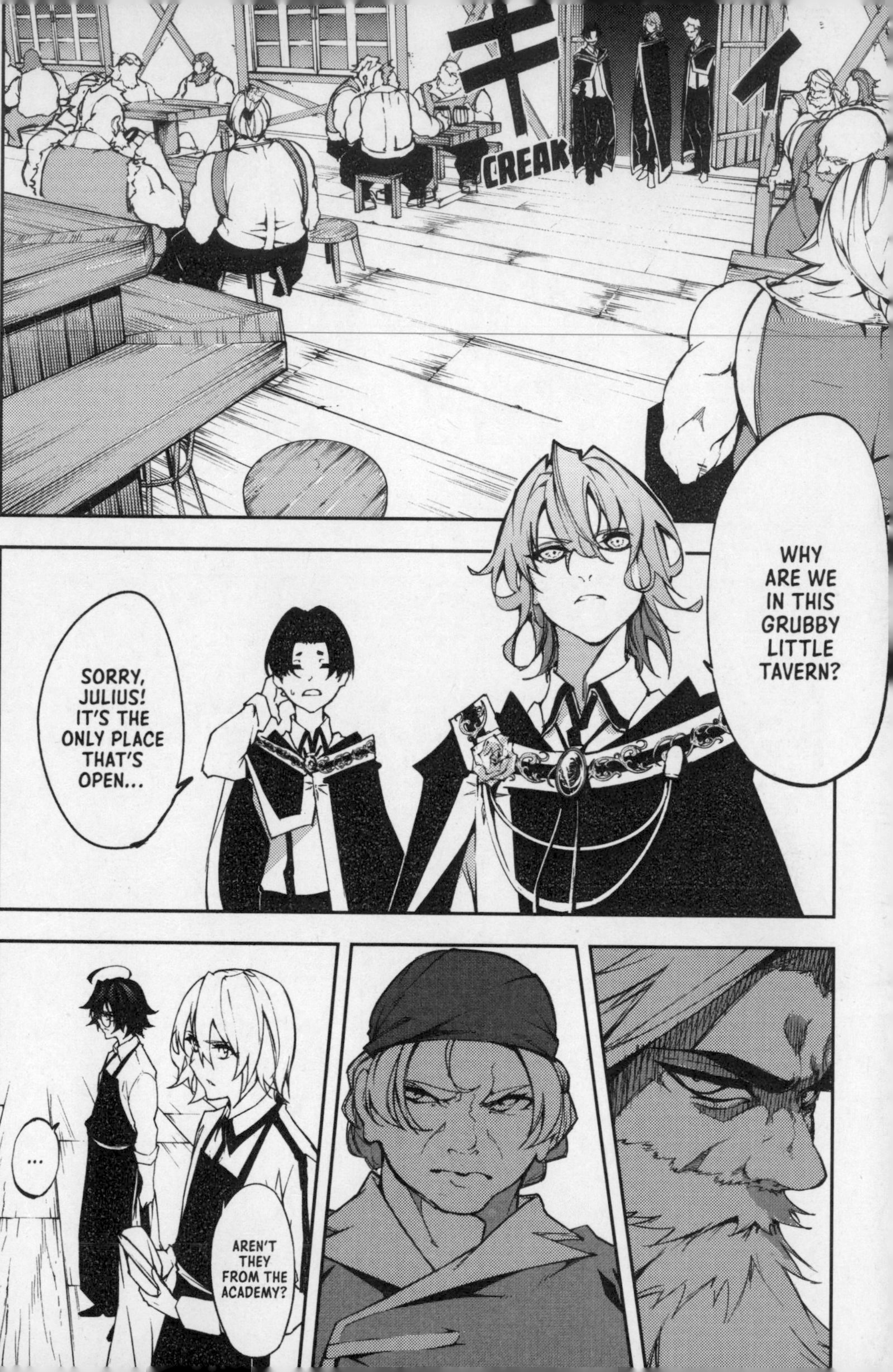
キイ
CREAK
WHY ARE WE IN THIS GRUBBY LITTLE TAVERN?
SORRY, JULIUS! IT'S THE ONLY PLACE THAT'S OPEN...
...
AREN'T THEY FROM THE ACADEMY?

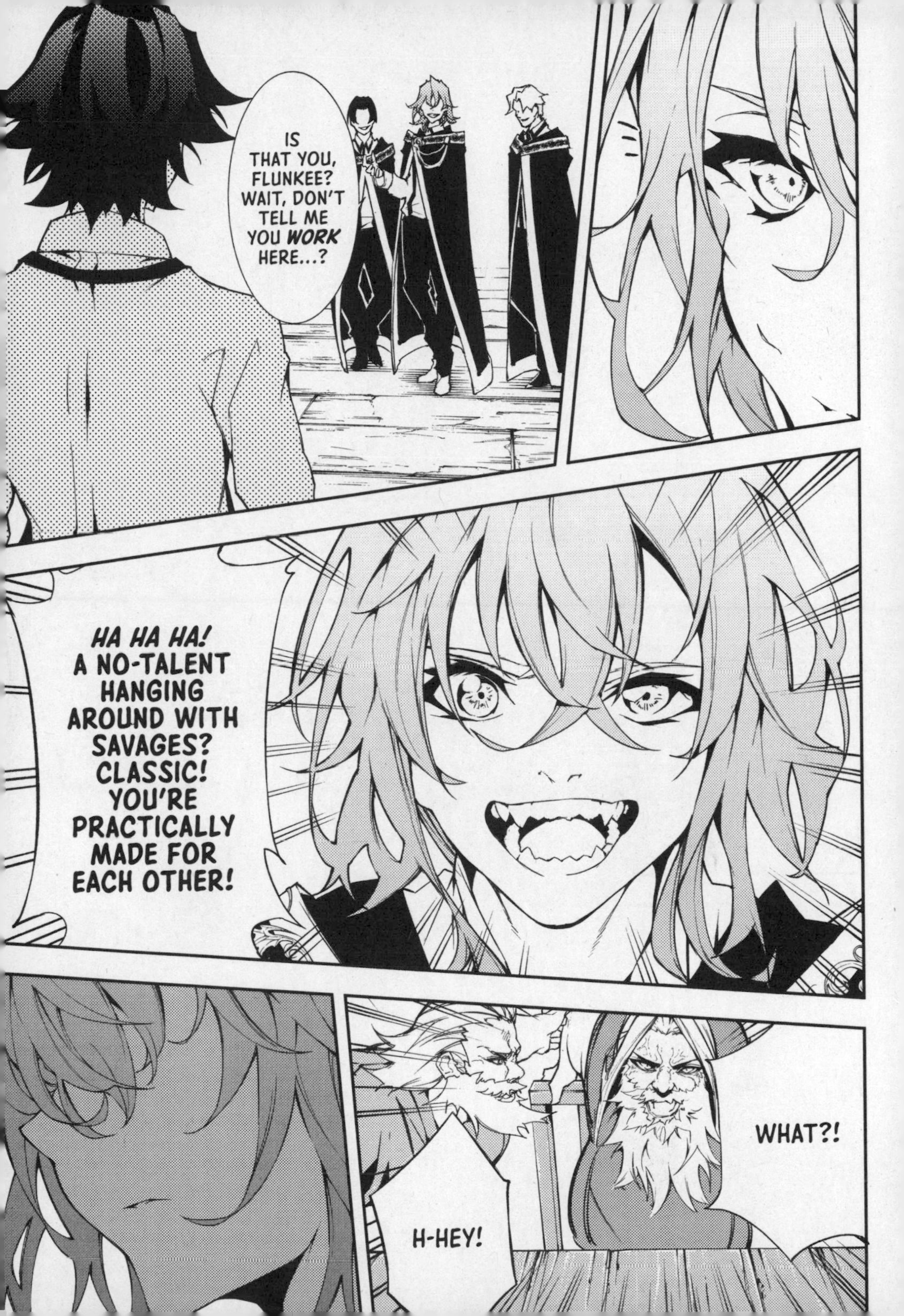
IS THAT YOU, FLUNKEE? WAIT, DON'T TELL ME YOU *WORK* HERE...?
HA HA HA! A NO-TALENT HANGING AROUND WITH SAVAGES? CLASSIC! YOU'RE PRACTICALLY MADE FOR EACH OTHER!
WHAT?!
H-HEY!

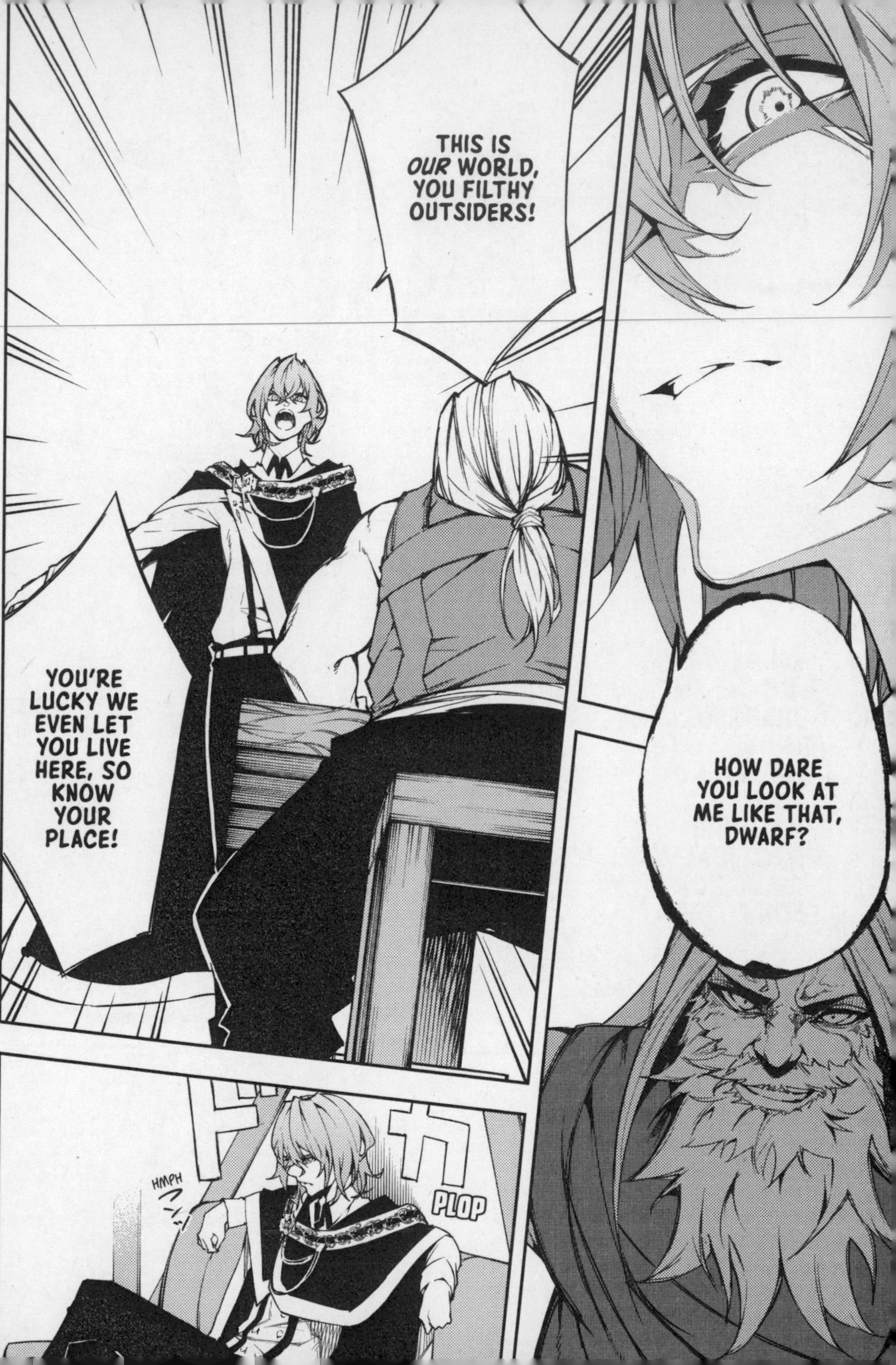
HOW DARE YOU LOOK AT ME LIKE THAT, DWARF?
THIS IS *OUR* WORLD, YOU FILTHY OUTSIDERS!
YOU'RE LUCKY WE EVEN LET YOU LIVE HERE, SO KNOW YOUR PLACE!
HMPH
PLOP

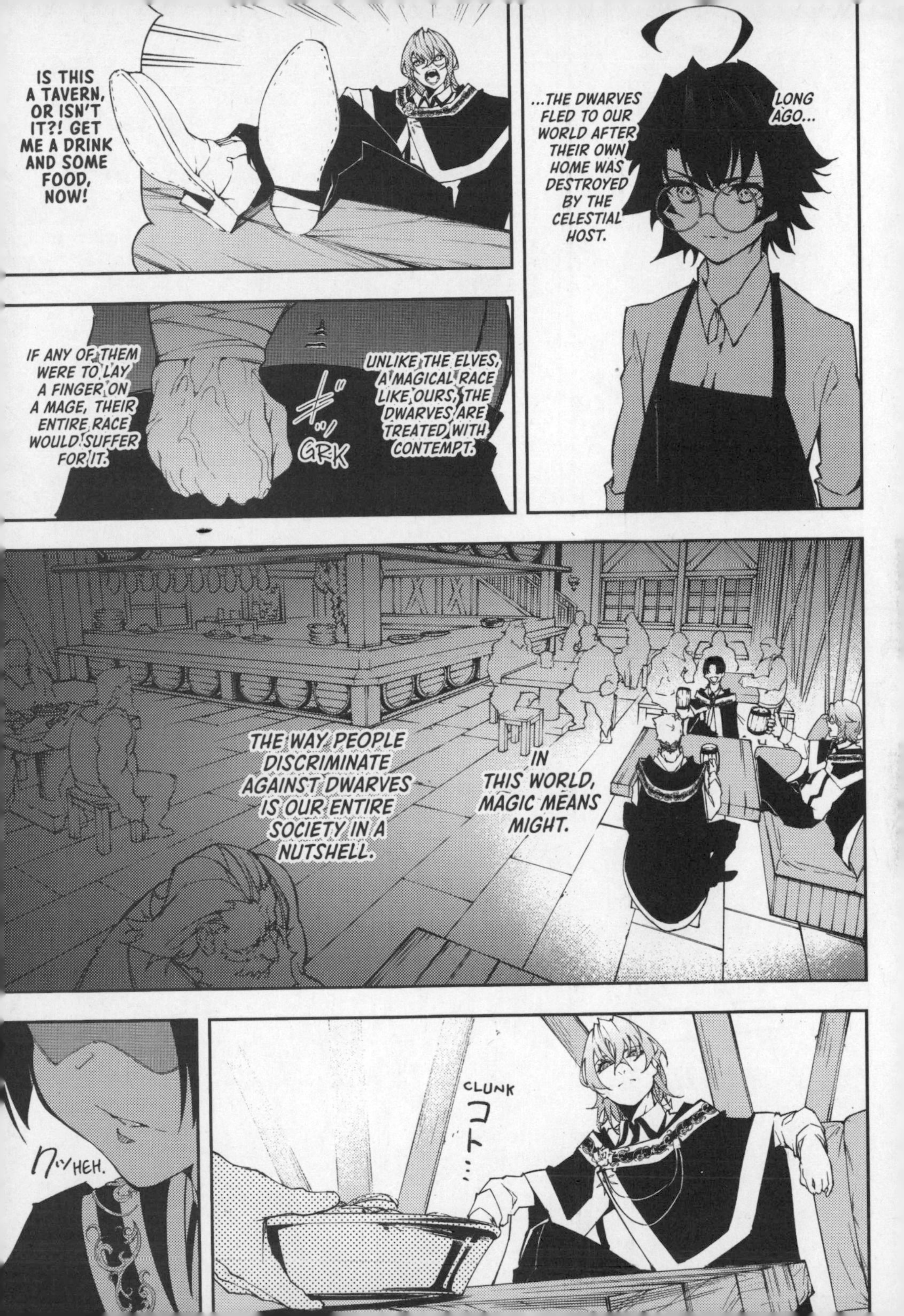

LONG AGO...
...THE DWARVES FLED TO OUR WORLD AFTER THEIR OWN HOME WAS DESTROYED BY THE CELESTIAL HOST.
IS THIS A TAVERN, OR ISN'T IT?! GET ME A DRINK AND SOME FOOD, NOW!
UNLIKE THE ELVES, A MAGICAL RACE LIKE OURS, THE DWARVES ARE TREATED WITH CONTEMPT.
ギッ
GRK
IF ANY OF THEM WERE TO LAY A FINGER ON A MAGE, THEIR ENTIRE RACE WOULD SUFFER FOR IT.
IN THIS WORLD, MAGIC MEANS MIGHT.
THE WAY PEOPLE DISCRIMINATE AGAINST DWARVES IS OUR ENTIRE SOCIETY IN A NUTSHELL.
CLUNK
コト…
ハッ
HEH.

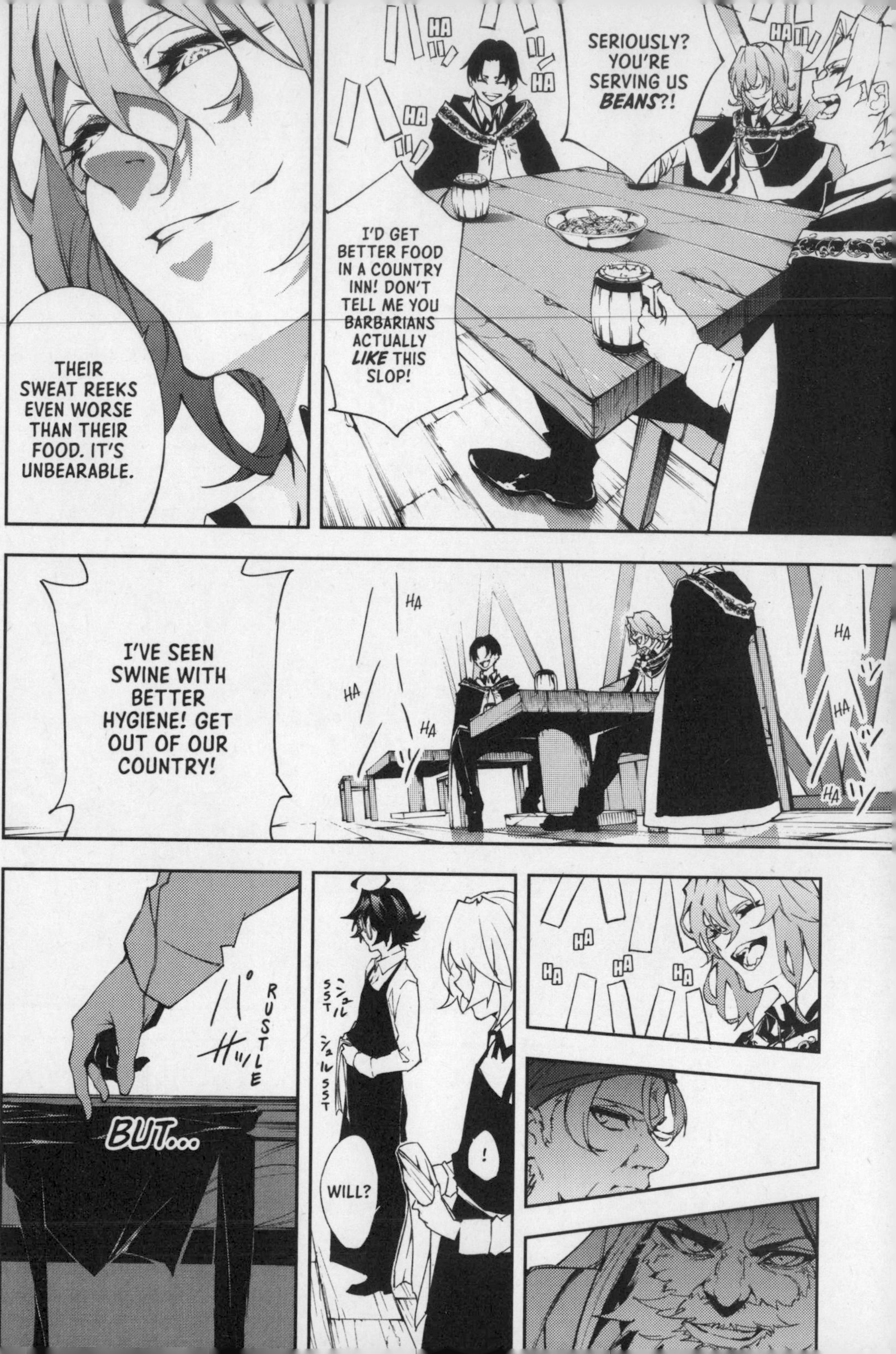
HA HA
SERIOUSLY? YOU'RE SERVING US BEANS?!
HA HA
HA HA
I'D GET BETTER FOOD IN A COUNTRY INN! DON'T TELL ME YOU BARBARIANS ACTUALLY LIKE THIS SLOP!
THEIR SWEAT REEKS EVEN WORSE THAN THEIR FOOD. IT'S UNBEARABLE.
HA HA HA
I'VE SEEN SWINE WITH BETTER HYGIENE! GET OUT OF OUR COUNTRY!
HA HA HA
HA HA HA HA
!
SST
SST
WILL?
RUSTLE
BUT...

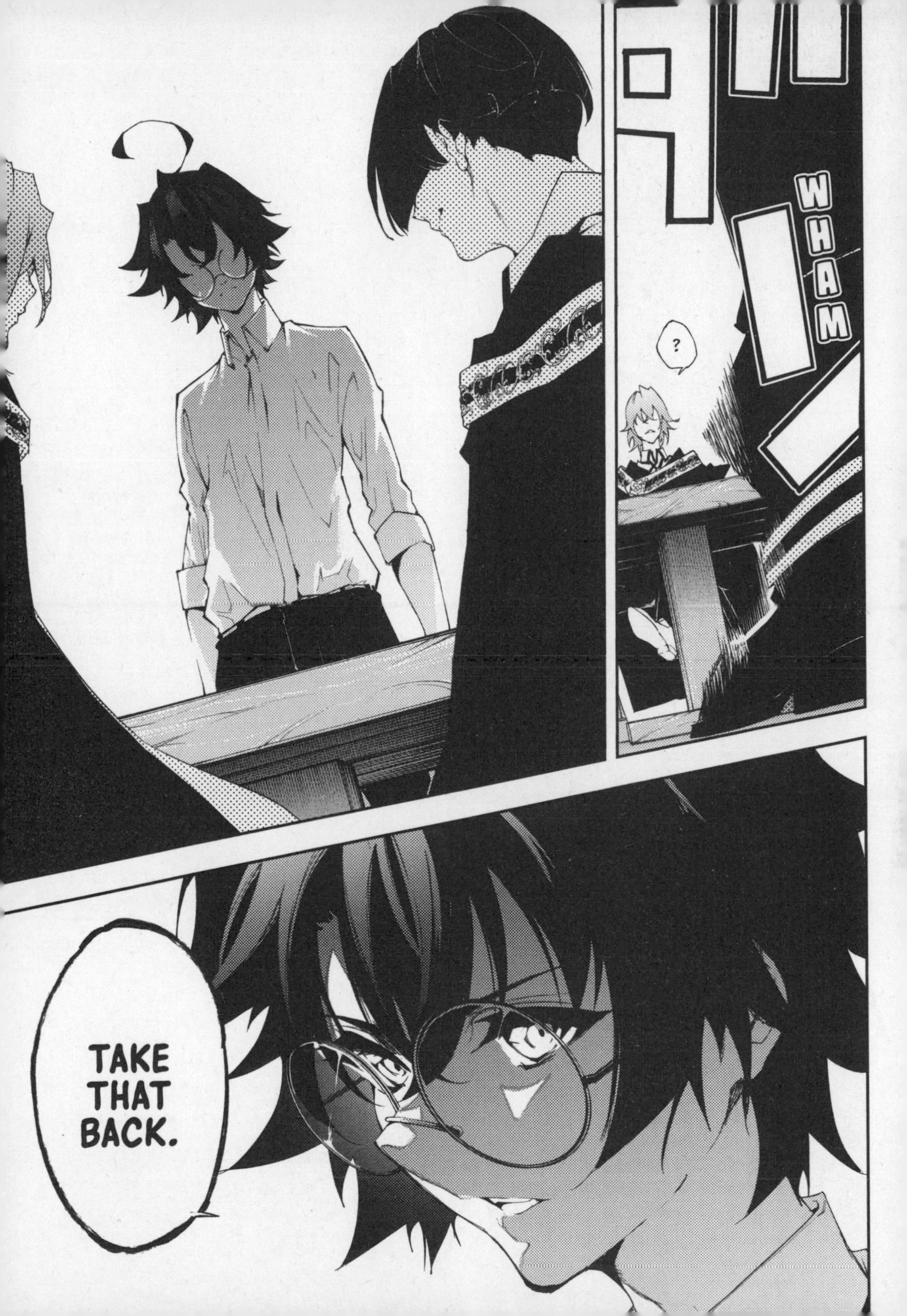
WHAM
?
TAKE THAT BACK.

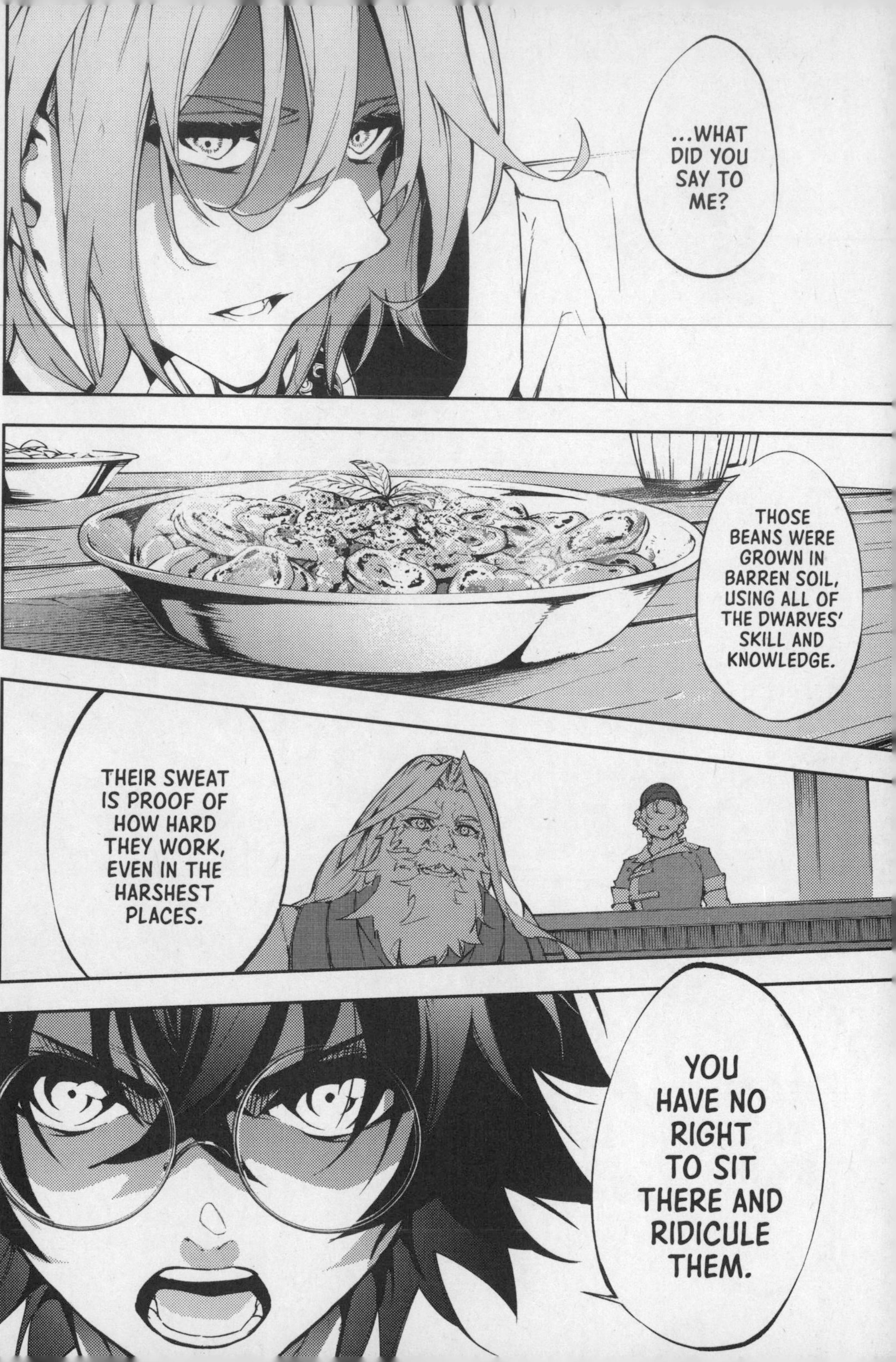
...WHAT DID YOU SAY TO ME?
THOSE BEANS WERE GROWN IN BARREN SOIL, USING ALL OF THE DWARVES' SKILL AND KNOWLEDGE.
THEIR SWEAT IS PROOF OF HOW HARD THEY WORK, EVEN IN THE HARSHEST PLACES.
YOU HAVE NO RIGHT TO SIT THERE AND RIDICULE THEM.

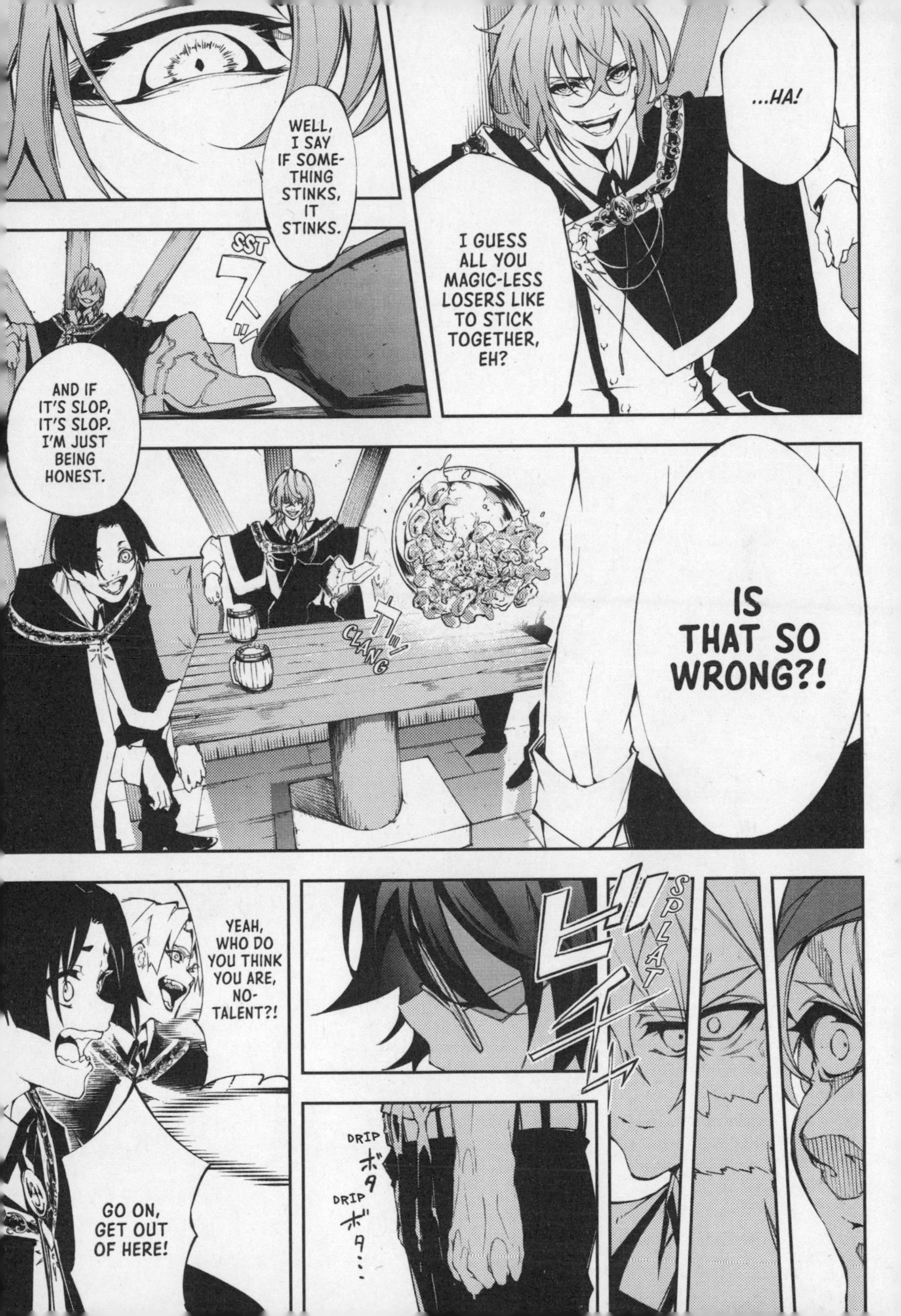
...HA!
I GUESS ALL YOU MAGIC-LESS LOSERS LIKE TO STICK TOGETHER, EH?
WELL, I SAY IF SOME-THING STINKS, IT STINKS.
SST
AND IF IT'S SLOP, IT'S SLOP. I'M JUST BEING HONEST.
IS THAT SO WRONG?!
CLANG
SPLAT
DRIP
DRIP
YEAH, WHO DO YOU THINK YOU ARE, NO-TALENT?!
GO ON, GET OUT OF HERE!

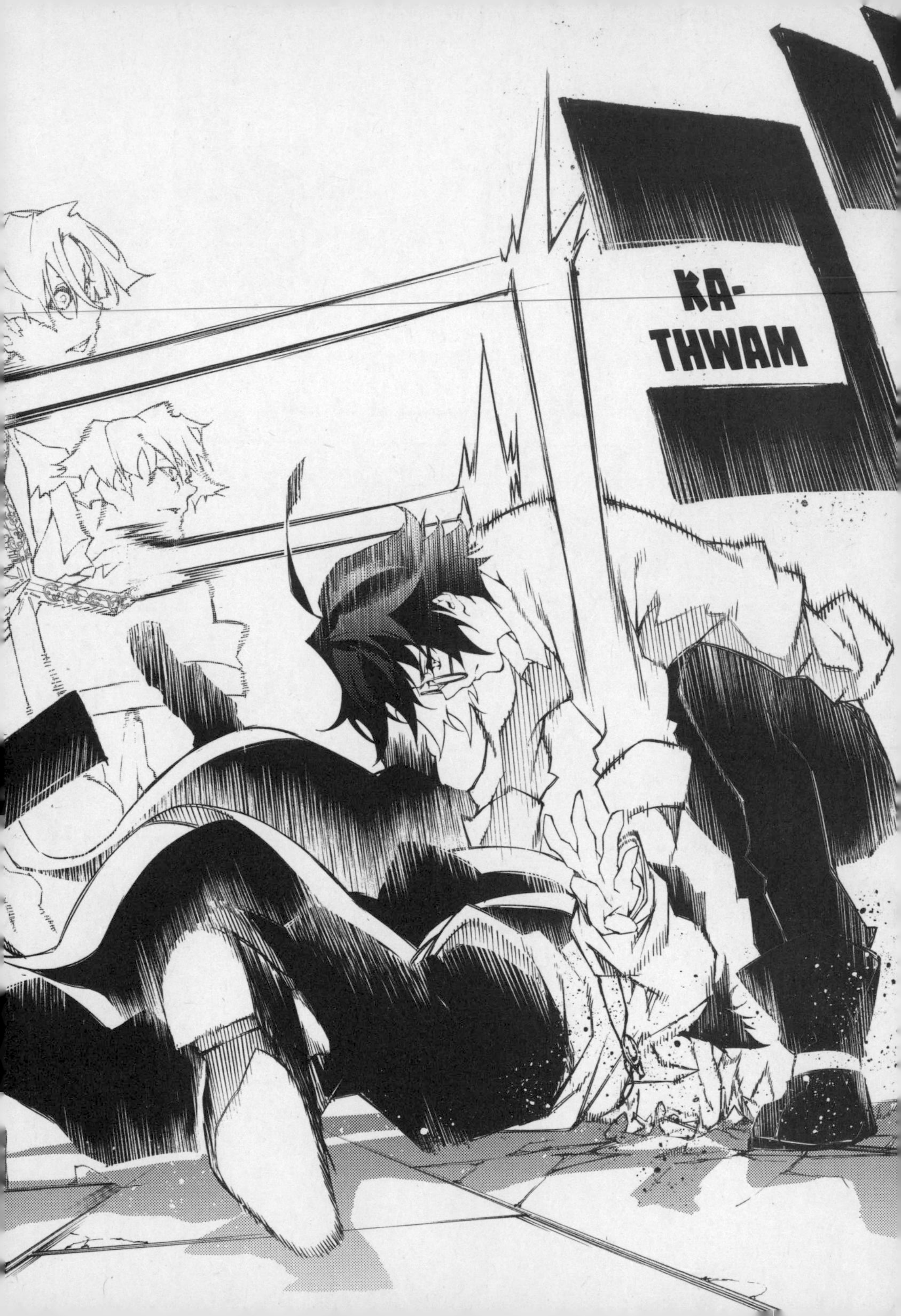
KA-
THWAM

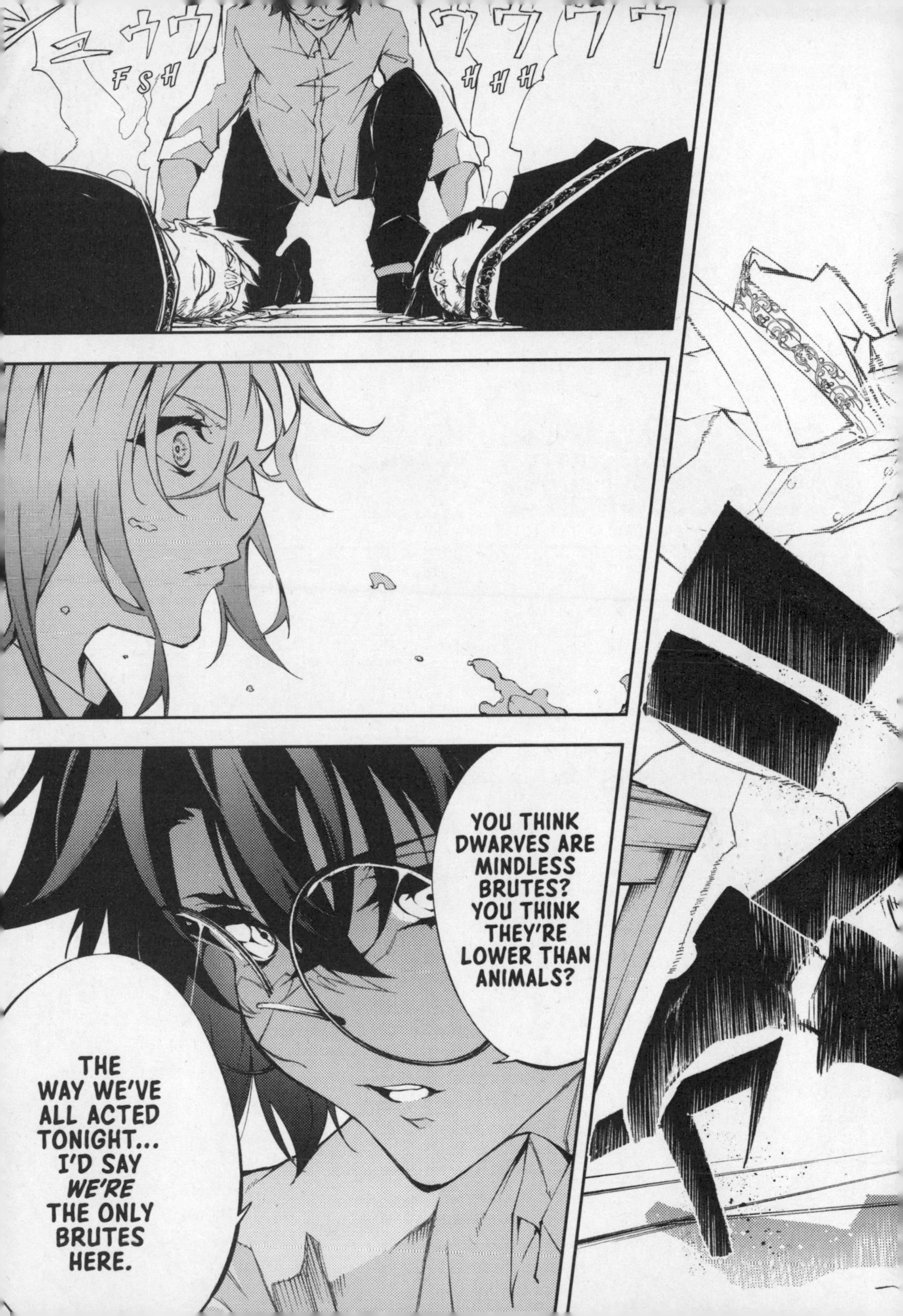
ウウウウ
HHH
ュウウ
FSH
YOU THINK DWARVES ARE MINDLESS BRUTES? YOU THINK THEY'RE LOWER THAN ANIMALS?
THE WAY WE'VE ALL ACTED TONIGHT... I'D SAY *WE'RE* THE ONLY BRUTES HERE.

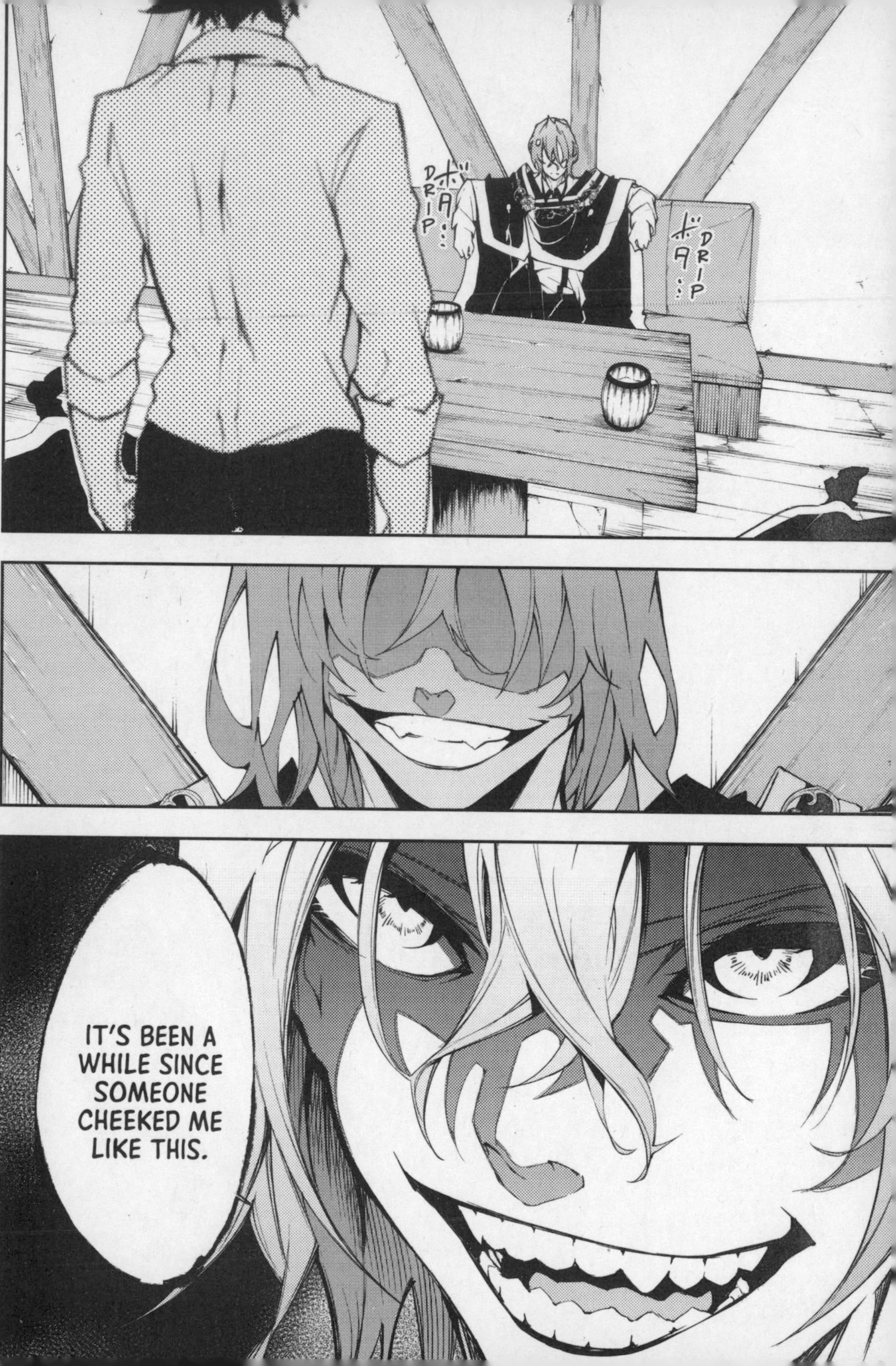
ボタ…
DRIP
ボタ…
DRIP
IT'S BEEN A WHILE SINCE SOMEONE CHEEKED ME LIKE THIS.

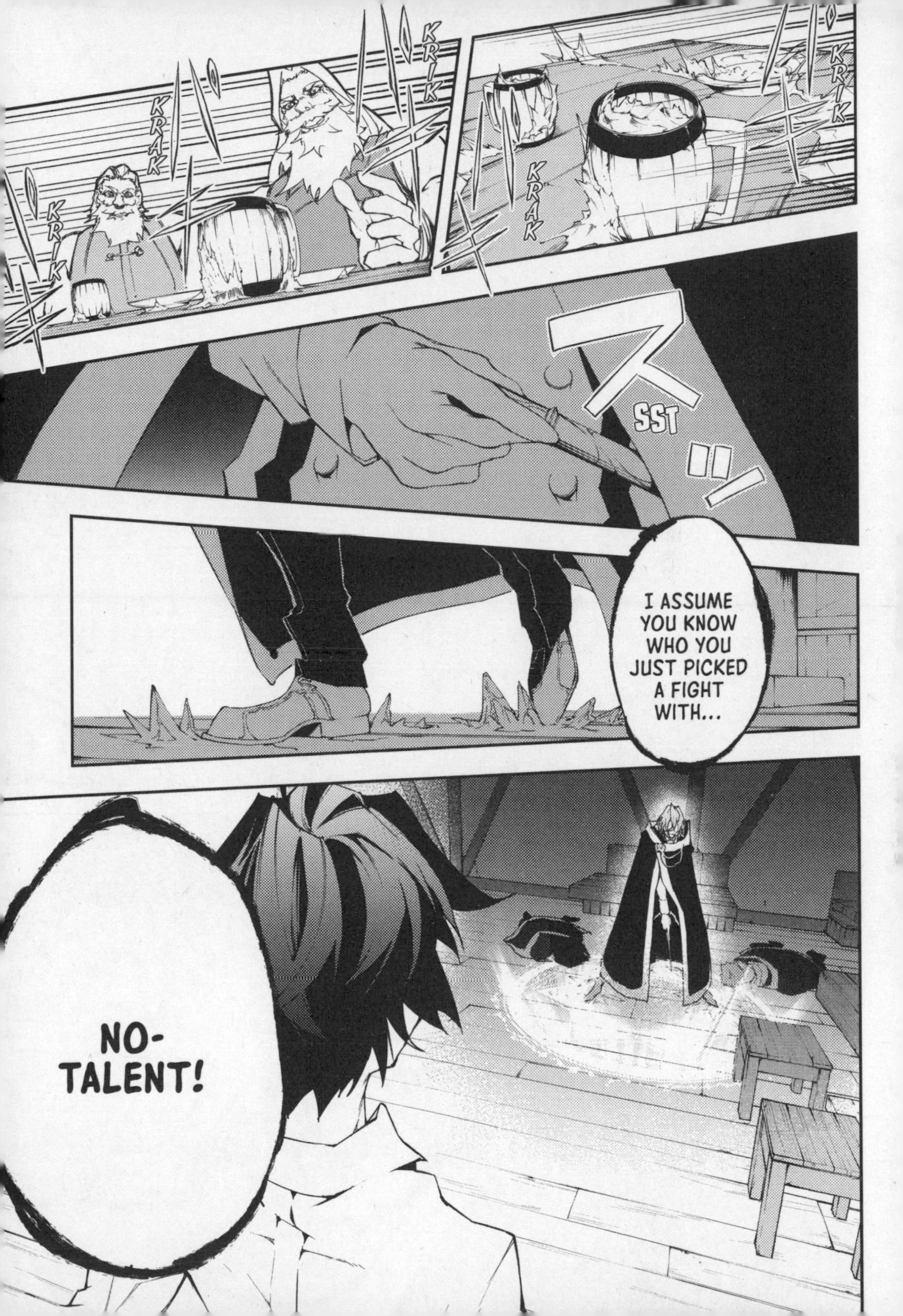
KRIK
KRAK
KRIK
KRAK
KRIK
スッ
SST
I ASSUME YOU KNOW WHO YOU JUST PICKED A FIGHT WITH...
NO-TALENT!

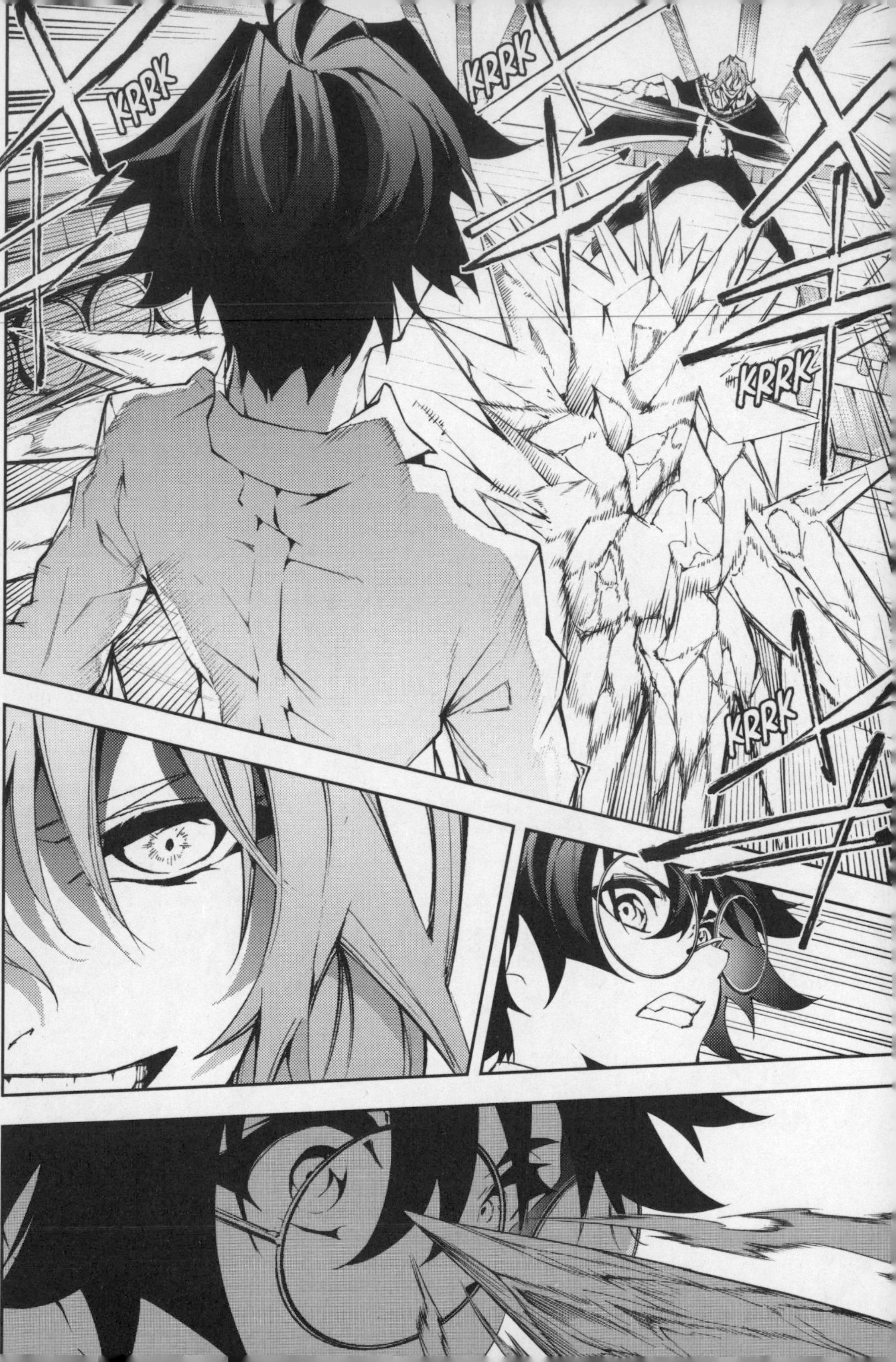
KRRK
KRRK
KRRK
KRRK

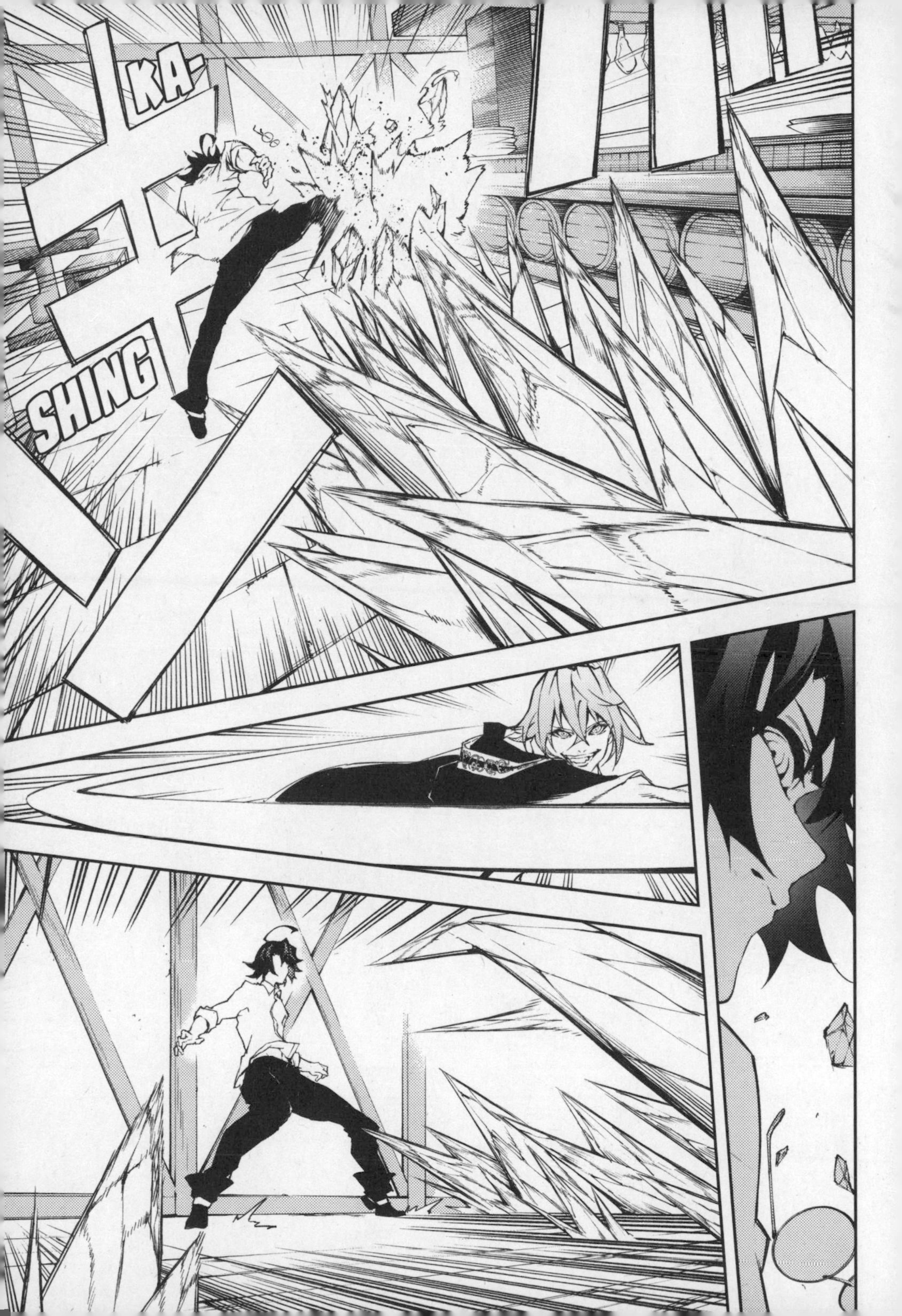
KA-
SHING

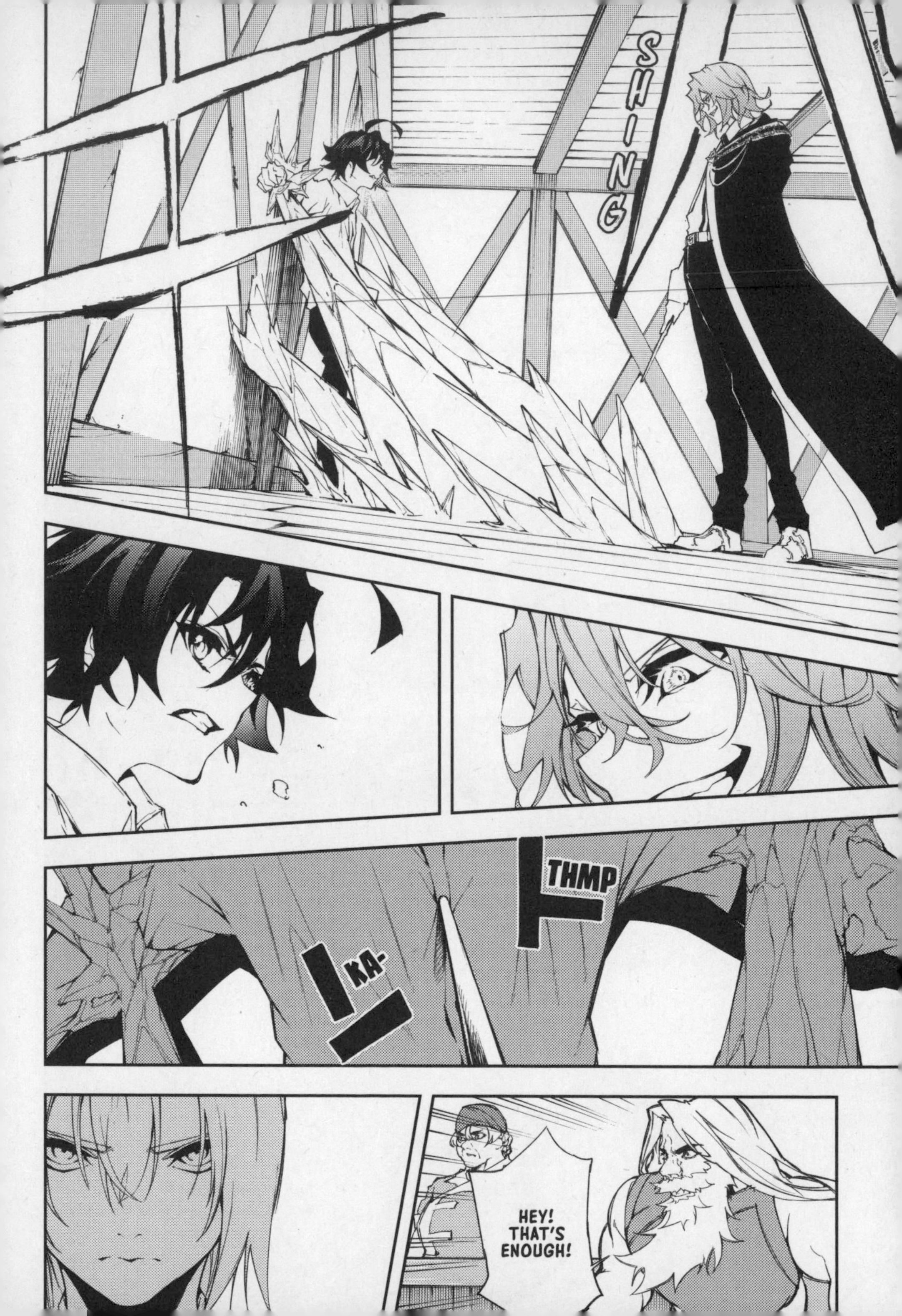
SHING
THMP
KA-
HEY! THAT'S ENOUGH!

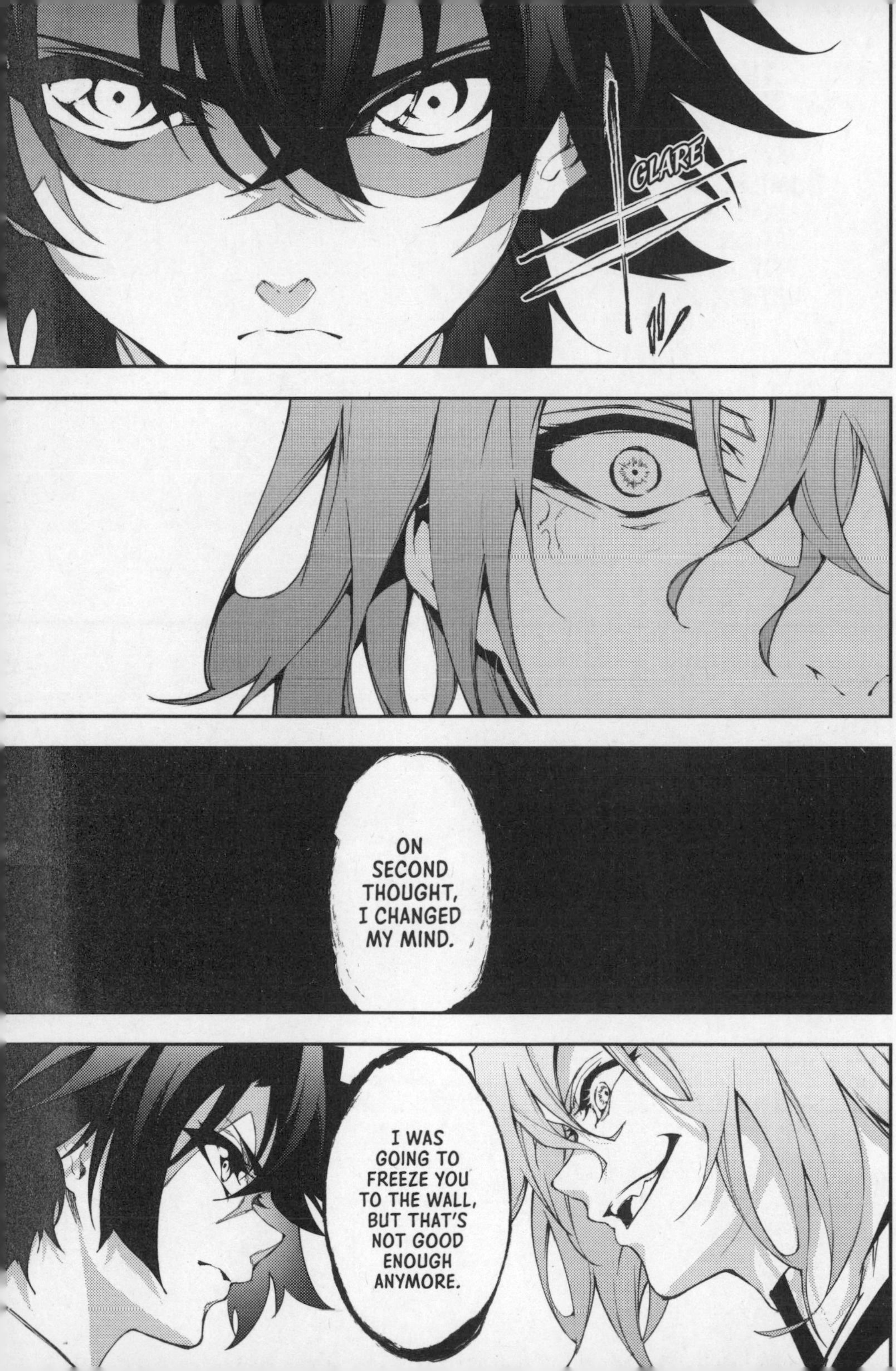
GLARE
ON SECOND THOUGHT, I CHANGED MY MIND.
I WAS GOING TO FREEZE YOU TO THE WALL, BUT THAT'S NOT GOOD ENOUGH ANYMORE.

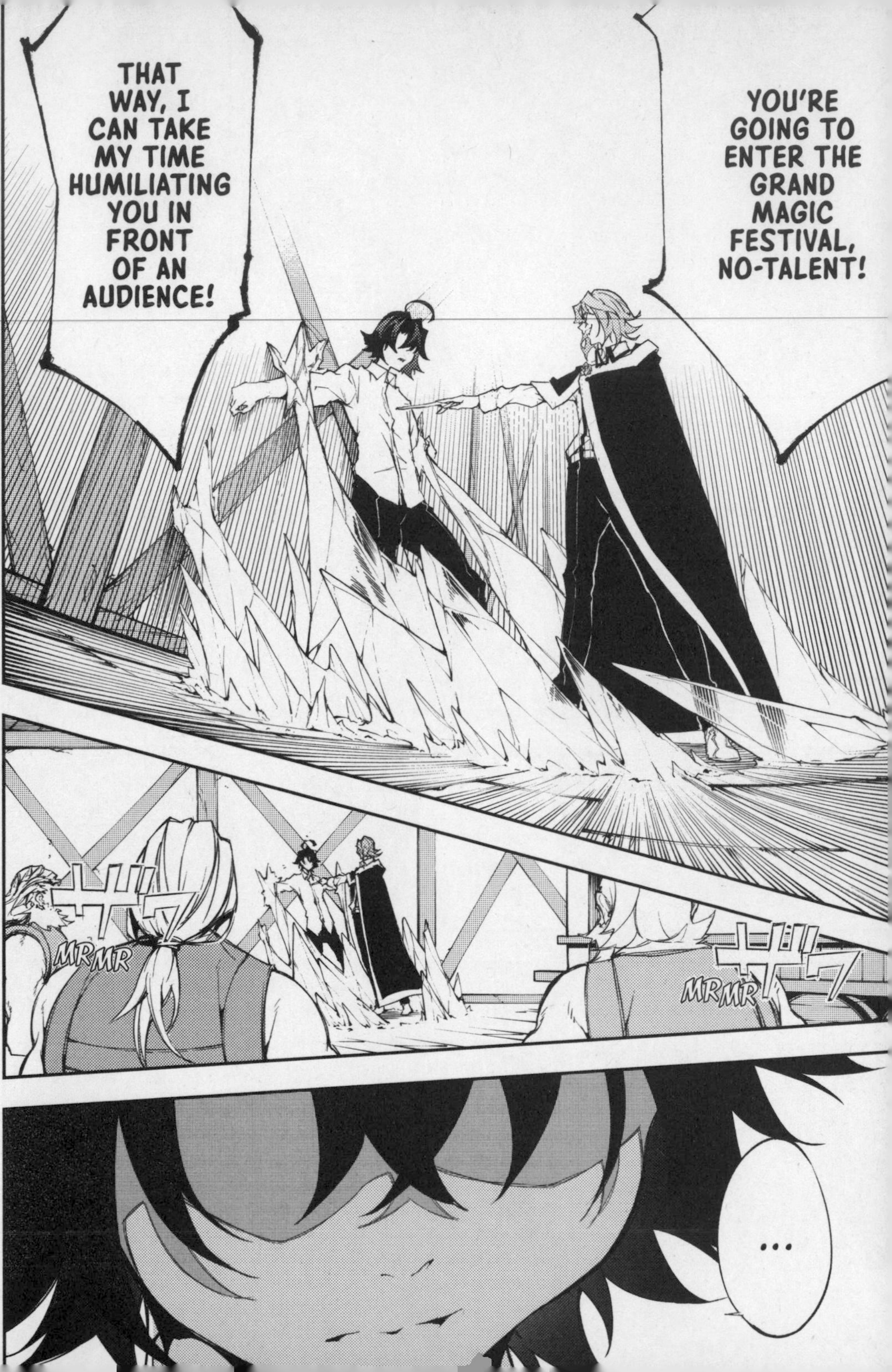
YOU'RE GOING TO ENTER THE GRAND MAGIC FESTIVAL, NO-TALENT!
THAT WAY, I CAN TAKE MY TIME HUMILIATING YOU IN FRONT OF AN AUDIENCE!
MRMR
MRMR
...

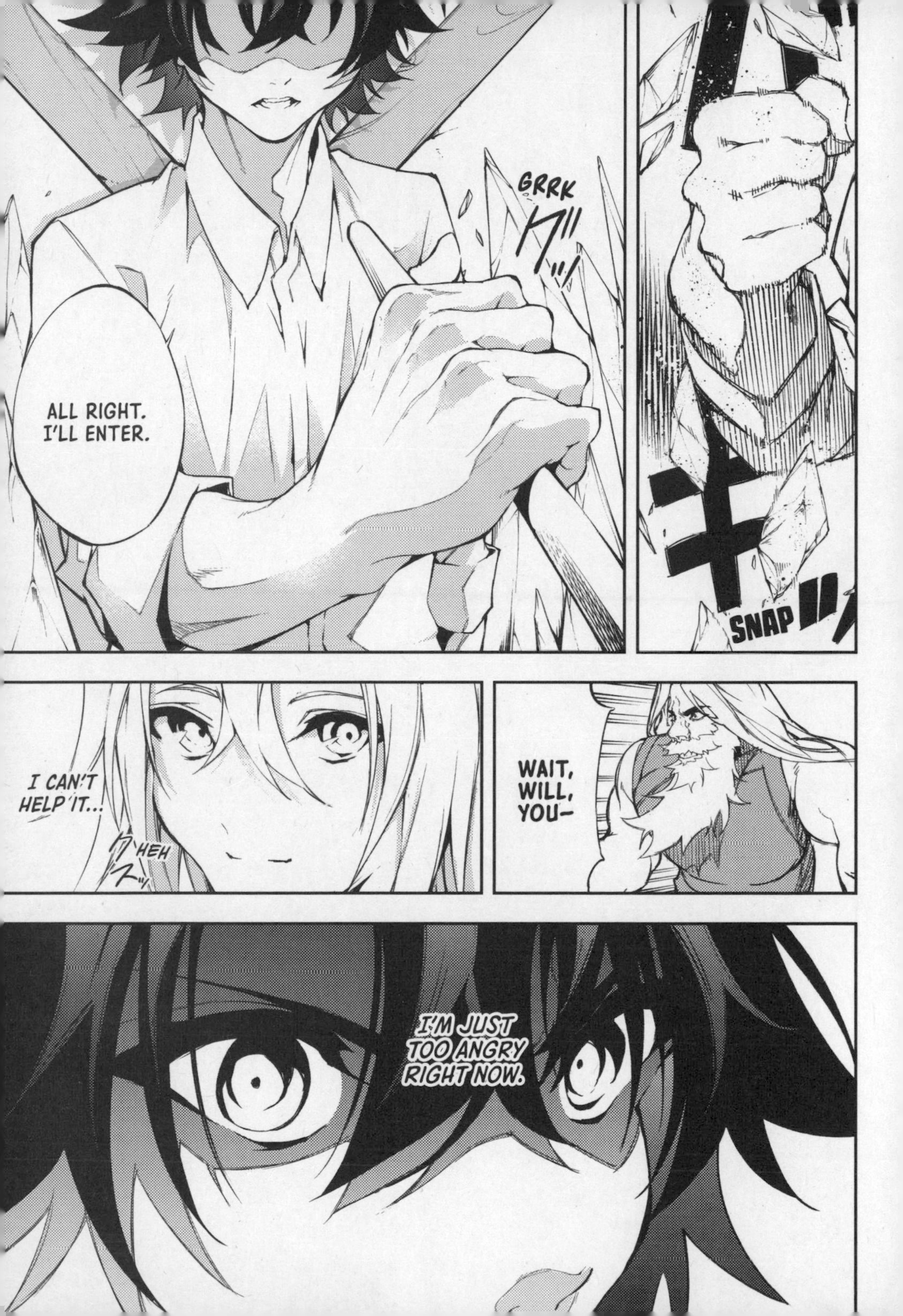
SNAP
GRRK
ALL RIGHT. I'LL ENTER.
WAIT, WILL, YOU–
I CAN'T HELP IT...
HEH
I'M JUST TOO ANGRY RIGHT NOW.

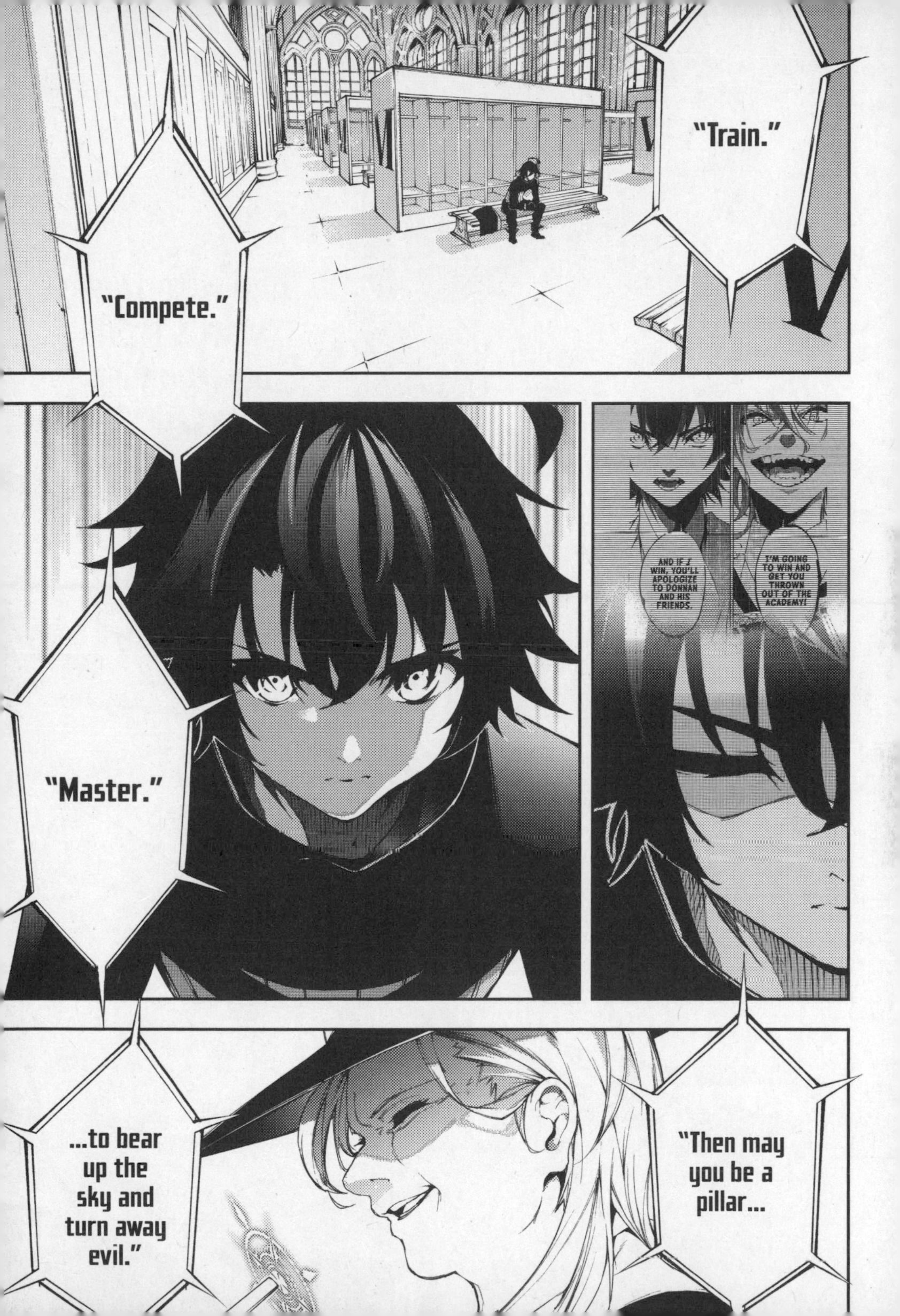
"Train."
"Compete."
I'M GOING TO WIN AND GET YOU THROWN OUT OF THE ACADEMY!
AND IF I WIN, YOU'LL APOLOGIZE TO DONNAN AND HIS FRIENDS.
"Master."
"Then may you be a pillar...
...to bear up the sky and turn away evil."

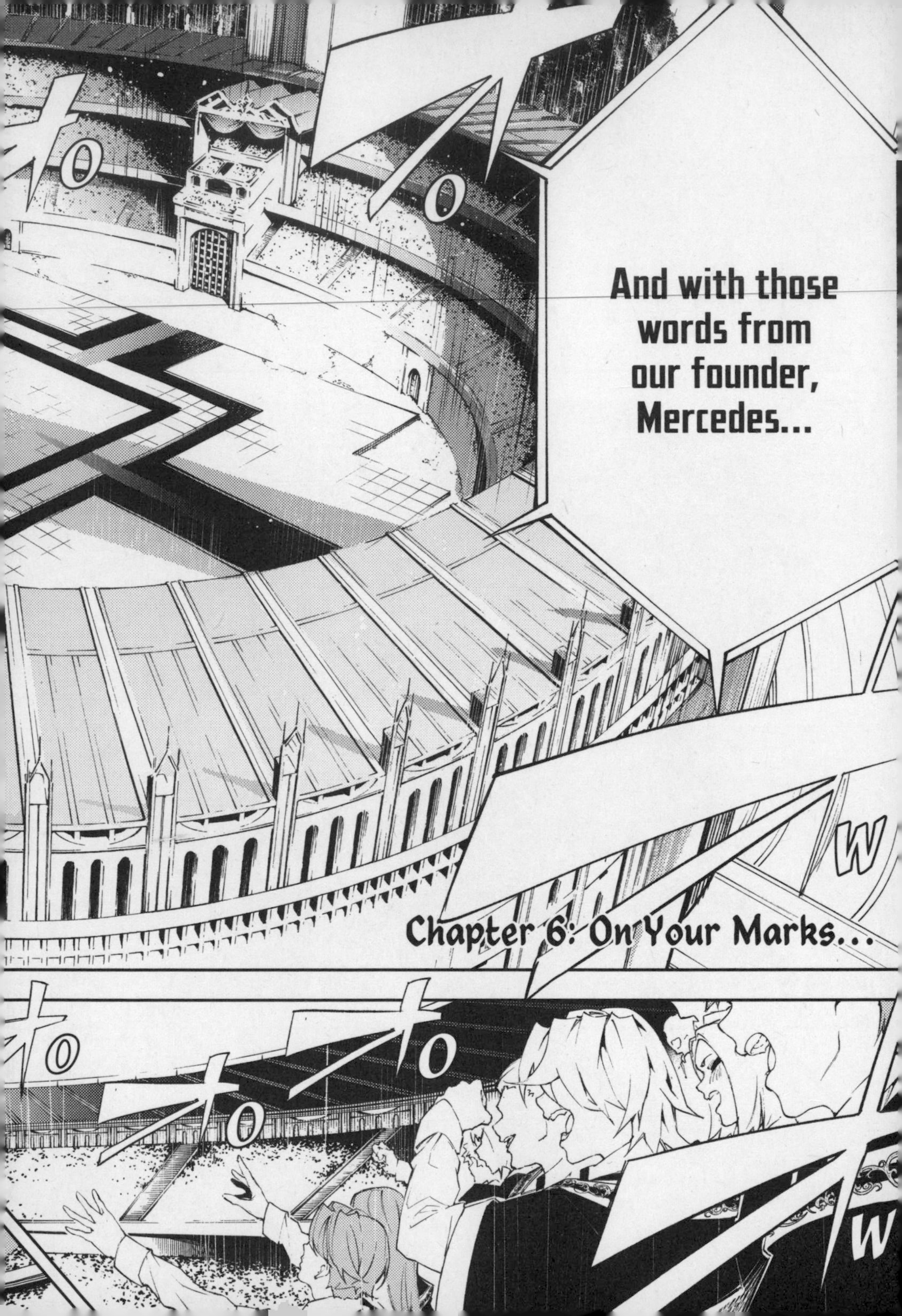
And with those words from our founder, Mercedes...
O
O
W
Chapter 6: On Your Marks...
O
O
O
W

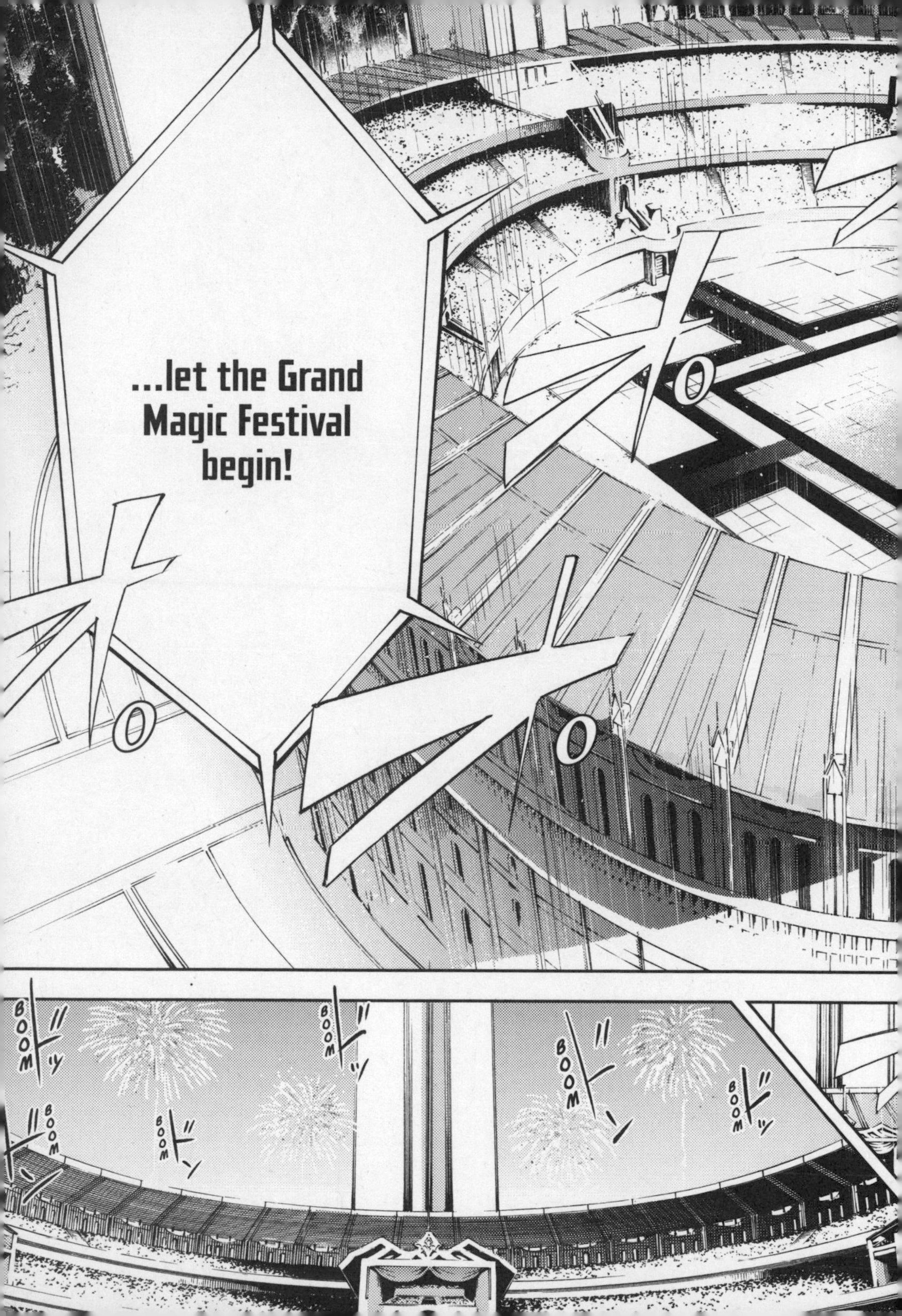
...let the Grand Magic Festival begin!
BOOM
BOOM
BOOM
BOOM
BOOM
BOOM

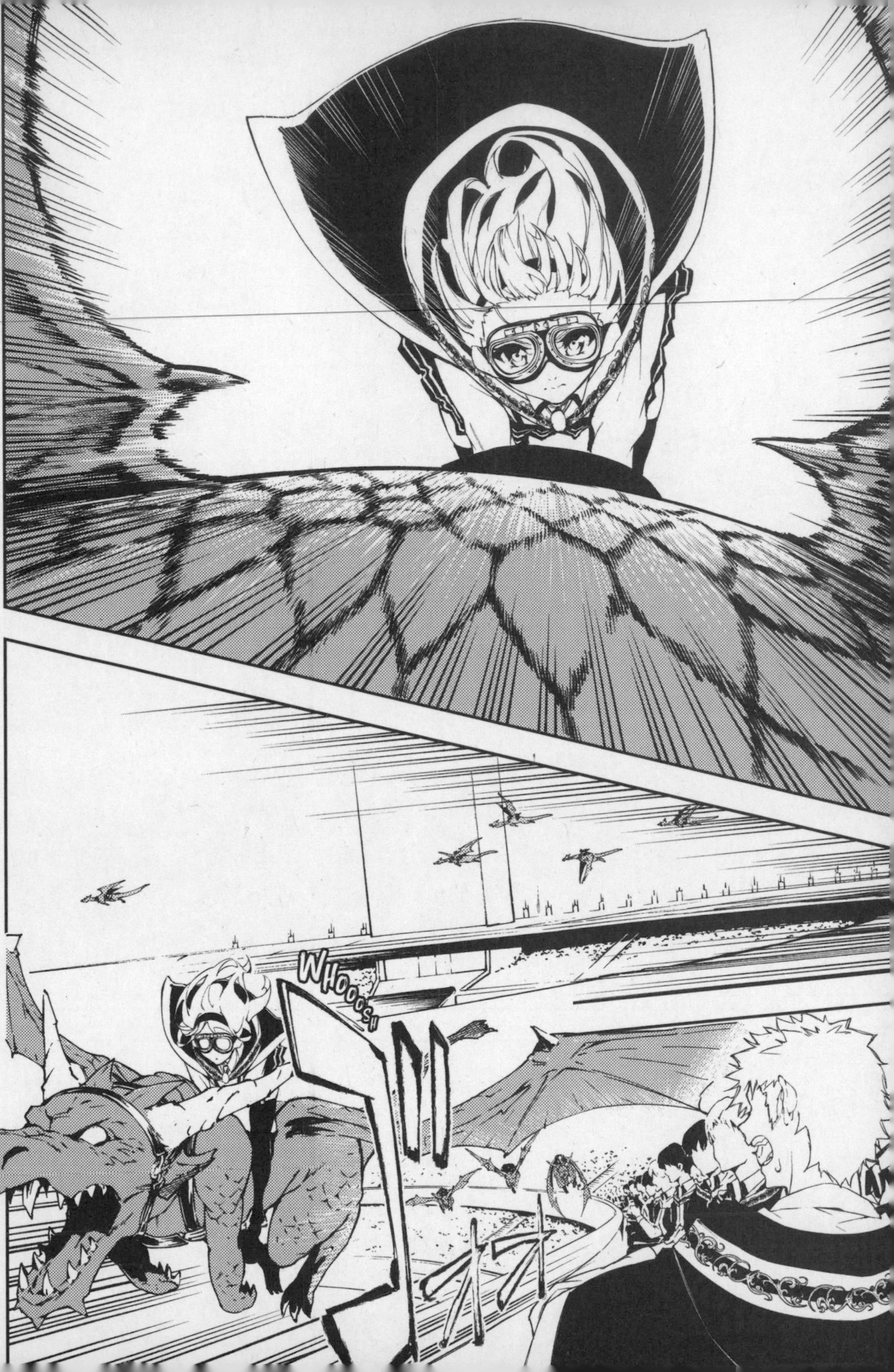
WHOOOSH

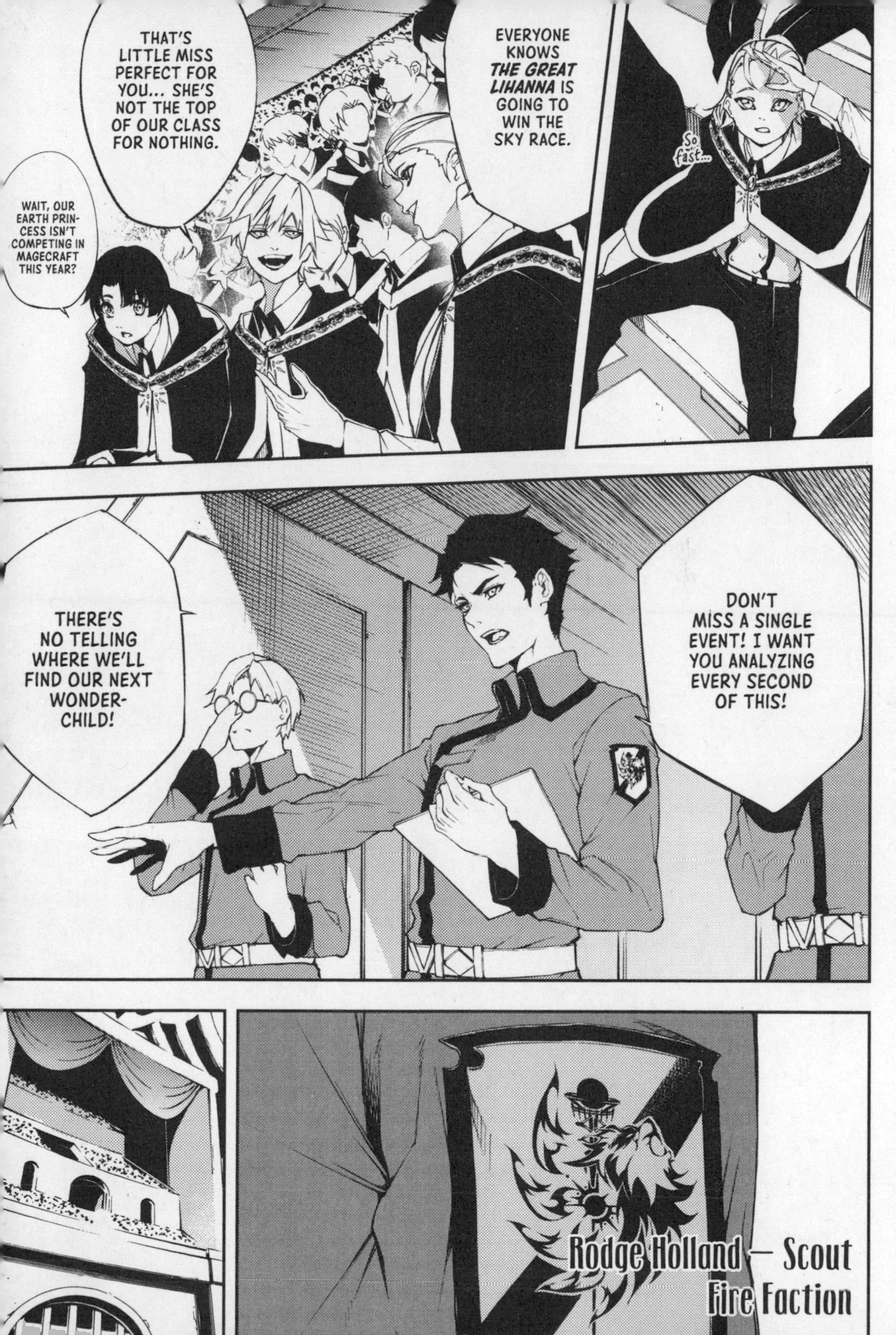
So fast...
EVERYONE KNOWS THE GREAT LIHANNA IS GOING TO WIN THE SKY RACE.
THAT'S LITTLE MISS PERFECT FOR YOU... SHE'S NOT THE TOP OF OUR CLASS FOR NOTHING.
WAIT, OUR EARTH PRINCESS ISN'T COMPETING IN MAGECRAFT THIS YEAR?
DON'T MISS A SINGLE EVENT! I WANT YOU ANALYZING EVERY SECOND OF THIS!
THERE'S NO TELLING WHERE WE'LL FIND OUR NEXT WONDER-CHILD!
Rodge Holland — Scout
Fire Faction

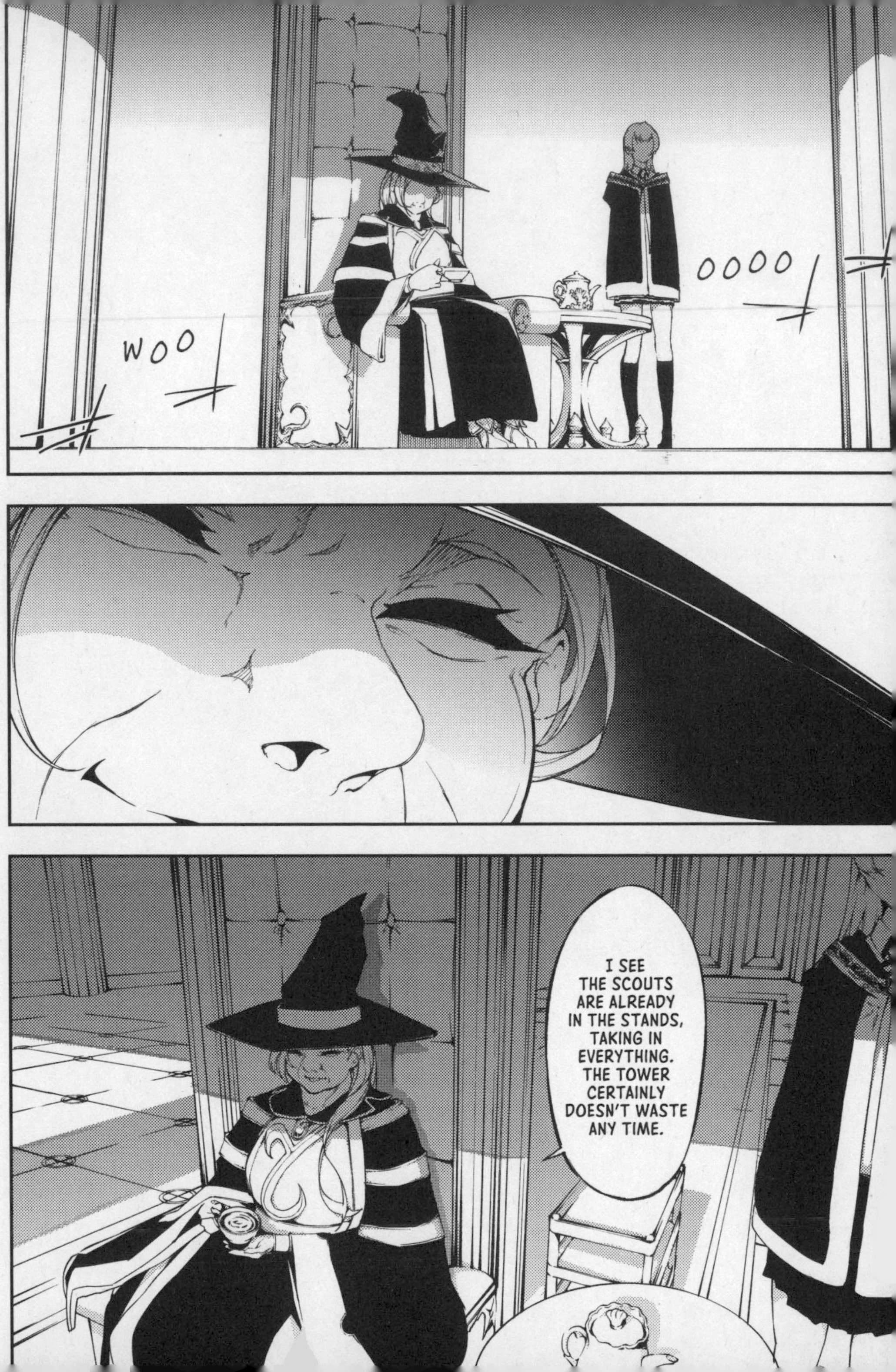
OOOO
WOO
I SEE THE SCOUTS ARE ALREADY IN THE STANDS, TAKING IN EVERYTHING. THE TOWER CERTAINLY DOESN'T WASTE ANY TIME.

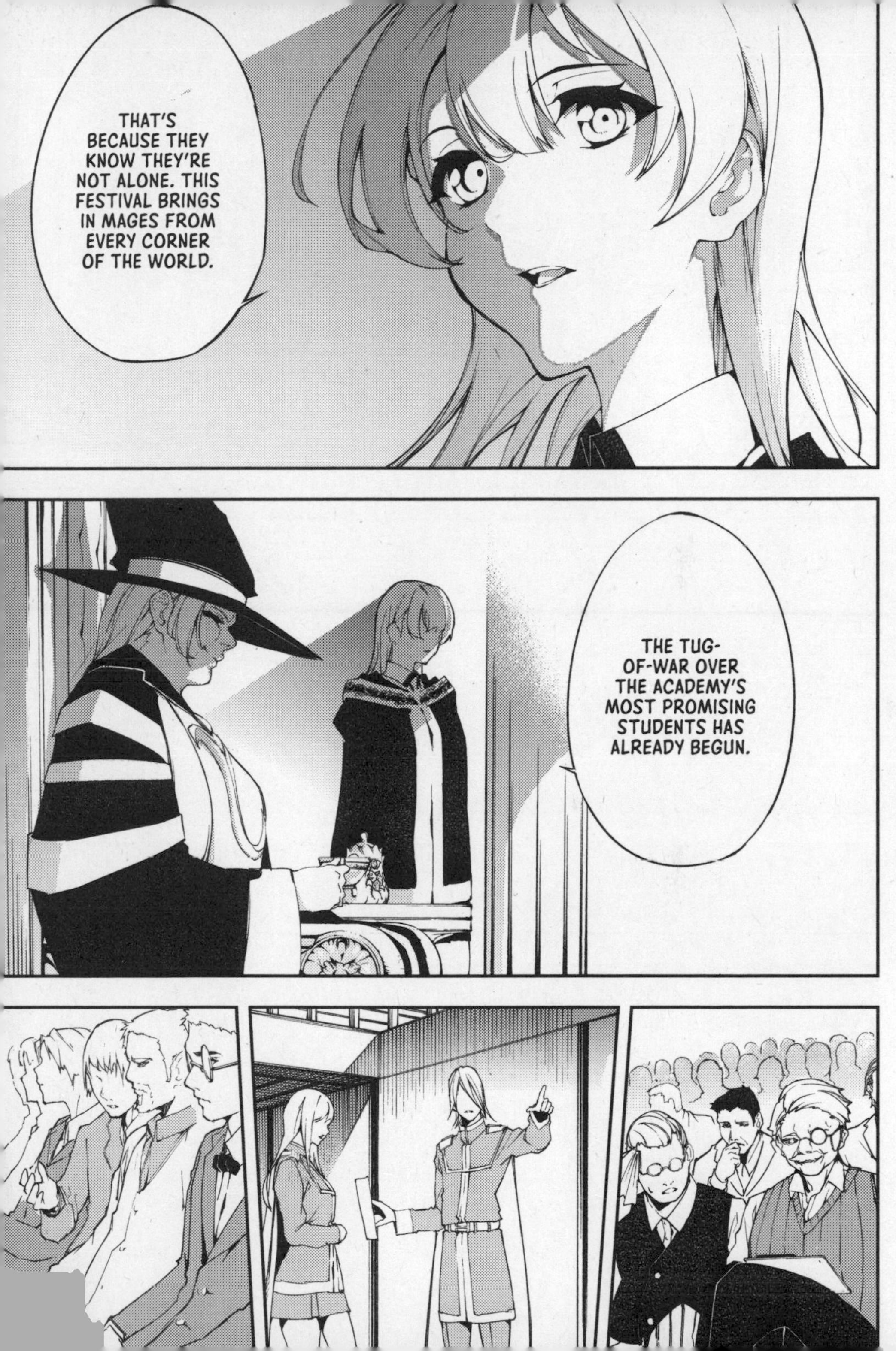
THAT'S BECAUSE THEY KNOW THEY'RE NOT ALONE. THIS FESTIVAL BRINGS IN MAGES FROM EVERY CORNER OF THE WORLD.
THE TUG-OF-WAR OVER THE ACADEMY'S MOST PROMISING STUDENTS HAS ALREADY BEGUN.

NOW, IF YOU'LL EXCUSE ME.

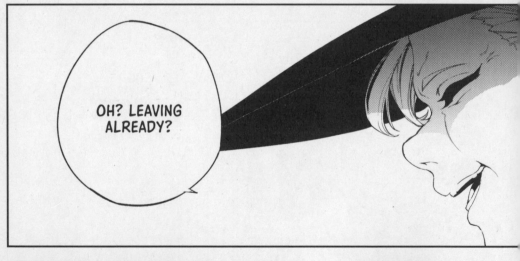

OH? LEAVING ALREADY?

YES. I'M AFRAID THE WATCHERS HAVE THEIR OWN WORK HERE.

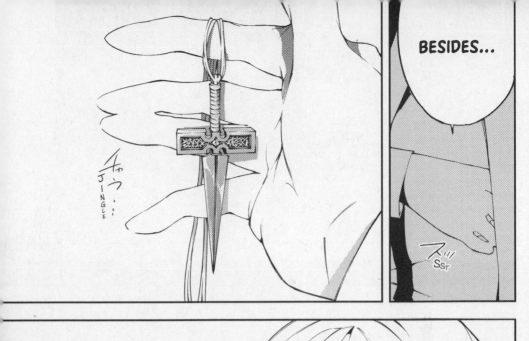

BESIDES...

...THERE'S A CERTAIN UPPER-CLASSMAN I'D LIKE TO CHEER FOR.

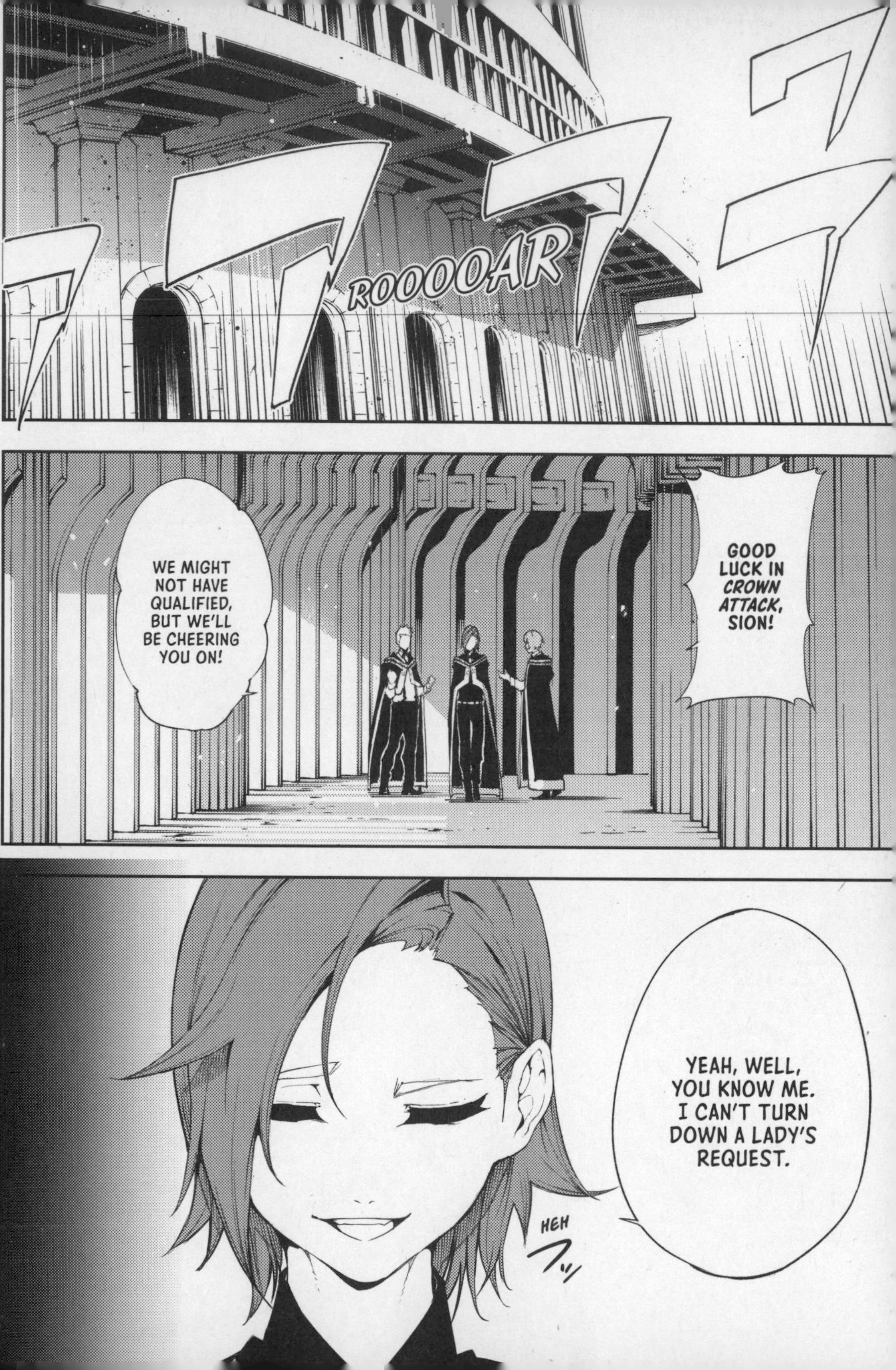
ROOOOAR
GOOD LUCK IN *CROWN ATTACK*, SION!
WE MIGHT NOT HAVE QUALIFIED, BUT WE'LL BE CHEERING YOU ON!
YEAH, WELL, YOU KNOW ME. I CAN'T TURN DOWN A LADY'S REQUEST.
HEH

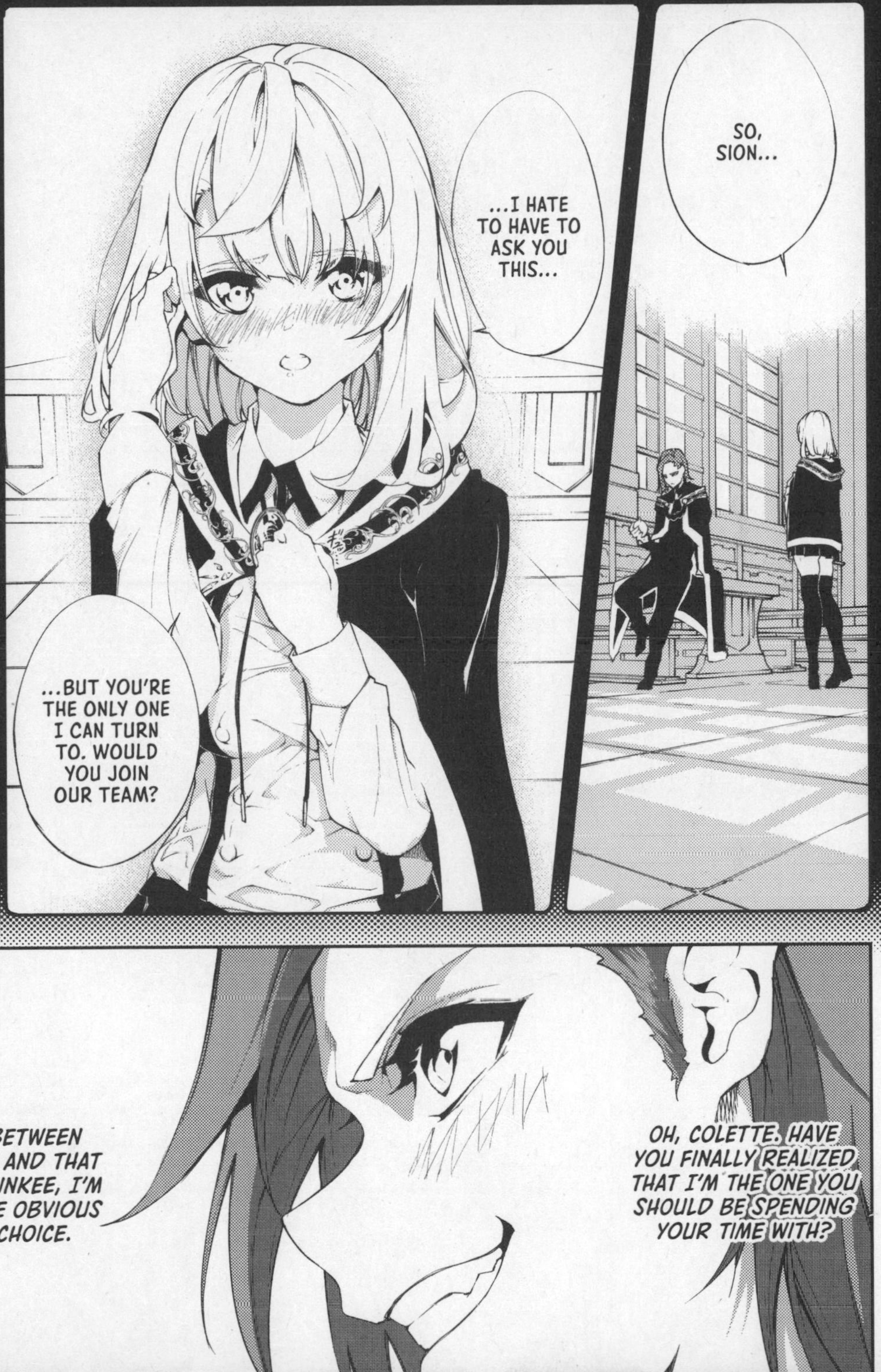
SO, SION...
...I HATE TO HAVE TO ASK YOU THIS...
...BUT YOU'RE THE ONLY ONE I CAN TURN TO. WOULD YOU JOIN OUR TEAM?
OH, COLETTE. HAVE YOU FINALLY REALIZED THAT I'M THE ONE YOU SHOULD BE SPENDING YOUR TIME WITH?
BETWEEN ME AND THAT FLUNKEE, I'M THE OBVIOUS CHOICE.

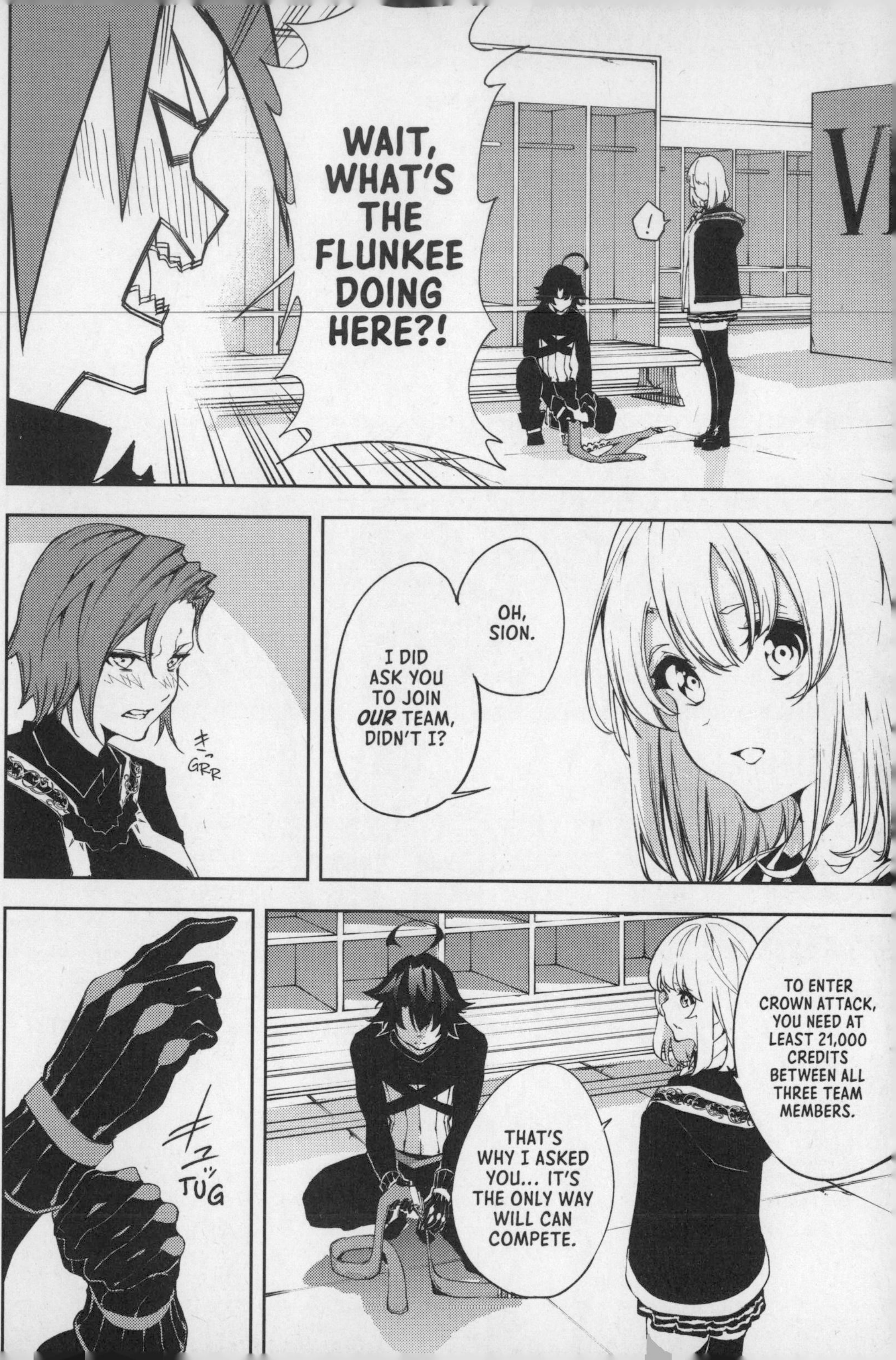
WAIT, WHAT'S THE FLUNKEE DOING HERE?!
!
OH, SION.
I DID ASK YOU TO JOIN *OUR* TEAM, DIDN'T I?
GRR
TO ENTER CROWN ATTACK, YOU NEED AT LEAST 21,000 CREDITS BETWEEN ALL THREE TEAM MEMBERS.
THAT'S WHY I ASKED YOU... IT'S THE ONLY WAY WILL CAN COMPETE.
TUG

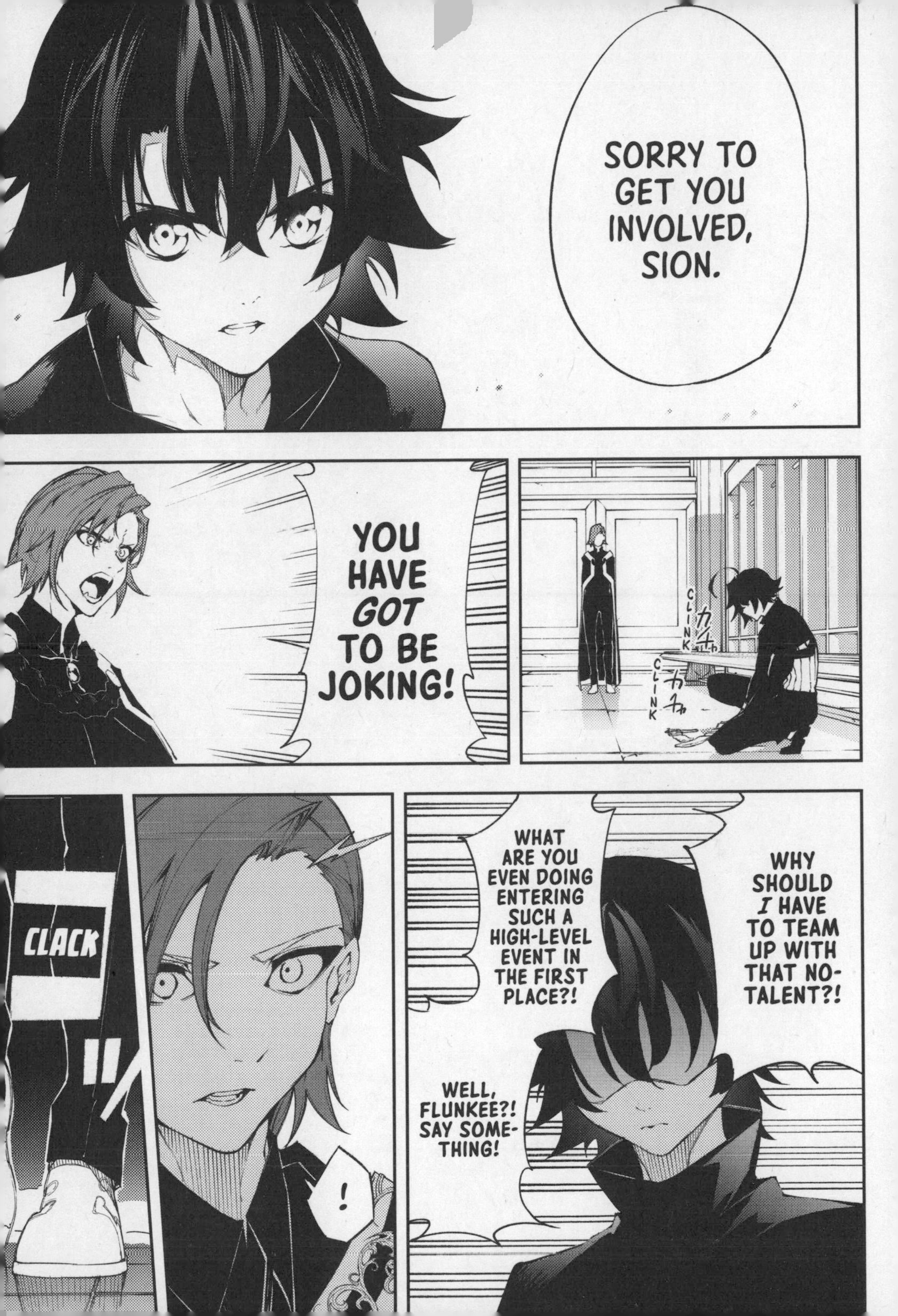
SORRY TO GET YOU INVOLVED, SION.
CLINK
CLINK
YOU HAVE *GOT* TO BE JOKING!
WHY SHOULD *I* HAVE TO TEAM UP WITH THAT NO-TALENT?!
WHAT ARE YOU EVEN DOING ENTERING SUCH A HIGH-LEVEL EVENT IN THE FIRST PLACE?!
WELL, FLUNKEE?! SAY SOMETHING!
!
CLACK

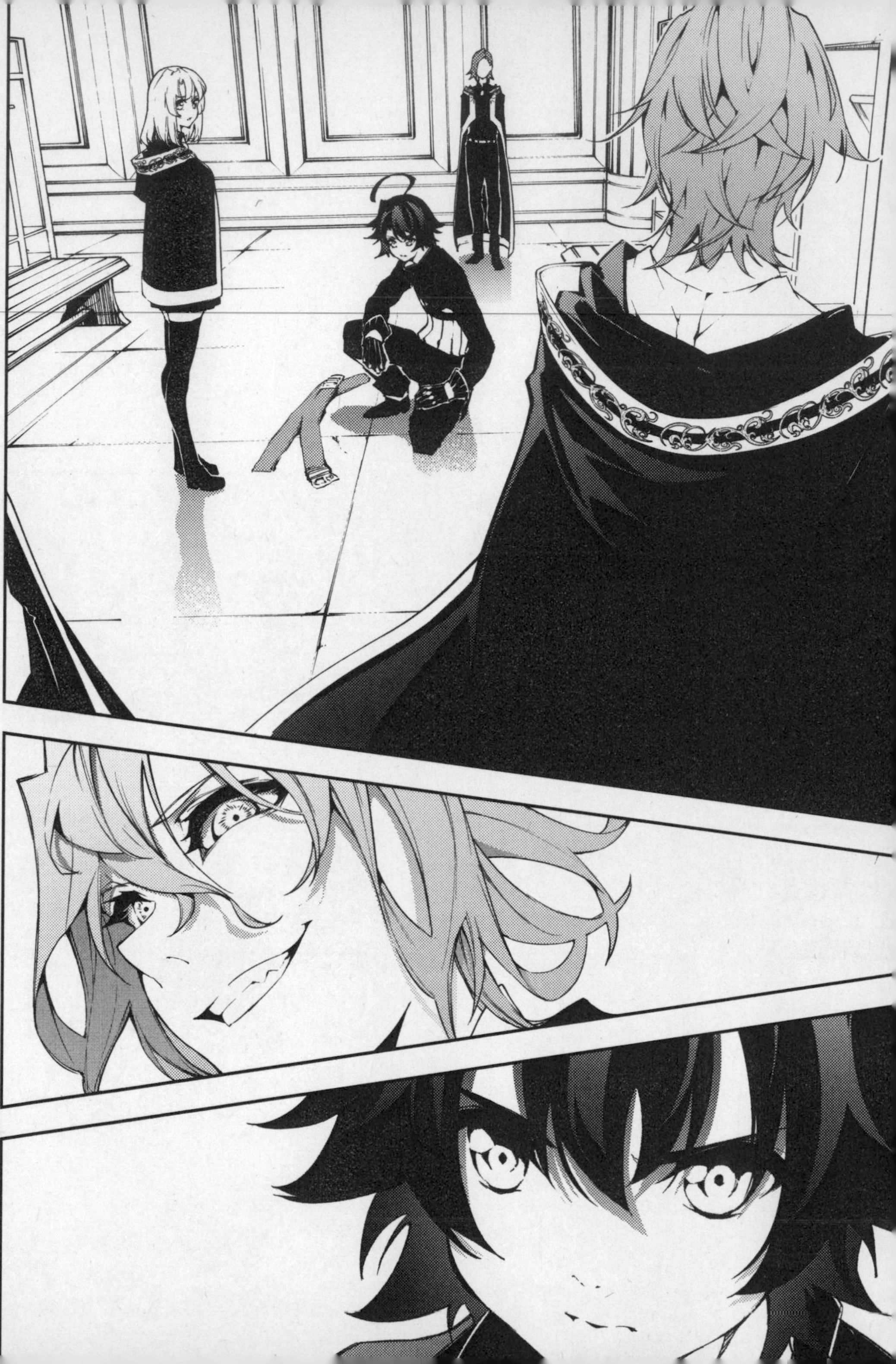

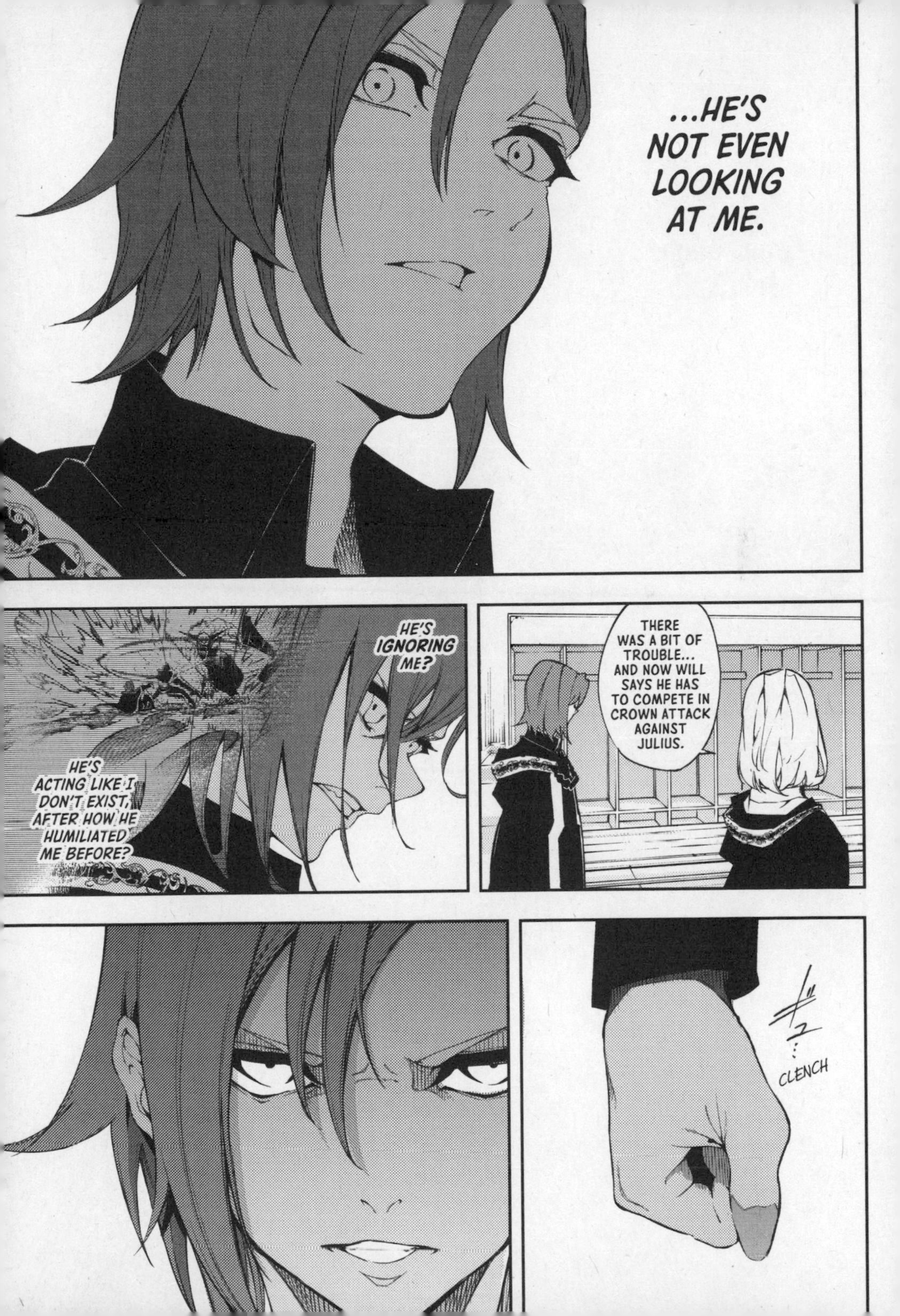
...HE'S NOT EVEN LOOKING AT ME.
THERE WAS A BIT OF TROUBLE... AND NOW WILL SAYS HE HAS TO COMPETE IN CROWN ATTACK AGAINST JULIUS.
HE'S IGNORING ME?
HE'S ACTING LIKE I DON'T EXIST, AFTER HOW HE HUMILIATED ME BEFORE?
CLENCH

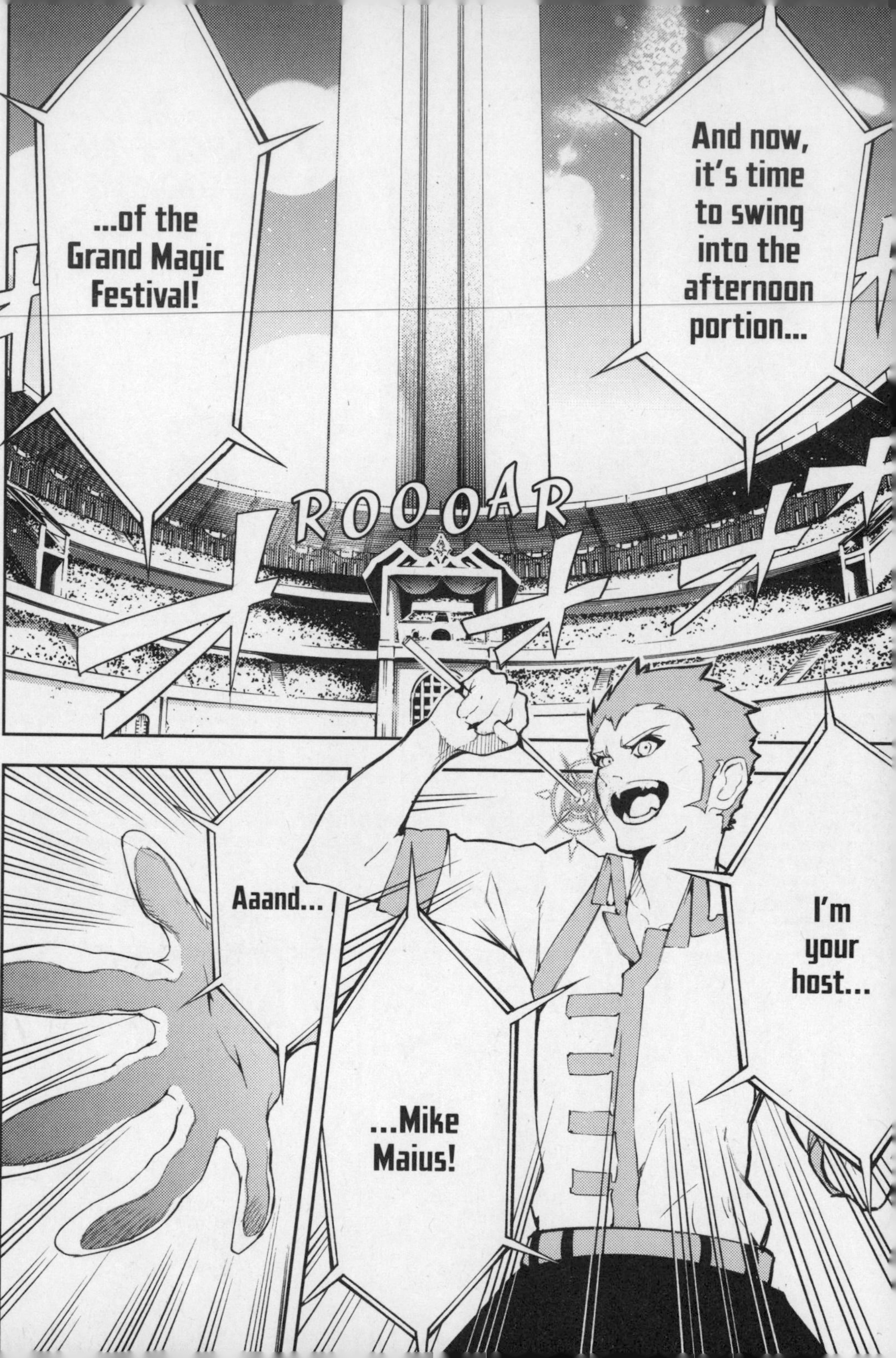
And now, it's time to swing into the afternoon portion...
...of the Grand Magic Festival!
ROOOAR
I'm your host...
Aaand...
...Mike Maius!

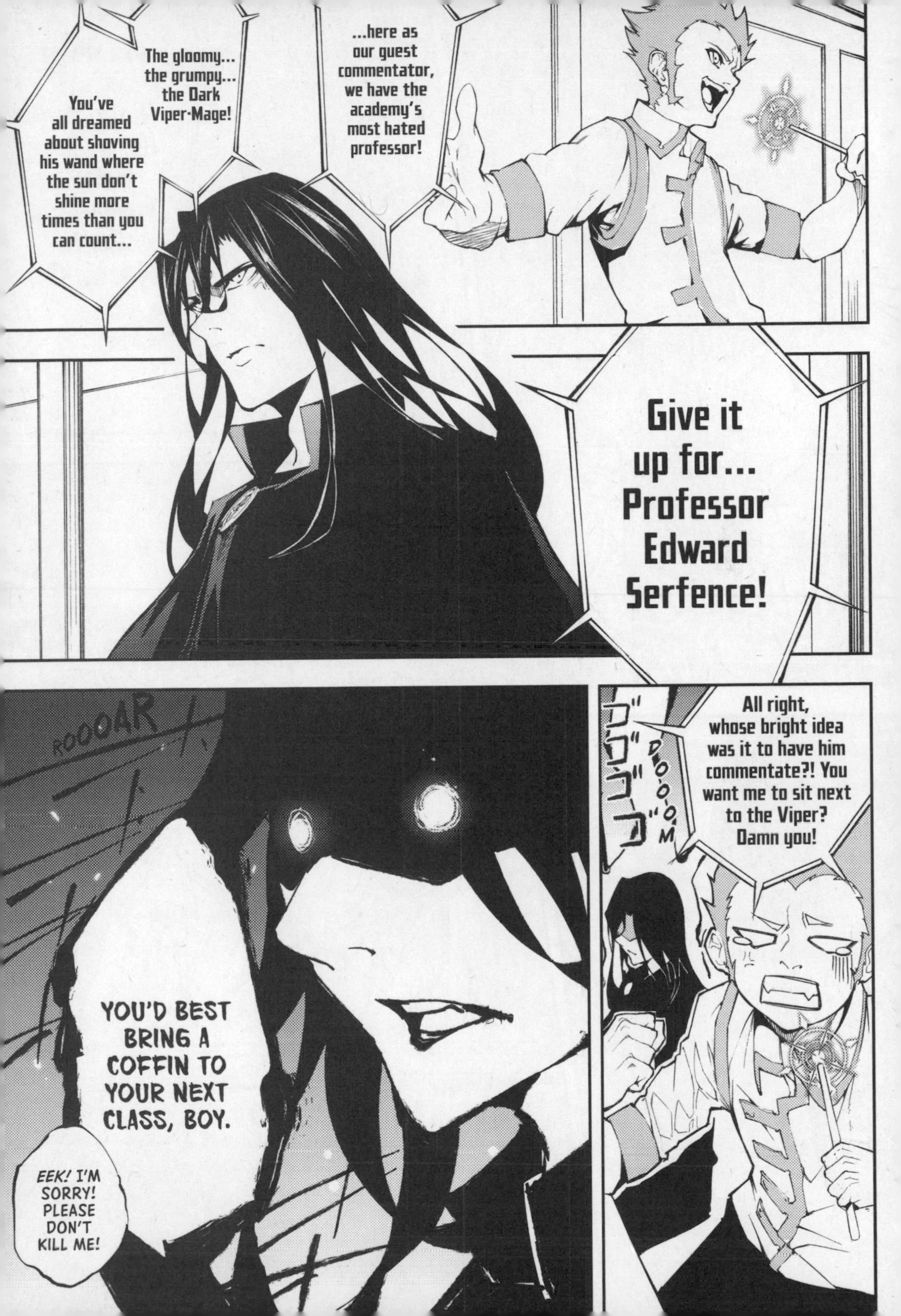
...here as our guest commentator, we have the academy's most hated professor!
The gloomy... the grumpy... the Dark Viper-Mage!
You've all dreamed about shoving his wand where the sun don't shine more times than you can count...
Give it up for... Professor Edward Serfence!
ゴゴゴゴ
DOO-O-O-OM
All right, whose bright idea was it to have him commentate?! You want me to sit next to the Viper? Damn you!
ROOOAR
YOU'D BEST BRING A COFFIN TO YOUR NEXT CLASS, BOY.
EEK! I'M SORRY! PLEASE DON'T KILL ME!

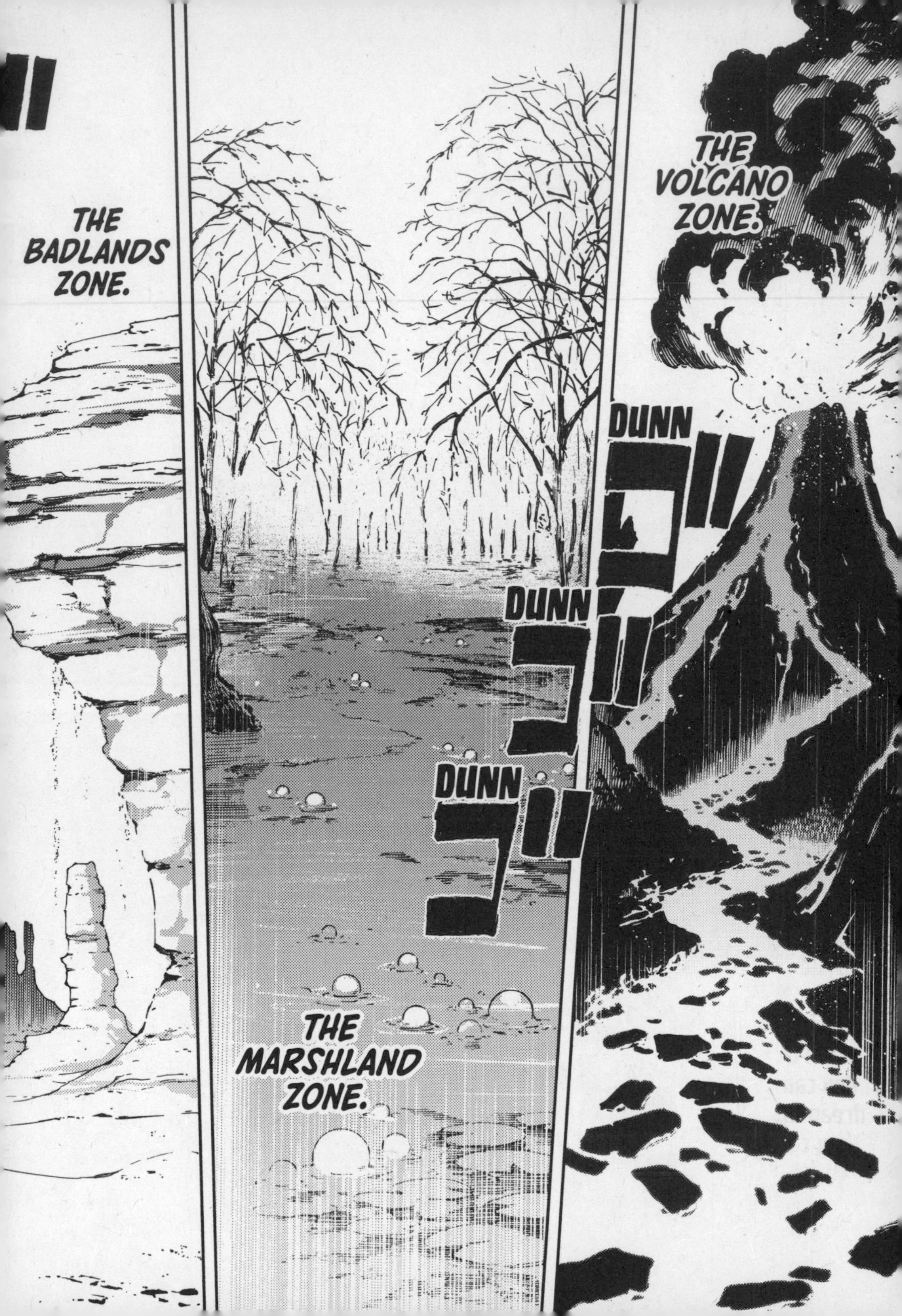
THE VOLCANO ZONE.
DUNN
ゴ
DUNN
ゴ
DUNN
ゴ
THE MARSHLAND ZONE.
THE BADLANDS ZONE.

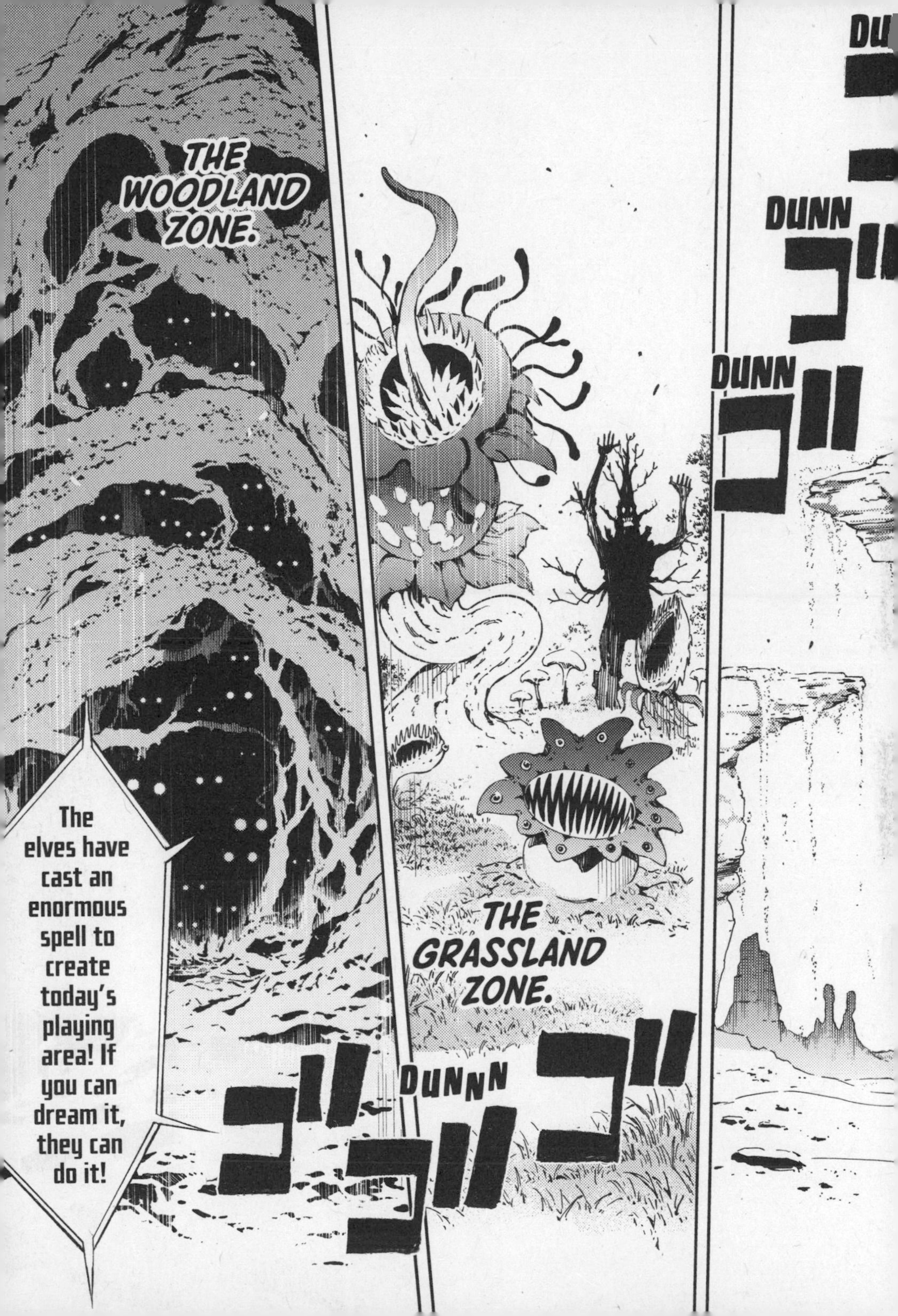
DUNN
DUNN
THE GRASSLAND ZONE.
DUNNN
THE WOODLAND ZONE.
The elves have cast an enormous spell to create today's playing area! If you can dream it, they can do it!

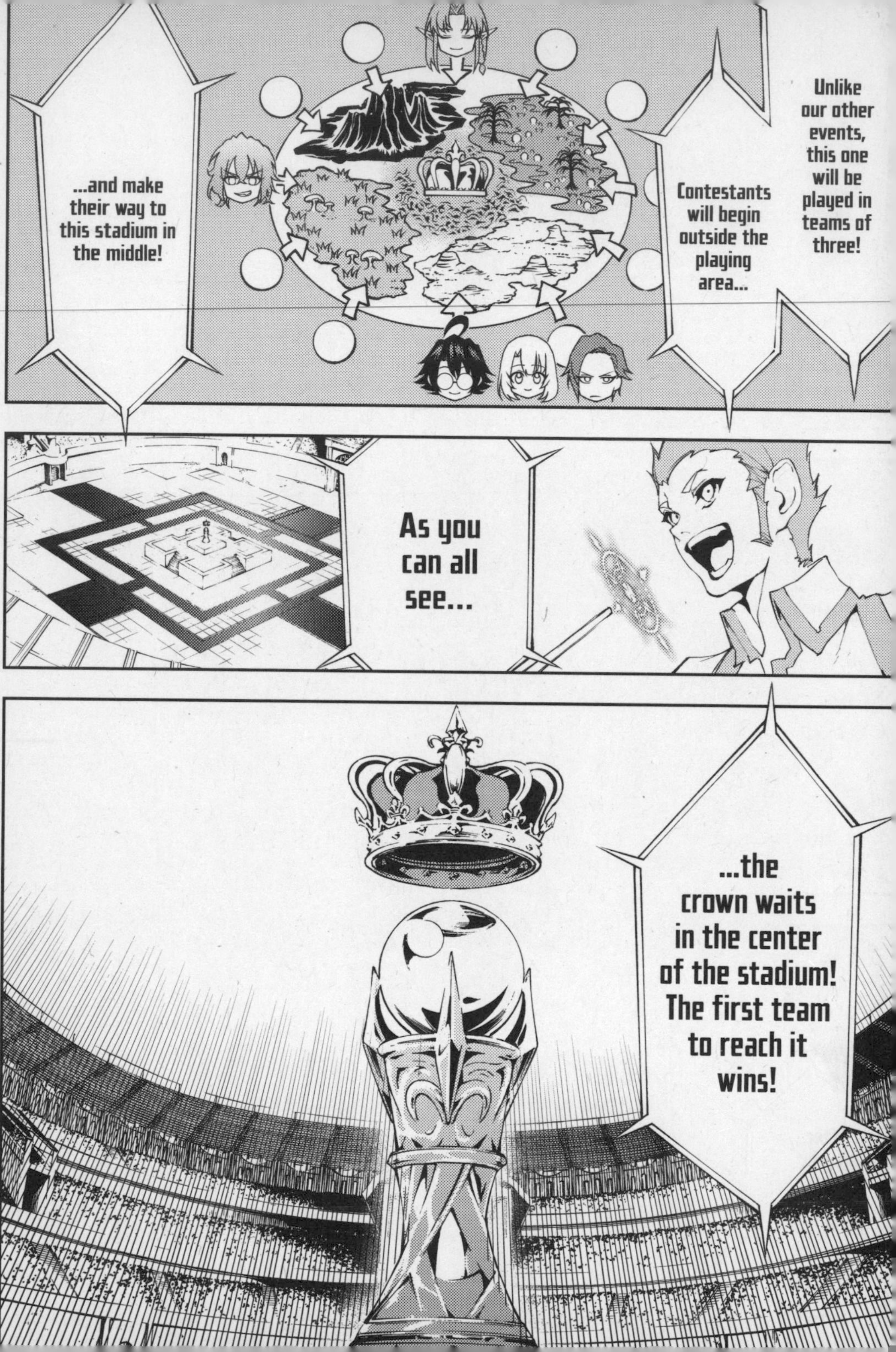
Unlike our other events, this one will be played in teams of three!
Contestants will begin outside the playing area...
...and make their way to this stadium in the middle!
As you can all see...
...the crown waits in the center of the stadium! The first team to reach it wins!

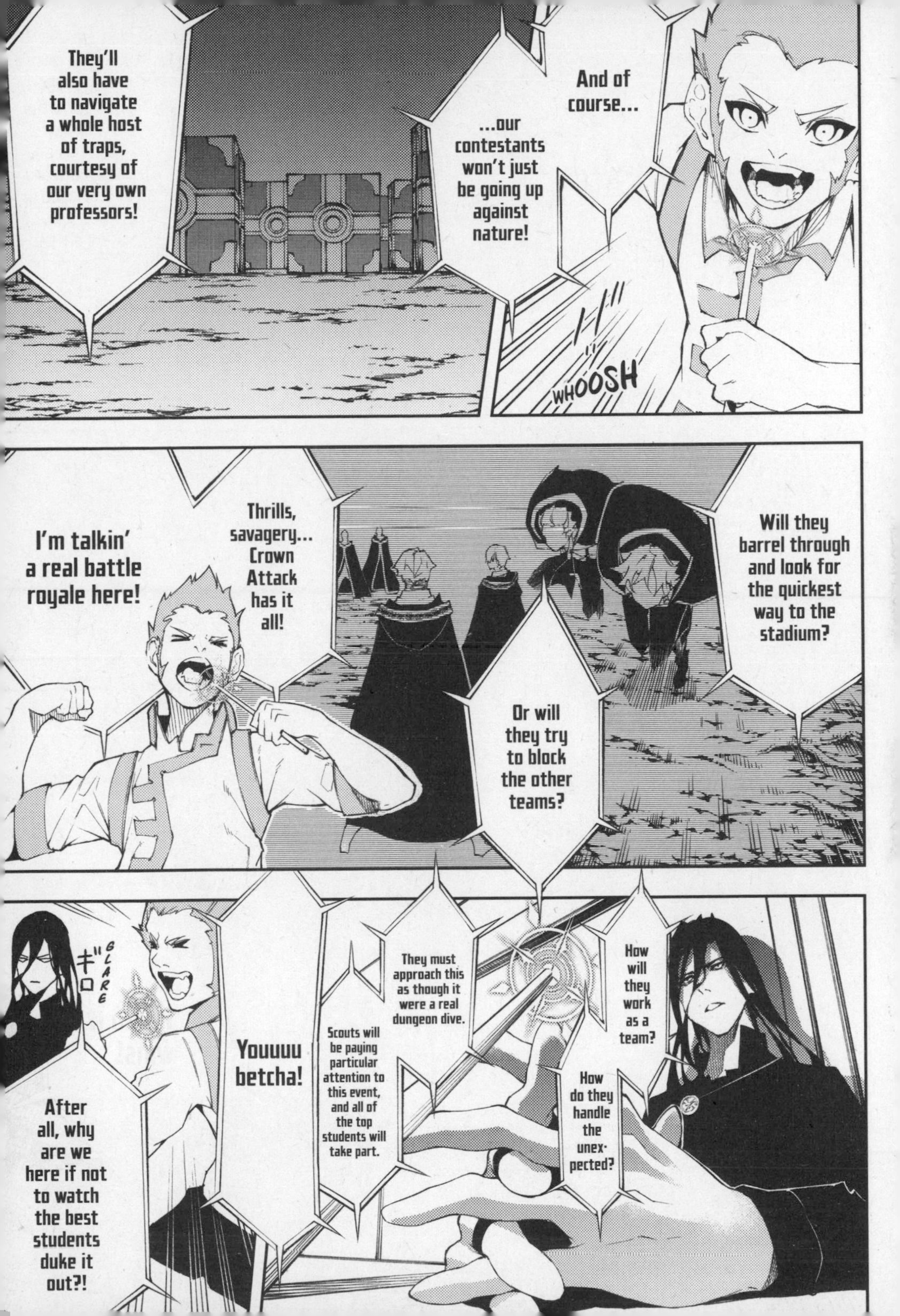
And of course...
...our contestants won't just be going up against nature!
WHOOSH
They'll also have to navigate a whole host of traps, courtesy of our very own professors!
Will they barrel through and look for the quickest way to the stadium?
Or will they try to block the other teams?
Thrills, savagery... Crown Attack has it all!
I'm talkin' a real battle royale here!
How will they work as a team?
How do they handle the unex-pected?
They must approach this as though it were a real dungeon dive.
Scouts will be paying particular attention to this event, and all of the top students will take part.
ギロ GLARE
Youuuu betcha!
After all, why are we here if not to watch the best students duke it out?!

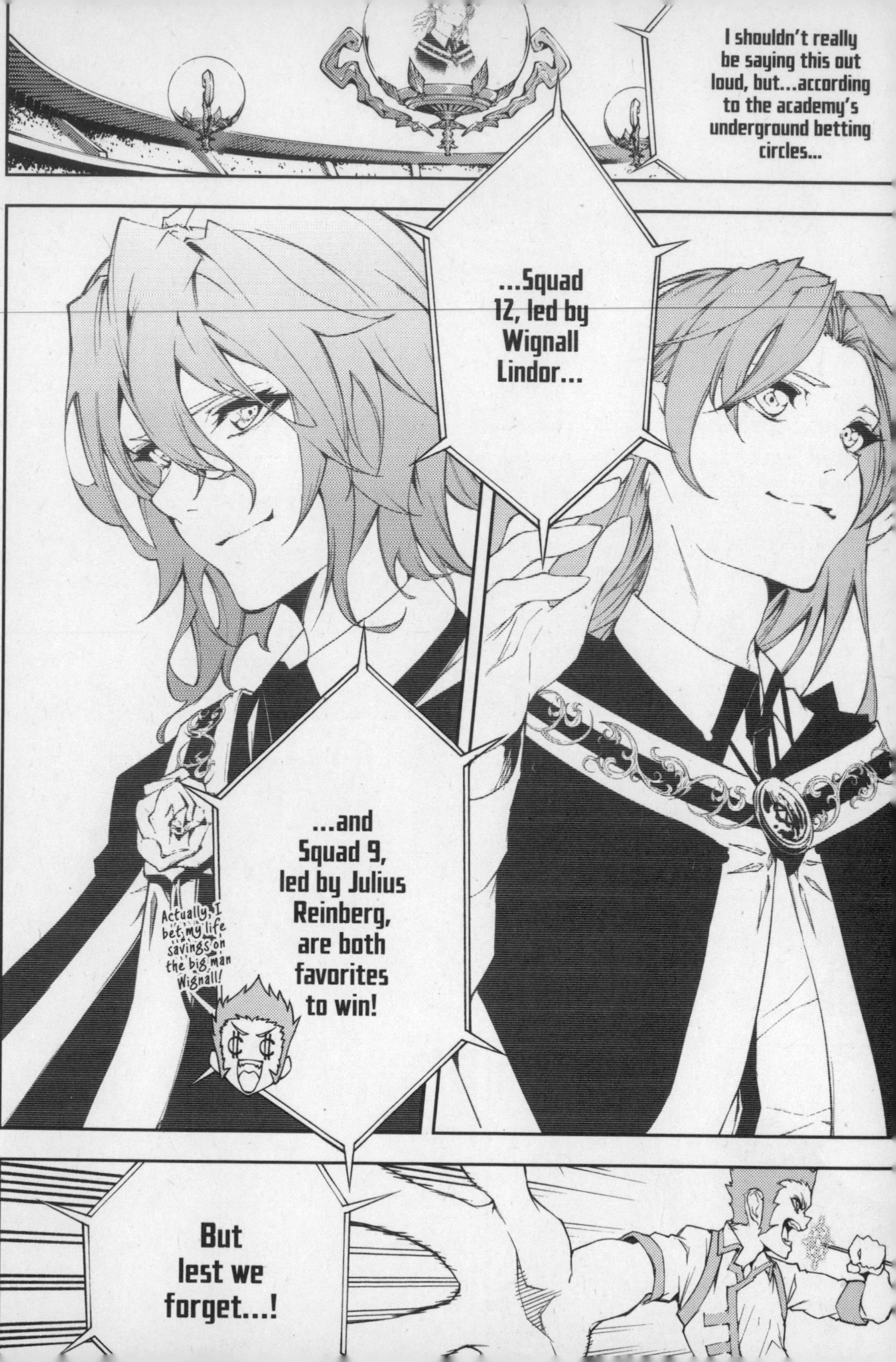
I shouldn't really be saying this out loud, but...according to the academy's underground betting circles...
...Squad 12, led by Wignall Lindor...
...and Squad 9, led by Julius Reinberg, are both favorites to win!
Actually, I bet my life savings on the big man Wignall!
But lest we forget...!

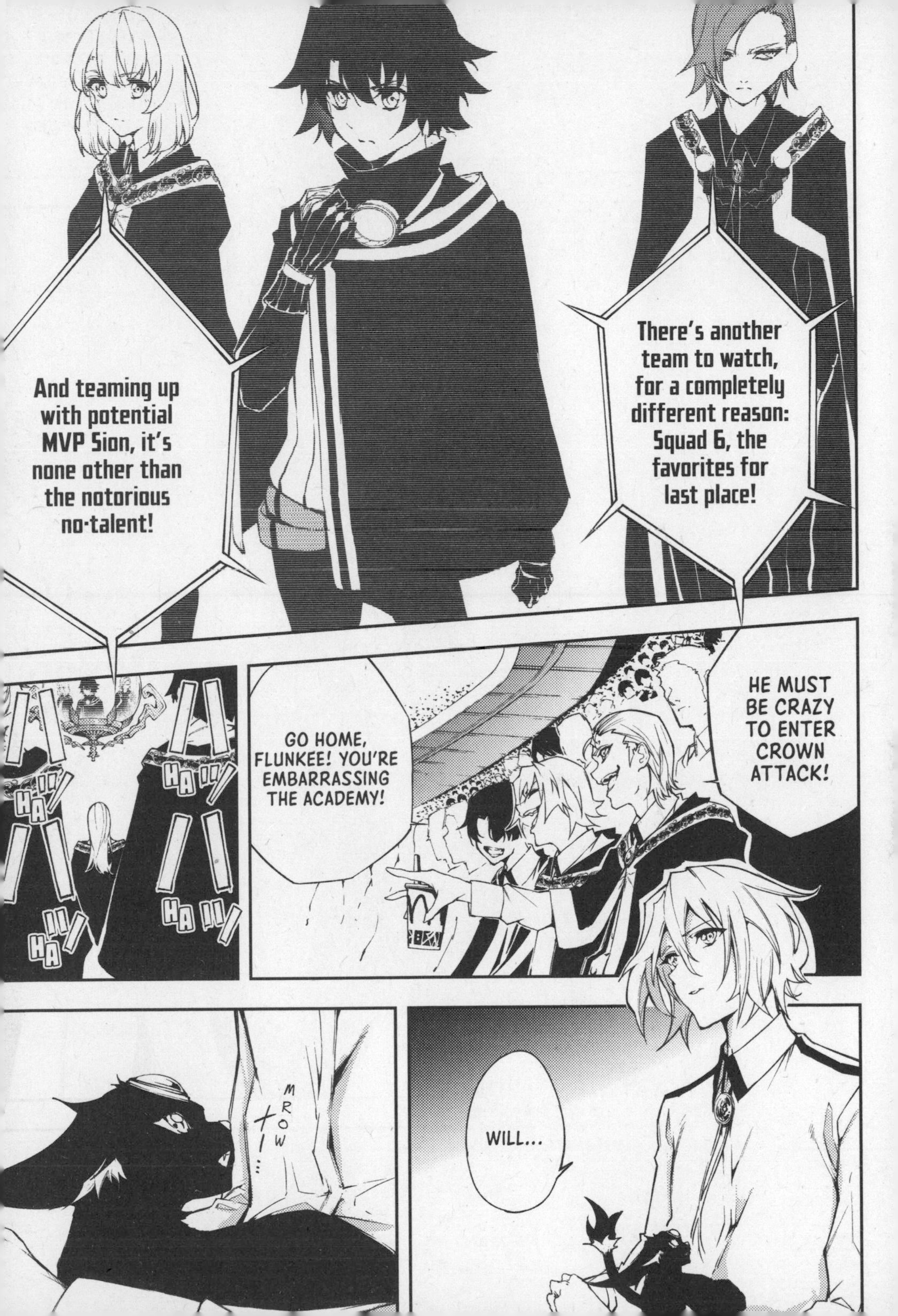
There's another team to watch, for a completely different reason: Squad 6, the favorites for last place!
And teaming up with potential MVP Sion, it's none other than the notorious no-talent!
HE MUST BE CRAZY TO ENTER CROWN ATTACK!
GO HOME, FLUNKEE! YOU'RE EMBARRASSING THE ACADEMY!
HA
HA
HA
HA
WILL...
MROW

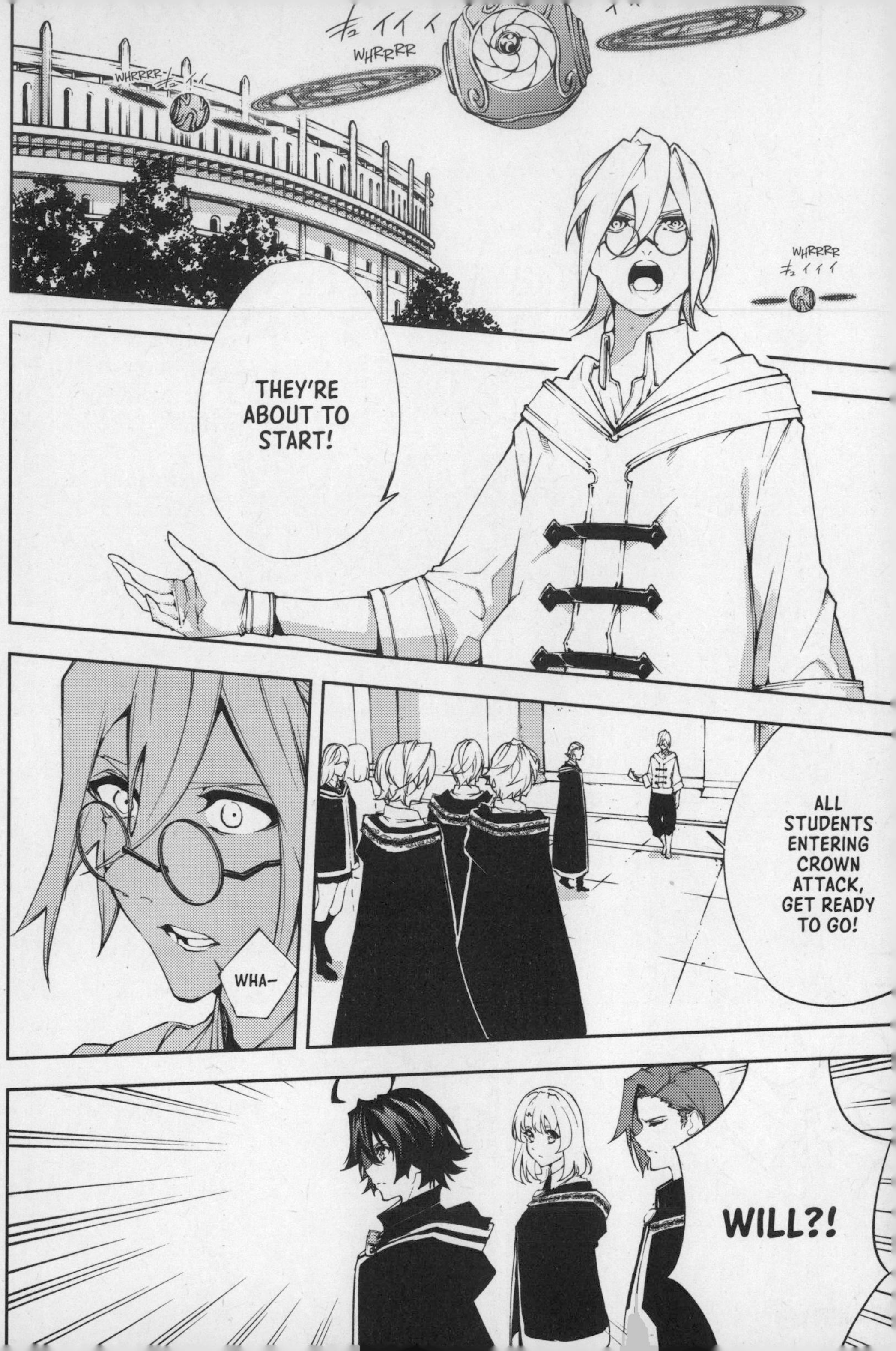

キュイイイ
WHRRRR
WHRRRR キュイイ
WHRRRR キュイイイ
THEY'RE ABOUT TO START!
ALL STUDENTS ENTERING CROWN ATTACK, GET READY TO GO!
WHA-
WILL?!

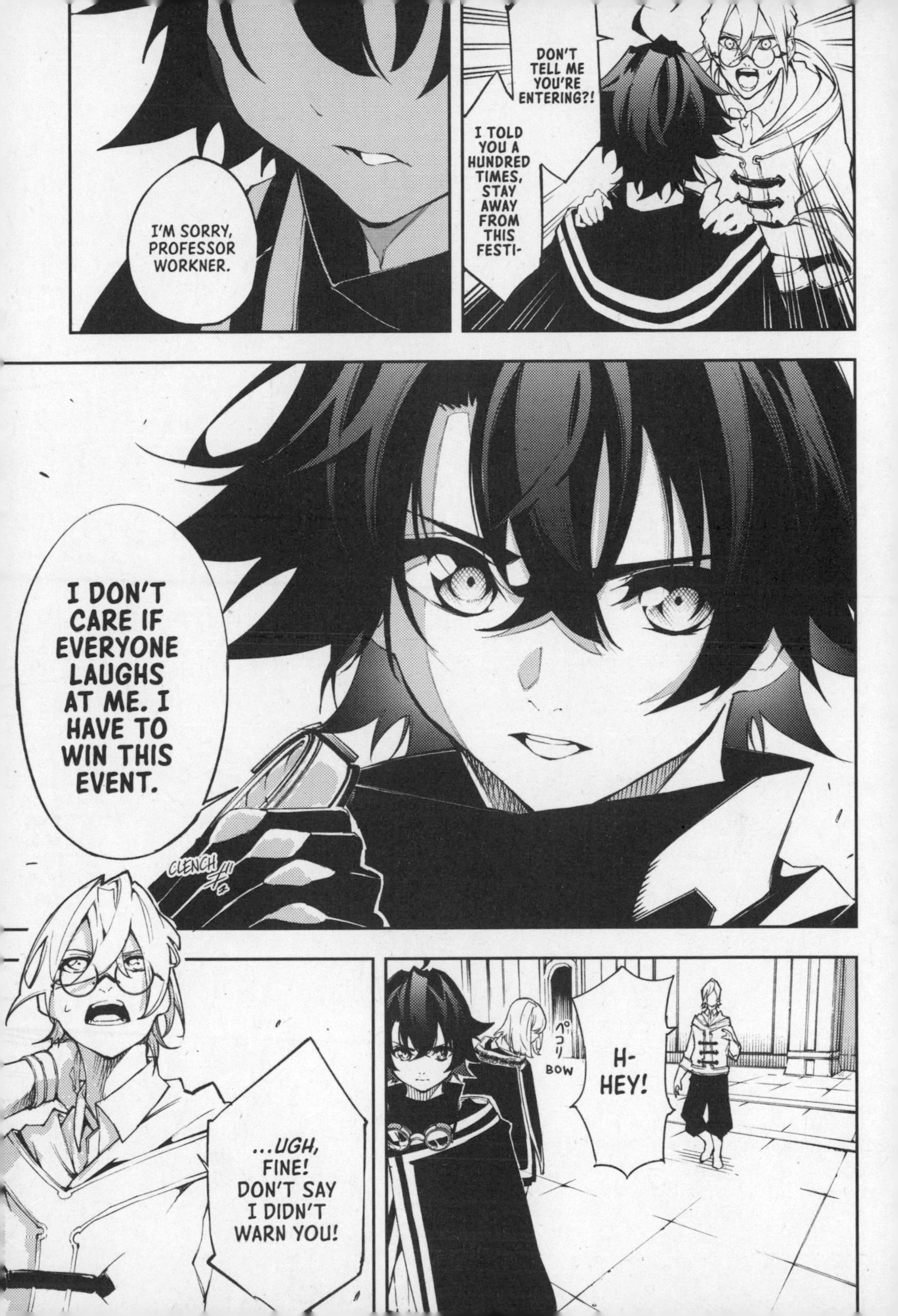
DON'T TELL ME YOU'RE ENTERING?!
I TOLD YOU A HUNDRED TIMES, STAY AWAY FROM THIS FESTI-
I'M SORRY, PROFESSOR WORKNER.
I DON'T CARE IF EVERYONE LAUGHS AT ME. I HAVE TO WIN THIS EVENT.
CLENCH
H-HEY!
ペコリ
BOW
...UGH, FINE! DON'T SAY I DIDN'T WARN YOU!

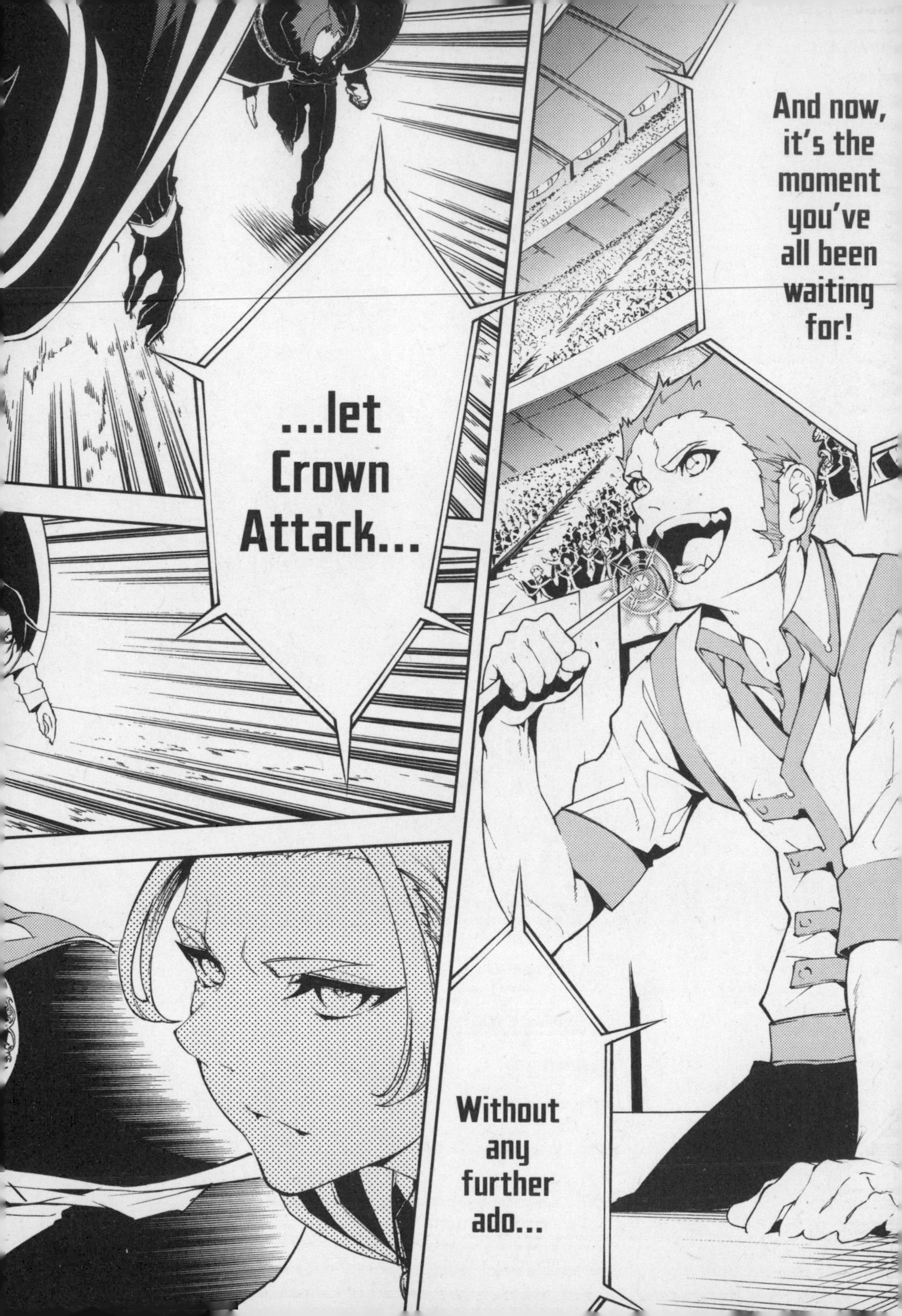
And now, it's the moment you've all been waiting for!
Without any further ado...
...let Crown Attack...

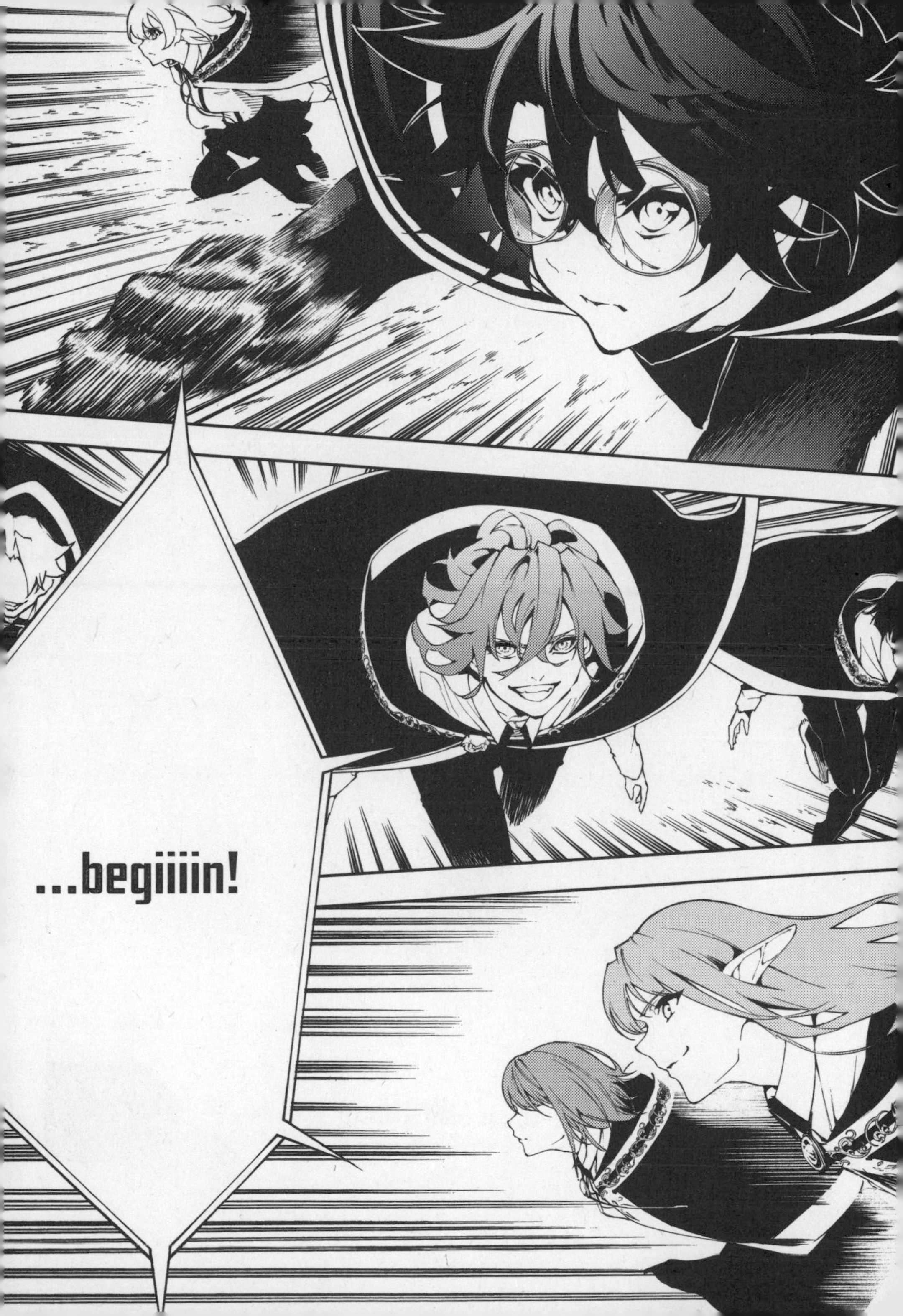
...begiiiin!

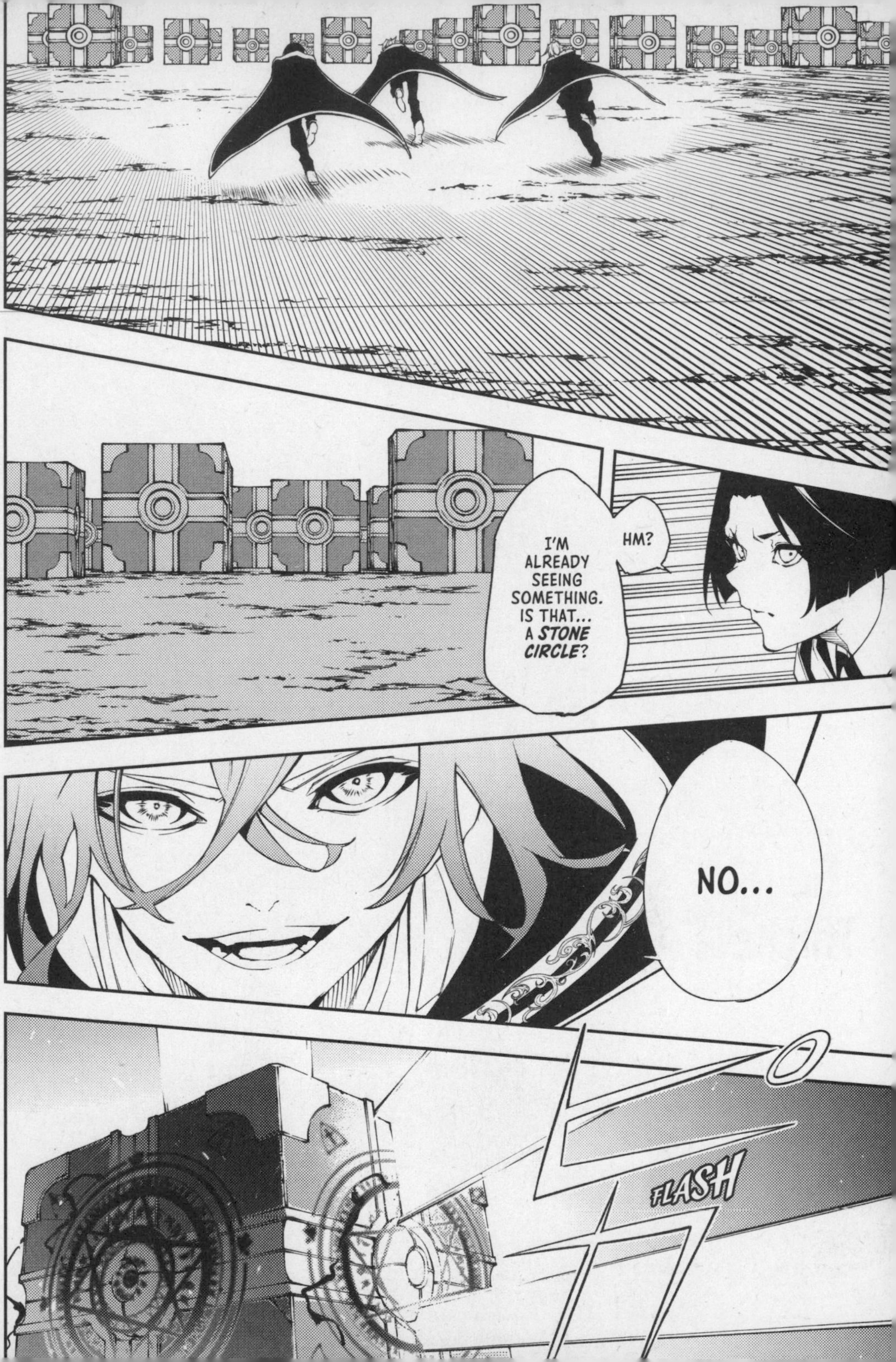
HM?
I'M ALREADY SEEING SOMETHING. IS THAT... A STONE CIRCLE?
NO...
FLASH

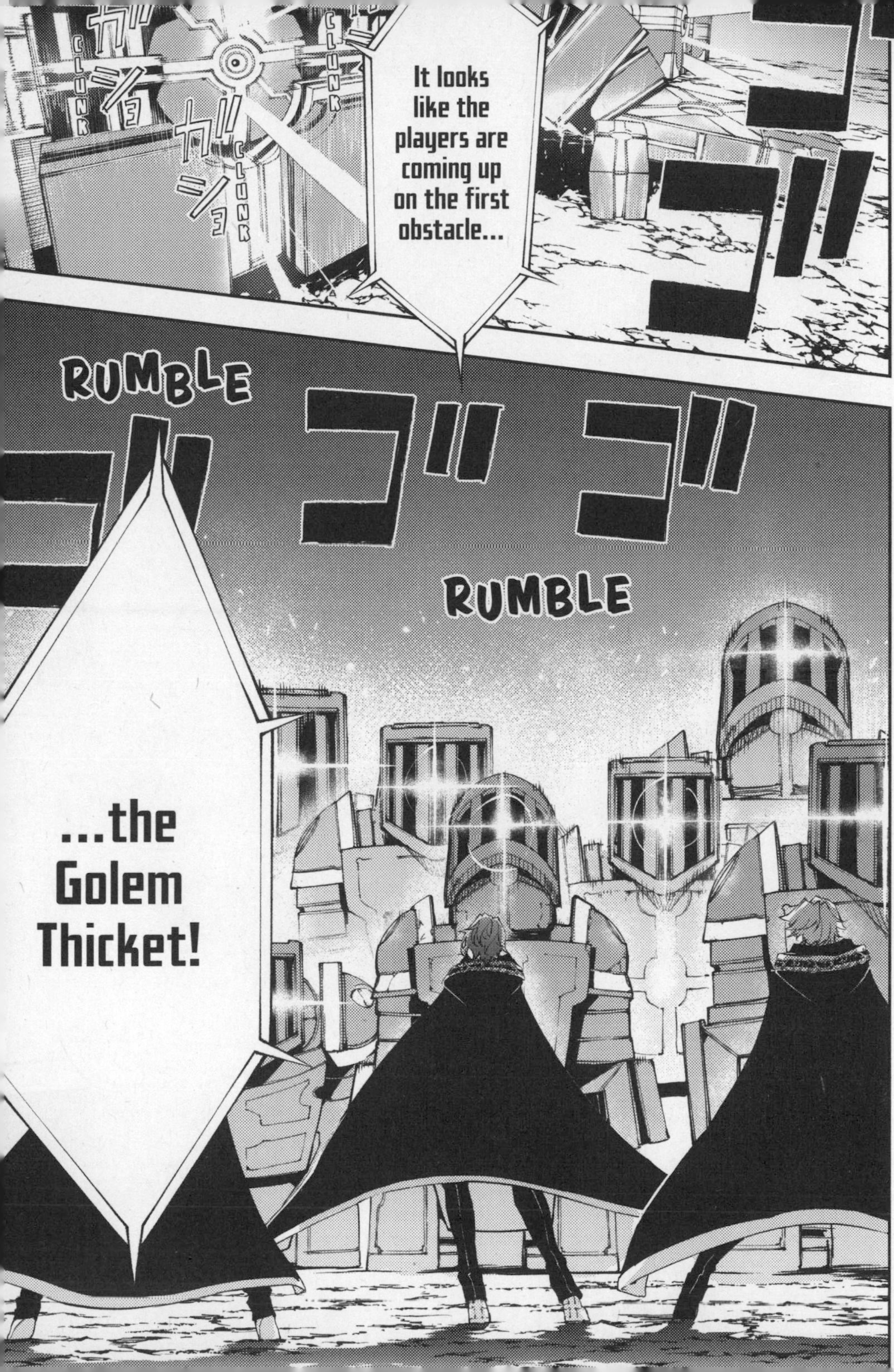
CLUNK
CLUNK
CLUNK
CLUNK
It looks like the players are coming up on the first obstacle...
RUMBLE
RUMBLE
...the Golem Thicket!

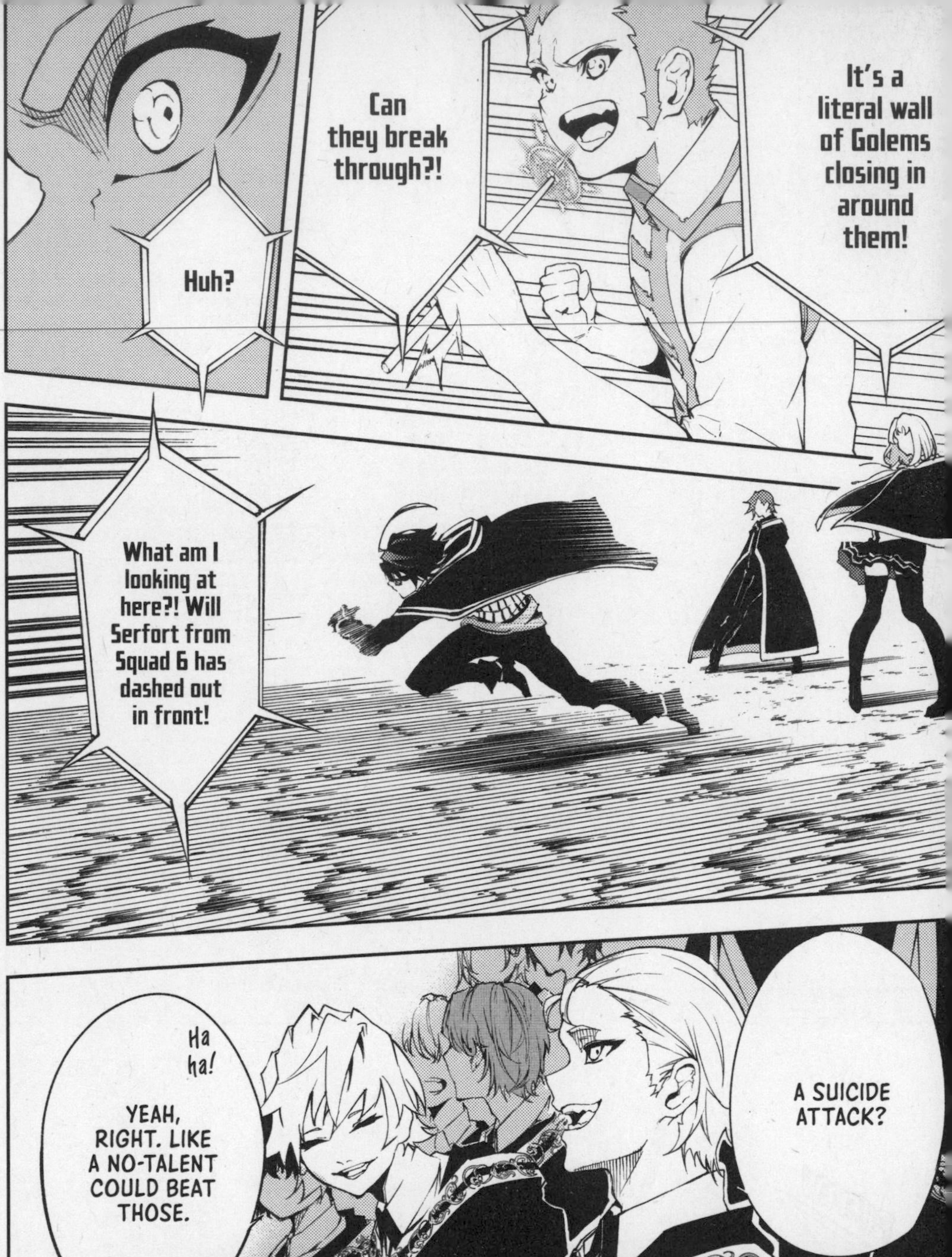
It's a literal wall of Golems closing in around them!
Can they break through?!
Huh?
What am I looking at here?! Will Serfort from Squad 6 has dashed out in front!
A SUICIDE ATTACK?
Ha ha!
YEAH, RIGHT. LIKE A NO-TALENT COULD BEAT THOSE.

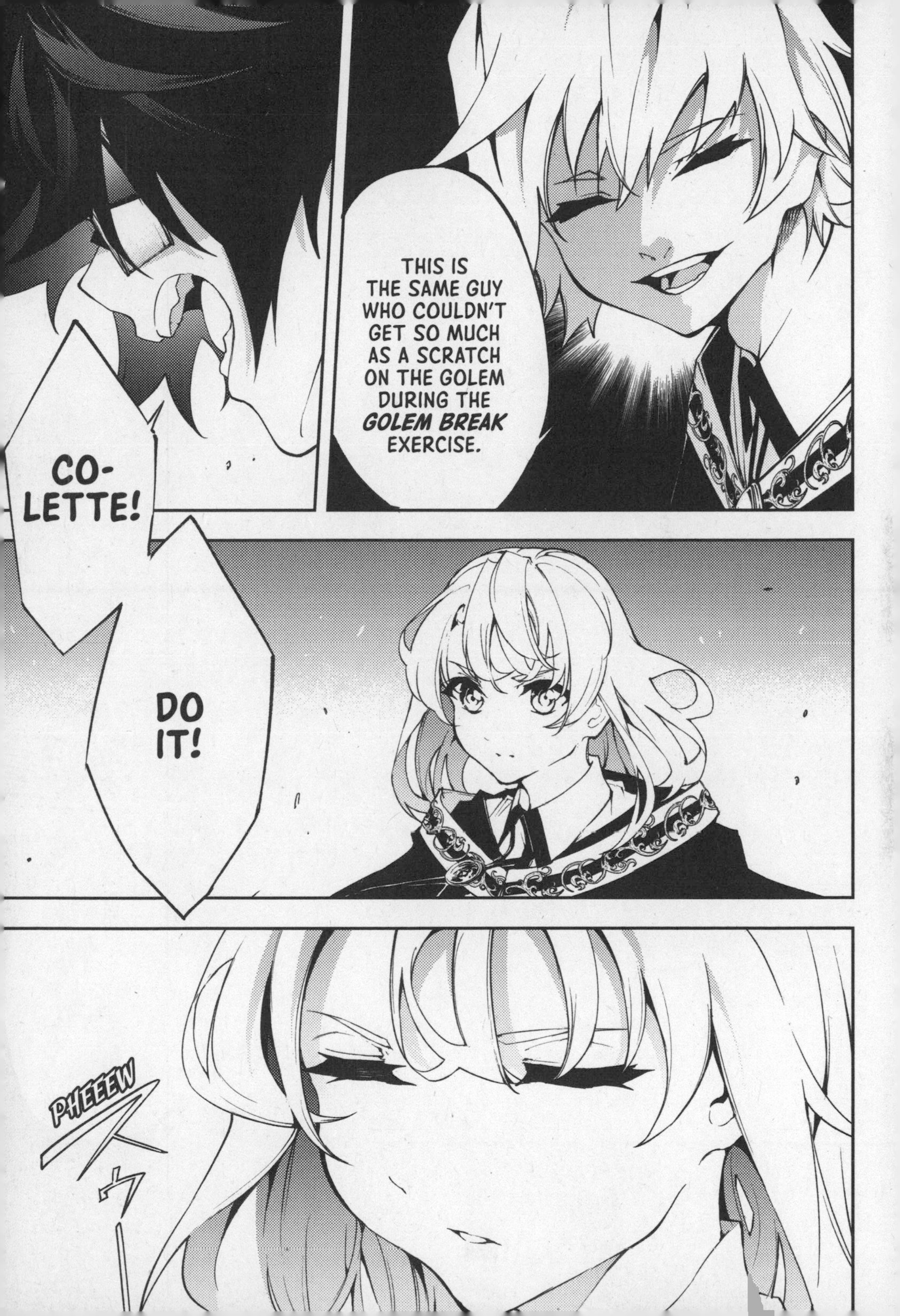
THIS IS THE SAME GUY WHO COULDN'T GET SO MUCH AS A SCRATCH ON THE GOLEM DURING THE GOLEM BREAK EXERCISE.
CO-LETTE!
DO IT!
PHEEEW

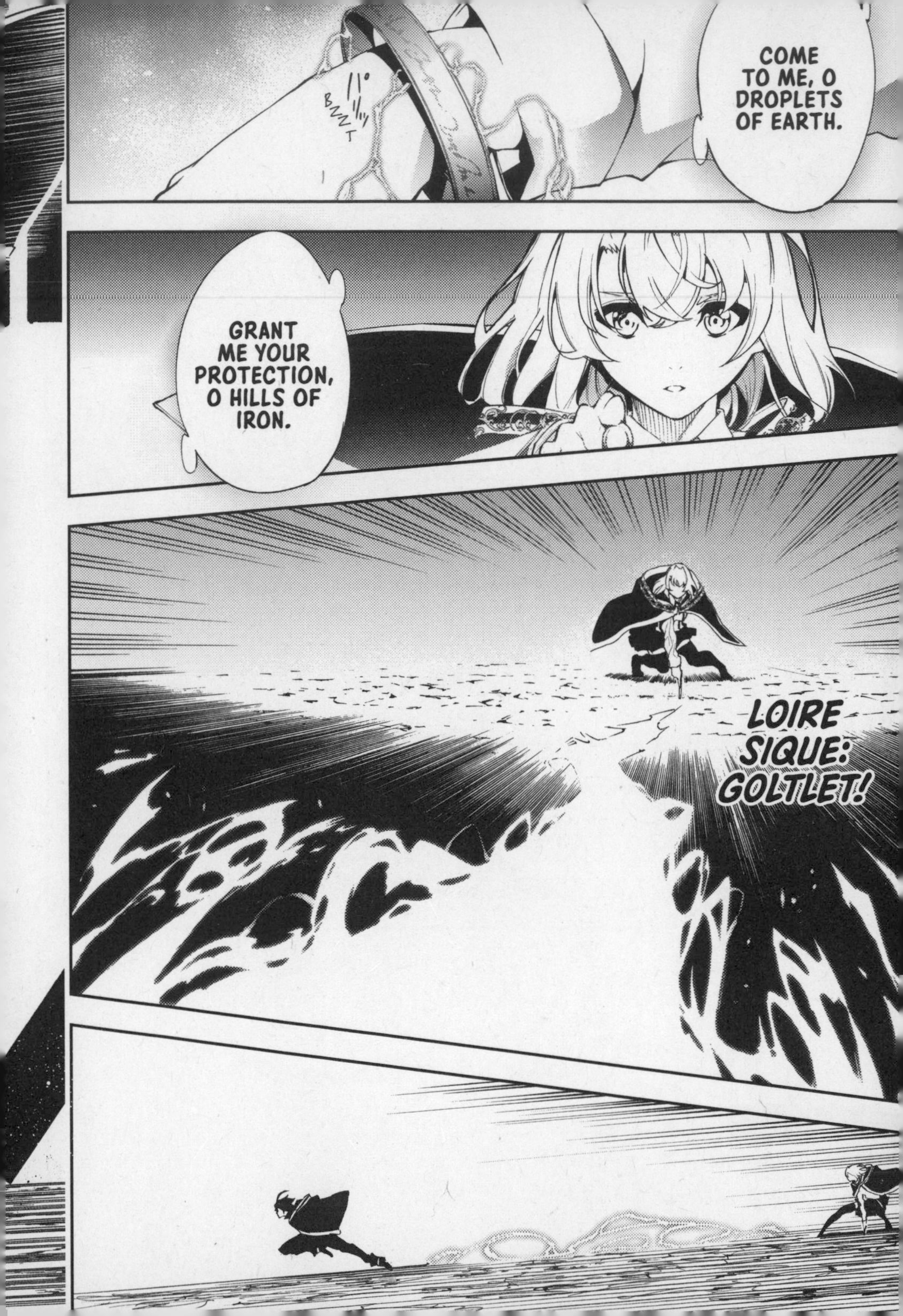
COME TO ME, O DROPLETS OF EARTH.
BZZZT
GRANT ME YOUR PROTECTION, O HILLS OF IRON.
LOIRE SIQUE: GOLTLET!

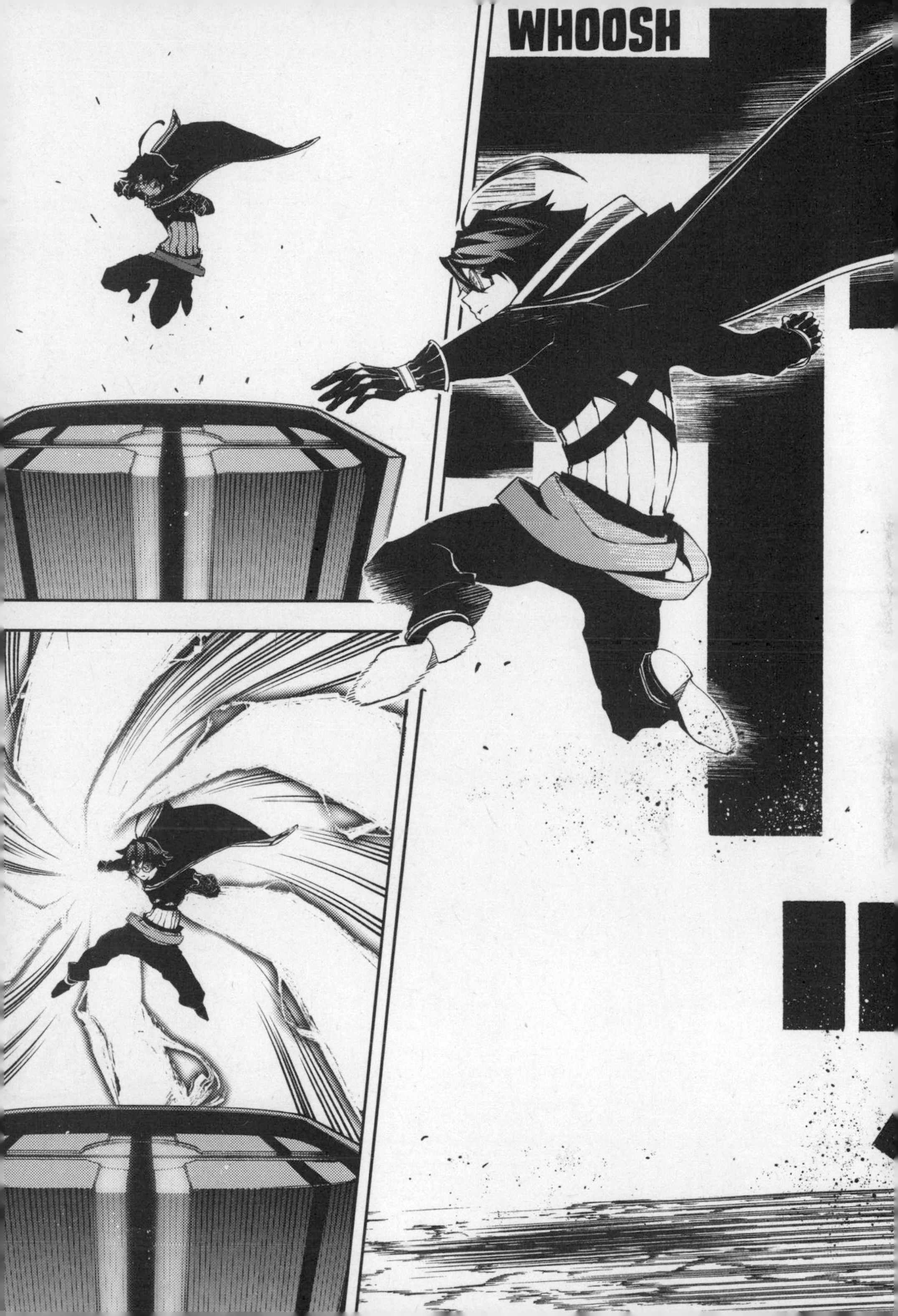
WHOOSH

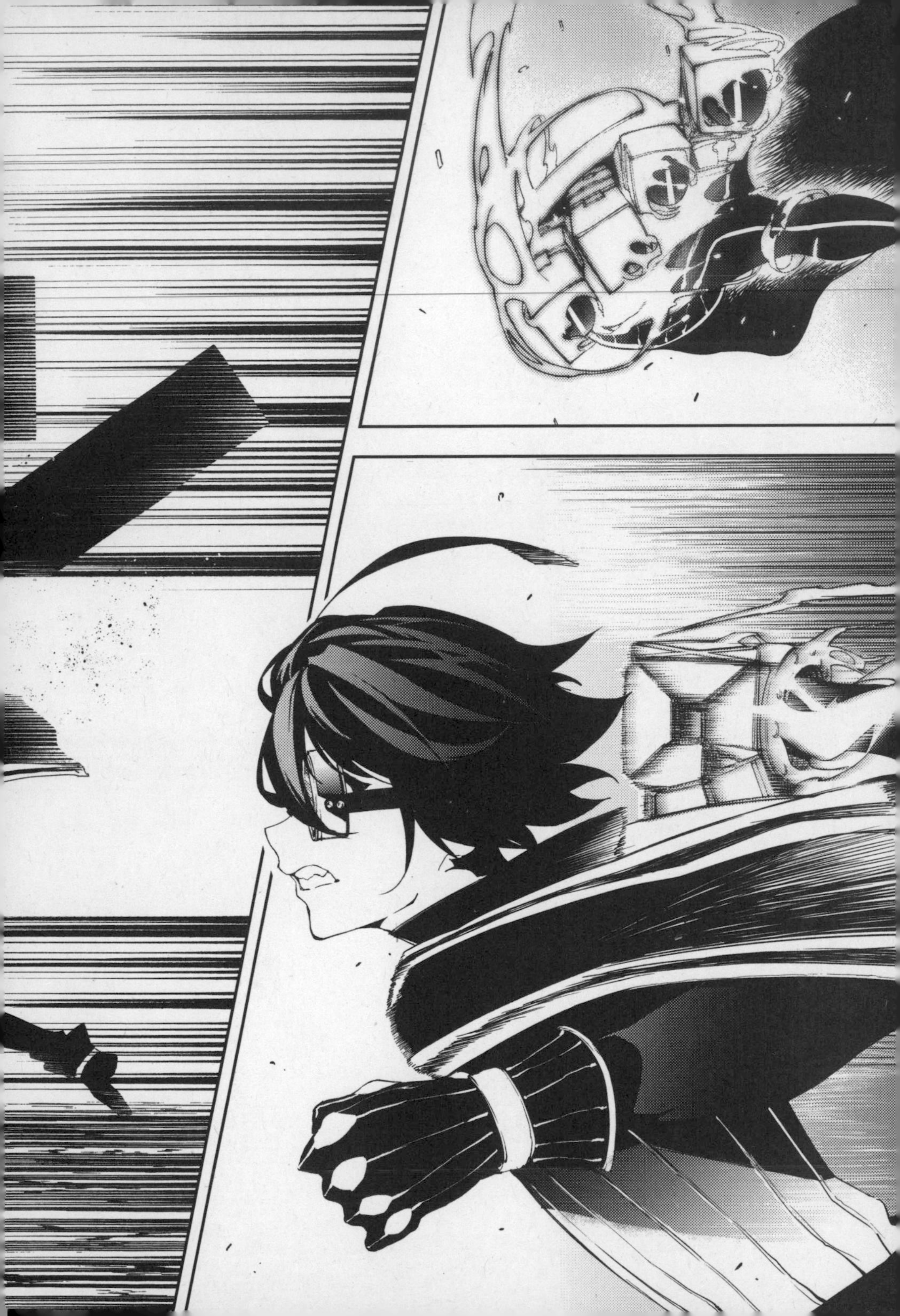

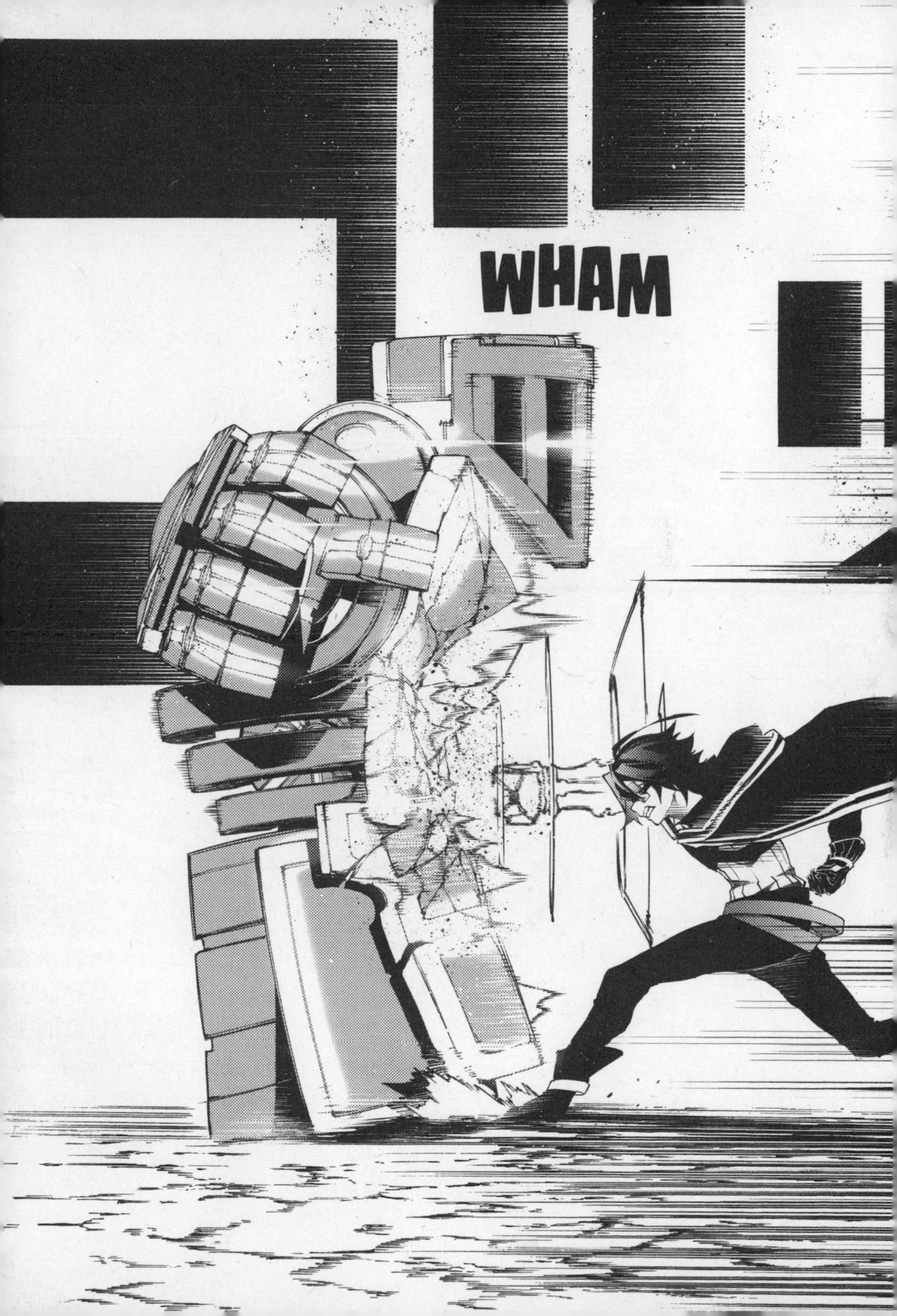
WHAM

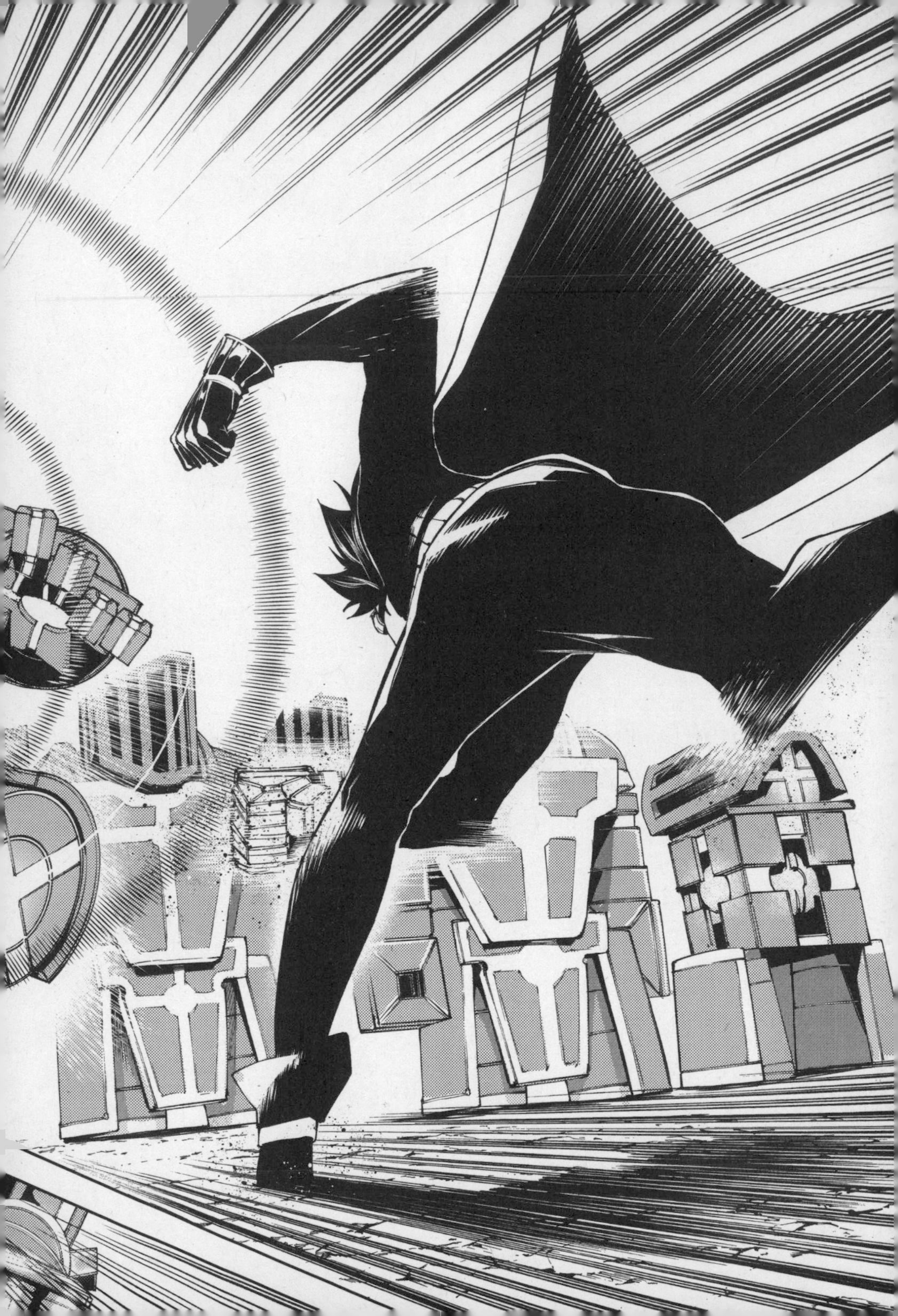

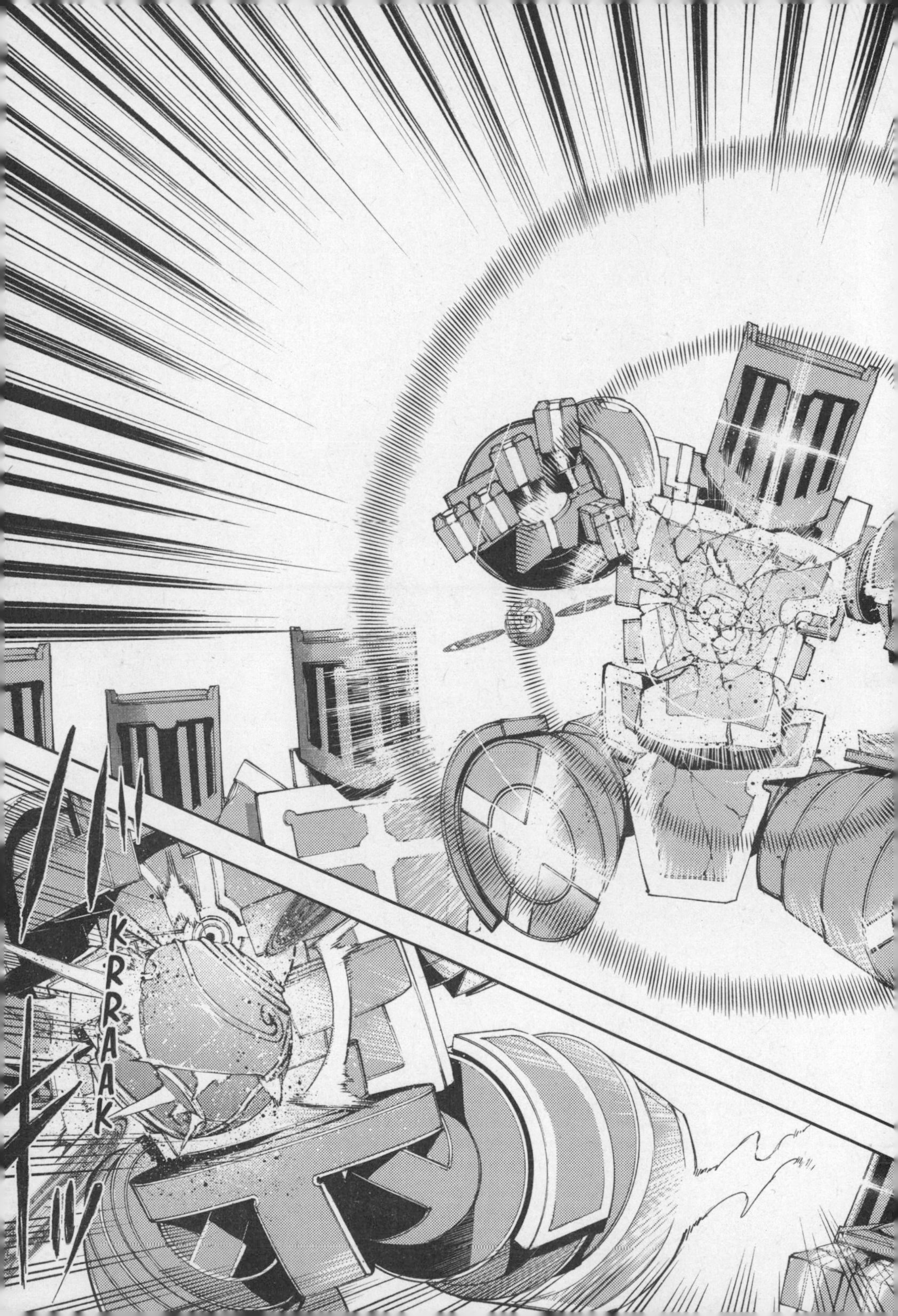
KRRAAK

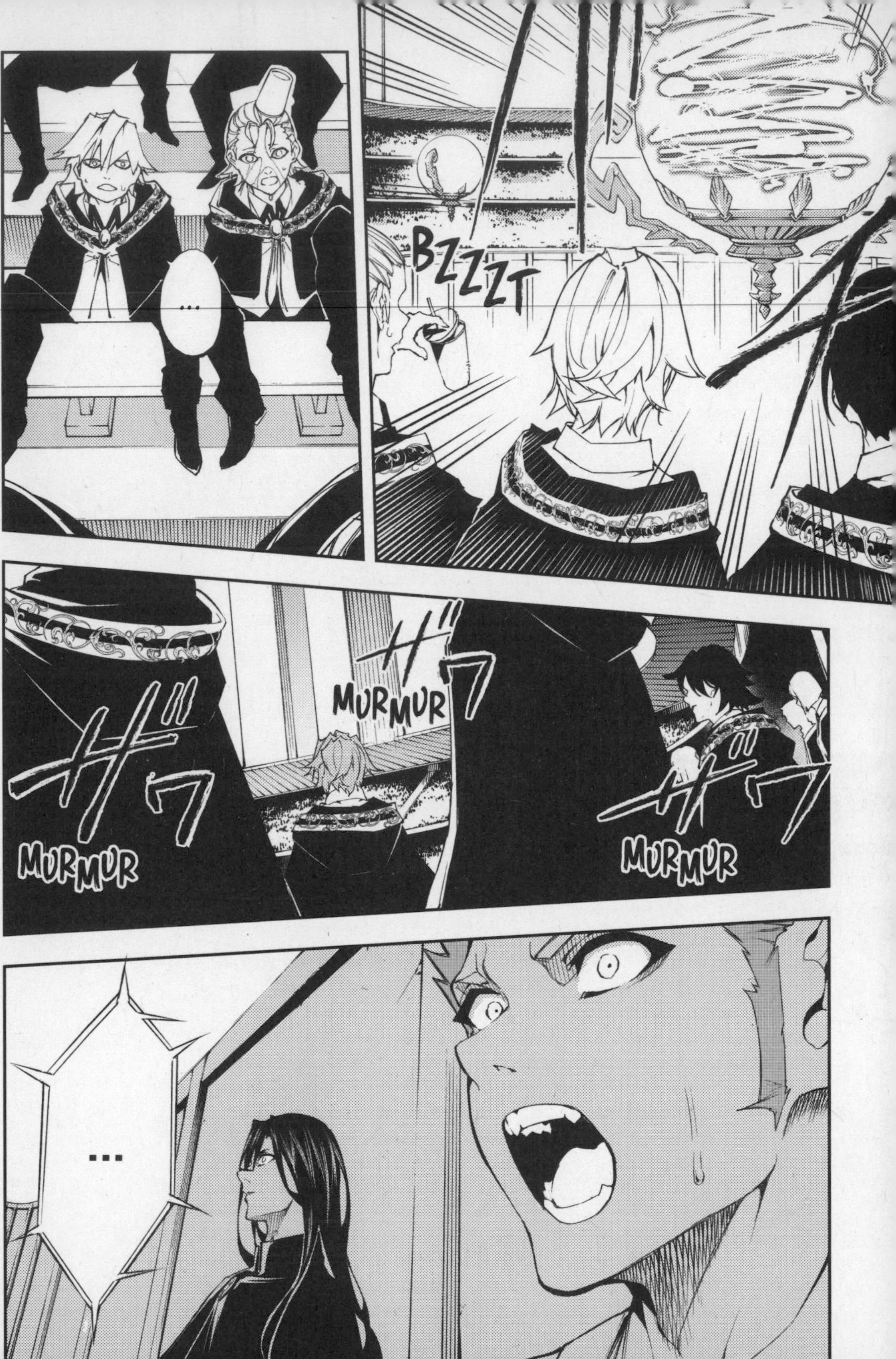
BZZZZT
...
ザワ
MURMUR
ザワ
MURMUR
ザワ
MURMUR
...

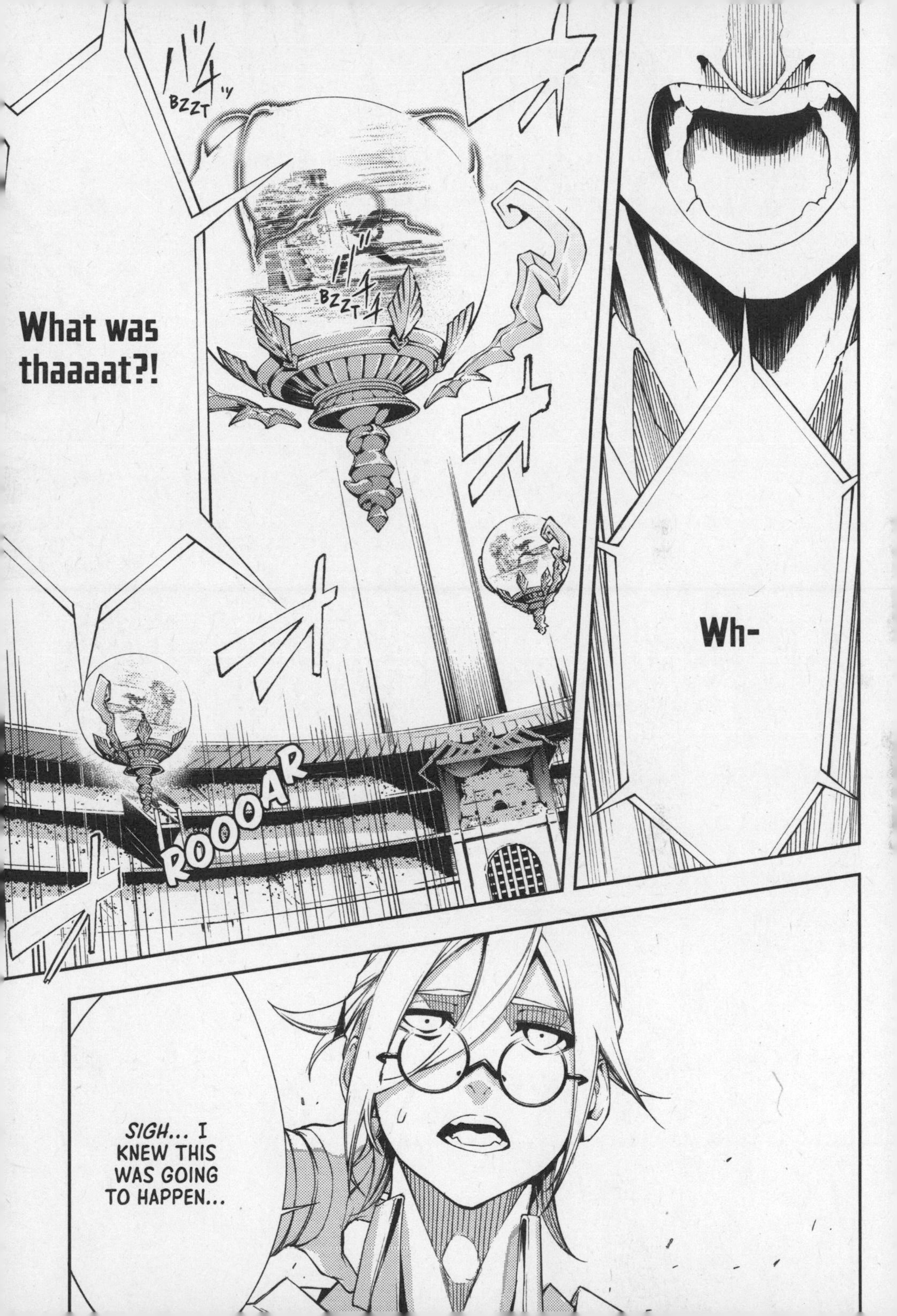
Wh-
BZZT
BZZT
What was thaaaat?!
ROOOAR
SIGH... I KNEW THIS WAS GOING TO HAPPEN...

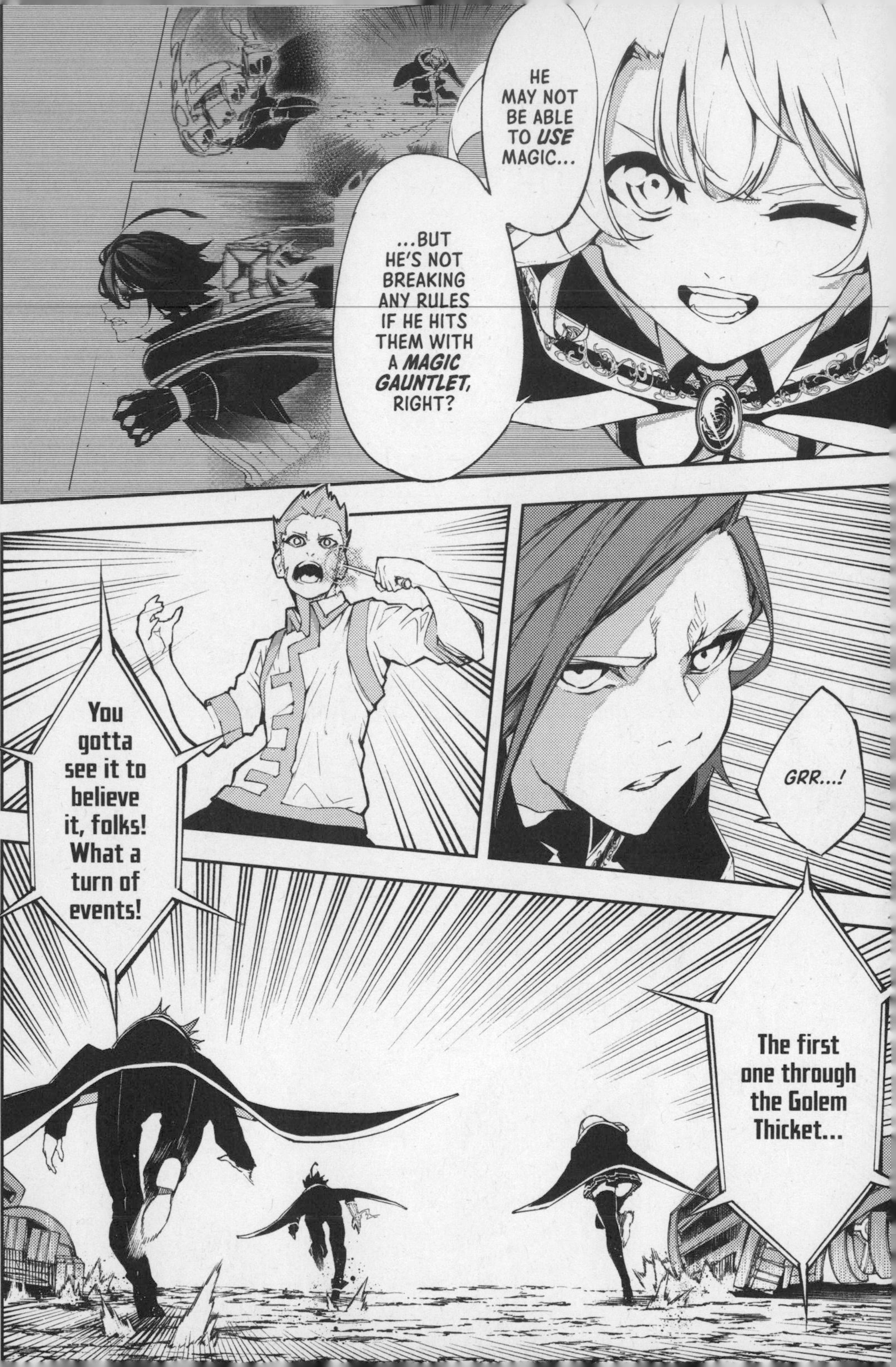
HE MAY NOT BE ABLE TO *USE* MAGIC...
...BUT HE'S NOT BREAKING ANY RULES IF HE HITS THEM WITH A *MAGIC GAUNTLET*, RIGHT?
GRR...!
You gotta see it to believe it, folks! What a turn of events!
The first one through the Golem Thicket...

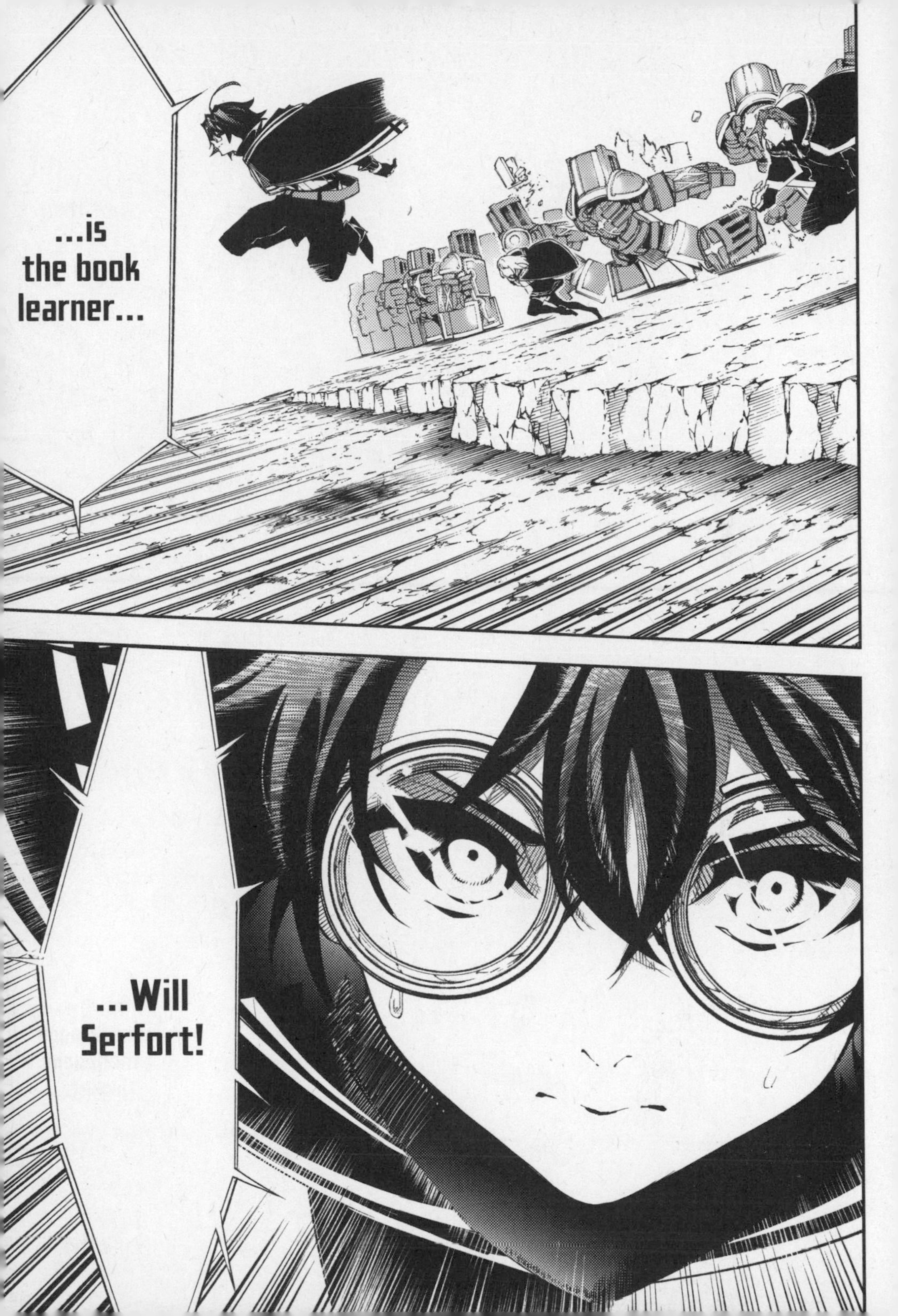
...is the book learner...
...Will Serfort!

Wistoria
Wand and Sword

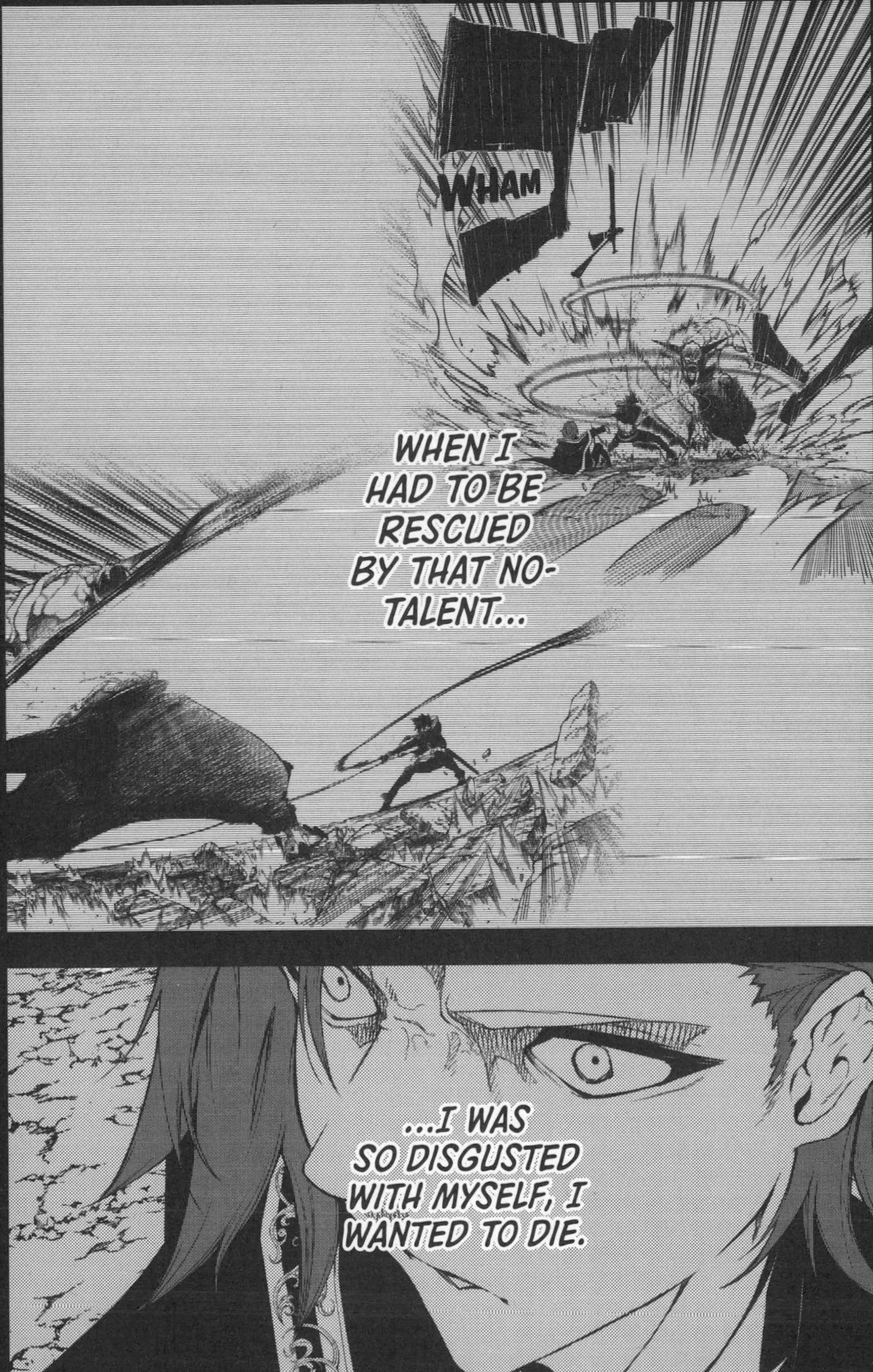
WHAM
WHEN I HAD TO BE RESCUED BY THAT NO-TALENT...
...I WAS SO DISGUSTED WITH MYSELF, I WANTED TO DIE.

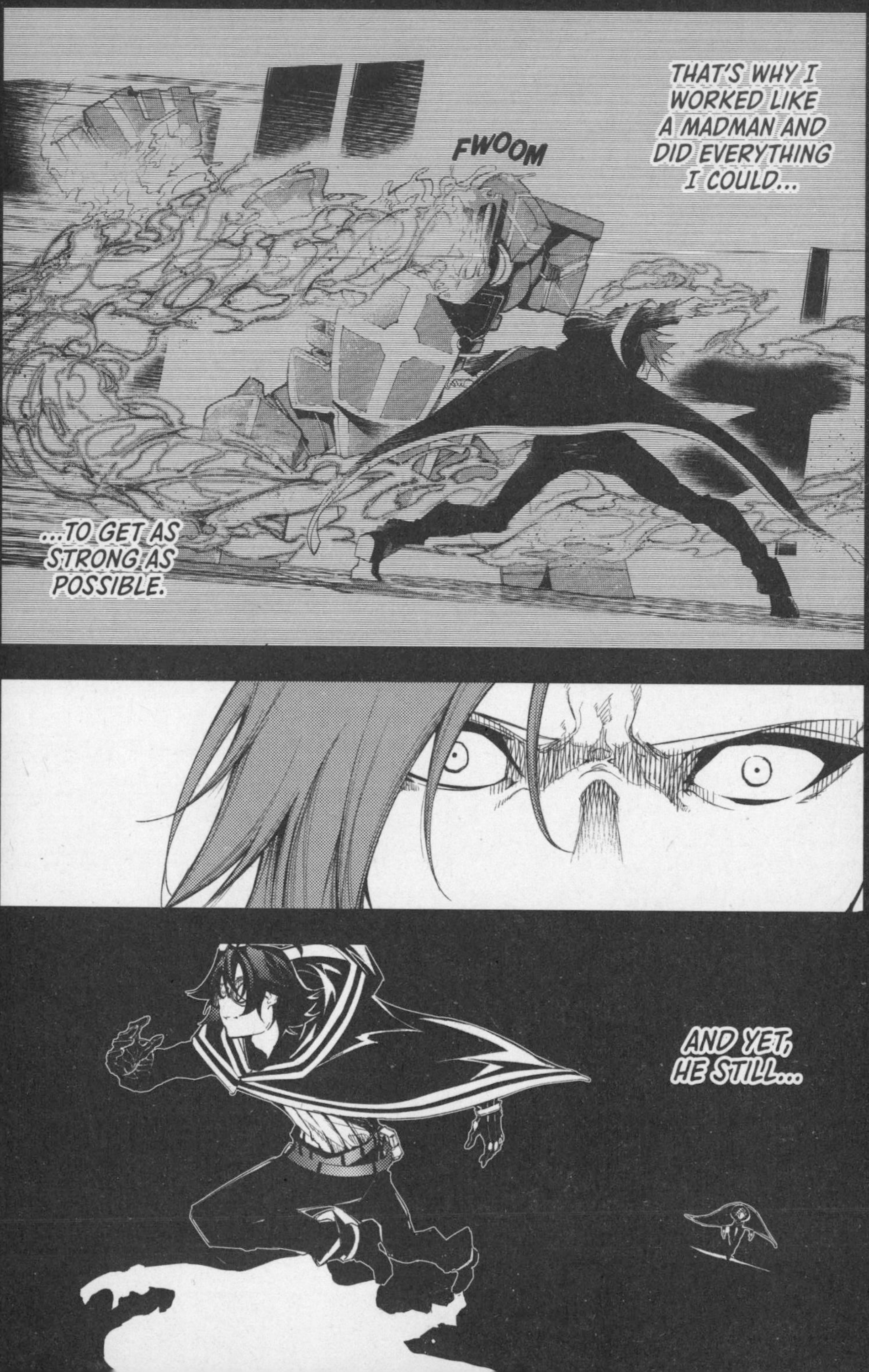
THAT'S WHY I WORKED LIKE A MADMAN AND DID EVERYTHING I COULD...
FWOOM
...TO GET AS STRONG AS POSSIBLE.
AND YET, HE STILL...

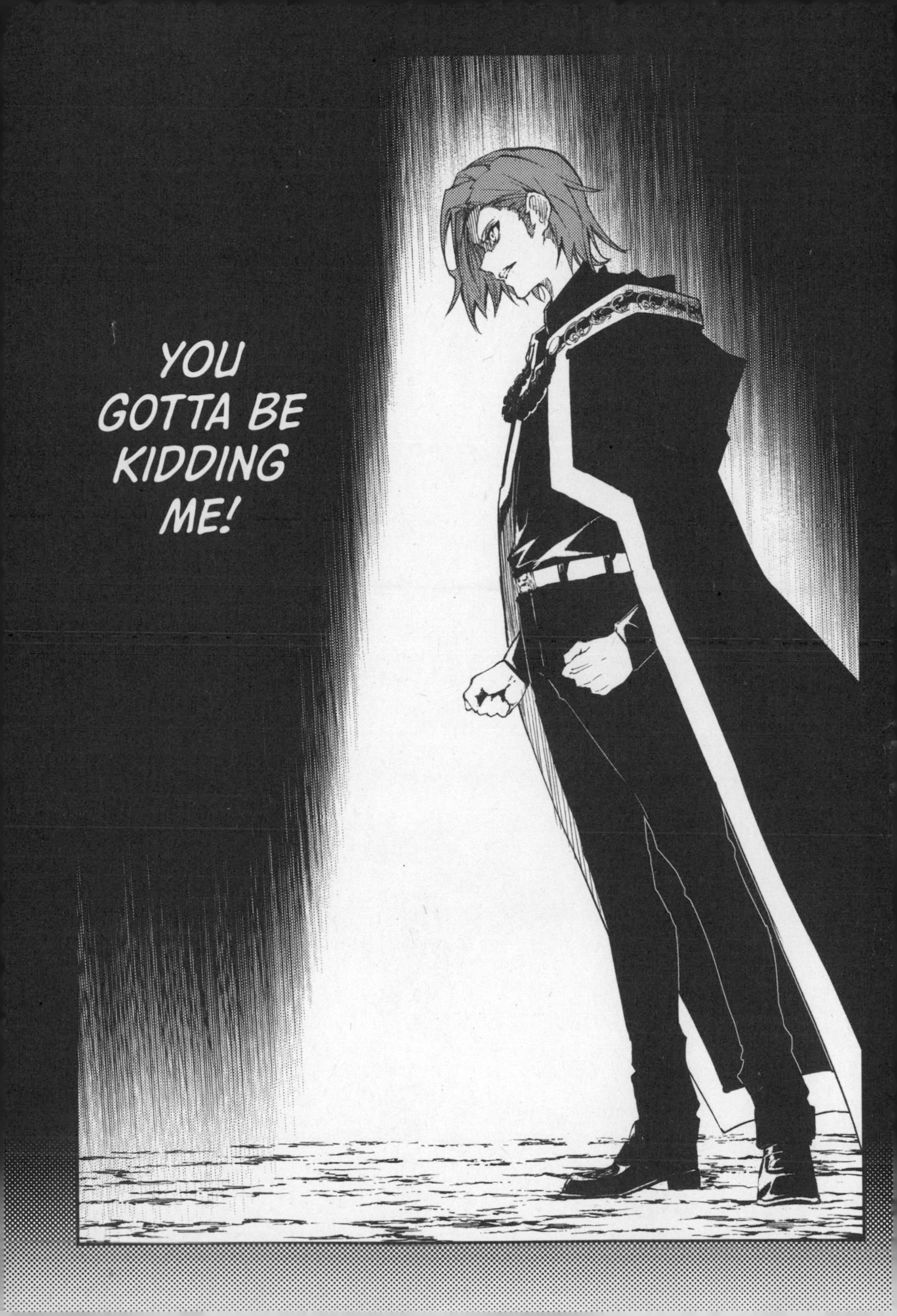
YOU GOTTA BE KIDDING ME!

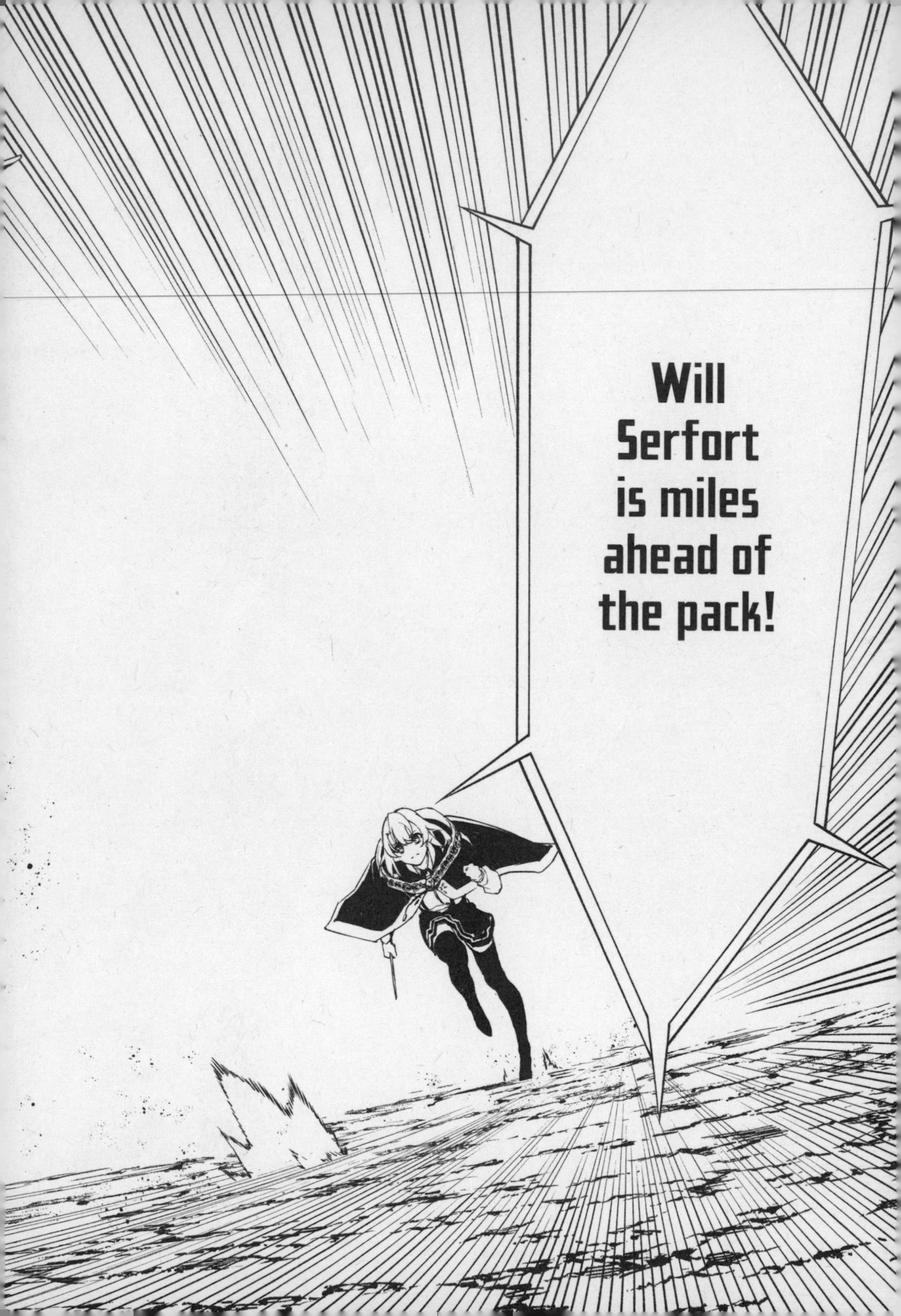
Will Serfort is miles ahead of the pack!

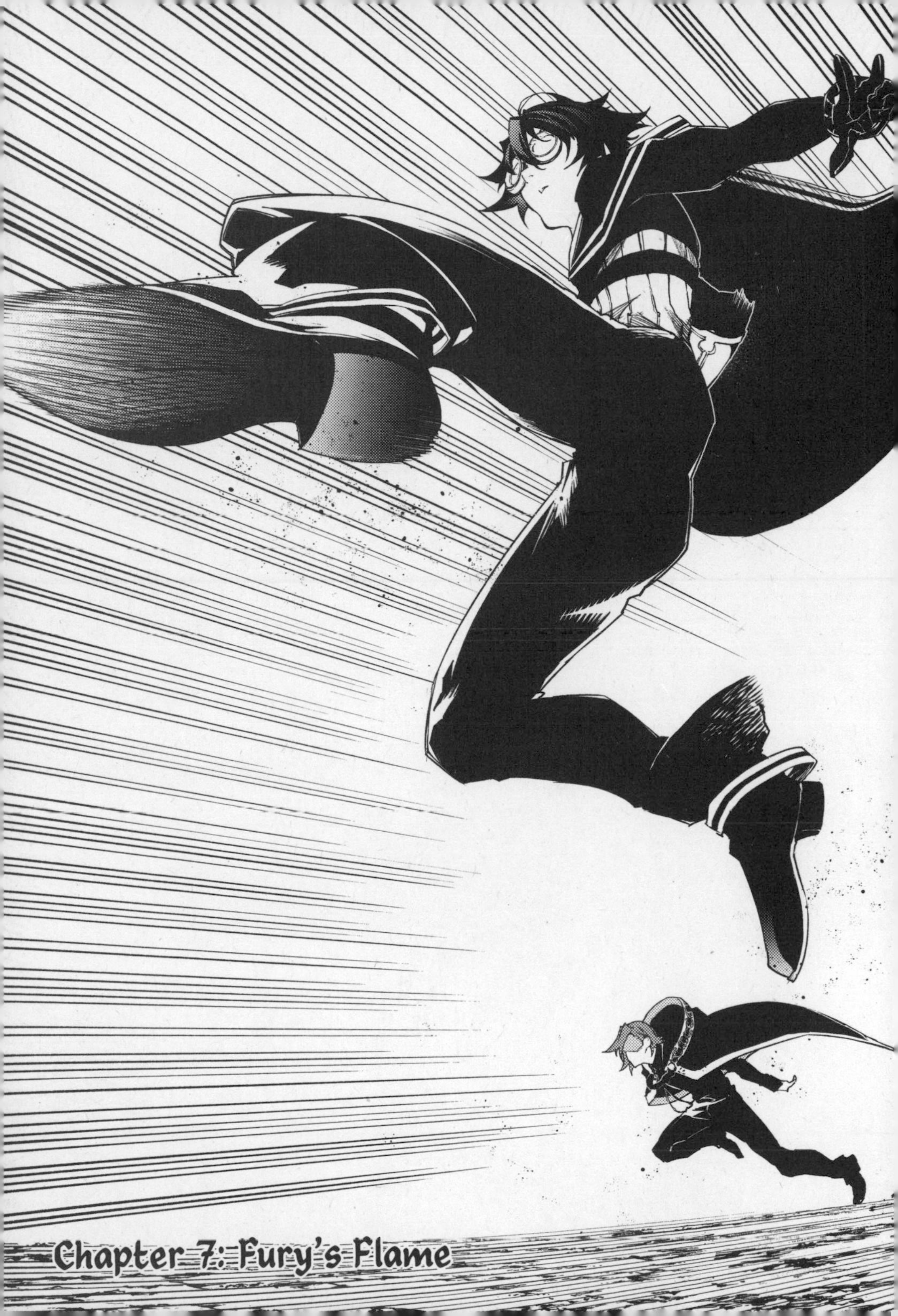
Chapter 7: Fury's Flame

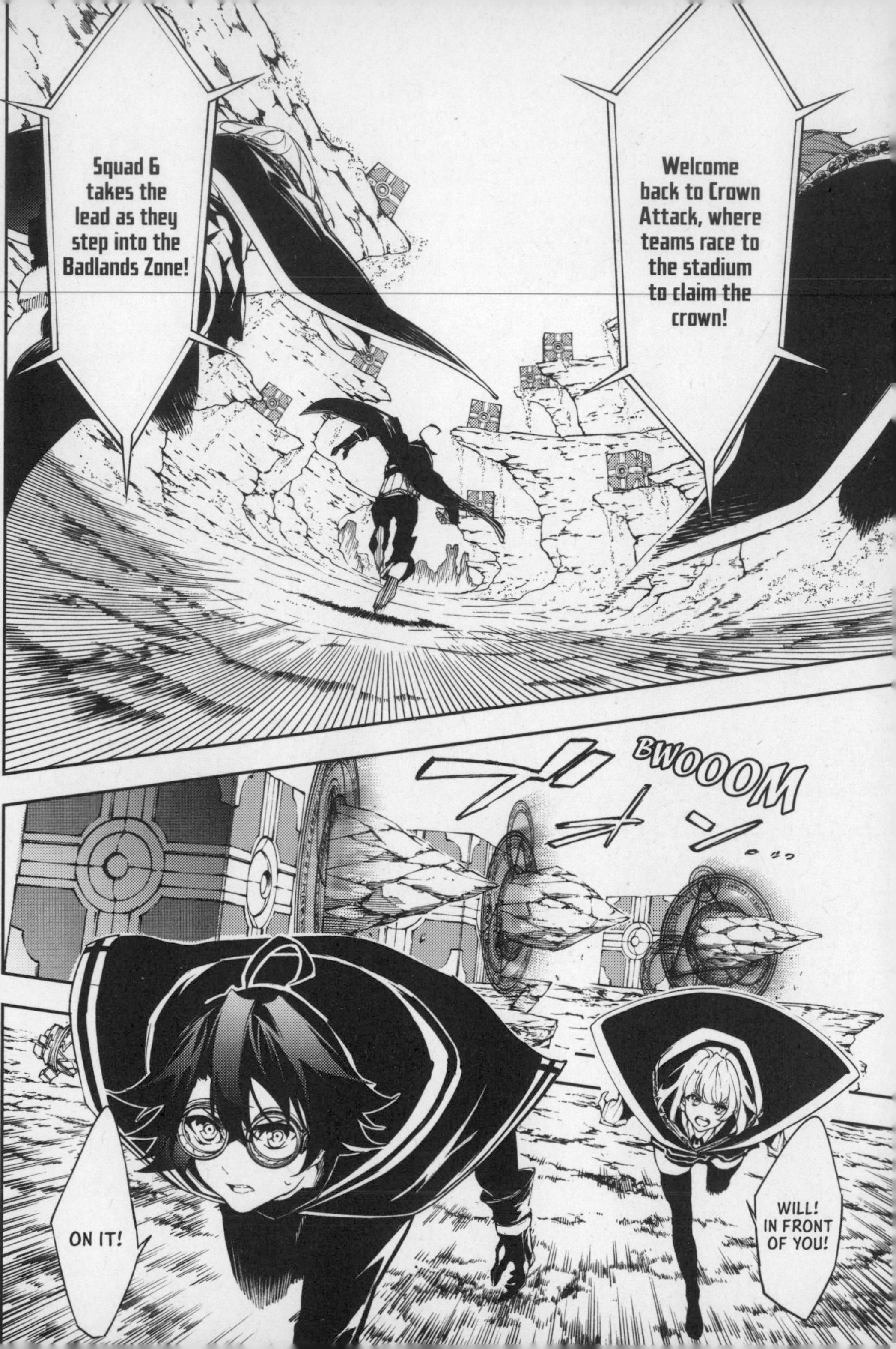
Welcome back to Crown Attack, where teams race to the stadium to claim the crown!
Squad 6 takes the lead as they step into the Badlands Zone!
BWOOOM
WILL! IN FRONT OF YOU!
ON IT!

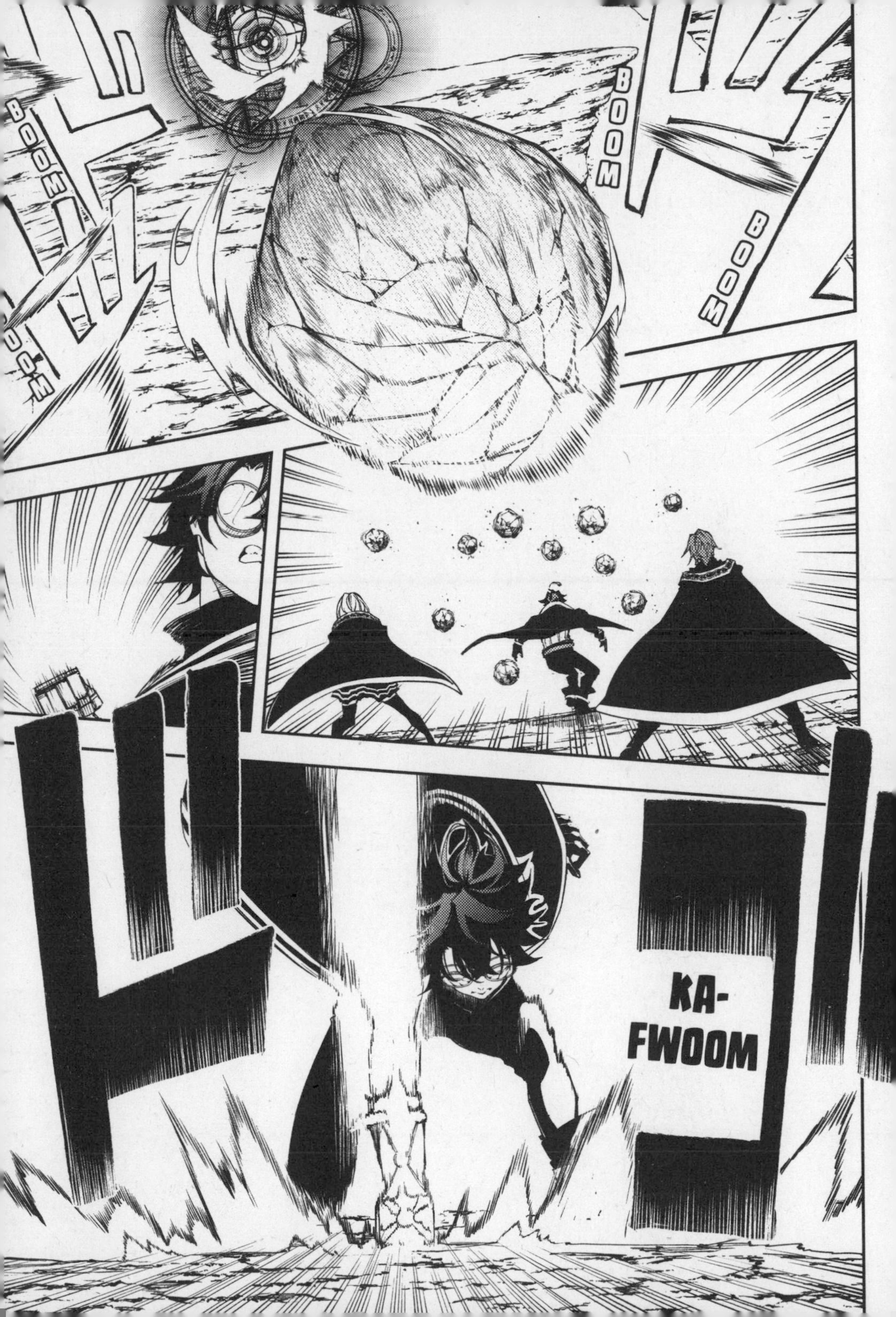
BOOM
BOOM
BOOM
BOOM
KA-
FWOOM

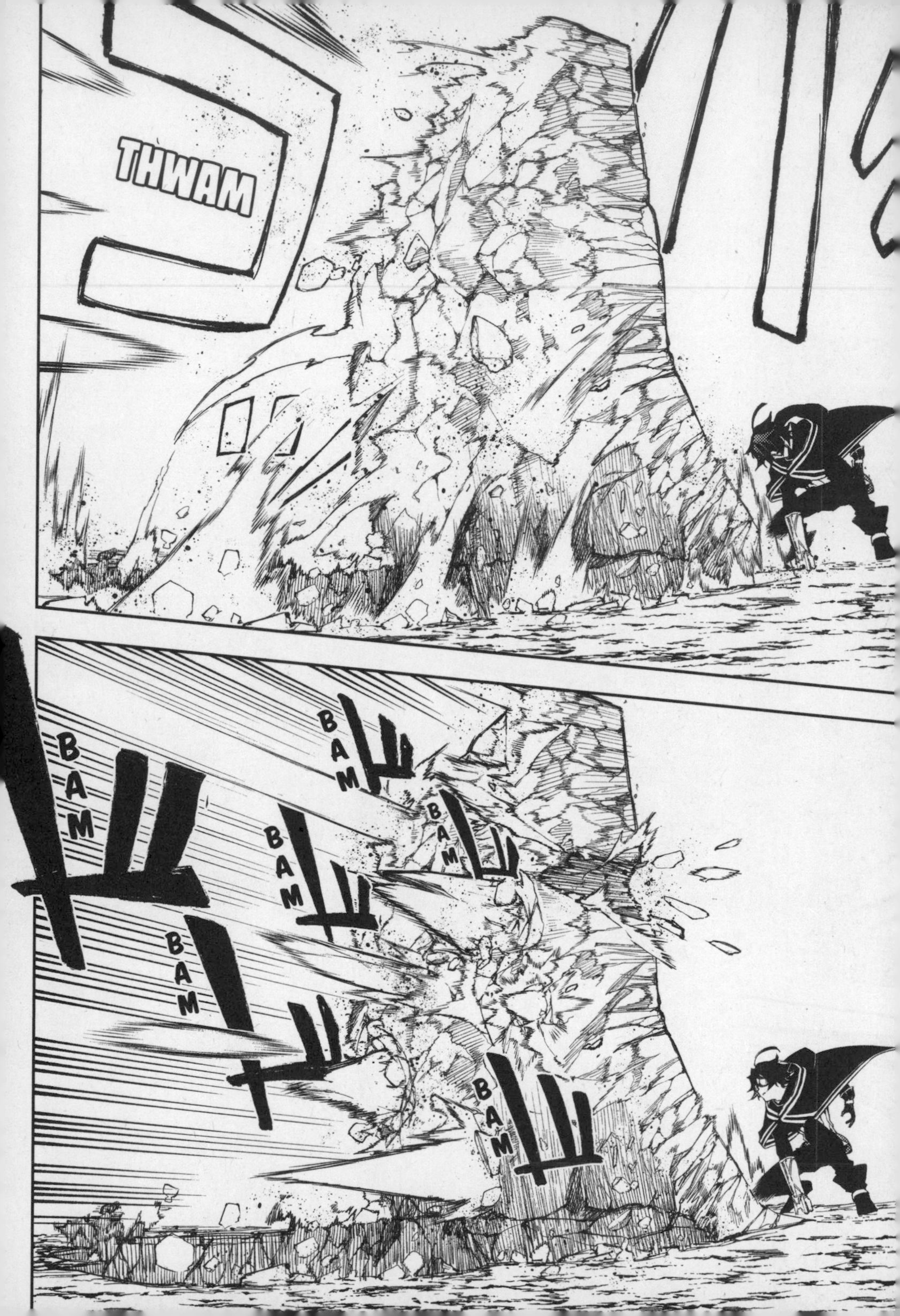
THWAM
BAM
BAM
BAM
BAM
BAM
BAM

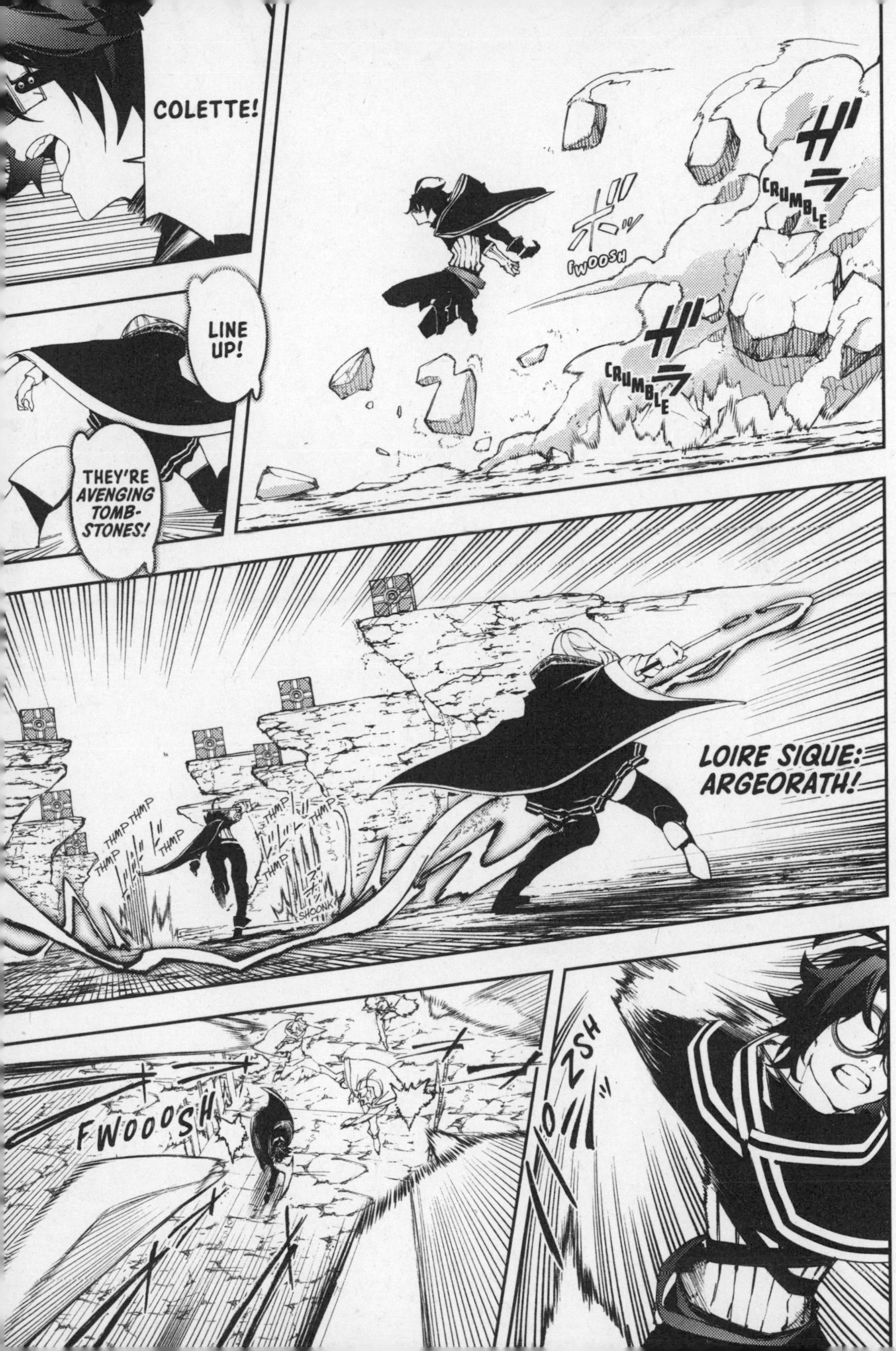
ボッ
FWOOSH
ガラ
CRUMBLE
ガラ
CRUMBLE
COLETTE!
LINE UP!
THEY'RE AVENGING TOMB-STONES!
LOIRE SIQUE: ARGEORATH!
THMP THMP
THMP
THMP
THMP
THMP
THMP
SHOONK
ZSH
FWOOOSH

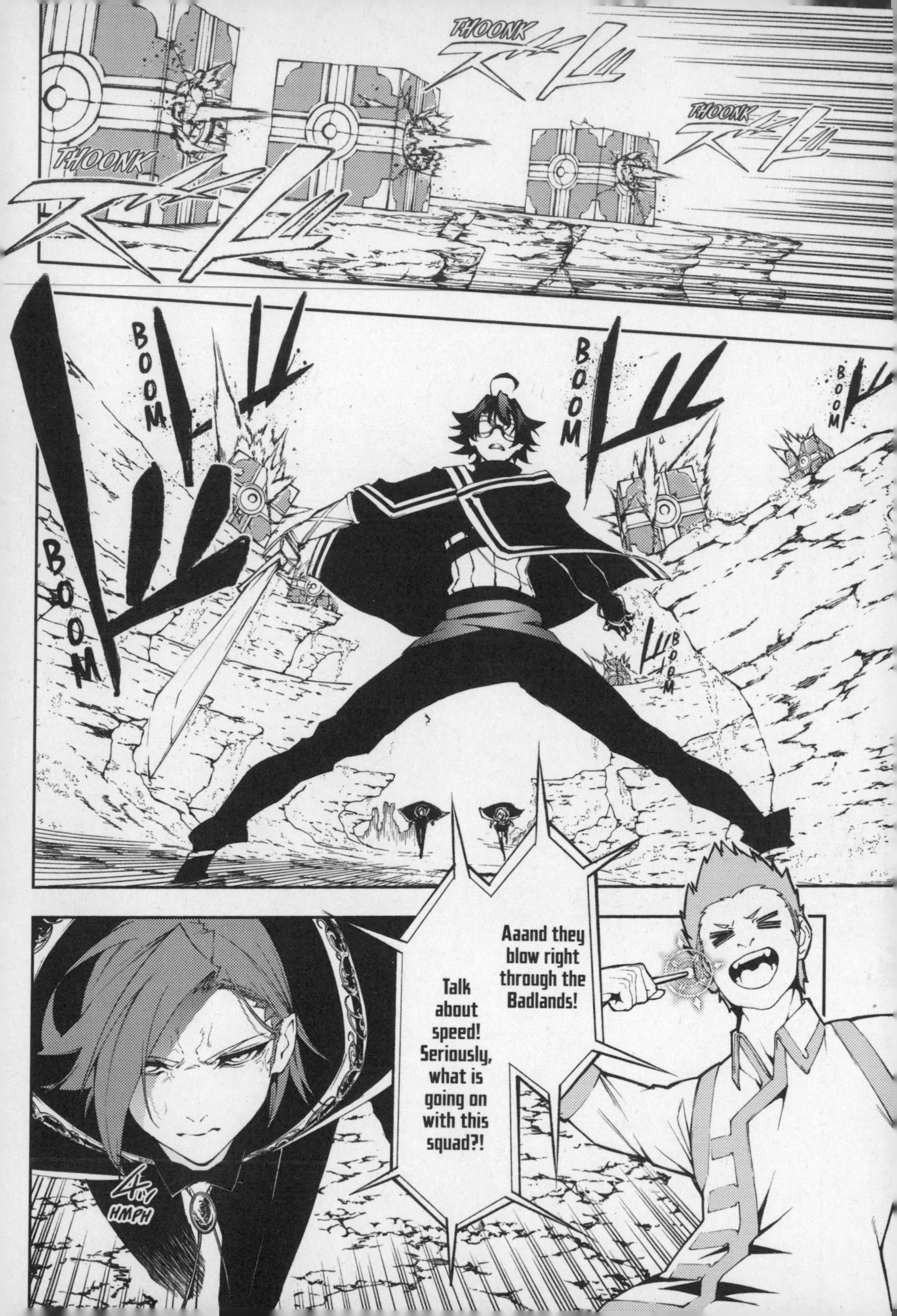
THOONK
THOONK
THOONK
BOOM
BOOM
BOOM
BOOM
BOOM
Aaand they blow right through the Badlands!
Talk about speed! Seriously, what is going on with this squad?!
HMPH

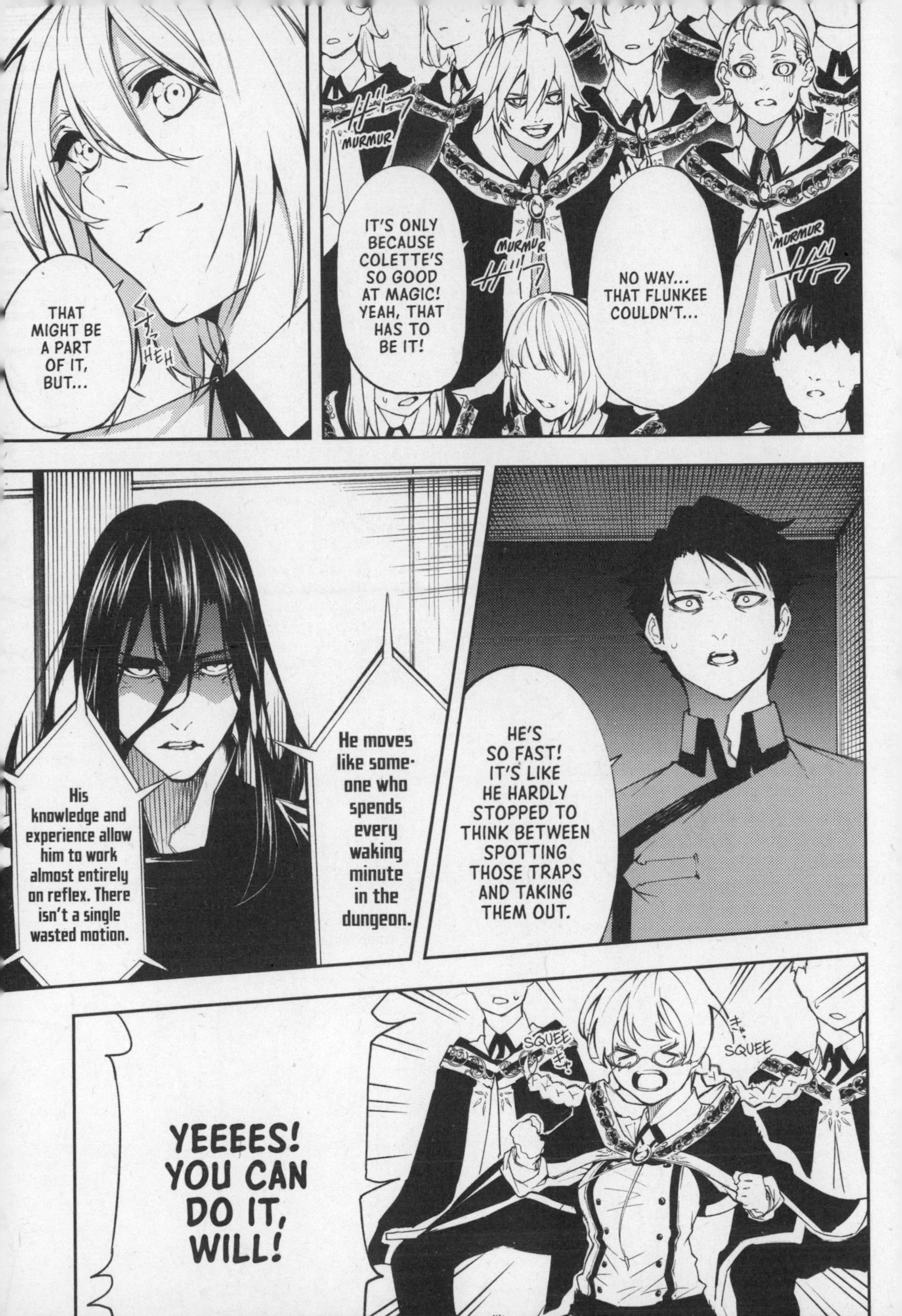
MURMUR
MURMUR
NO WAY... THAT FLUNKEE COULDN'T...
MURMUR
IT'S ONLY BECAUSE COLETTE'S SO GOOD AT MAGIC! YEAH, THAT HAS TO BE IT!
HEH
THAT MIGHT BE A PART OF IT, BUT...
HE'S SO FAST! IT'S LIKE HE HARDLY STOPPED TO THINK BETWEEN SPOTTING THOSE TRAPS AND TAKING THEM OUT.
He moves like some-one who spends every waking minute in the dungeon.
His knowledge and experience allow him to work almost entirely on reflex. There isn't a single wasted motion.
SQUEE
SQUEE
YEEEES! YOU CAN DO IT, WILL!

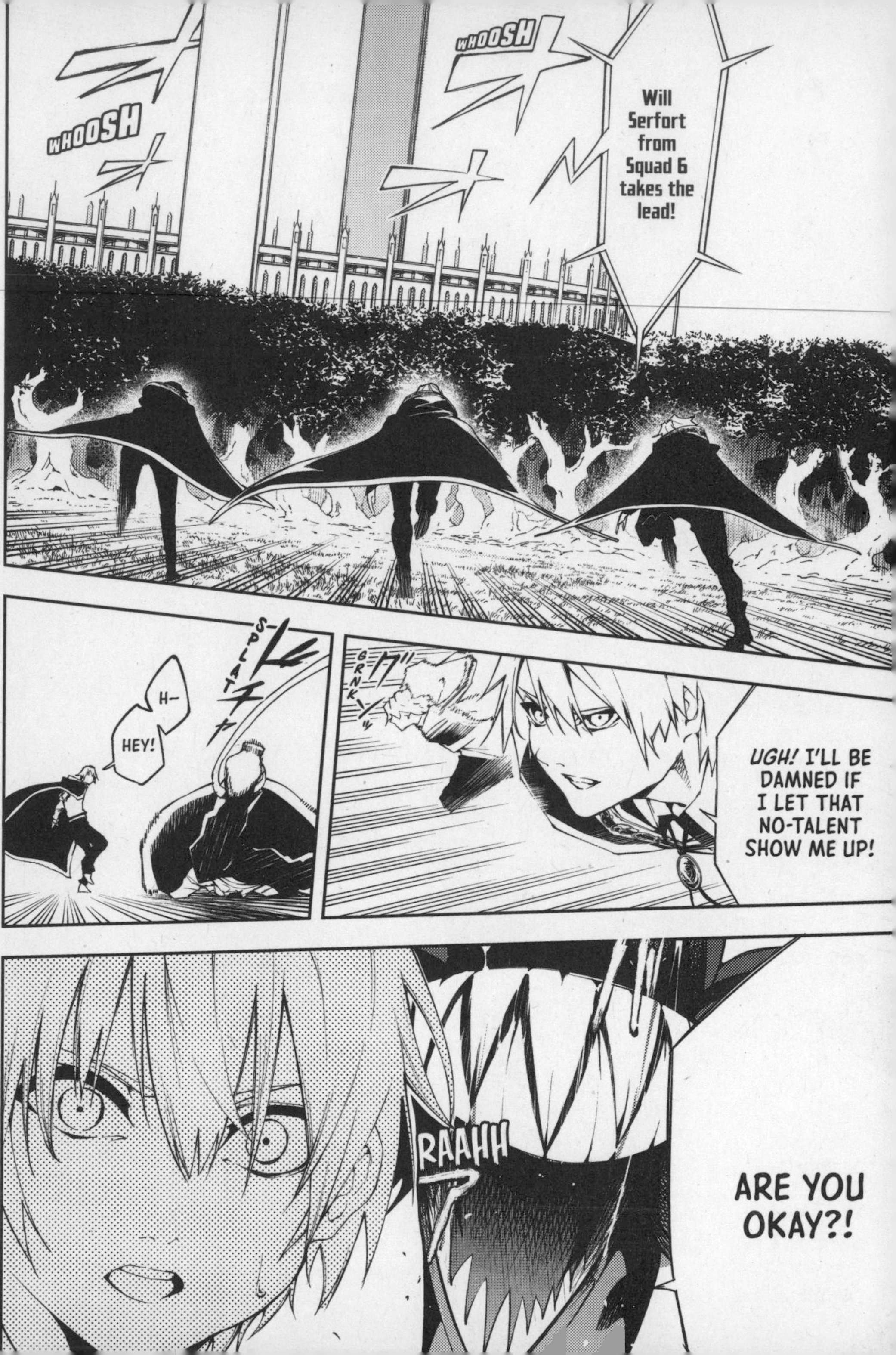
WHOOSH
Will Serfort from Squad 6 takes the lead!
WHOOSH
GRNK
UGH! I'LL BE DAMNED IF I LET THAT NO-TALENT SHOW ME UP!
SPLAT
H— HEY!
ARE YOU OKAY?!
RAAHH

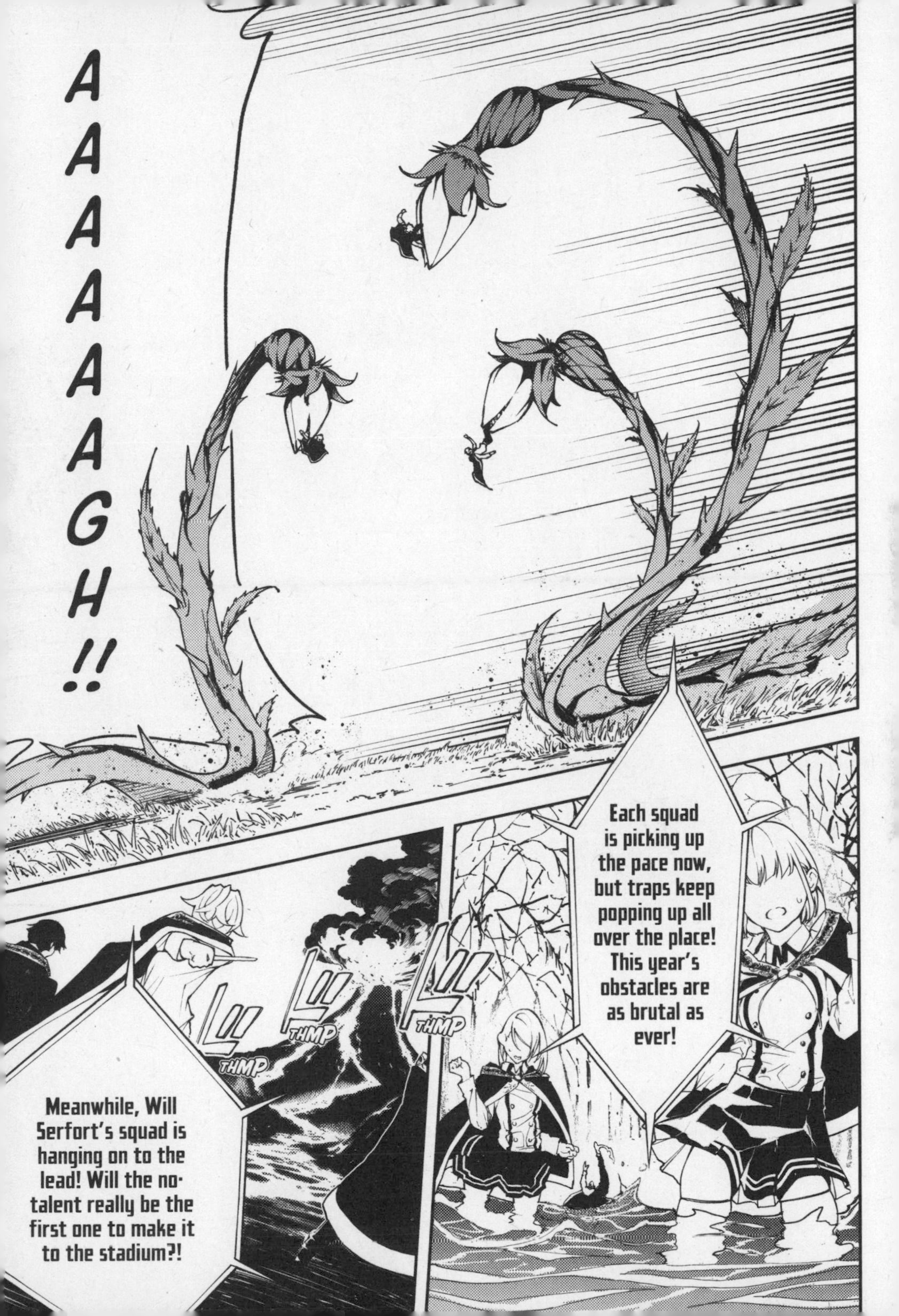
AAAAAAAGH!!
Each squad is picking up the pace now, but traps keep popping up all over the place! This year's obstacles are as brutal as ever!
THMP
THMP
THMP
Meanwhile, Will Serfort's squad is hanging on to the lead! Will the no-talent really be the first one to make it to the stadium?!

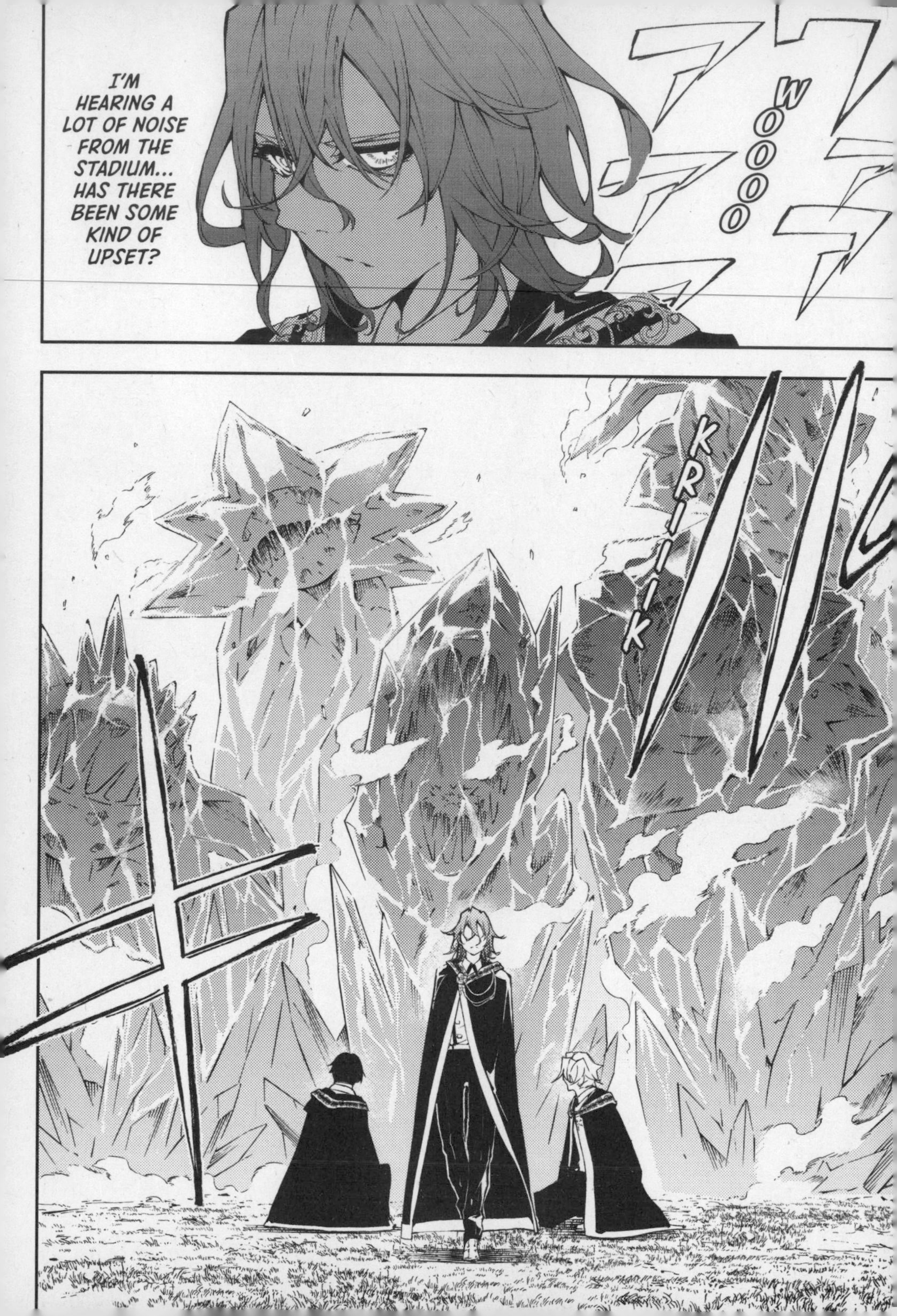
WOOOOO
I'M HEARING A LOT OF NOISE FROM THE STADIUM... HAS THERE BEEN SOME KIND OF UPSET?
KRIIIIK

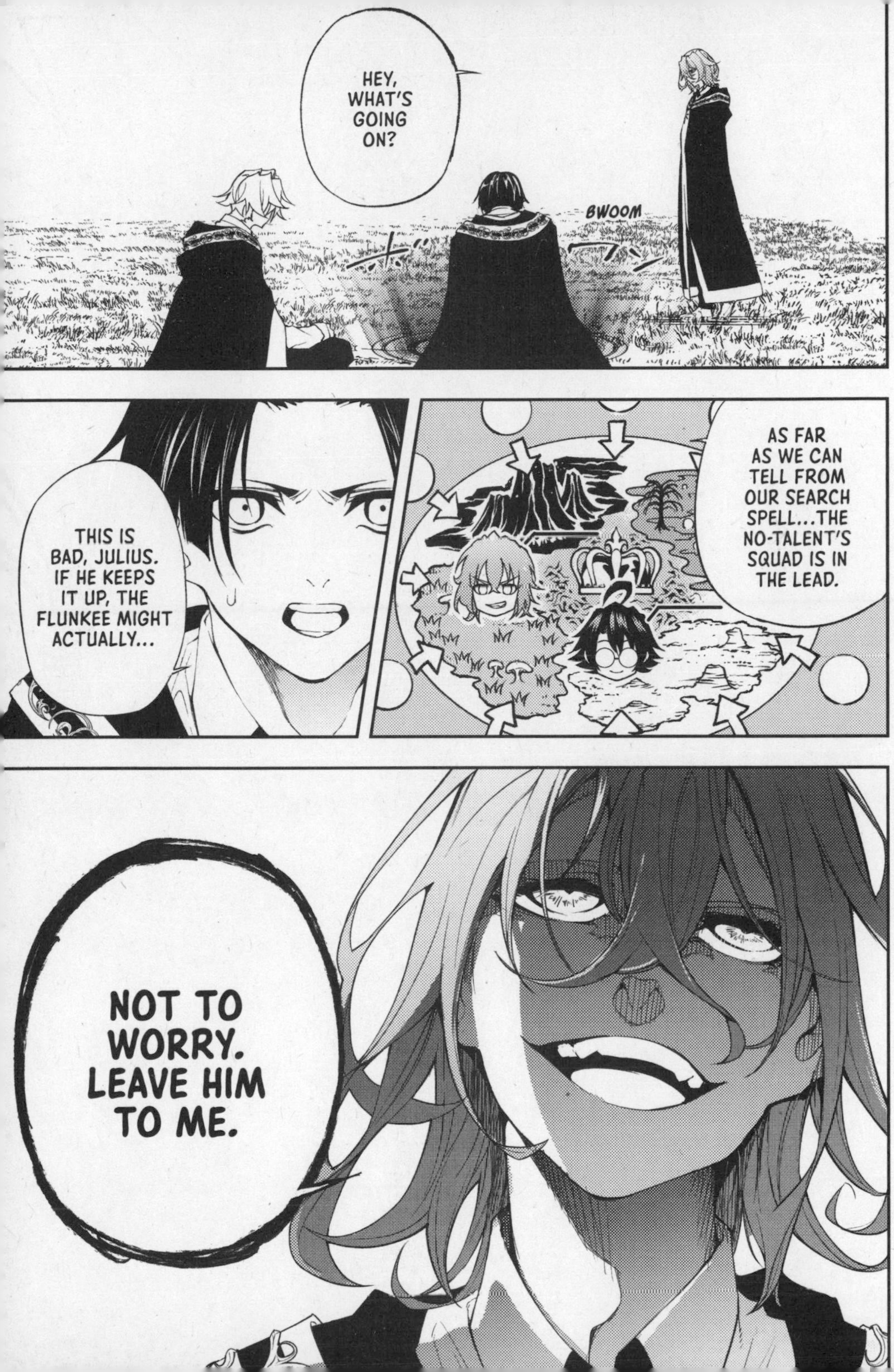
HEY, WHAT'S GOING ON?
BWOOM
AS FAR AS WE CAN TELL FROM OUR SEARCH SPELL...THE NO-TALENT'S SQUAD IS IN THE LEAD.
THIS IS BAD, JULIUS. IF HE KEEPS IT UP, THE FLUNKEE MIGHT ACTUALLY...
NOT TO WORRY. LEAVE HIM TO ME.

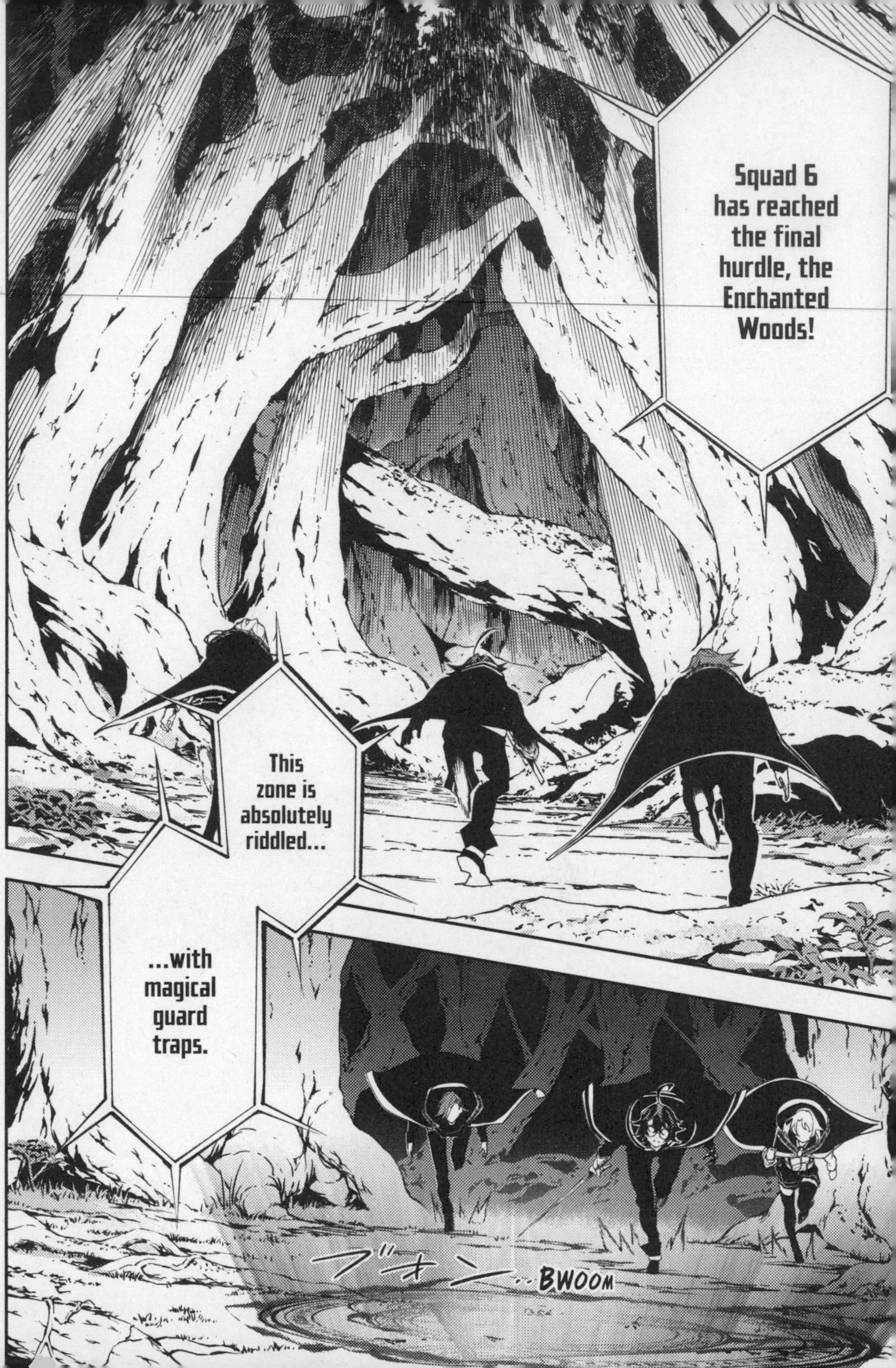
Squad 6 has reached the final hurdle, the Enchanted Woods!
This zone is absolutely riddled...
...with magical guard traps.
ブオン...
BWOOM

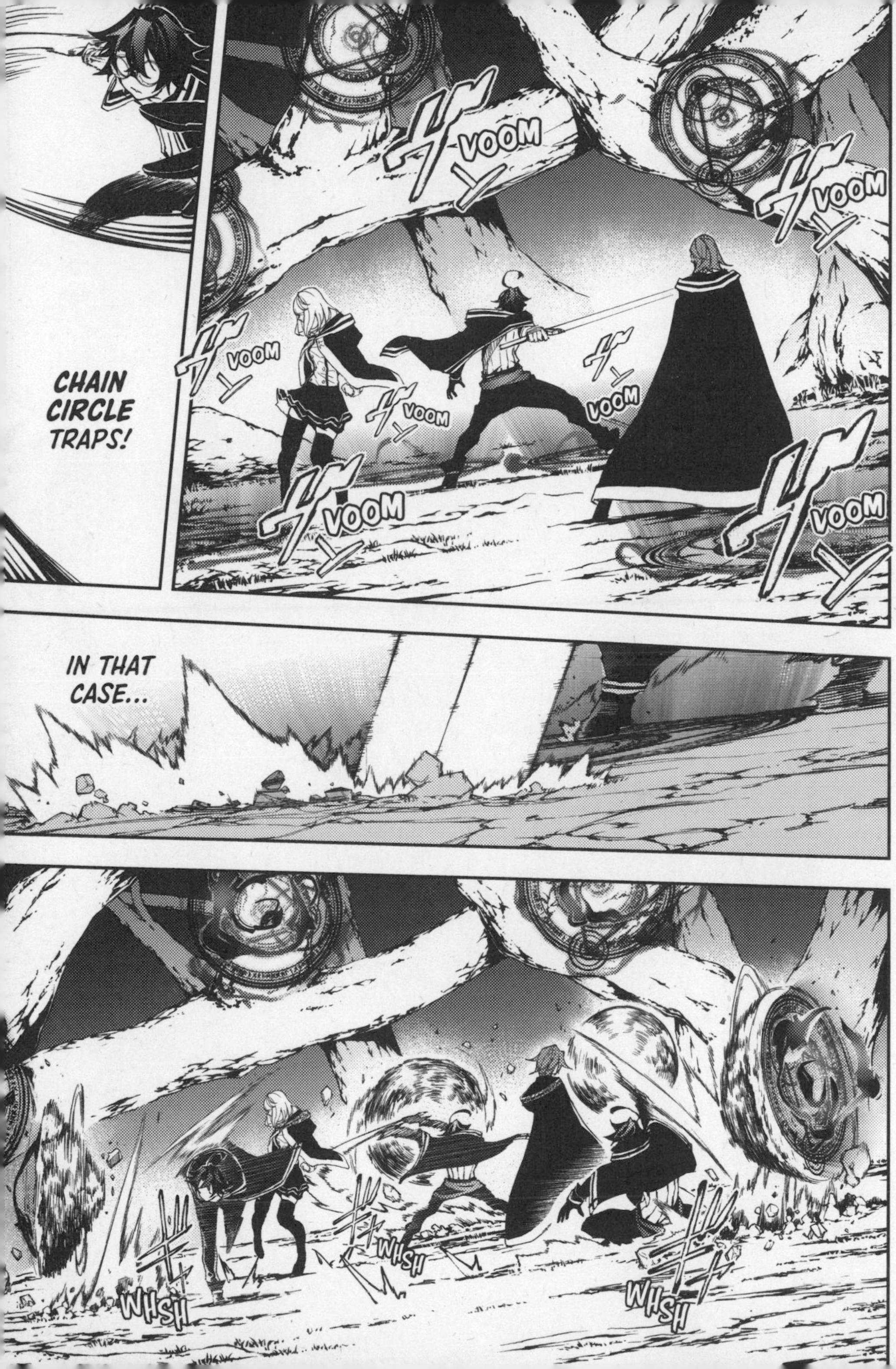
VOOM
VOOM
VOOM
VOOM
VOOM
VOOM
VOOM
CHAIN CIRCLE TRAPS!
IN THAT CASE...
WHSH
WHSH
WHSH

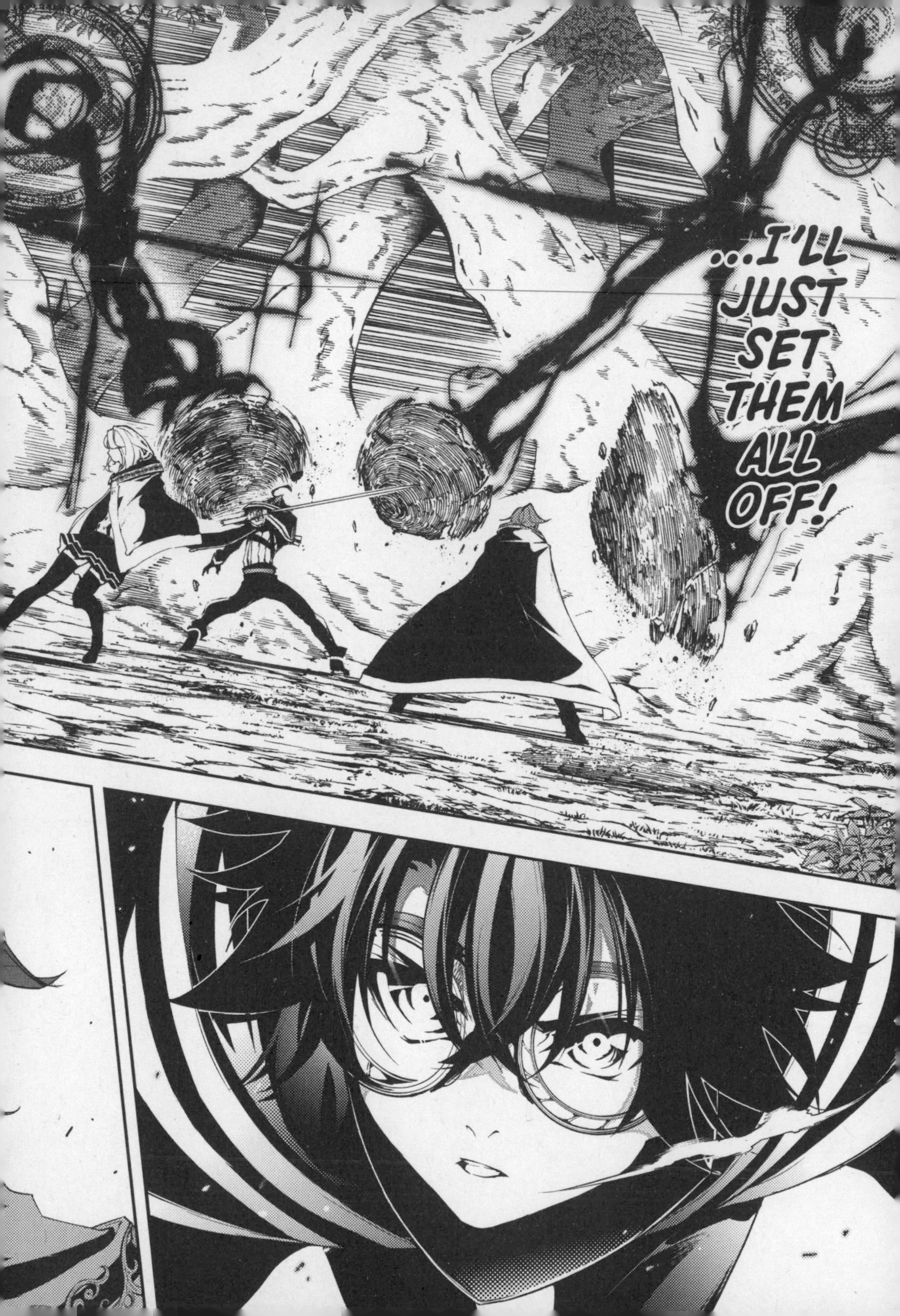
...I'LL JUST SET THEM ALL OFF!

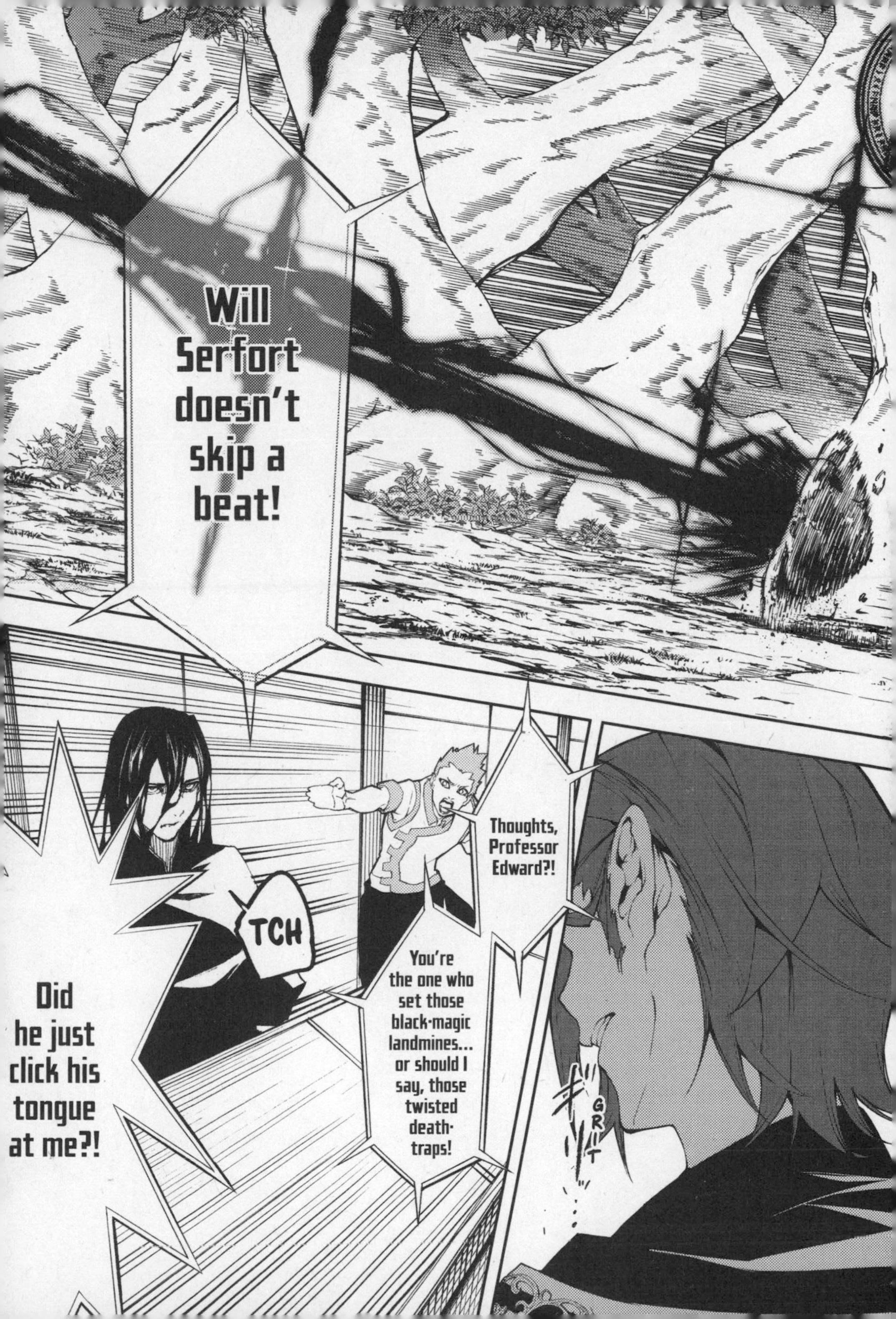
Will Serfort doesn't skip a beat!
GRIT
Thoughts, Professor Edward?!
You're the one who set those black-magic landmines... or should I say, those twisted death-traps!
TCH
Did he just click his tongue at me?!

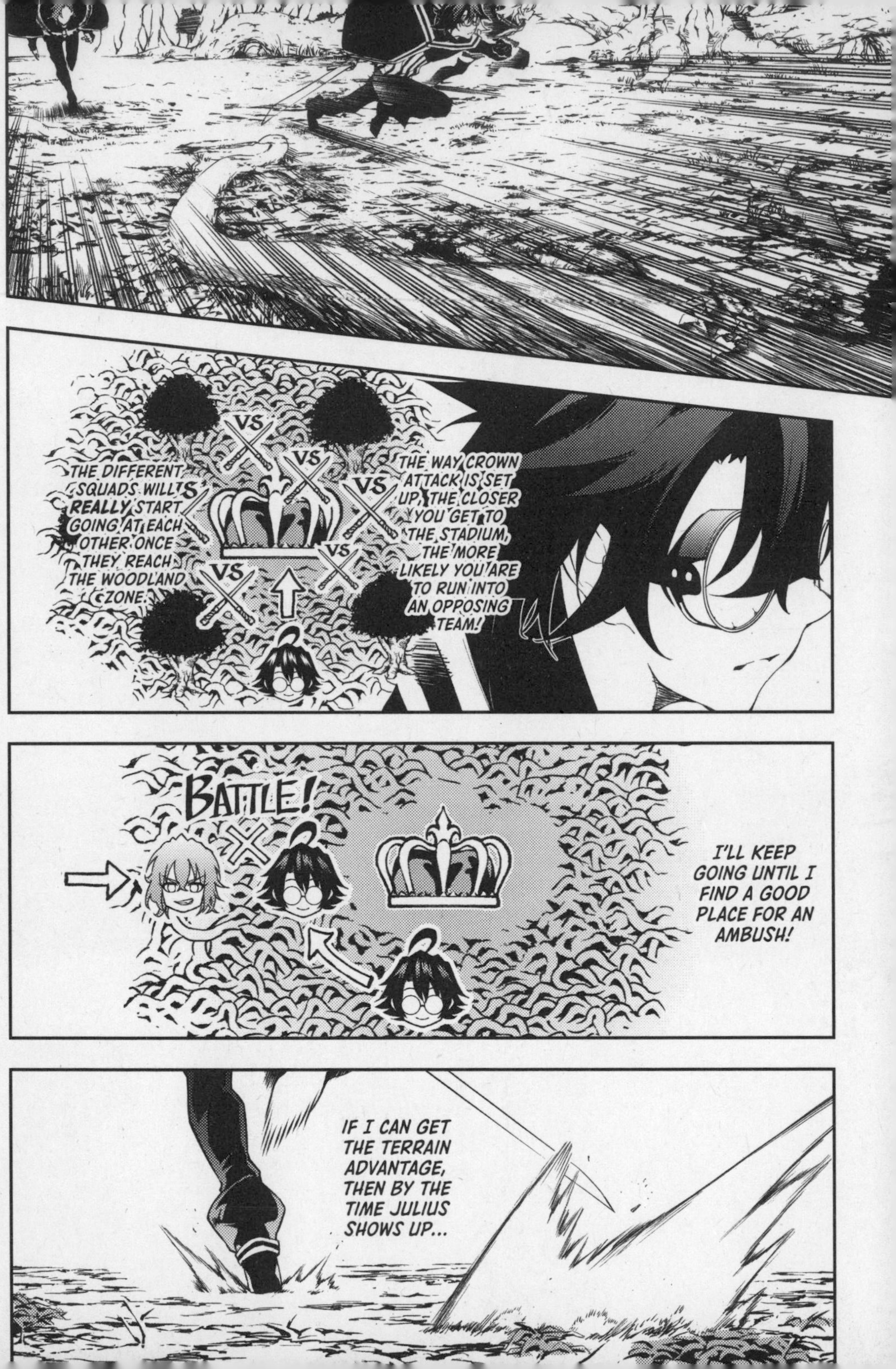
THE WAY CROWN ATTACK IS SET UP, THE CLOSER YOU GET TO THE STADIUM, THE MORE LIKELY YOU ARE TO RUN INTO AN OPPOSING TEAM!
THE DIFFERENT SQUADS WILL REALLY START GOING AT EACH OTHER ONCE THEY REACH THE WOODLAND ZONE.
VS
VS
VS
VS
VS
I'LL KEEP GOING UNTIL I FIND A GOOD PLACE FOR AN AMBUSH!
BATTLE!
IF I CAN GET THE TERRAIN ADVANTAGE, THEN BY THE TIME JULIUS SHOWS UP...

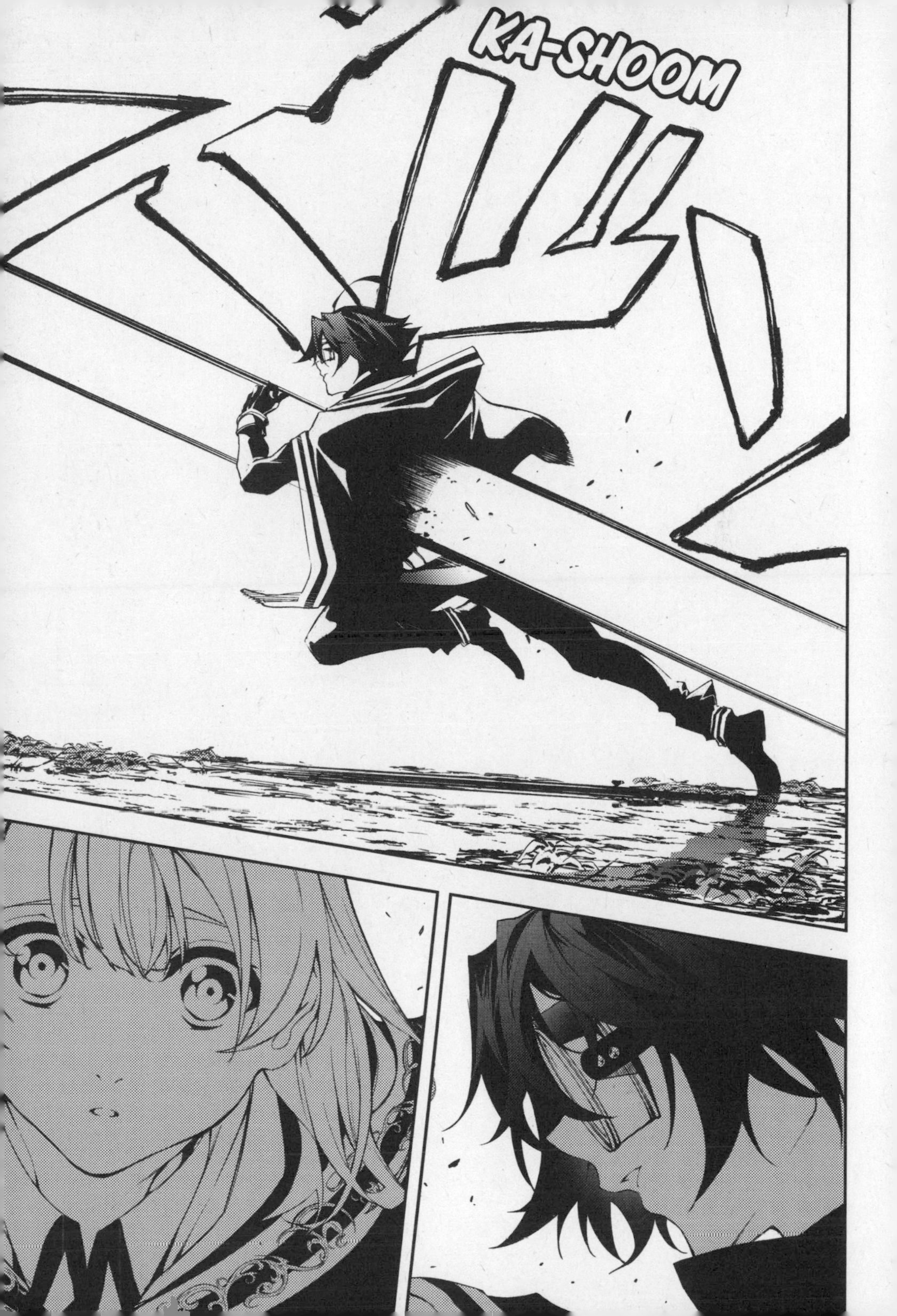
KA-SHOOM

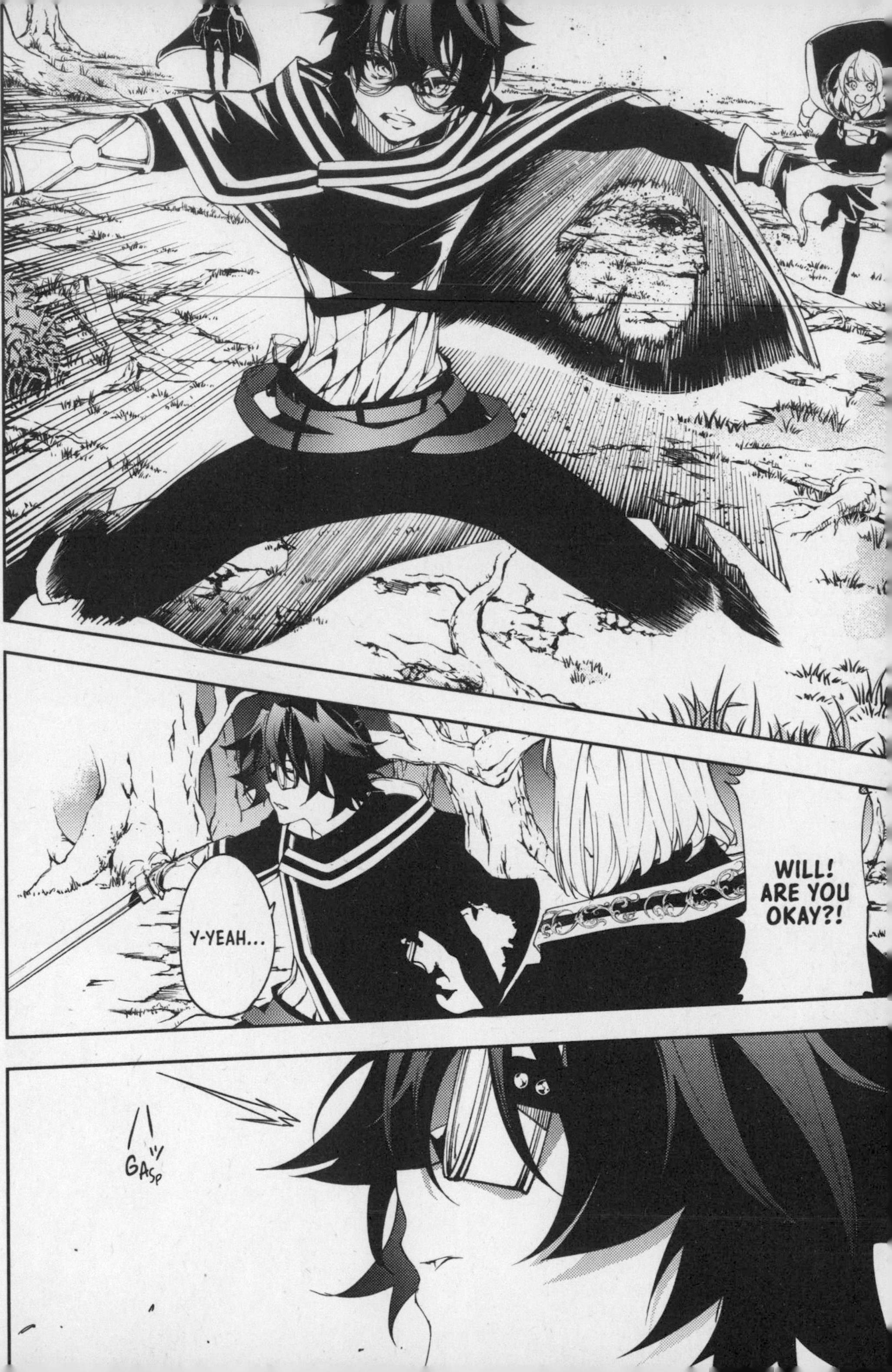
WILL! ARE YOU OKAY?!
Y-YEAH...
GASP

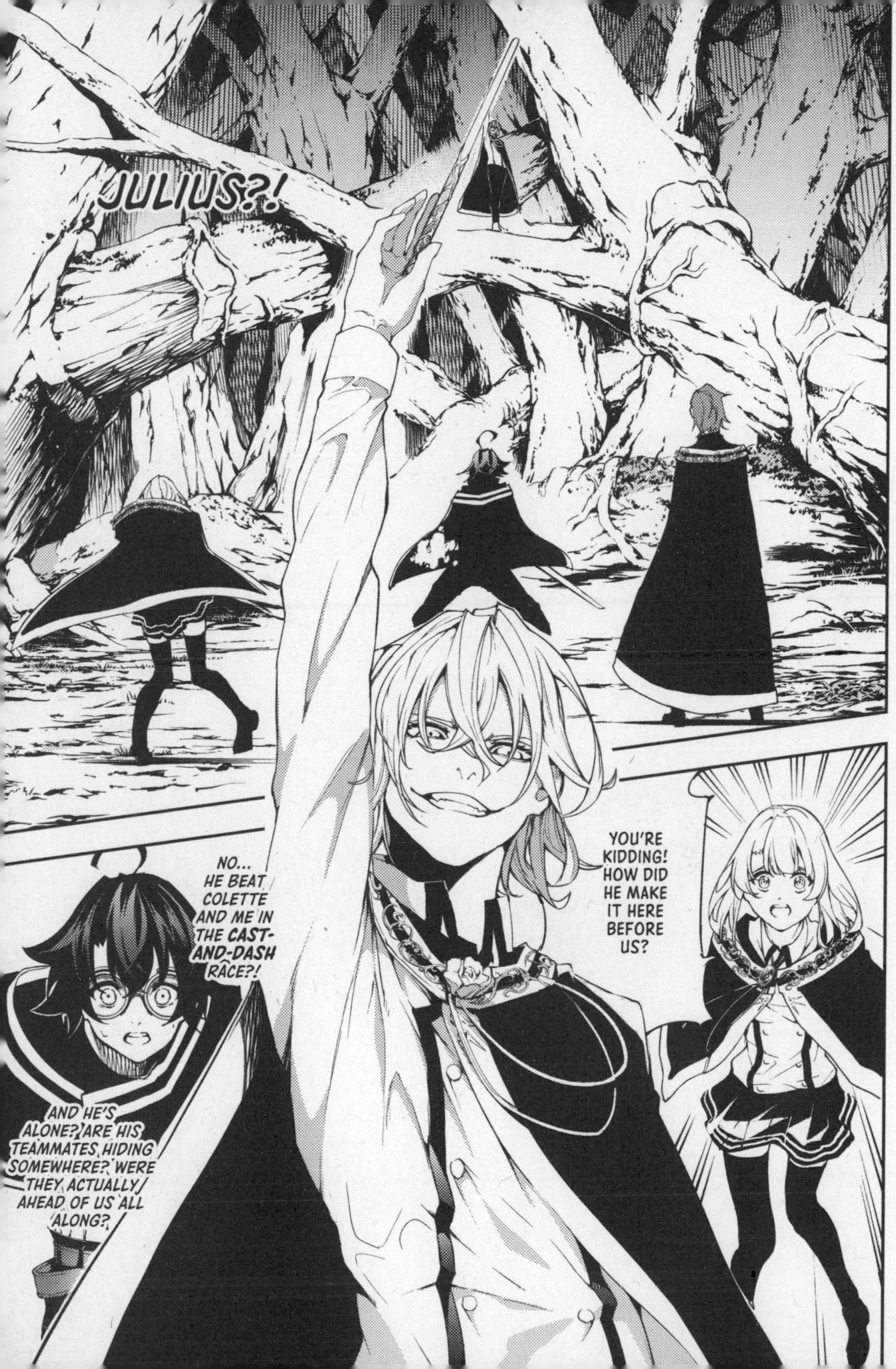
JULIUS?!
YOU'RE KIDDING! HOW DID HE MAKE IT HERE BEFORE US?
NO... HE BEAT COLETTE AND ME IN THE CAST-AND-DASH RACE?!
AND HE'S ALONE? ARE HIS TEAMMATES HIDING SOMEWHERE? WERE THEY ACTUALLY AHEAD OF US ALL ALONG?

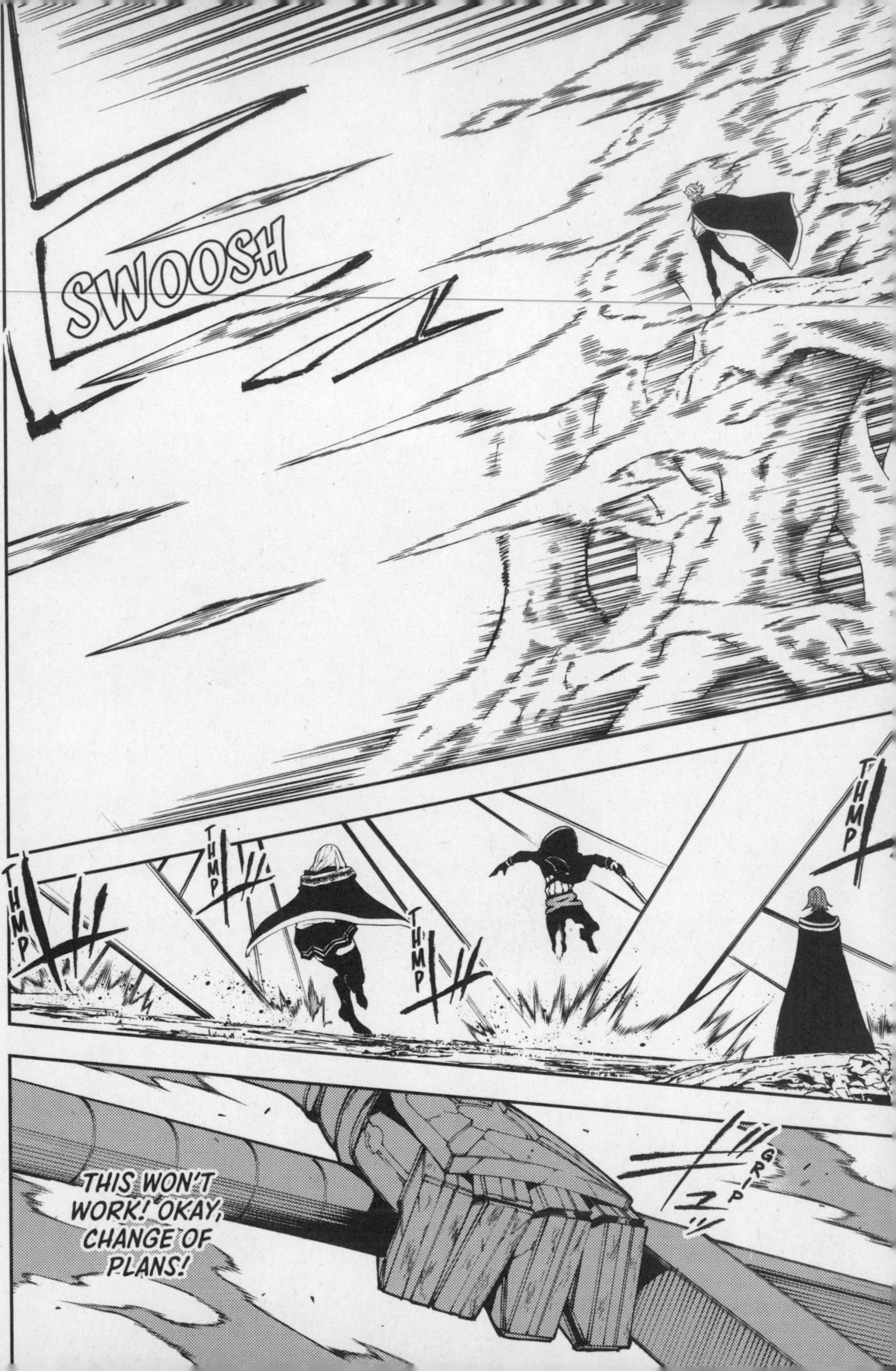
SWOOSH
THMP
THMP
THMP
THMP
GRIP
THIS WON'T WORK! OKAY, CHANGE OF PLANS!

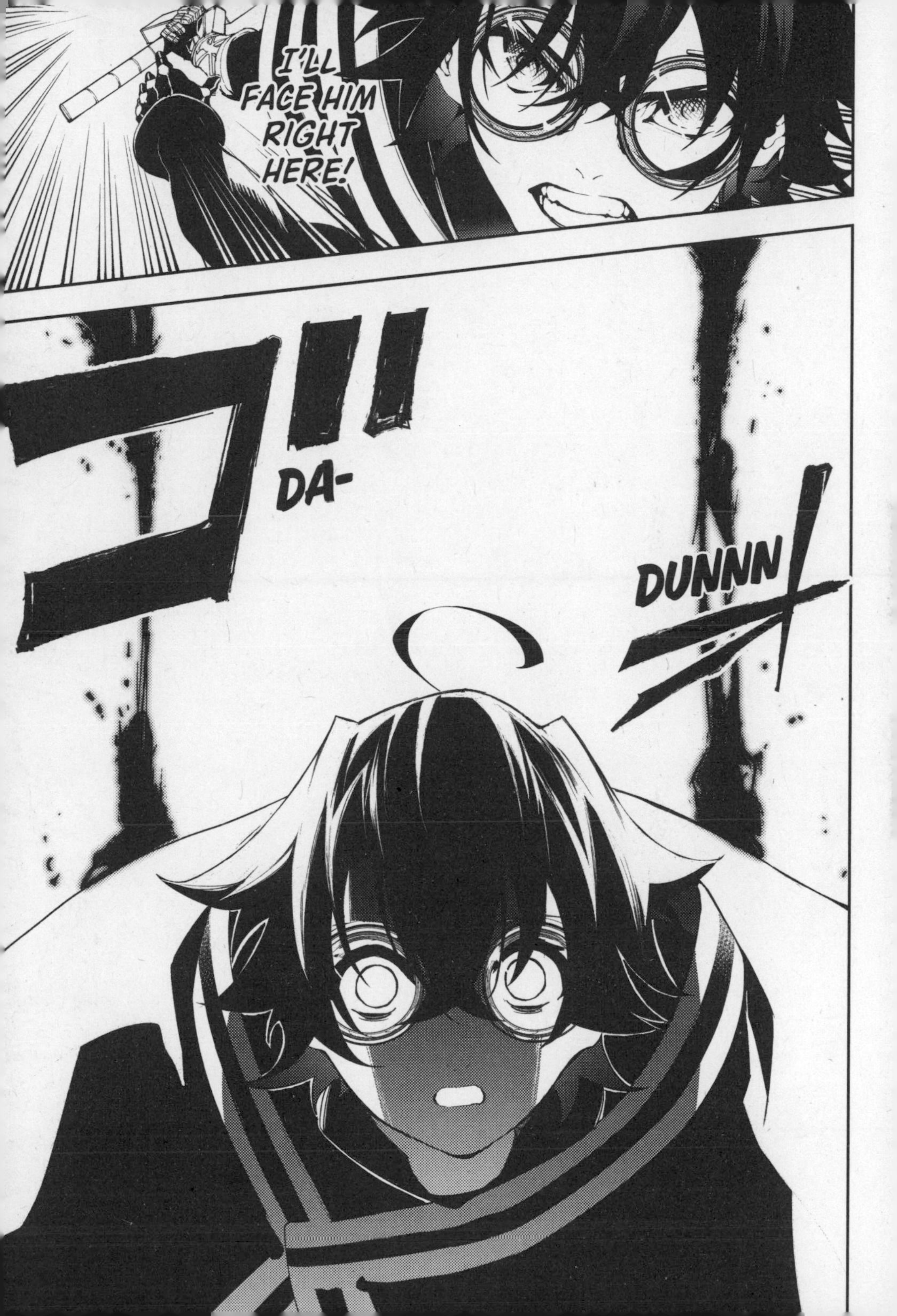
I'LL FACE HIM RIGHT HERE!
DA-
DUNNN!

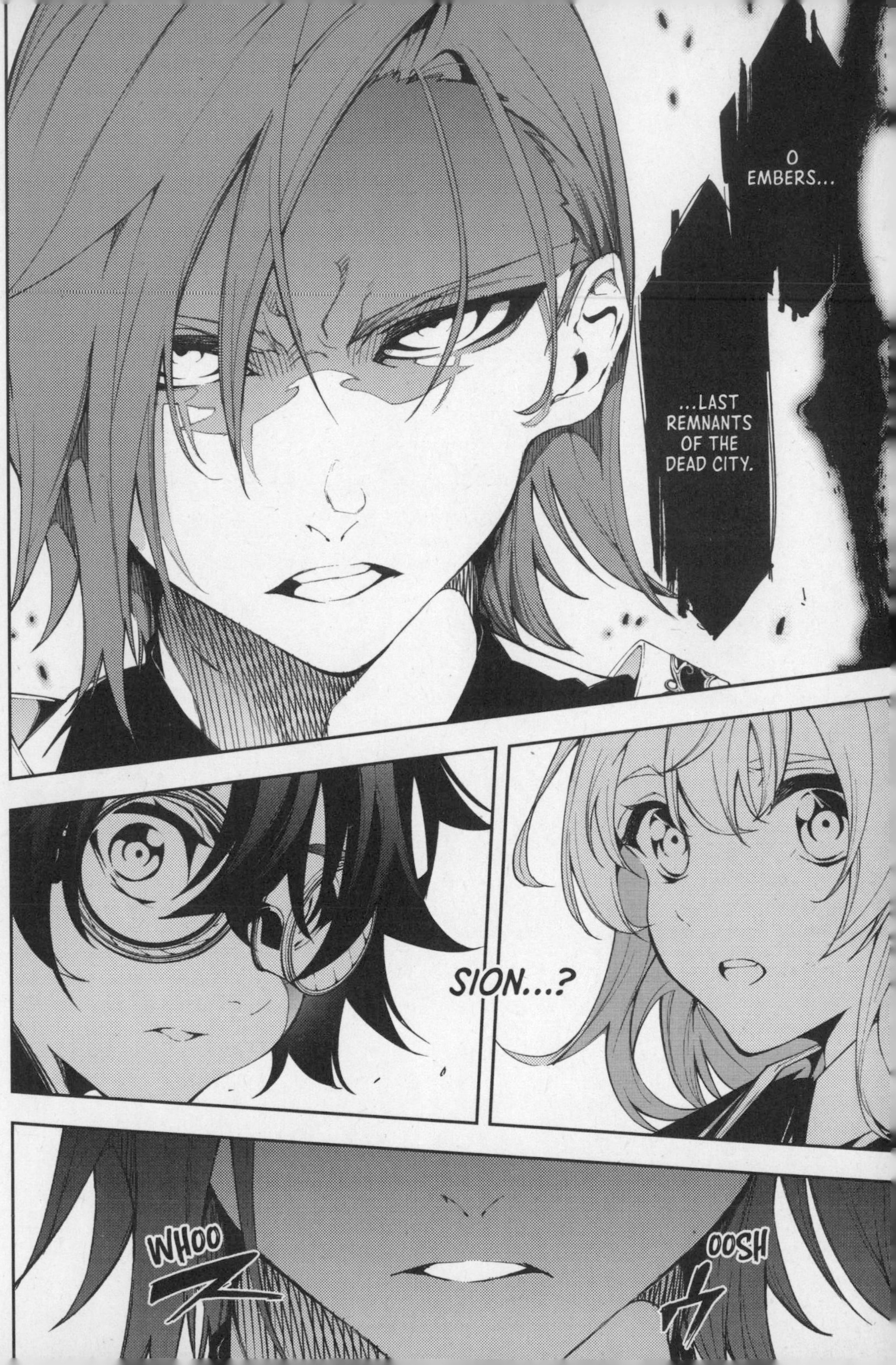
O EMBERS...
...LAST REMNANTS OF THE DEAD CITY.
SION...?
WHOO
OOSH

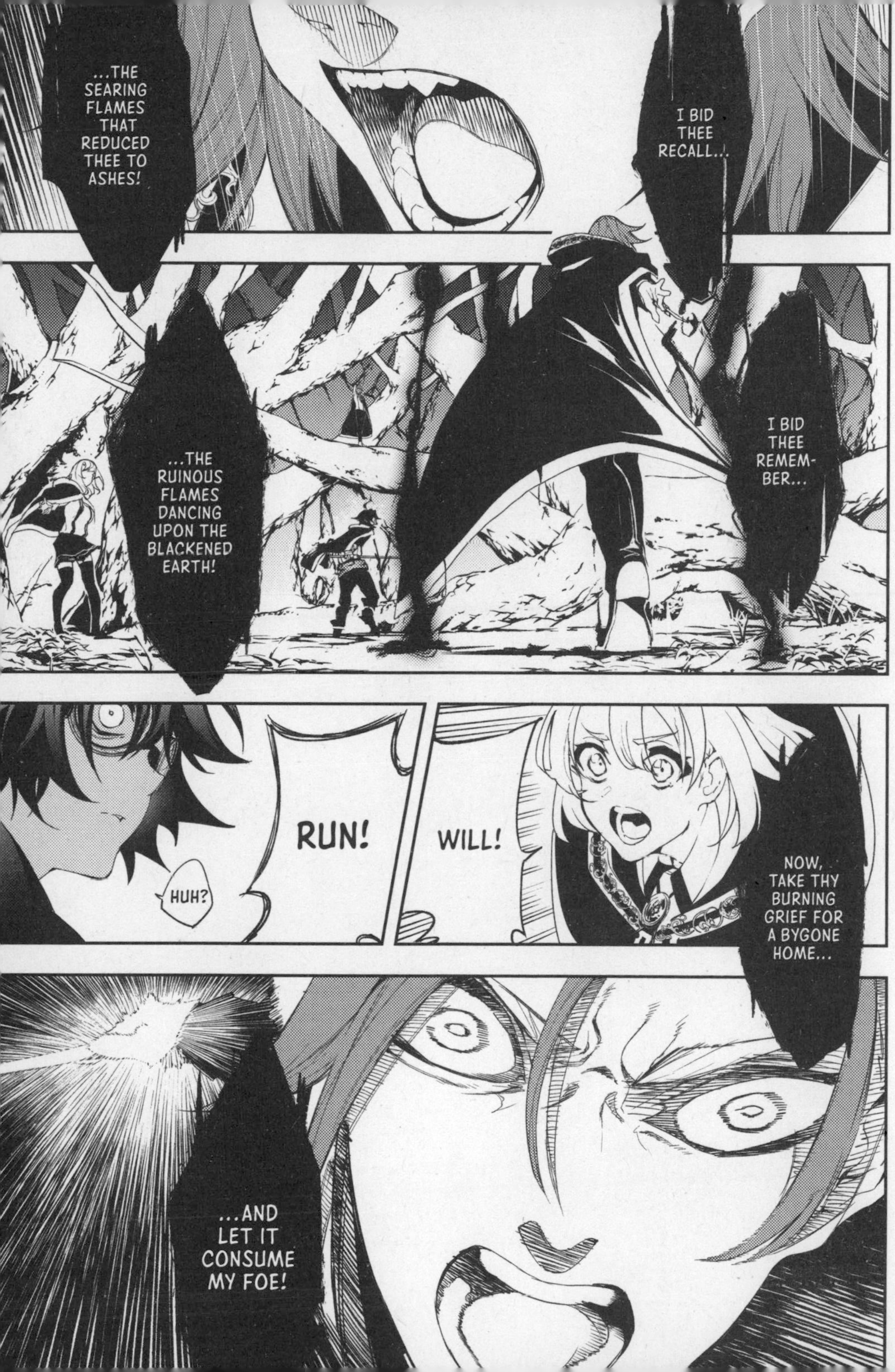
I BID THEE RECALL...
...THE SEARING FLAMES THAT REDUCED THEE TO ASHES!
I BID THEE REMEMBER...
...THE RUINOUS FLAMES DANCING UPON THE BLACKENED EARTH!
NOW, TAKE THY BURNING GRIEF FOR A BYGONE HOME...
WILL!
RUN!
HUH?
...AND LET IT CONSUME MY FOE!

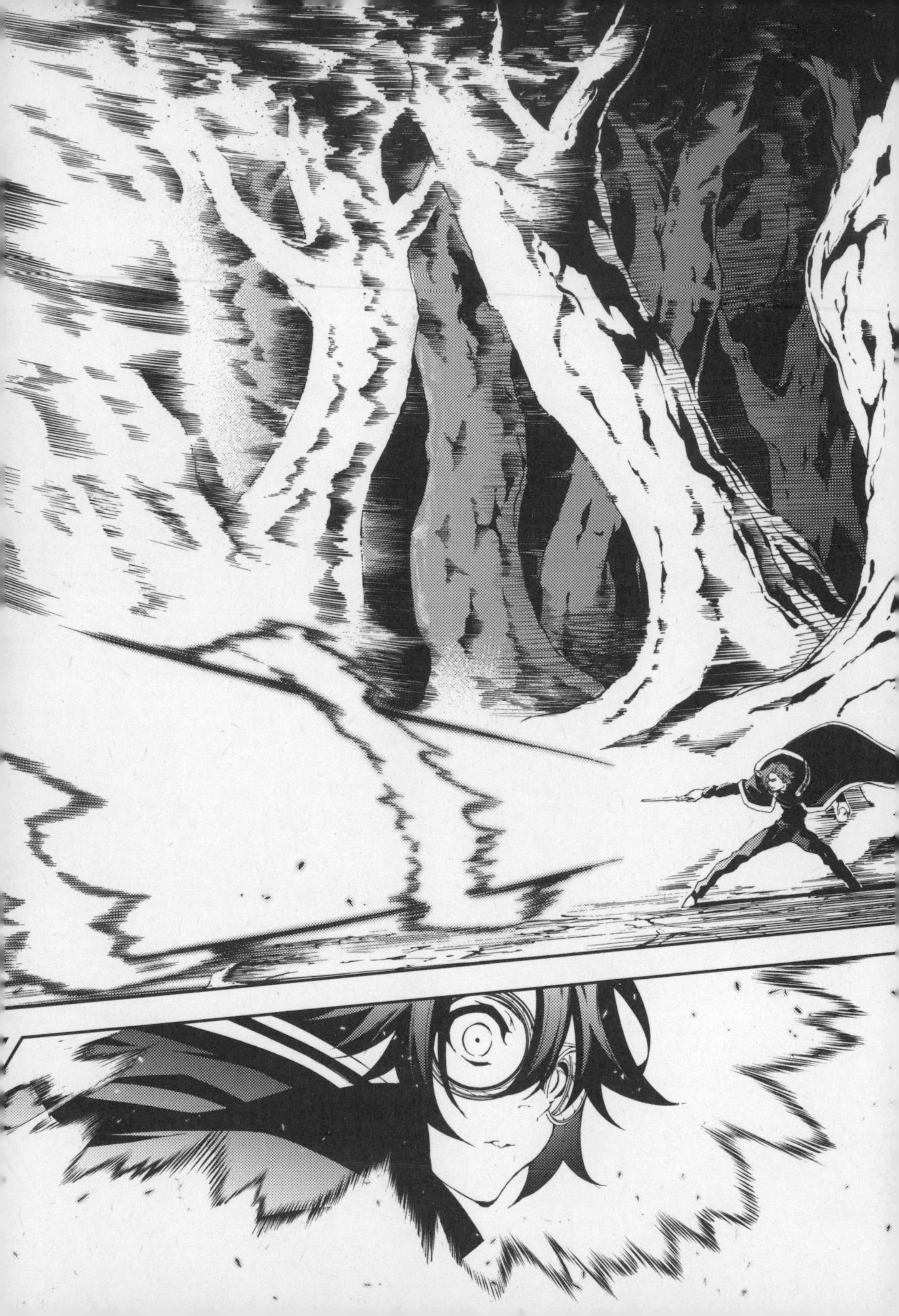

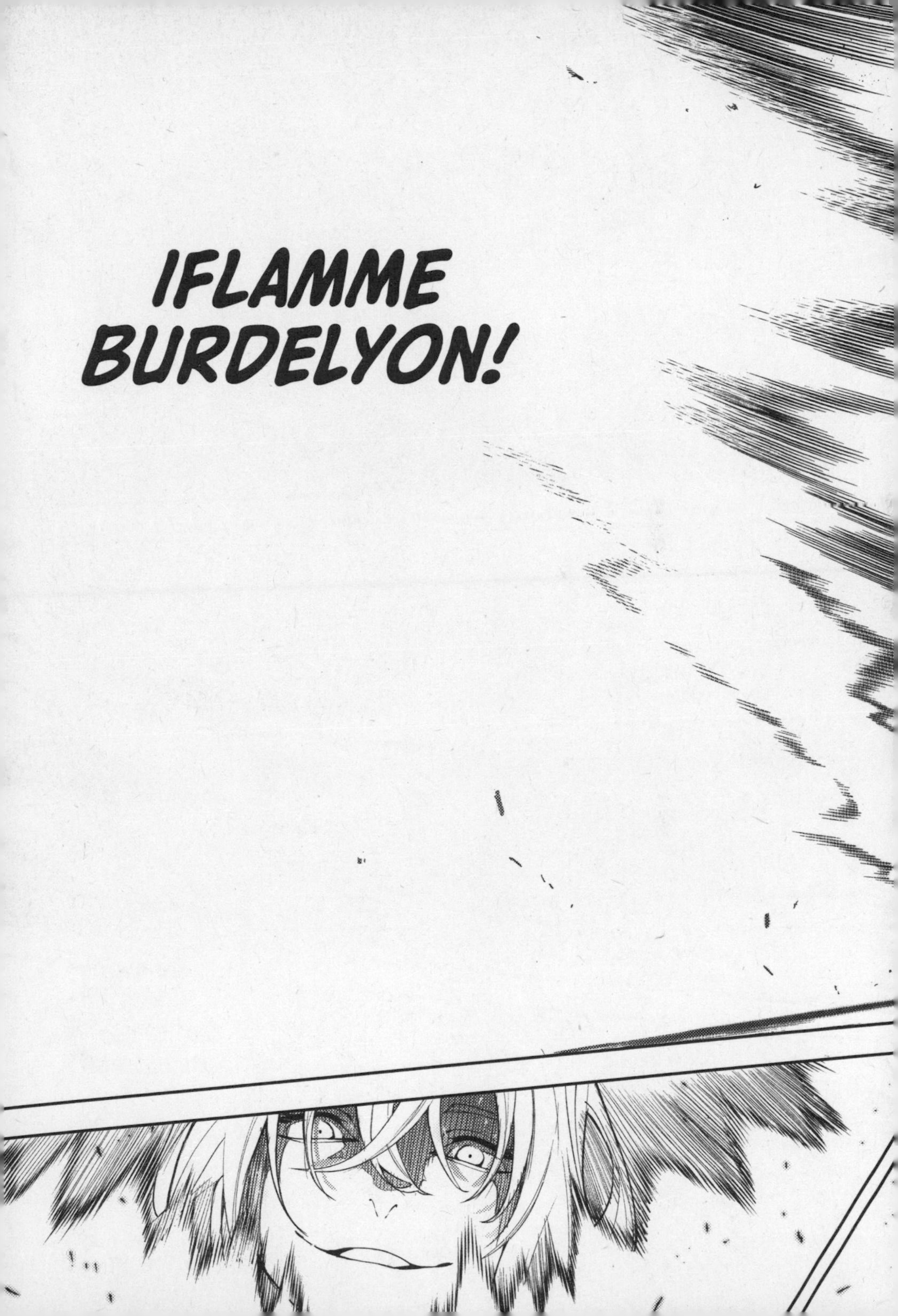
IFLAMME BURDELYON!

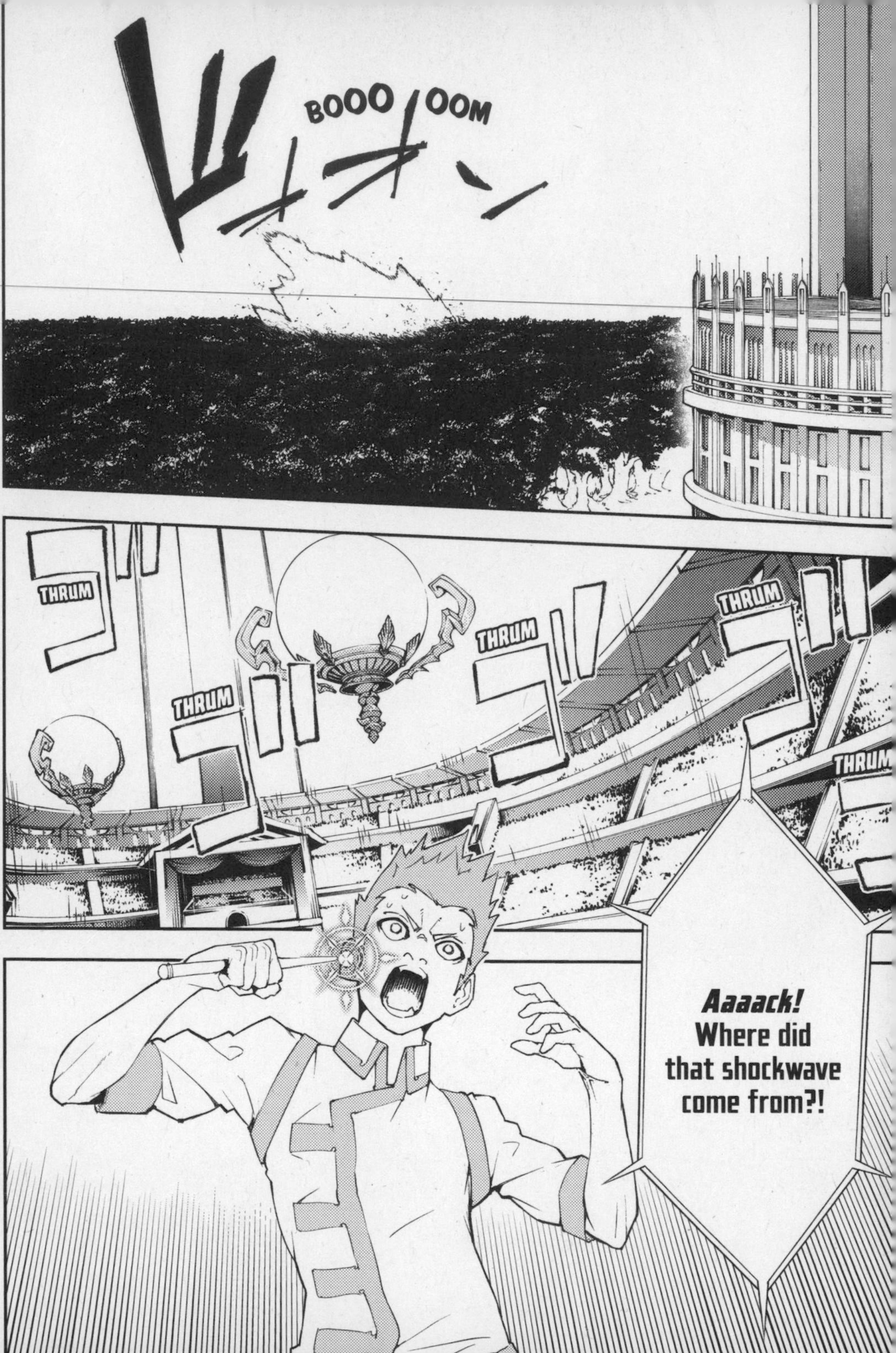
BOOO OOM
THRUM
THRUM
THRUM
THRUM
THRUM
Aaaack! Where did that shockwave come from?!

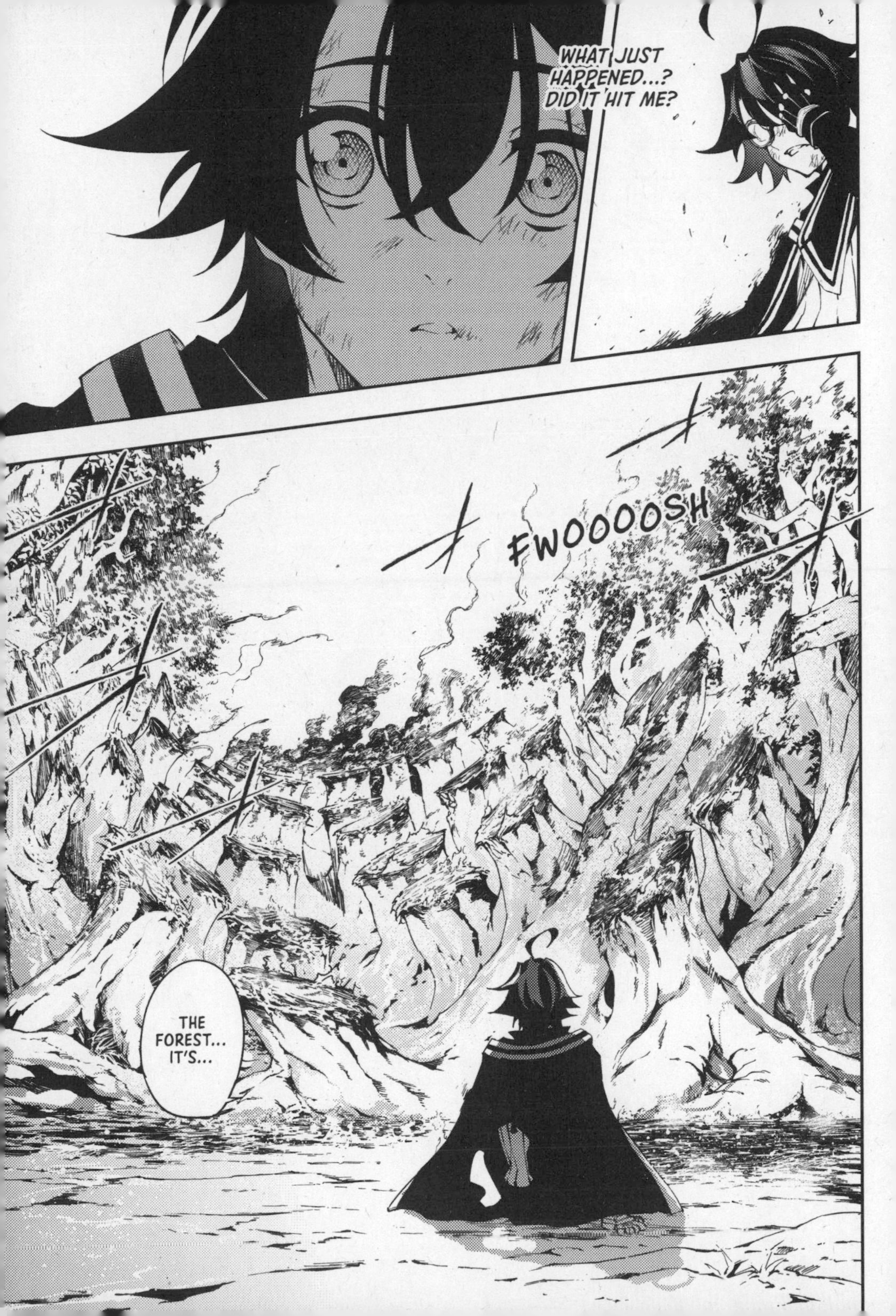
WHAT JUST HAPPENED...? DID IT HIT ME?
FWOOOOSH
THE FOREST... IT'S...

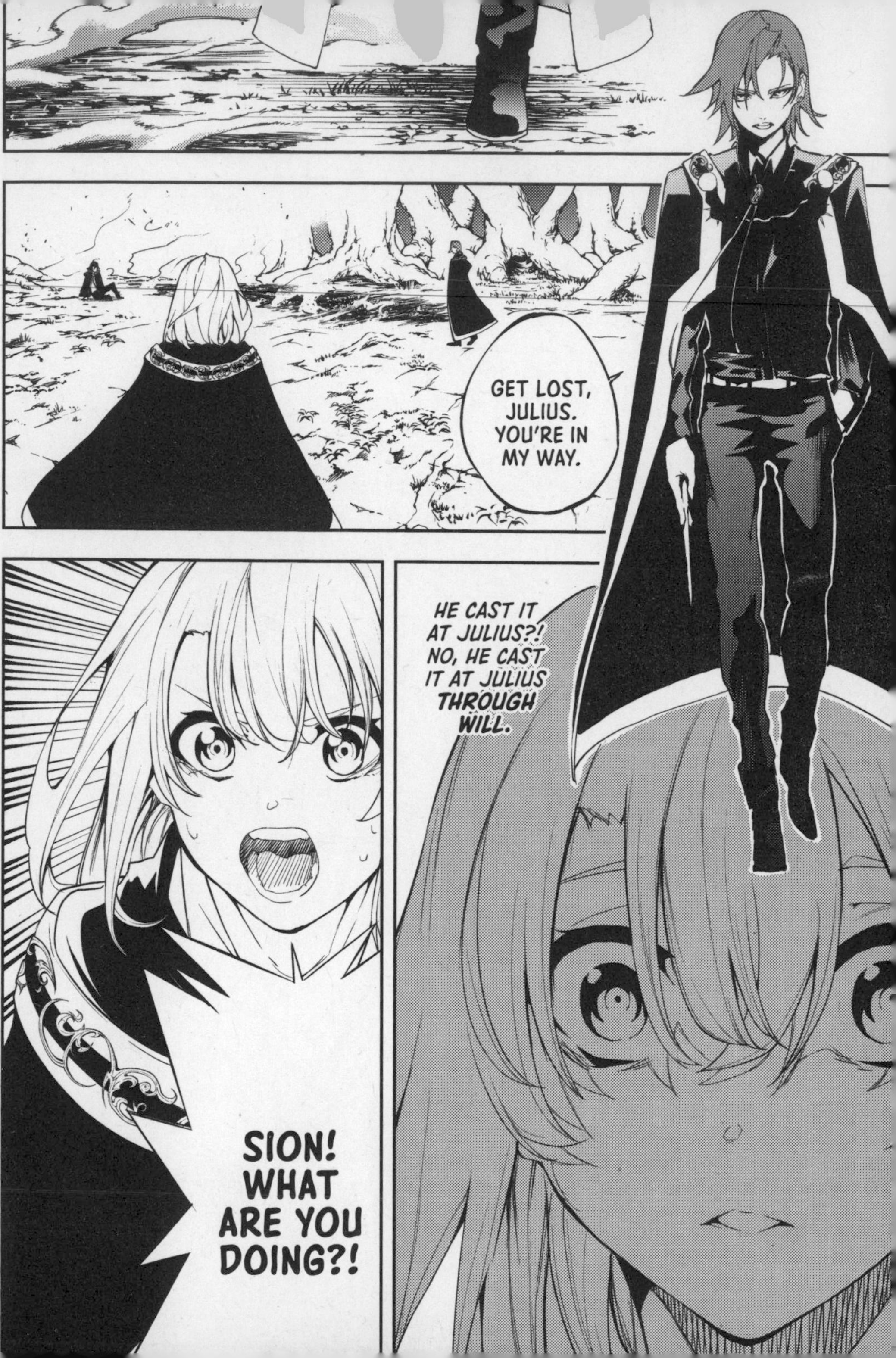
GET LOST, JULIUS. YOU'RE IN MY WAY.
HE CAST IT AT JULIUS?! NO, HE CAST IT AT JULIUS THROUGH WILL.
SION! WHAT ARE YOU DOING?!

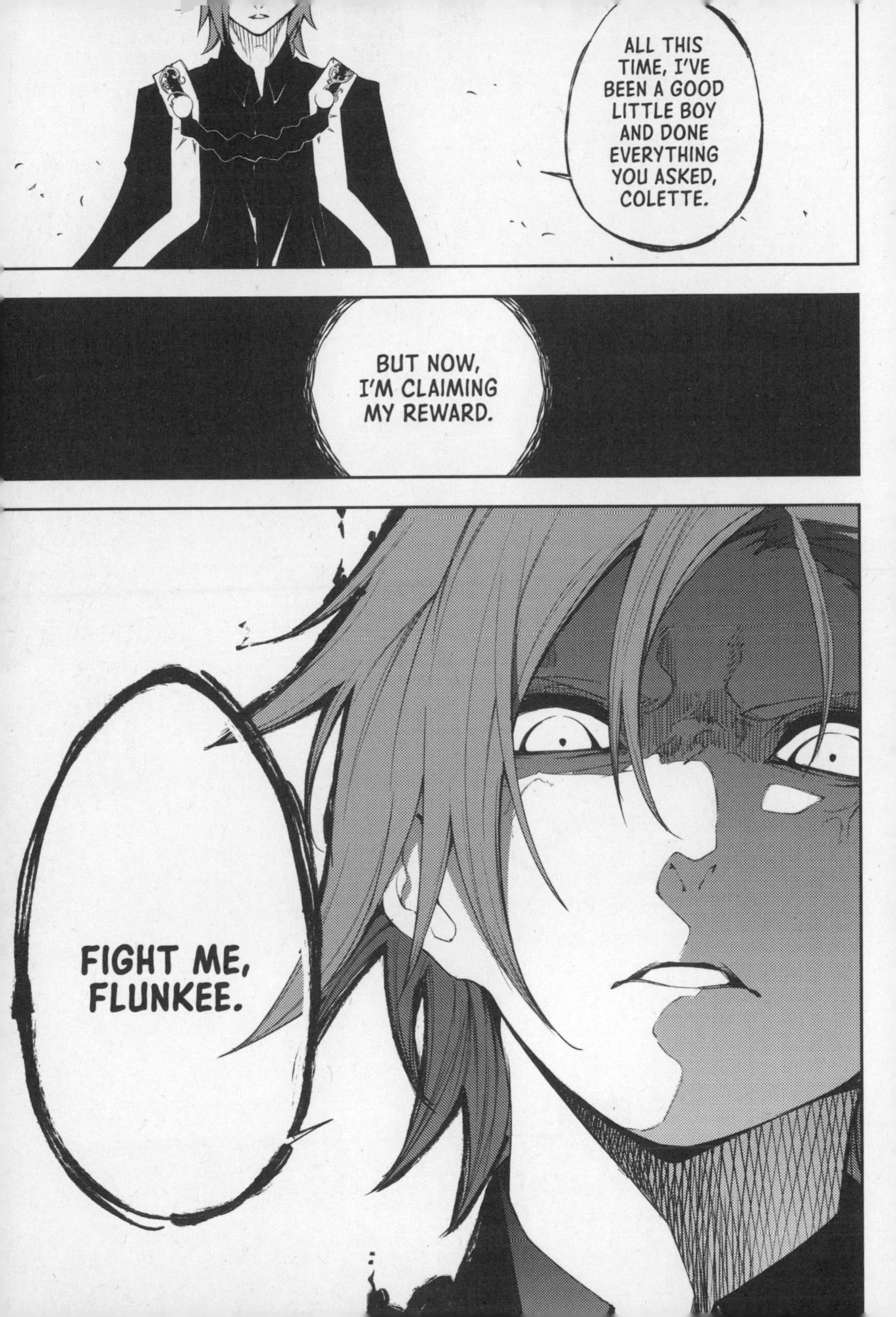
ALL THIS TIME, I'VE BEEN A GOOD LITTLE BOY AND DONE EVERYTHING YOU ASKED, COLETTE.
BUT NOW, I'M CLAIMING MY REWARD.
FIGHT ME, FLUNKEE.

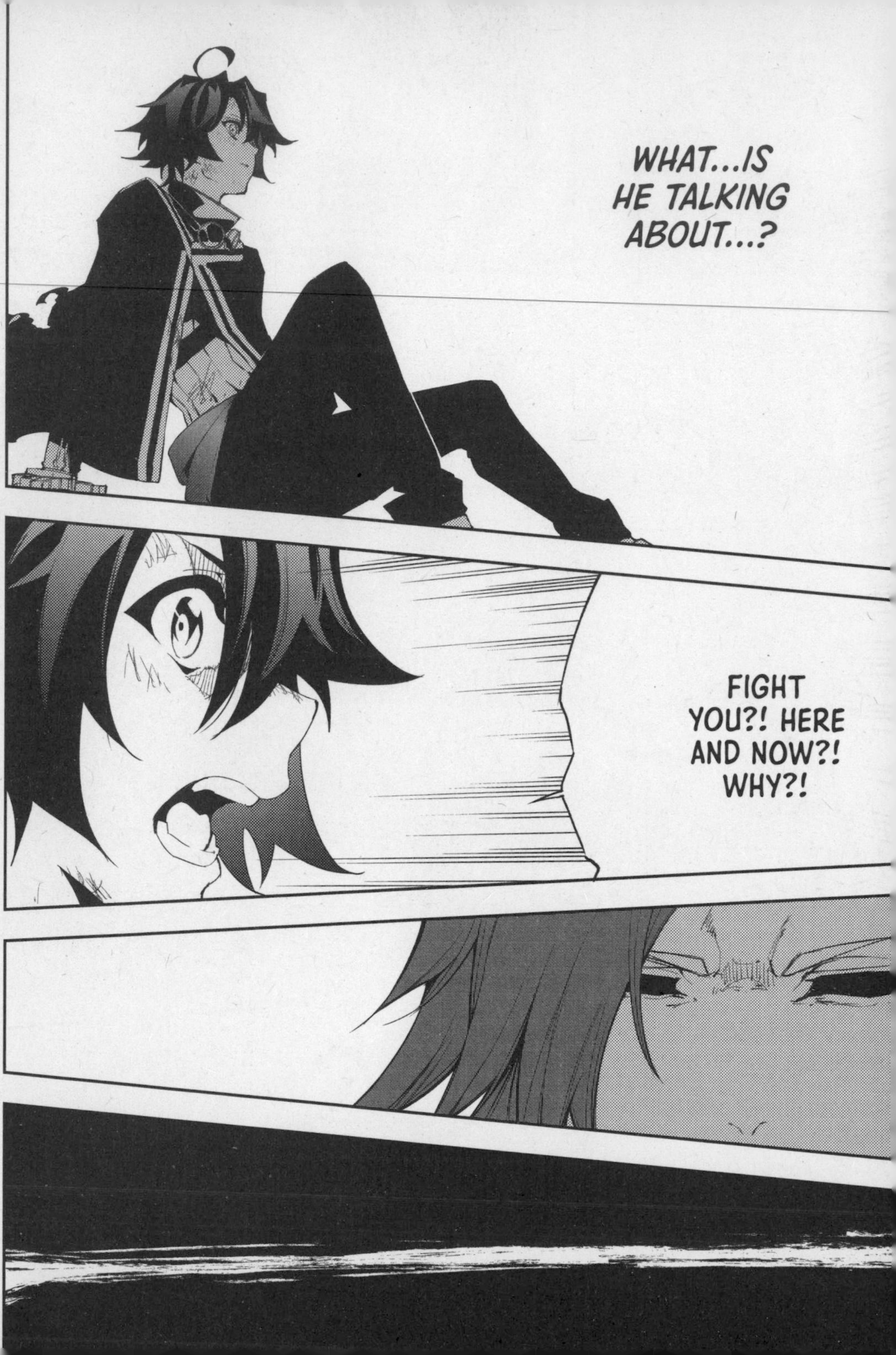
WHAT...IS
HE TALKING
ABOUT...?
FIGHT
YOU?! HERE
AND NOW?!
WHY?!

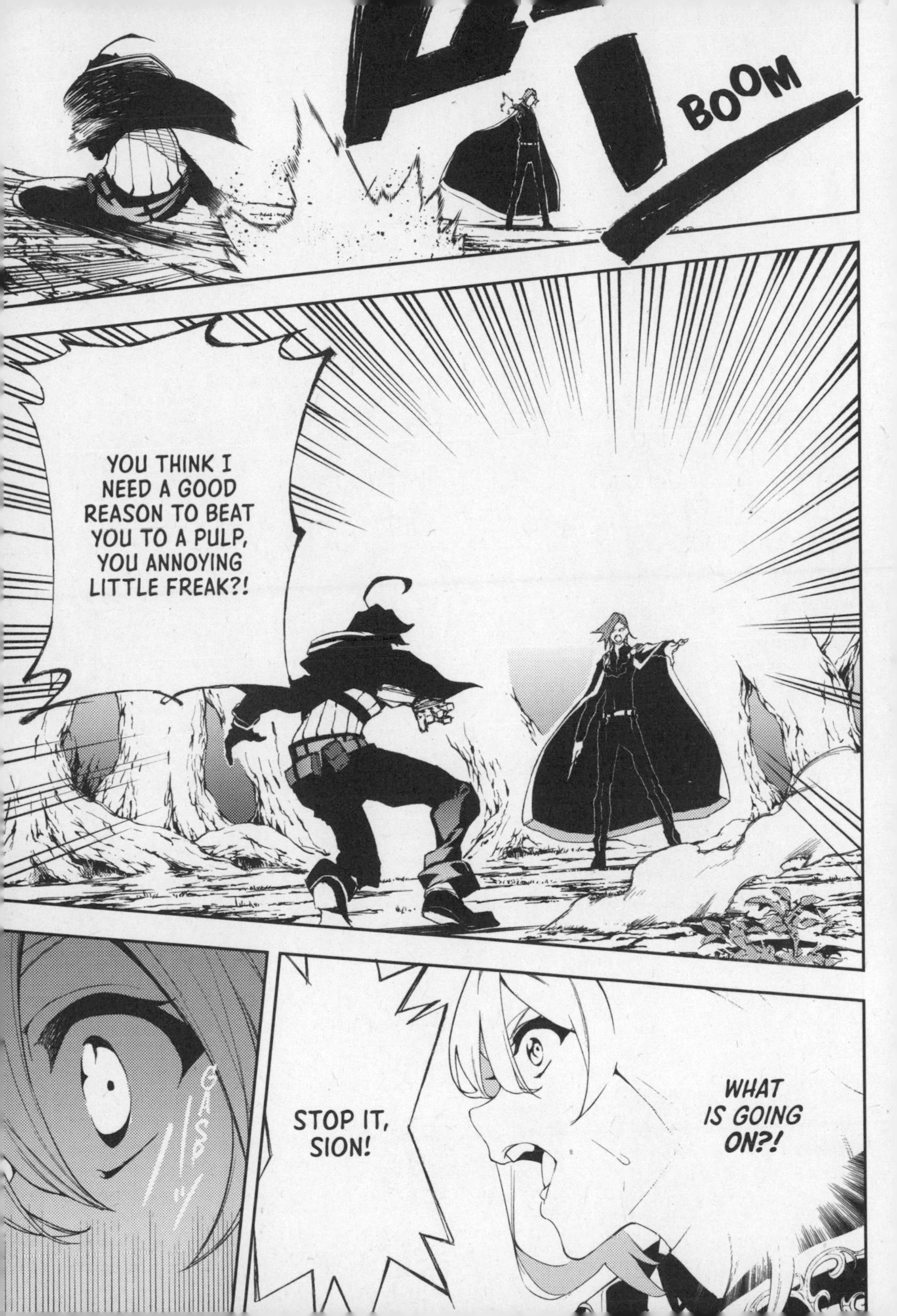
BOOM
YOU THINK I NEED A GOOD REASON TO BEAT YOU TO A PULP, YOU ANNOYING LITTLE FREAK?!
WHAT IS GOING ON?!
STOP IT, SION!
GASP

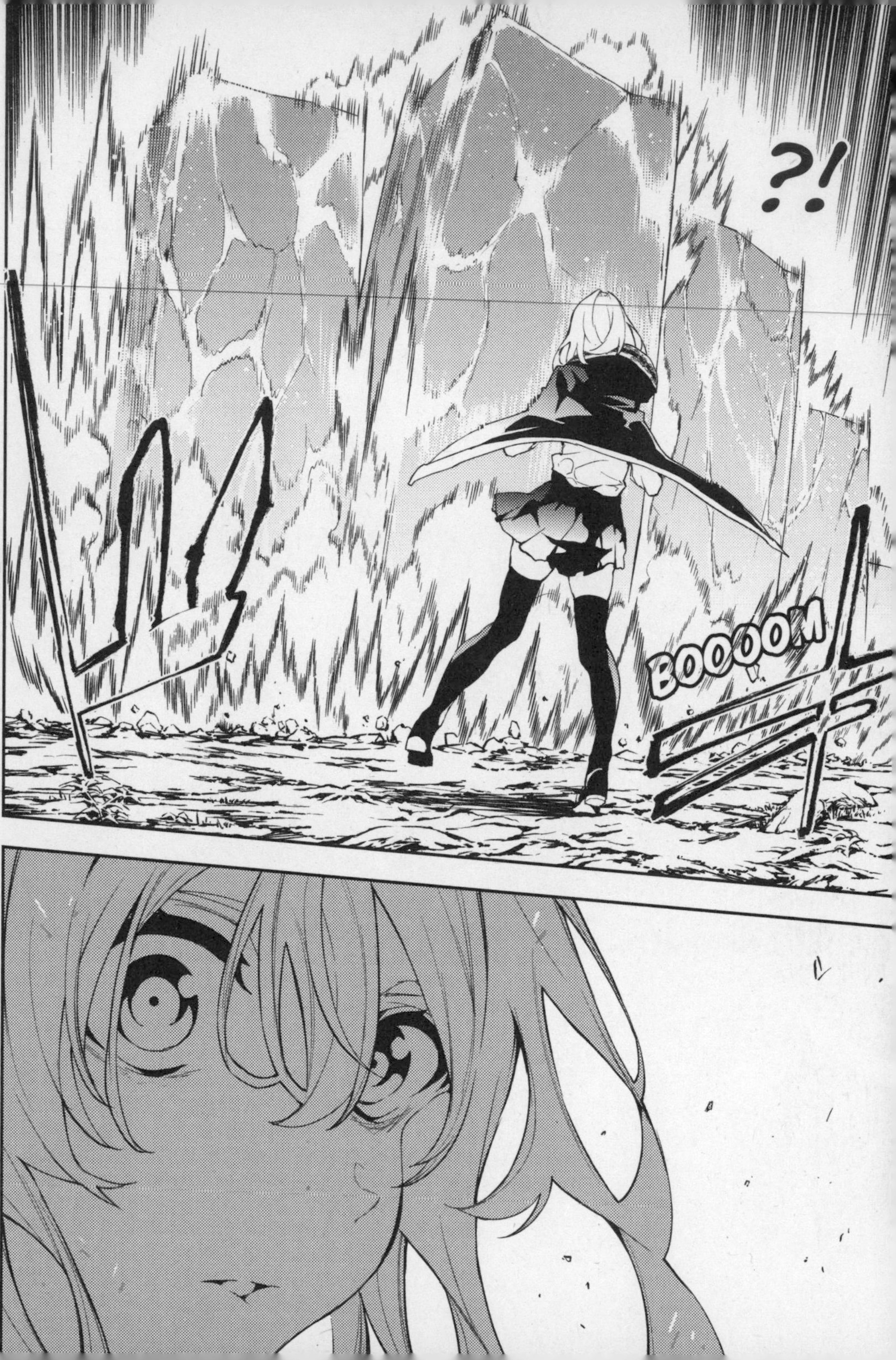
?!
BOOOOM

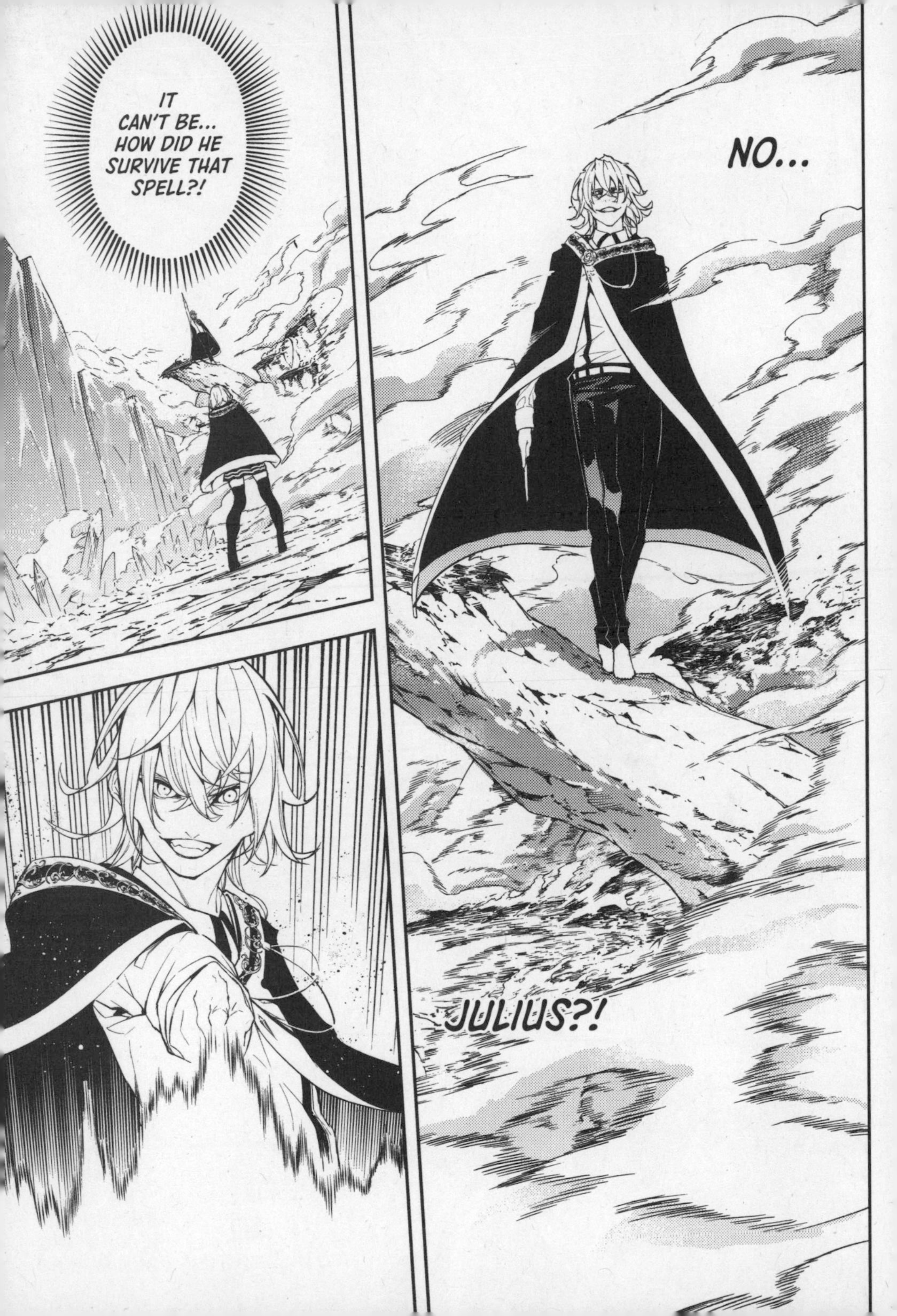
NO...
JULIUS?!
IT CAN'T BE... HOW DID HE SURVIVE THAT SPELL?!

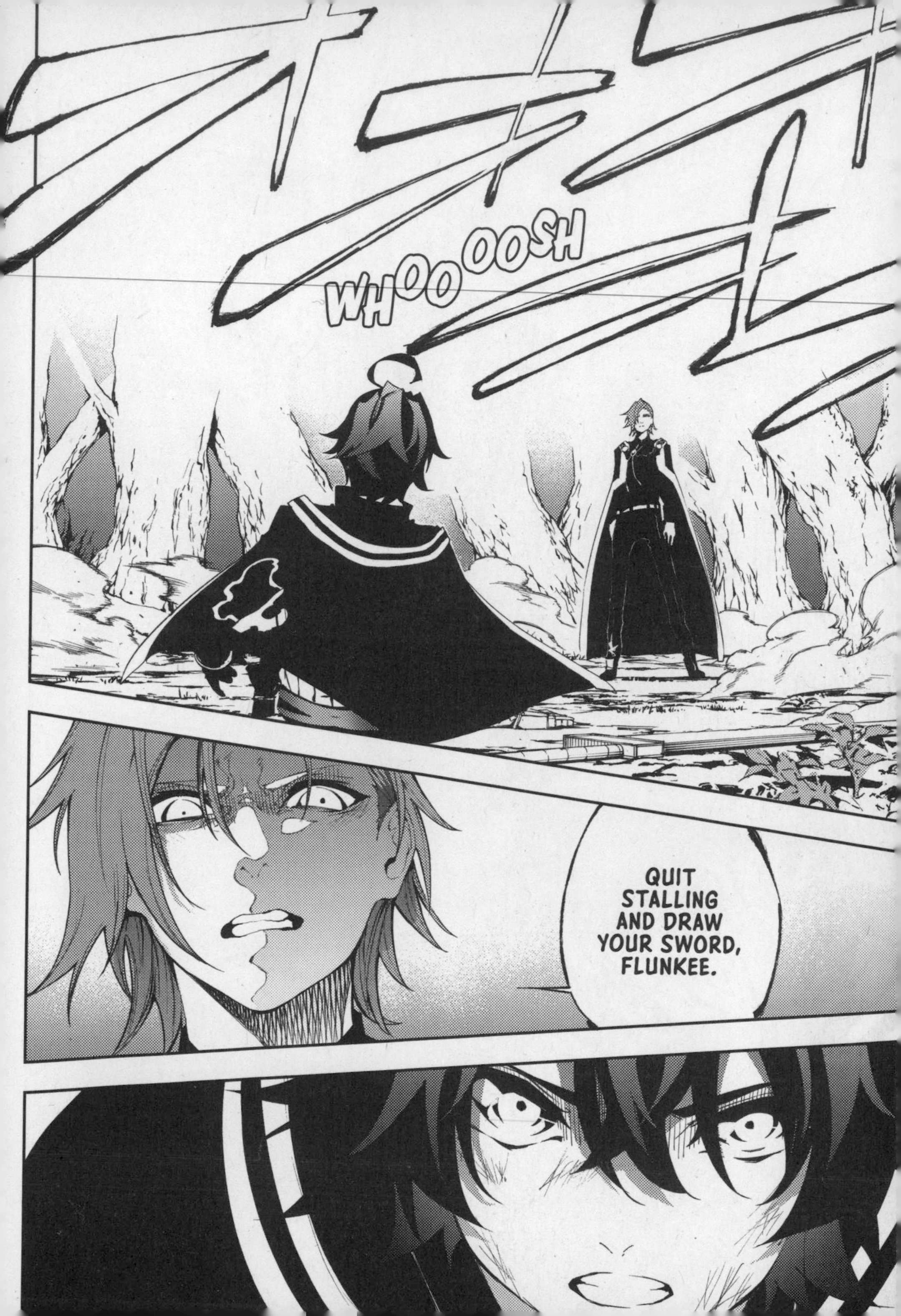
WHOOOOSH
QUIT STALLING AND DRAW YOUR SWORD, FLUNKEE.

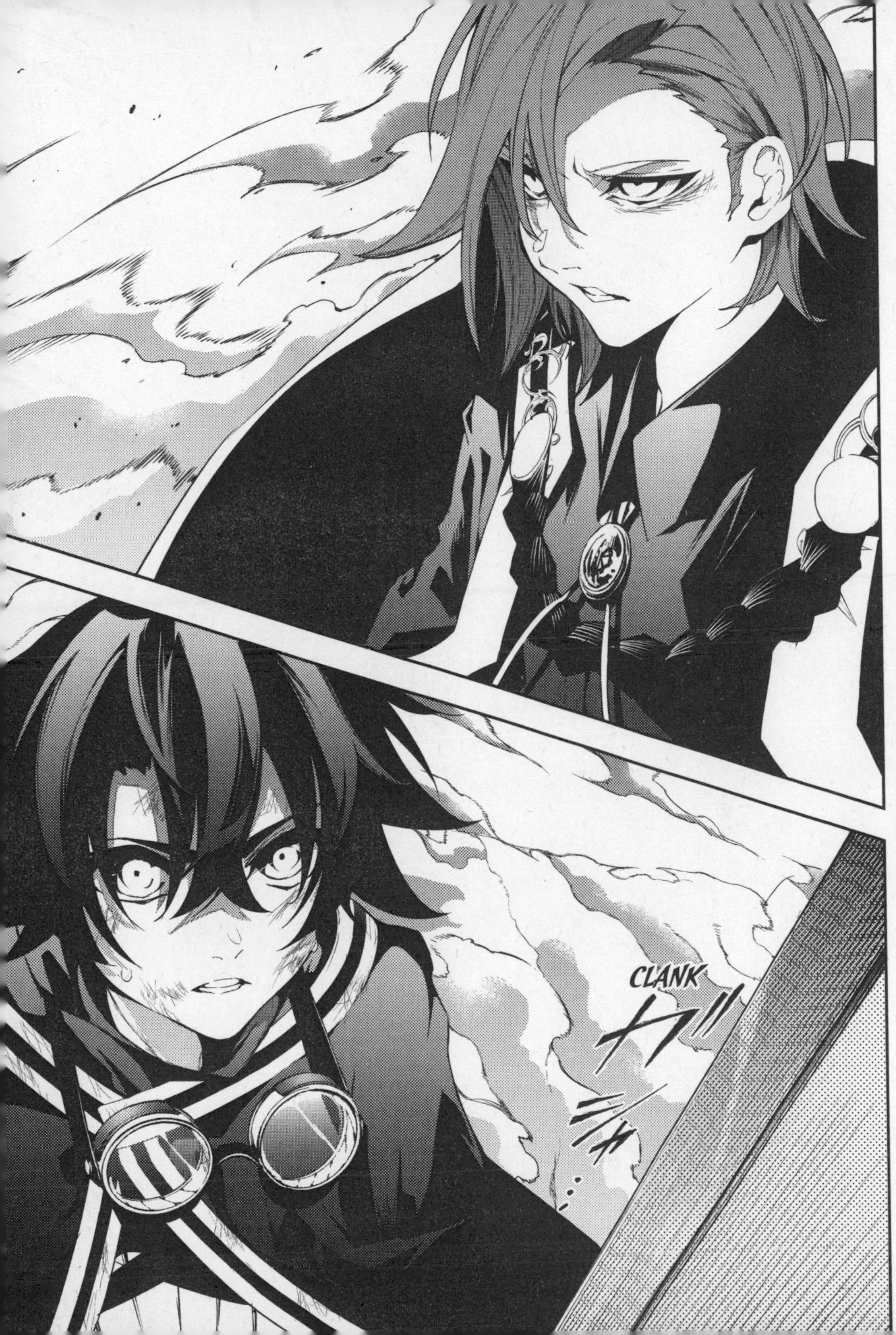
CLANK

Wistoria
Wand and Sword

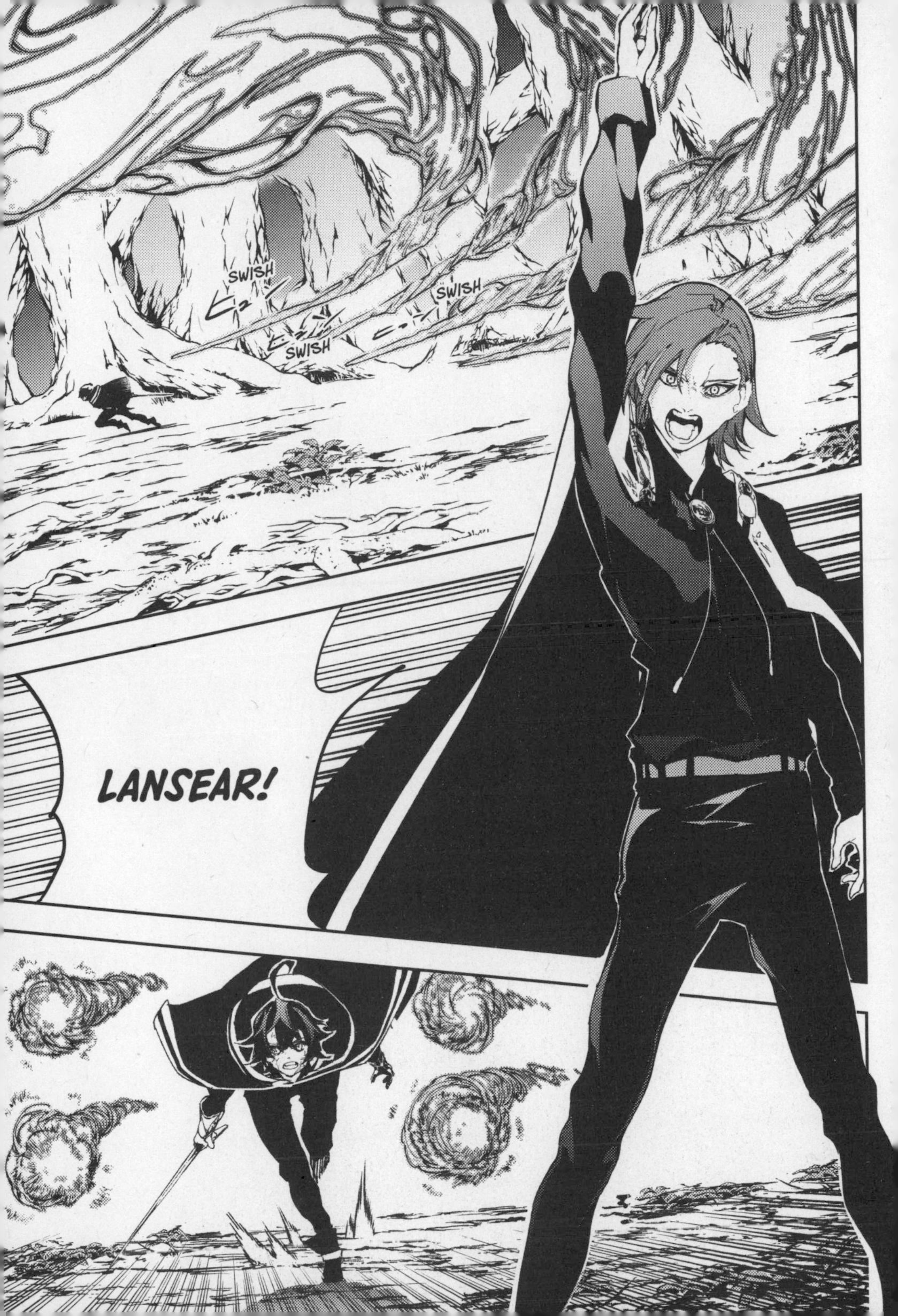
SWISH
SWISH
SWISH
LANSEAR!

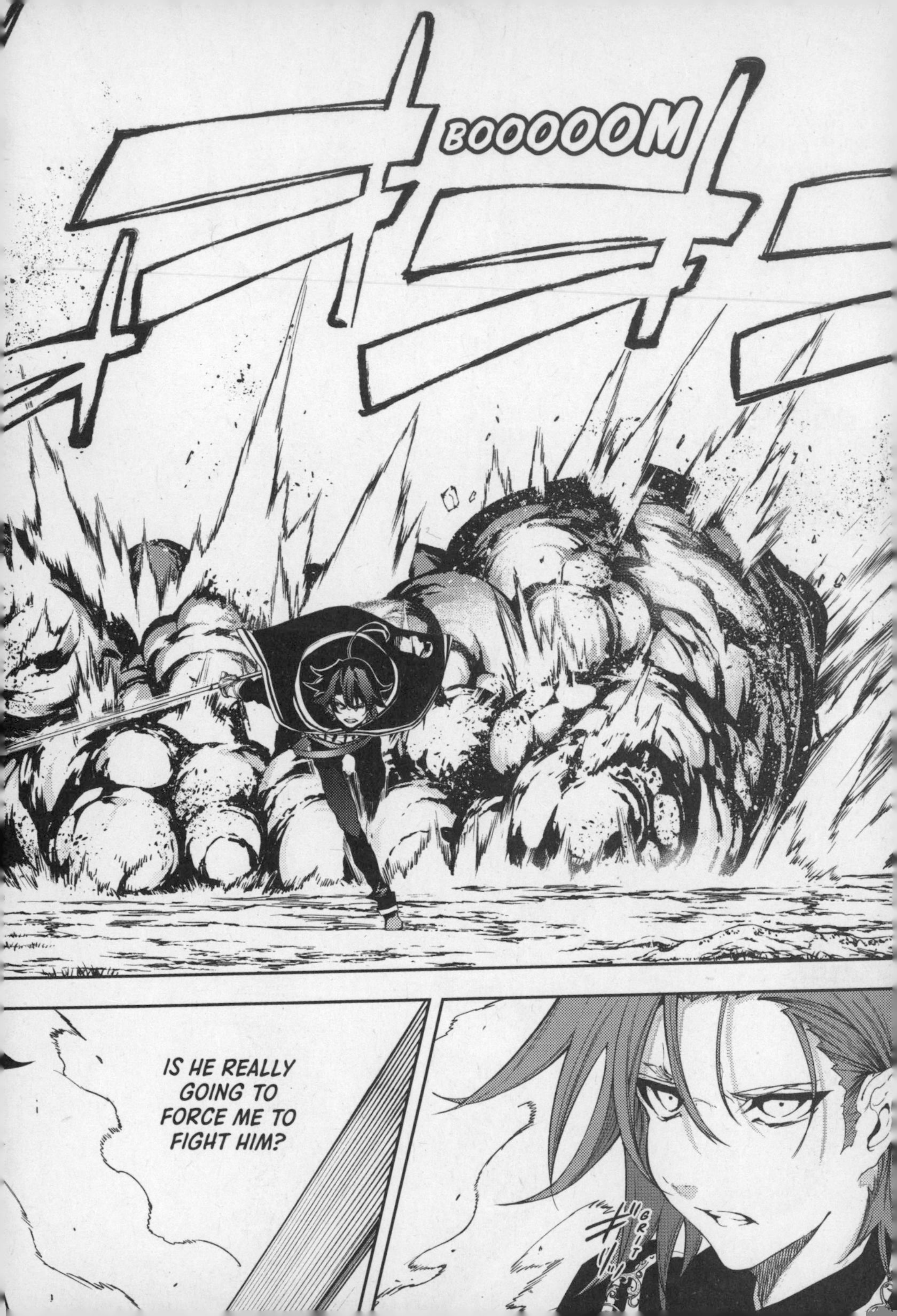
BOOOOOM
IS HE REALLY GOING TO FORCE ME TO FIGHT HIM?
GRIT

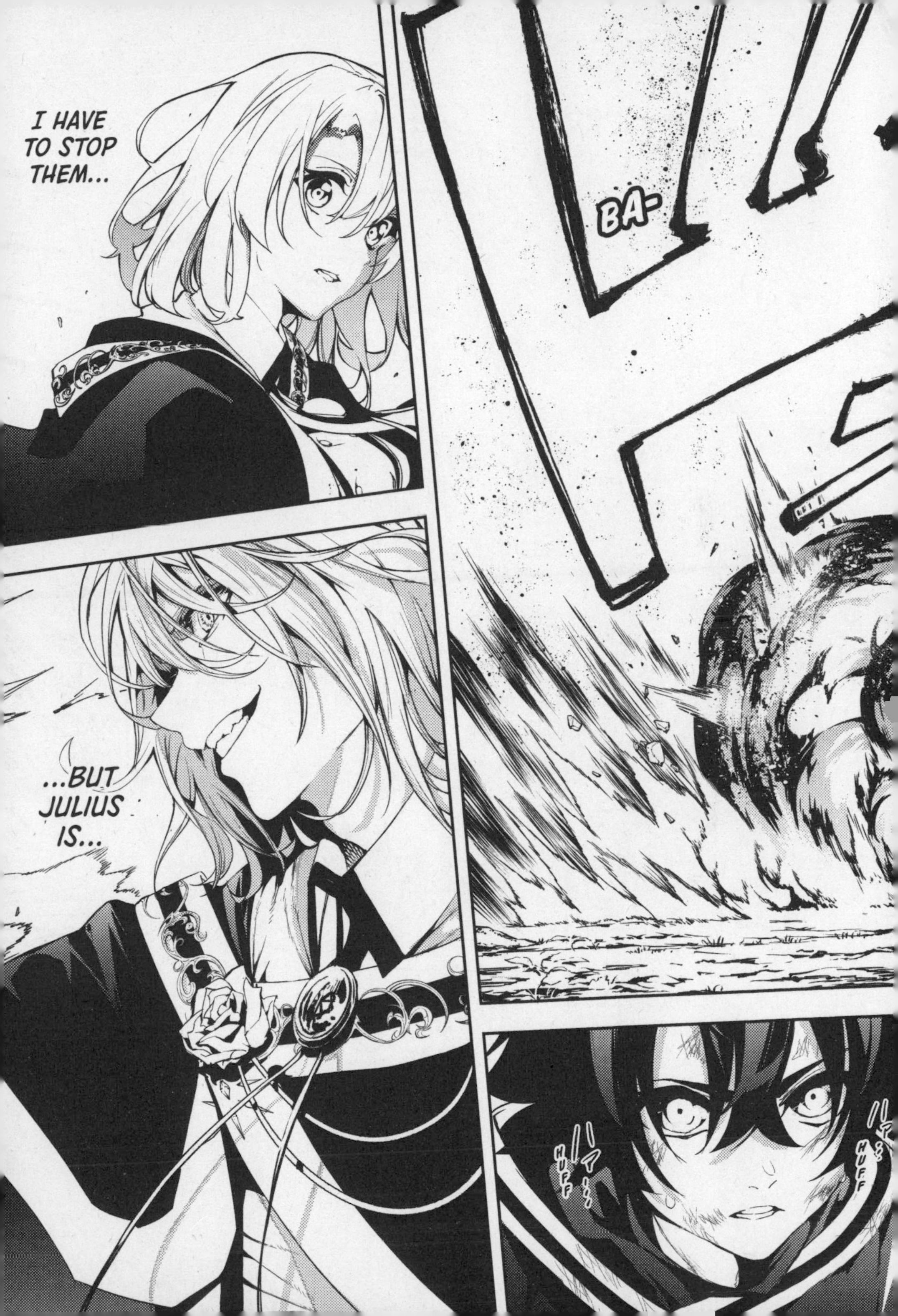
BA-
I HAVE TO STOP THEM...
...BUT JULIUS IS...
HUFF
HUFF

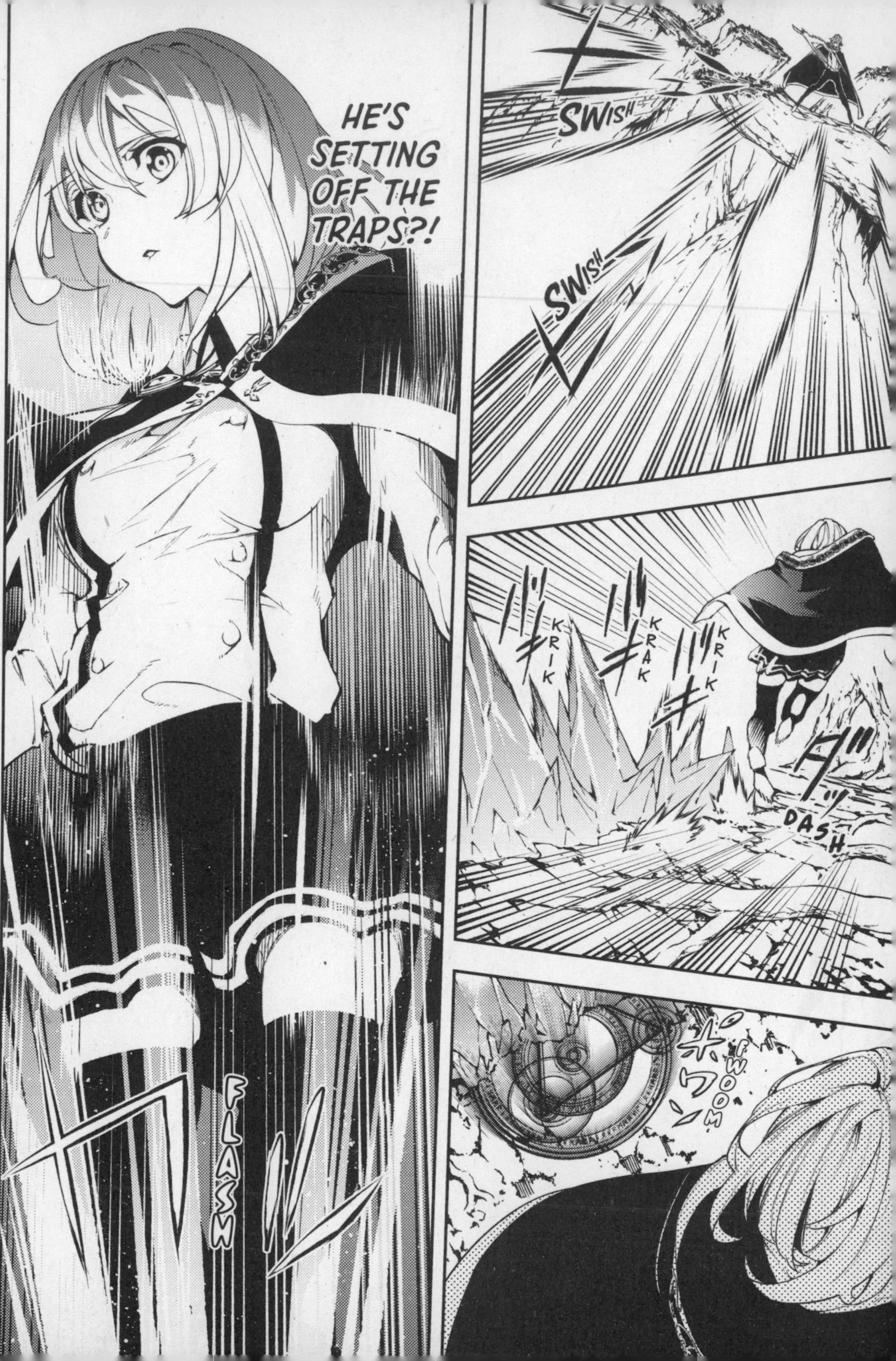
SWISH
SWISH
KRIK
KRAK
KRIK
DASH
FWOOM
HE'S SETTING OFF THE TRAPS?!
FLASH

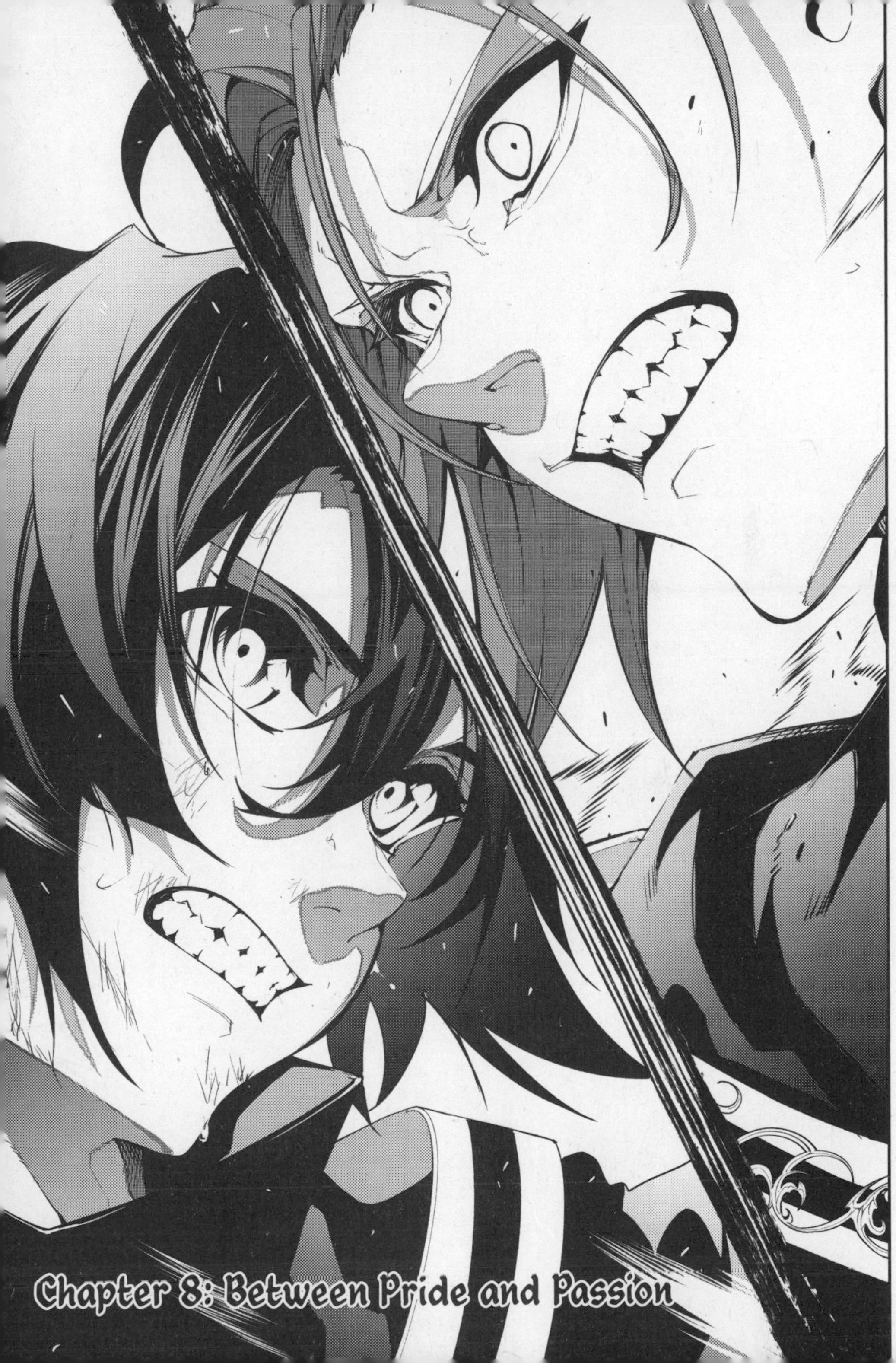

Chapter 8: Between Pride and Passion

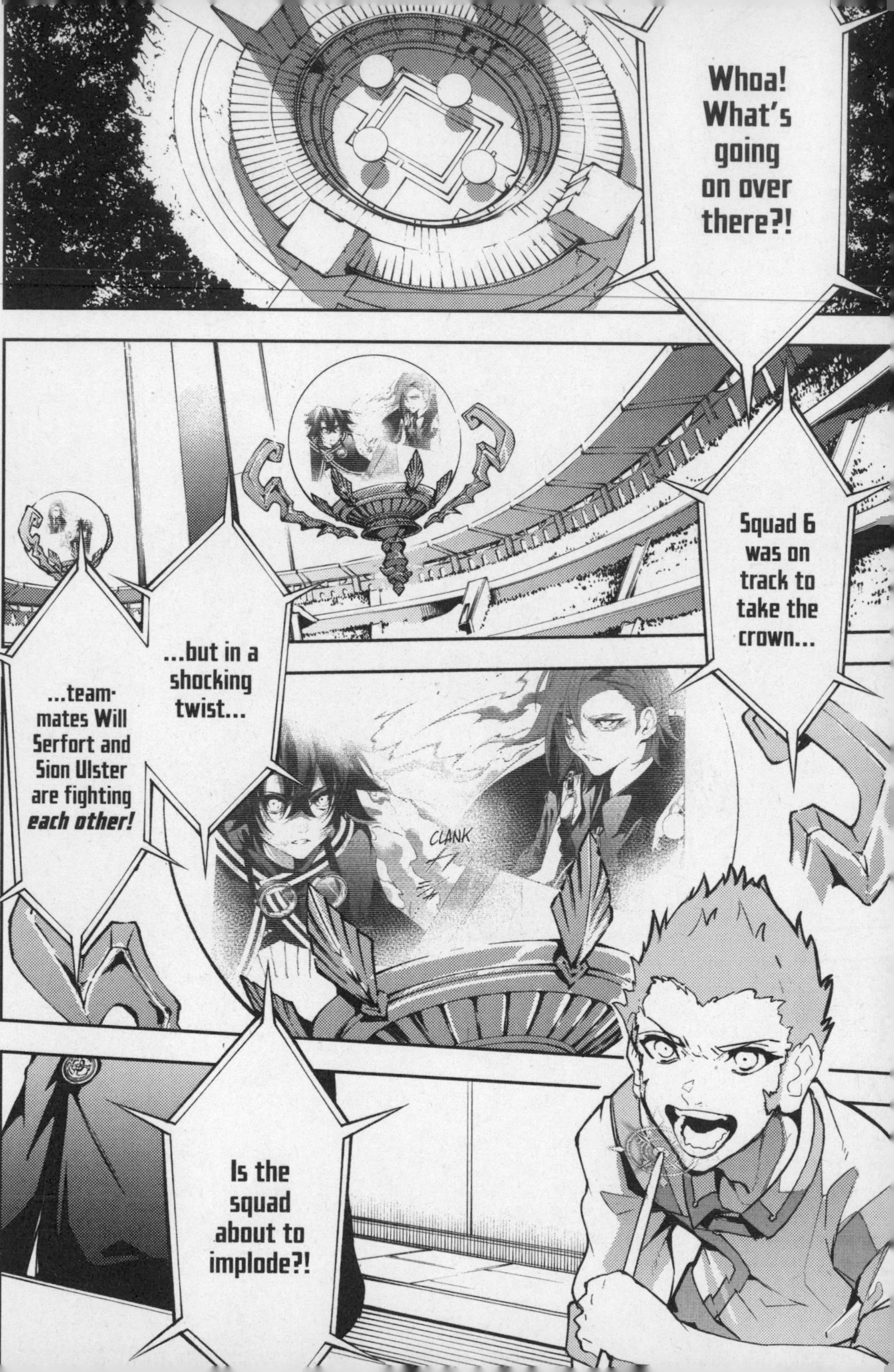
Whoa! What's going on over there?!
Squad 6 was on track to take the crown...
...but in a shocking twist...
...team-mates Will Serfort and Sion Ulster are fighting *each other!*
CLANK
Is the squad about to implode?!

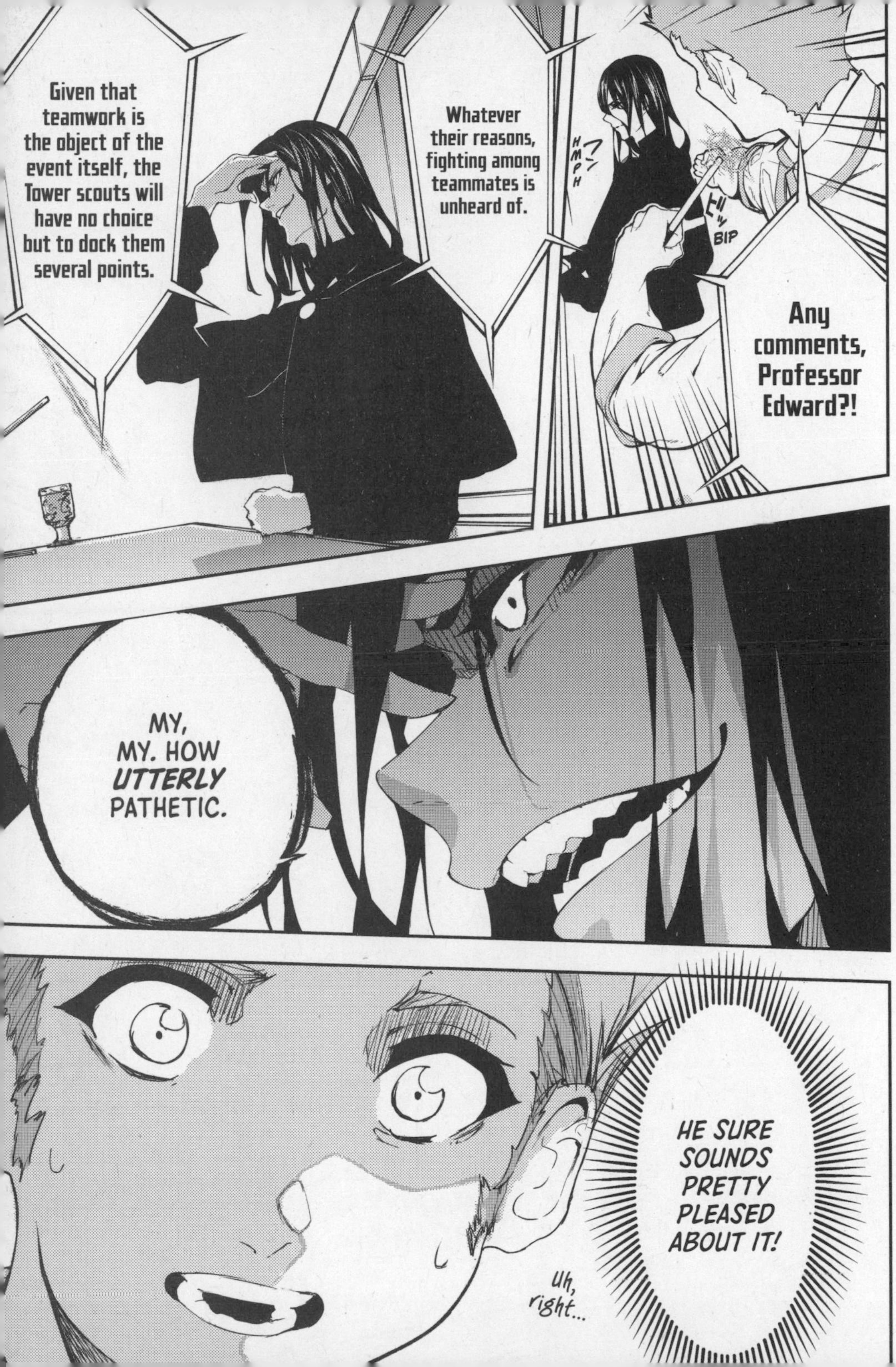
HMPH
BIP
Any comments, Professor Edward?!
Whatever their reasons, fighting among teammates is unheard of.
Given that teamwork is the object of the event itself, the Tower scouts will have no choice but to dock them several points.
MY, MY. HOW *UTTERLY* PATHETIC.
HE SURE SOUNDS PRETTY PLEASED ABOUT IT!
Uh, right...

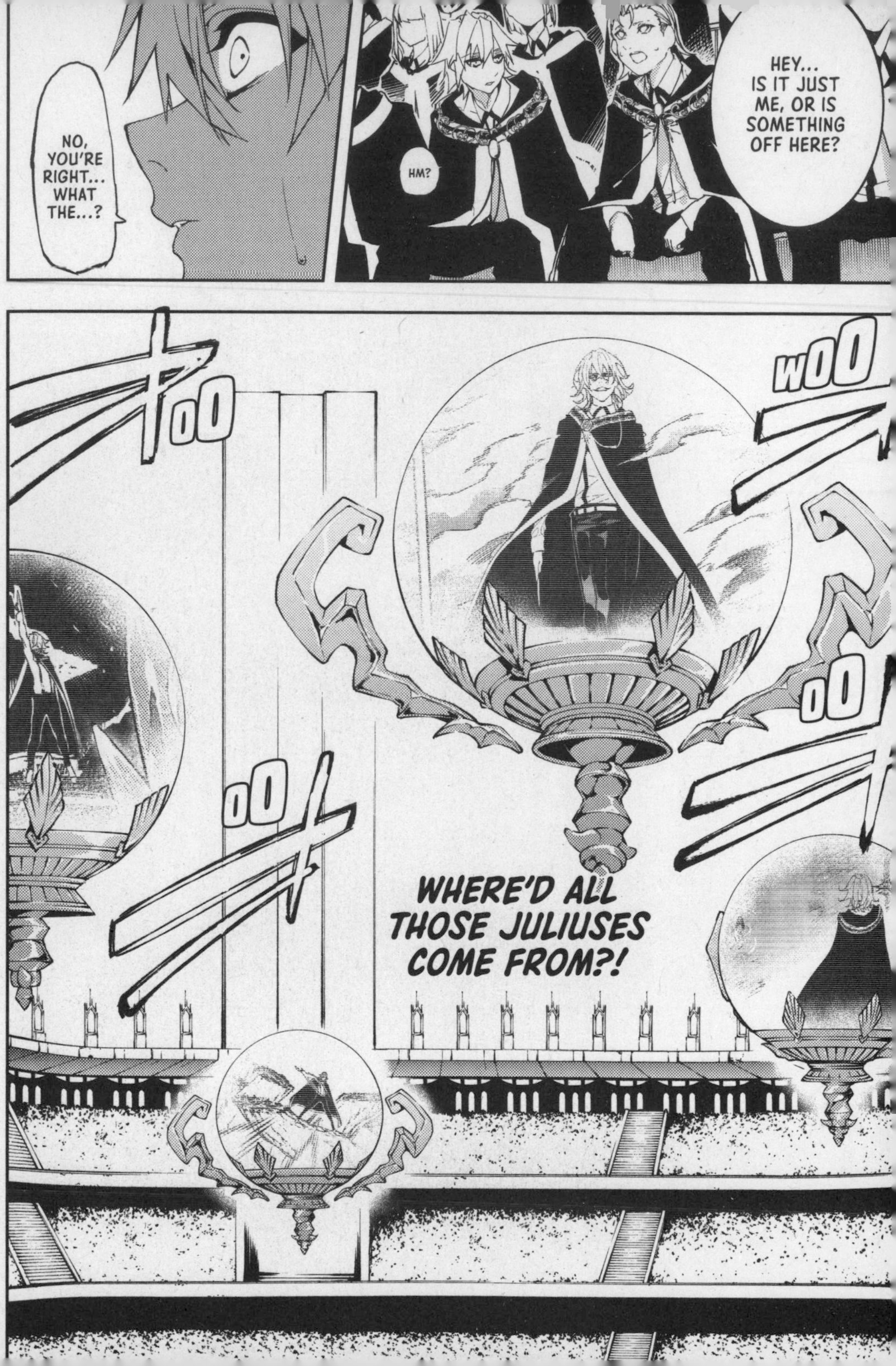
HEY... IS IT JUST ME, OR IS SOMETHING OFF HERE?
HM?
NO, YOU'RE RIGHT... WHAT THE...?
wOO
OO
oO
oO
WHERE'D ALL THOSE JULIUSES COME FROM?!

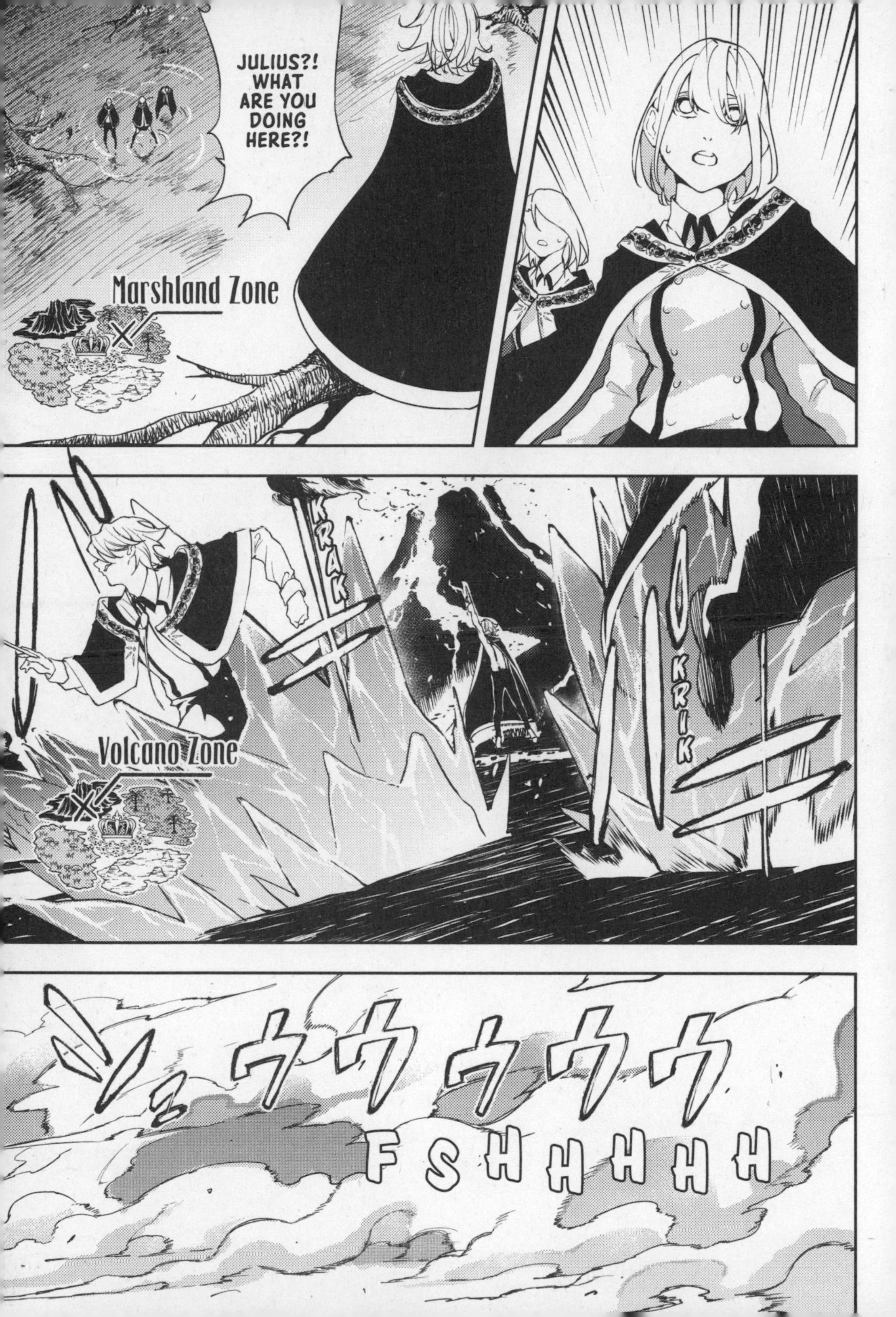
JULIUS?! WHAT ARE YOU DOING HERE?!
Marshland Zone
KRIK
KRAK
Volcano Zone
シュウウウウウ
FSHHHHHH

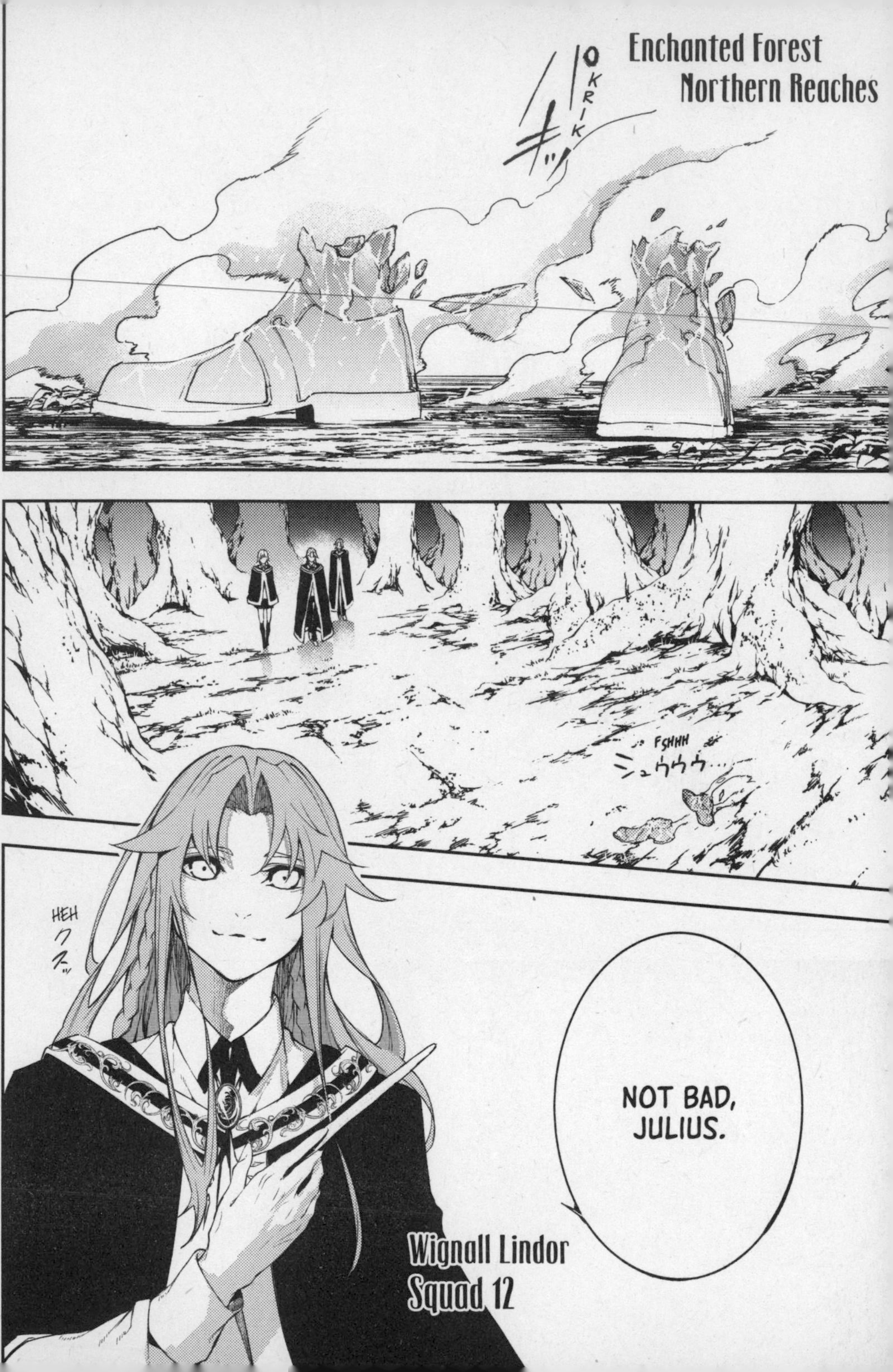
Enchanted Forest
Northern Reaches
KRIK
キッ
FSHHH
シュウウウ…
HEH
クスッ
NOT BAD, JULIUS.
Wignall Lindor
Squad 12

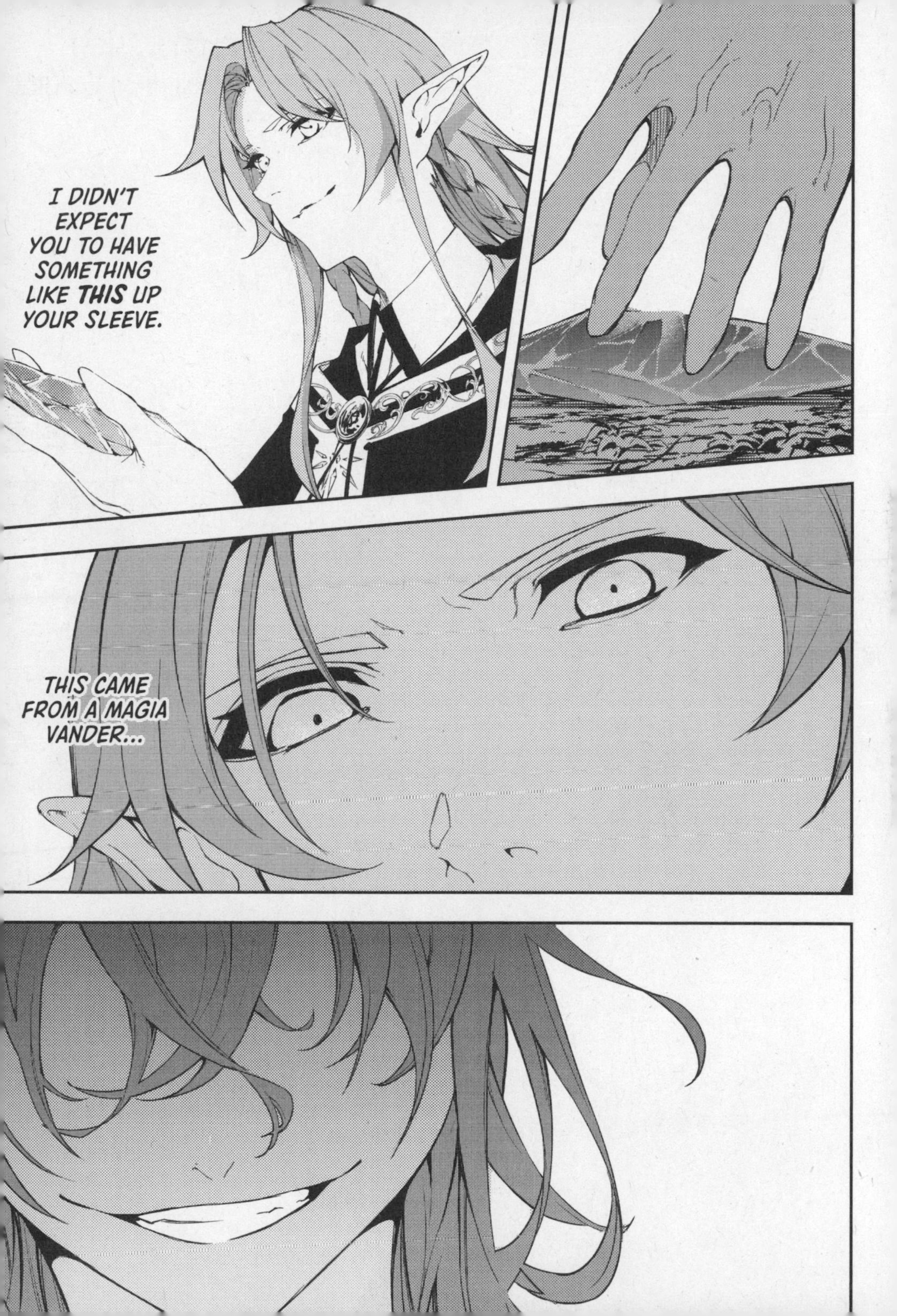
I DIDN'T EXPECT YOU TO HAVE SOMETHING LIKE **THIS** UP YOUR SLEEVE.
THIS CAME FROM A MAGIA VANDER...

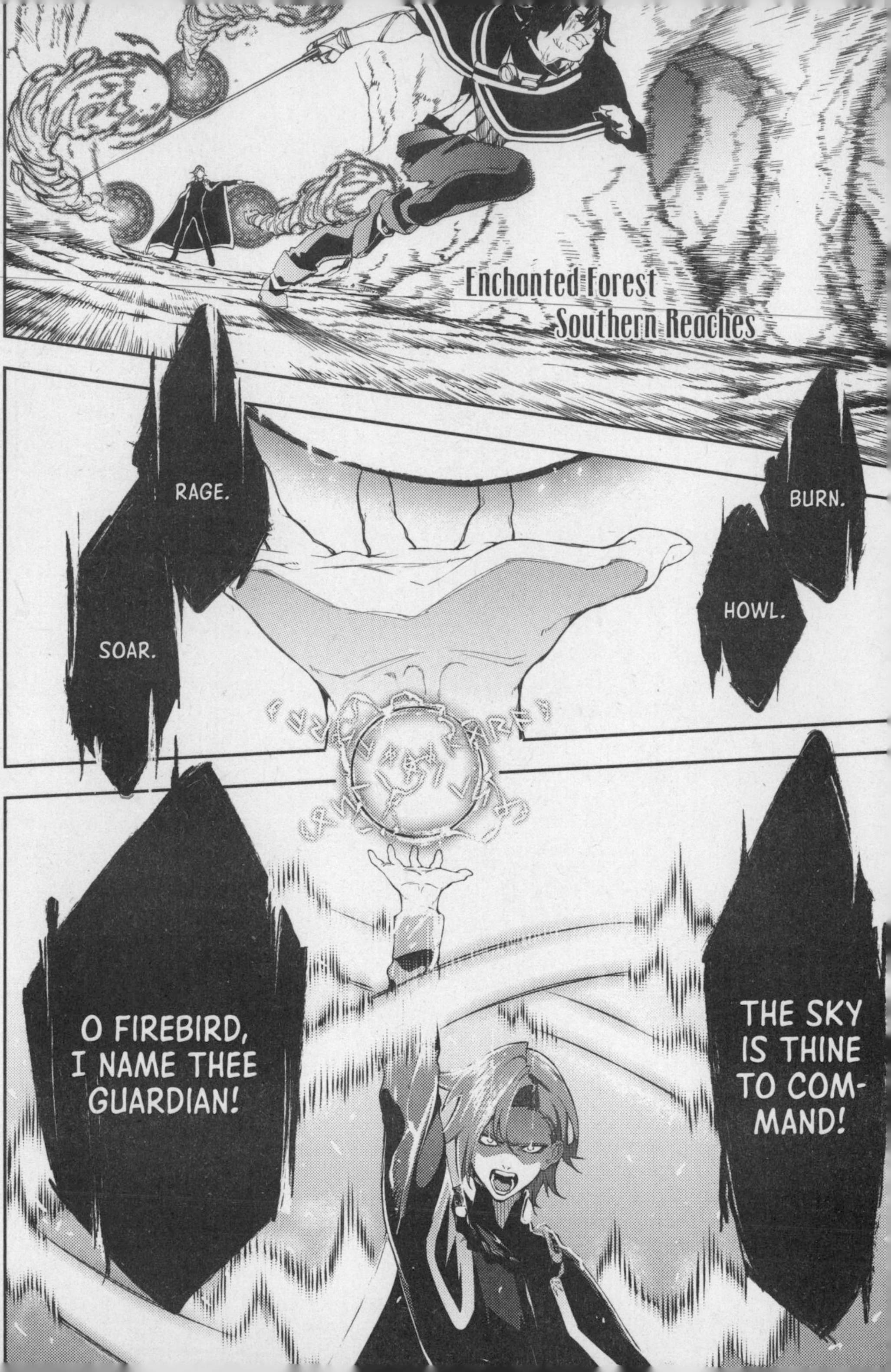
Enchanted Forest
Southern Reaches
BURN.
HOWL.
RAGE.
SOAR.
THE SKY IS THINE TO COM-MAND!
O FIREBIRD, I NAME THEE GUARDIAN!

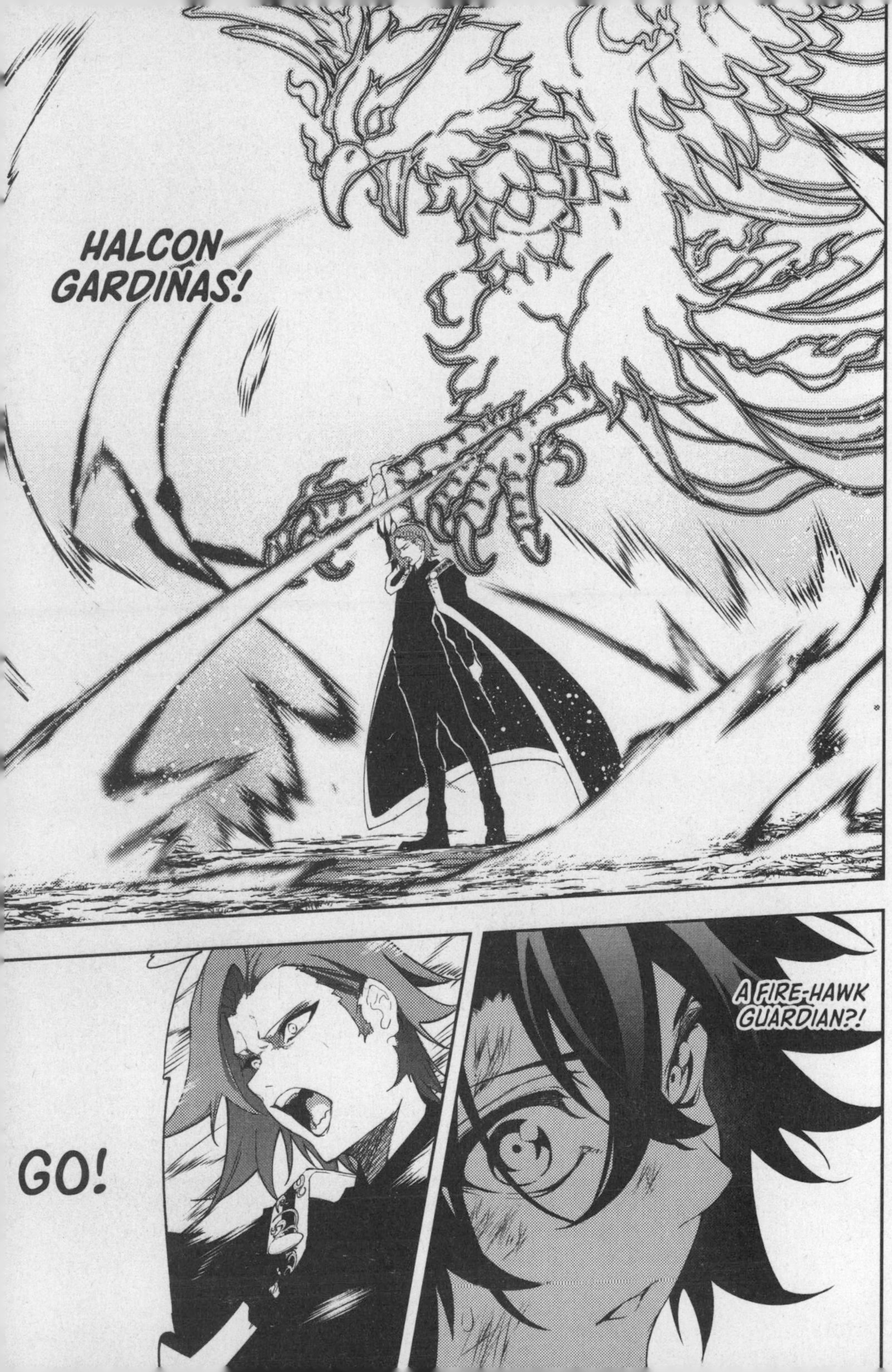
HALCON GARDIÑAS!
A FIRE-HAWK GUARDIAN?!
GO!

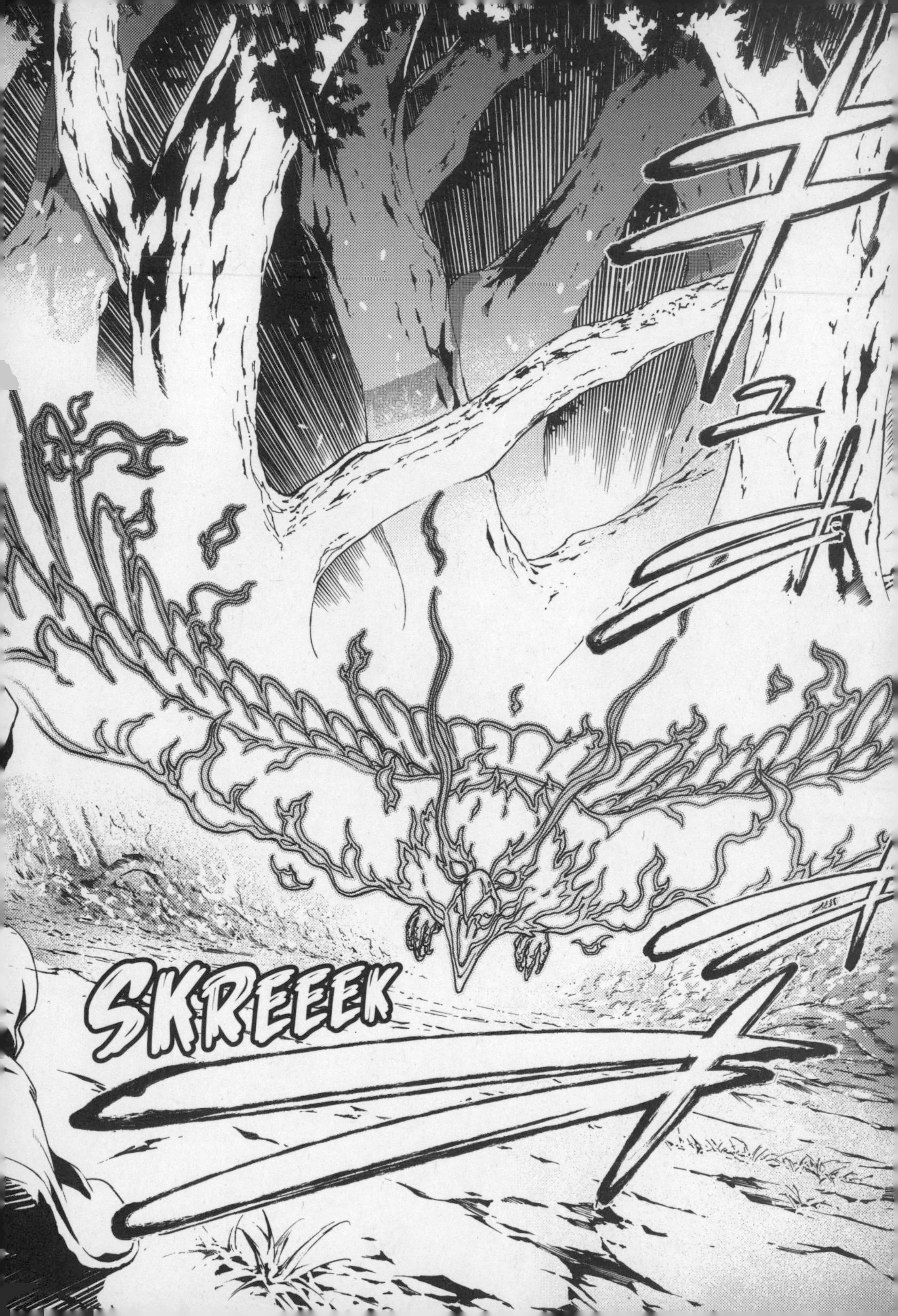
SKREEEK

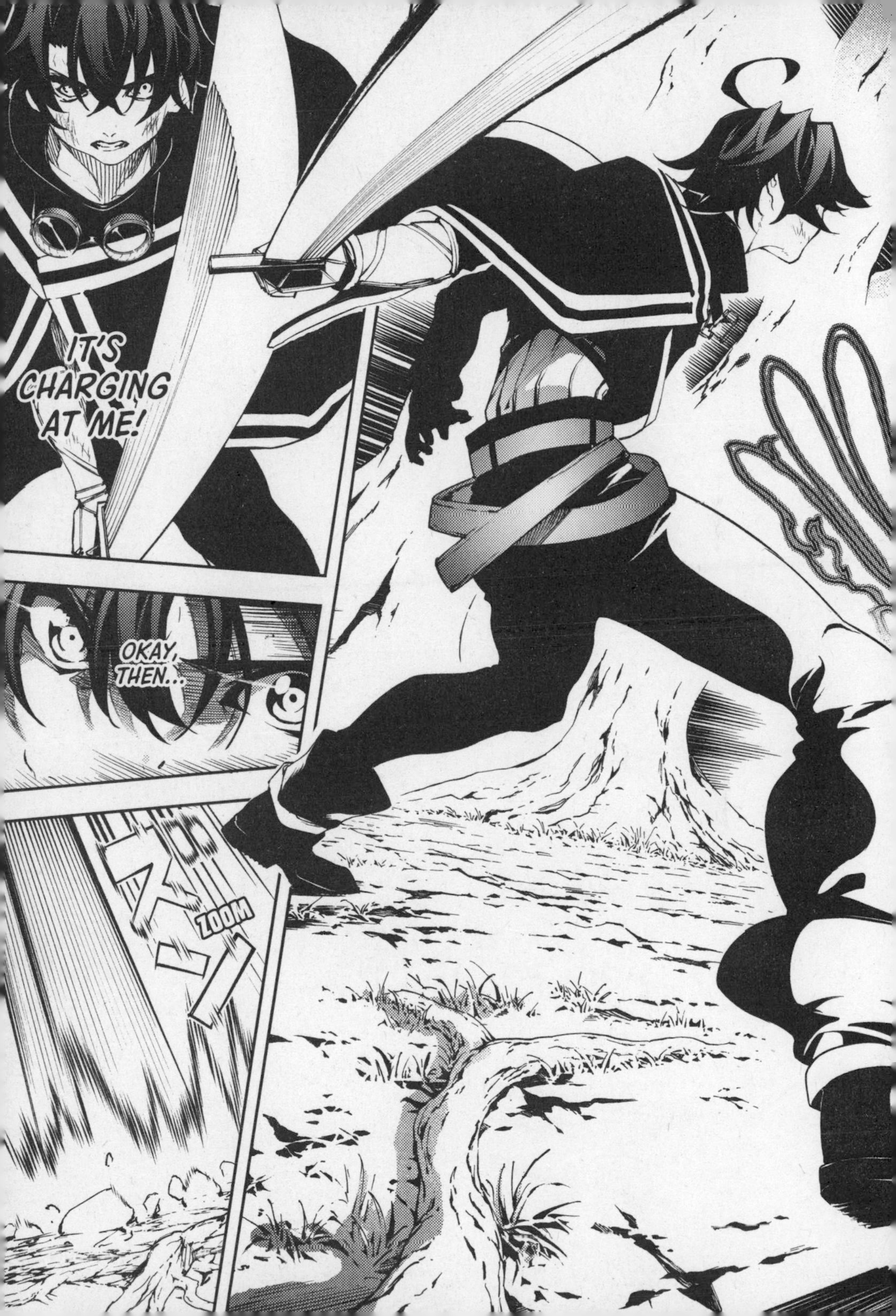
IT'S CHARGING AT ME!
OKAY, THEN...
ZOOM

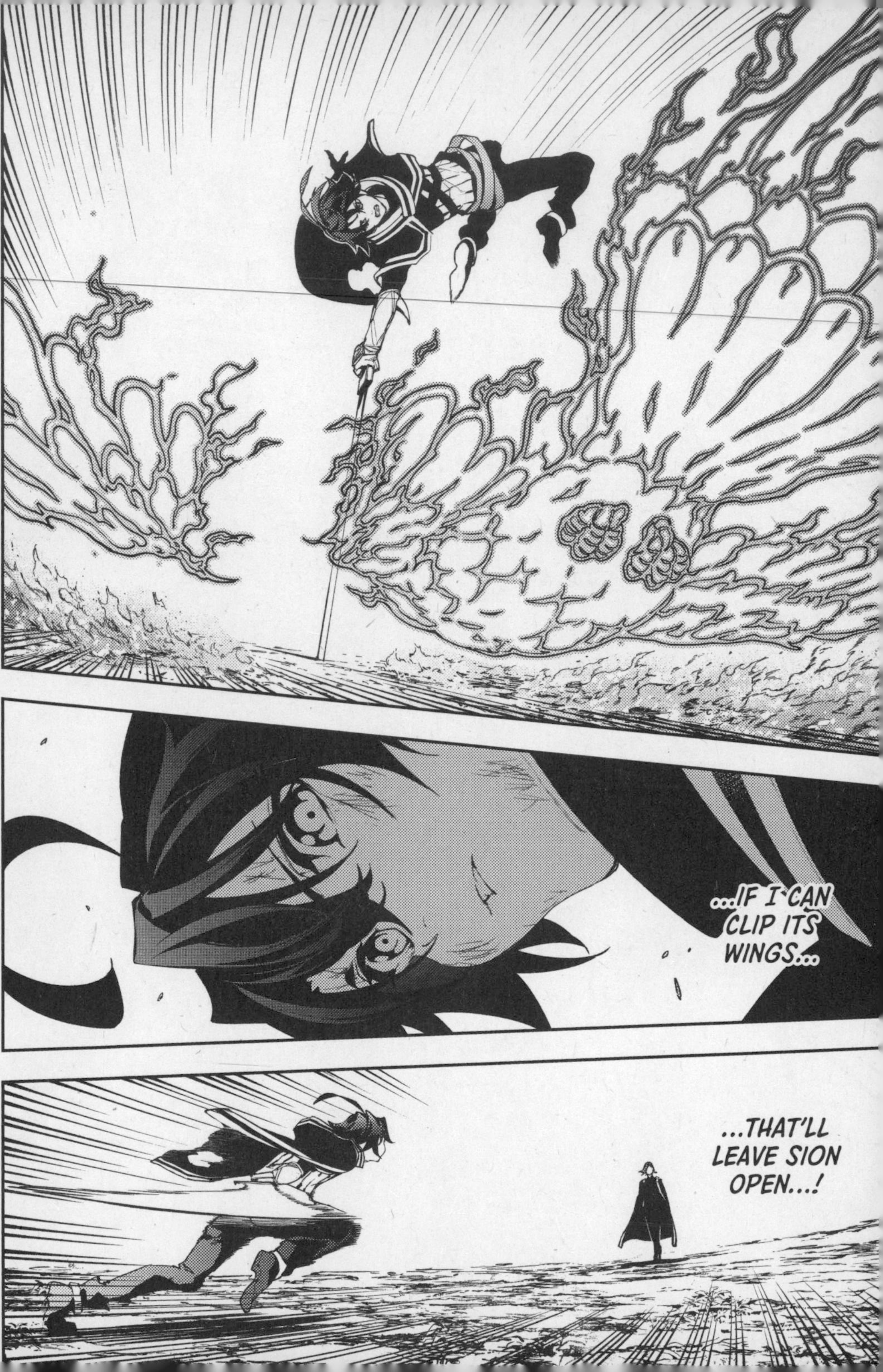
...IF I CAN CLIP ITS WINGS...
...THAT'LL LEAVE SION OPEN...!

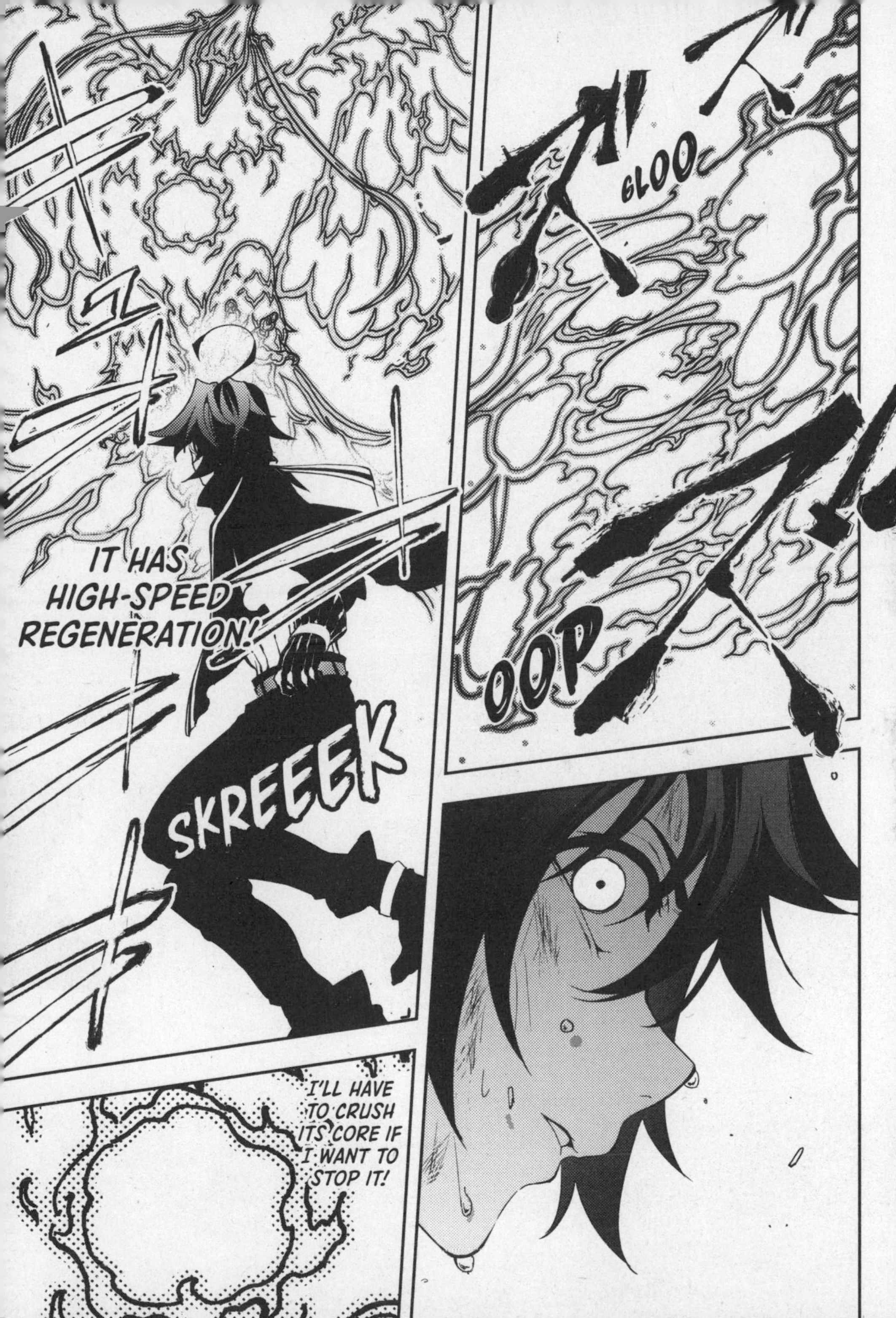
GLOO
OOP
IT HAS HIGH-SPEED REGENERATION!
SKREEEK
I'LL HAVE TO CRUSH ITS CORE IF I WANT TO STOP IT!

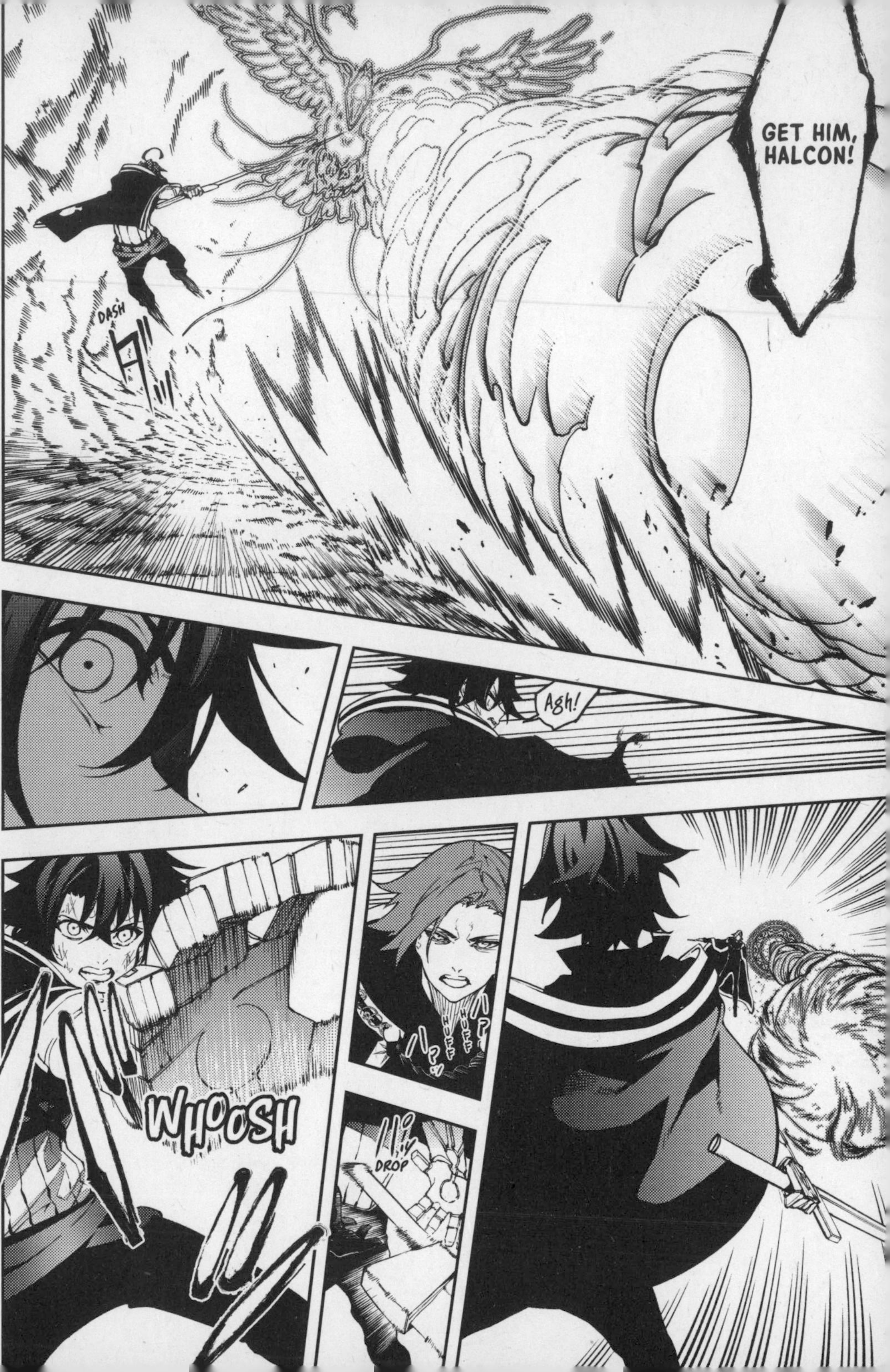
GET HIM, HALCON!
DASH
Agh!
HUFF HUFF
WHOOSH
DROP

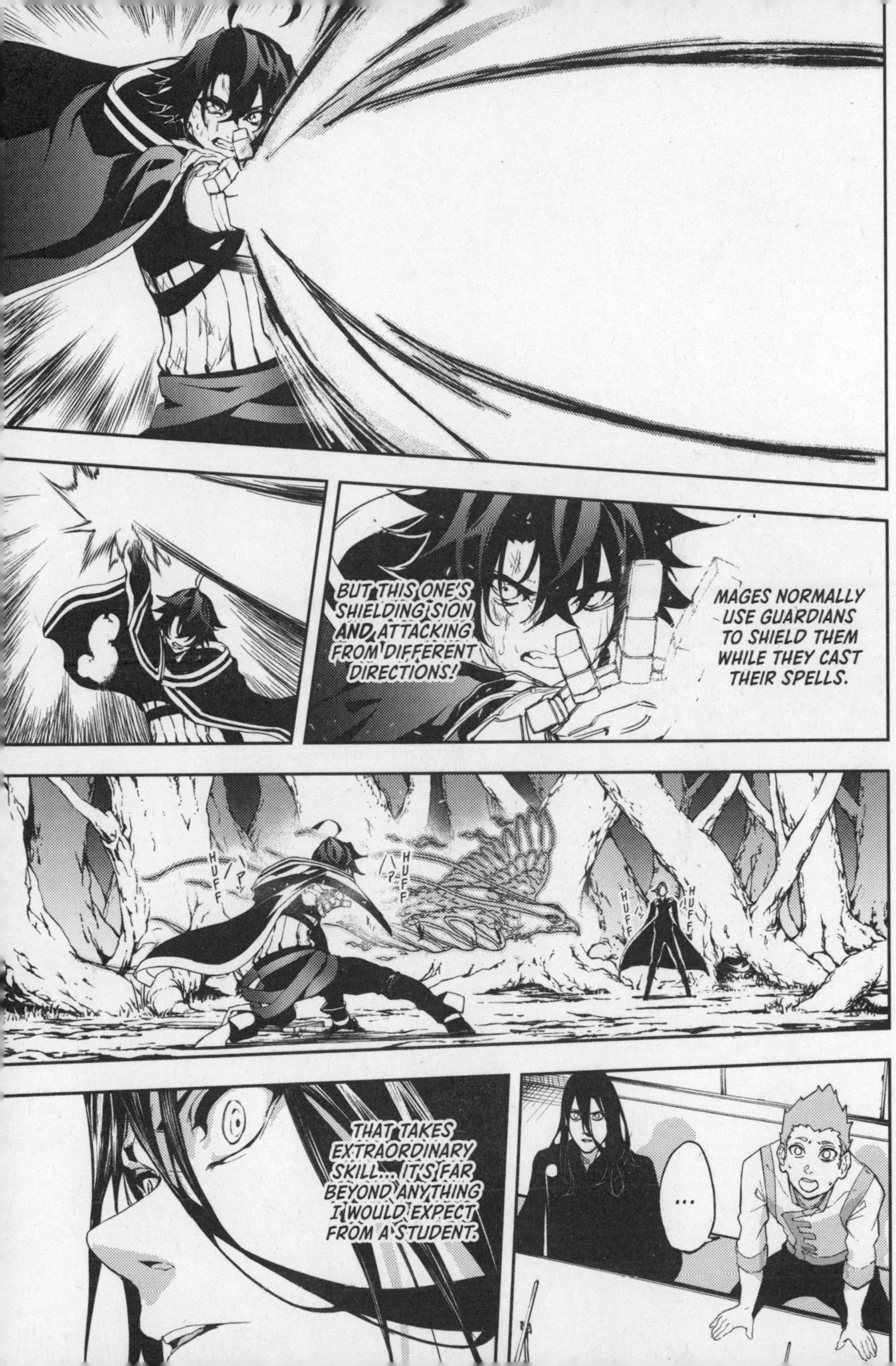
MAGES NORMALLY USE GUARDIANS TO SHIELD THEM WHILE THEY CAST THEIR SPELLS.
BUT THIS ONE'S SHIELDING SION AND ATTACKING FROM DIFFERENT DIRECTIONS!
HUFF HUFF
HUFF HUFF
...
THAT TAKES EXTRAORDINARY SKILL... IT'S FAR BEYOND ANYTHING I WOULD EXPECT FROM A STUDENT.

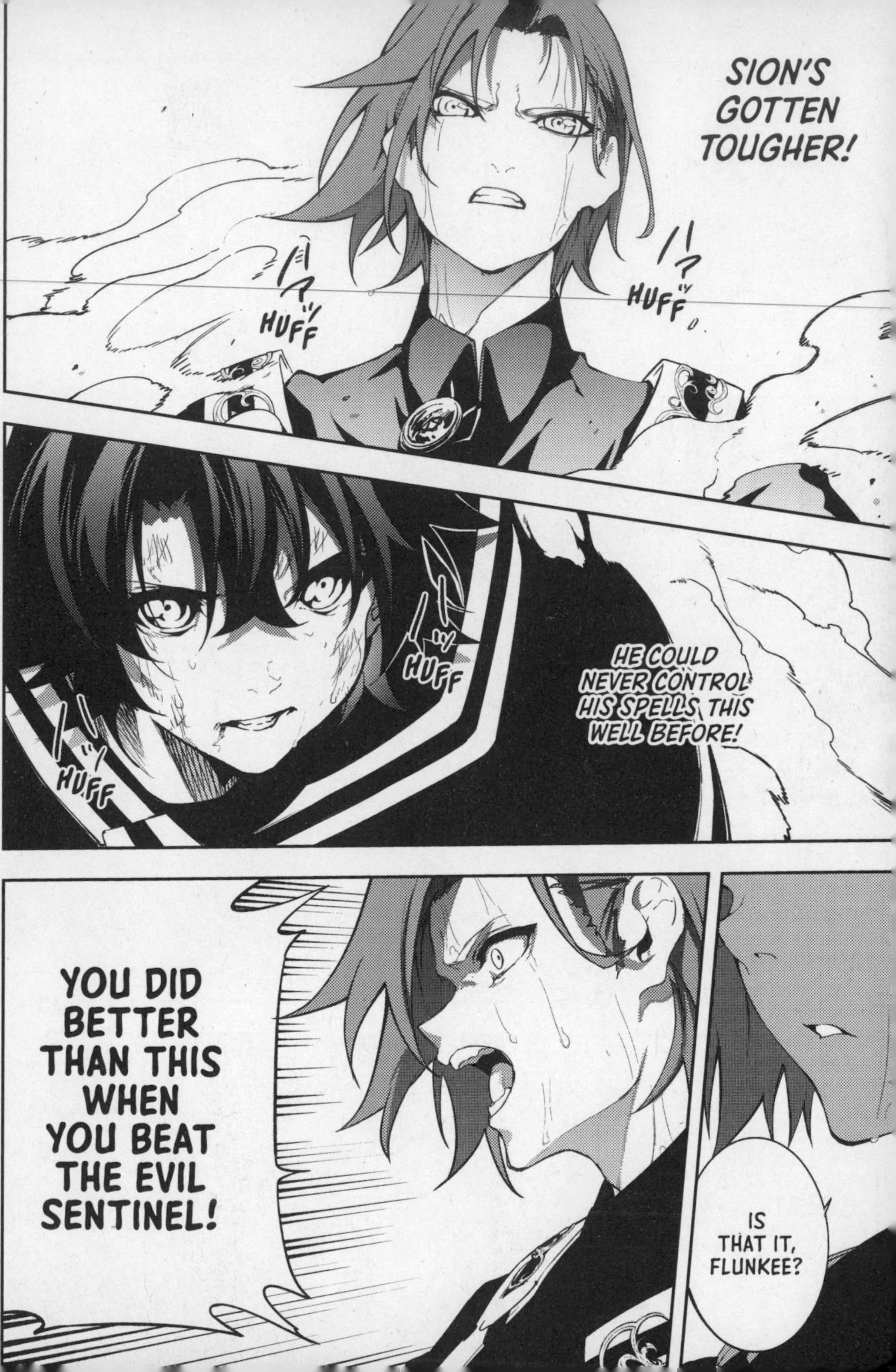
SION'S GOTTEN TOUGHER!
HUFF
HUFF
HE COULD NEVER CONTROL HIS SPELLS THIS WELL BEFORE!
HUFF
HUFF
YOU DID BETTER THAN THIS WHEN YOU BEAT THE EVIL SENTINEL!
IS THAT IT, FLUNKEE?

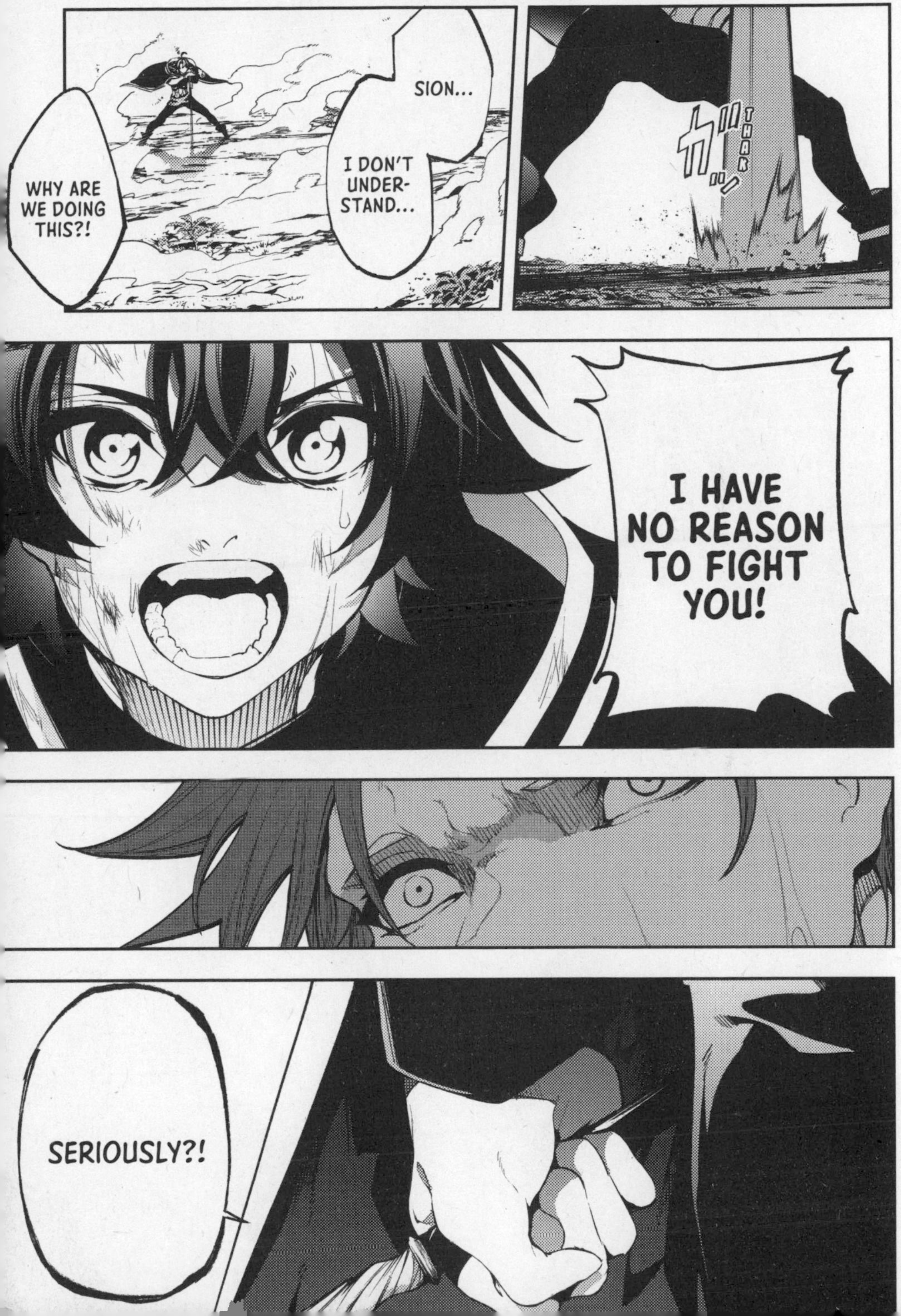
THAK
SION...
I DON'T UNDER-STAND...
WHY ARE WE DOING THIS?!
I HAVE NO REASON TO FIGHT YOU!
SERIOUSLY?!

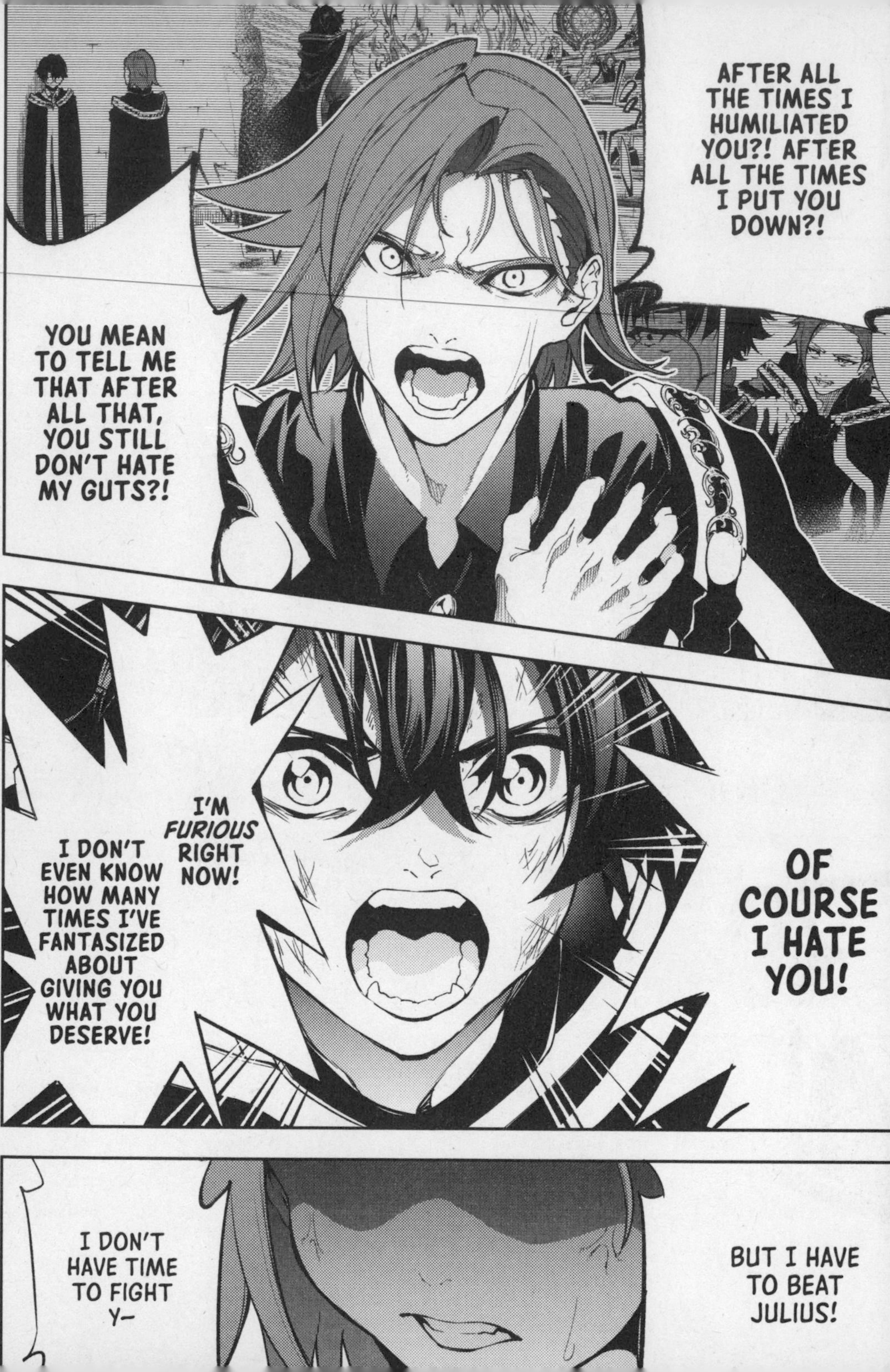
AFTER ALL THE TIMES I HUMILIATED YOU?! AFTER ALL THE TIMES I PUT YOU DOWN?!
YOU MEAN TO TELL ME THAT AFTER ALL THAT, YOU STILL DON'T HATE MY GUTS?!
OF COURSE I HATE YOU!
I'M *FURIOUS* RIGHT NOW!
I DON'T EVEN KNOW HOW MANY TIMES I'VE FANTASIZED ABOUT GIVING YOU WHAT YOU DESERVE!
BUT I HAVE TO BEAT JULIUS!
I DON'T HAVE TIME TO FIGHT Y—

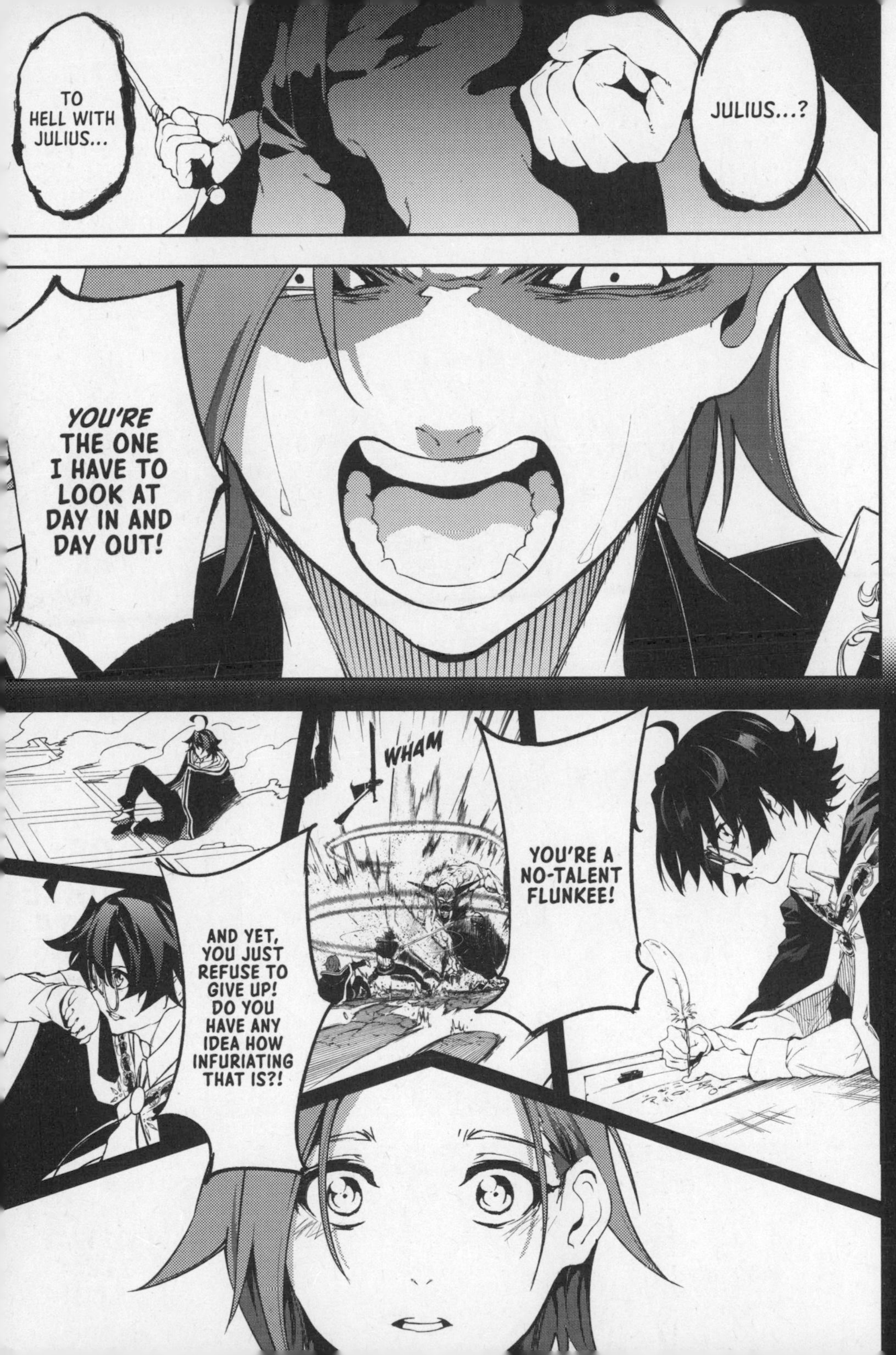
JULIUS...?
TO HELL WITH JULIUS...
YOU'RE THE ONE I HAVE TO LOOK AT DAY IN AND DAY OUT!
YOU'RE A NO-TALENT FLUNKEE!
WHAM
AND YET, YOU JUST REFUSE TO GIVE UP! DO YOU HAVE ANY IDEA HOW INFURIATING THAT IS?!

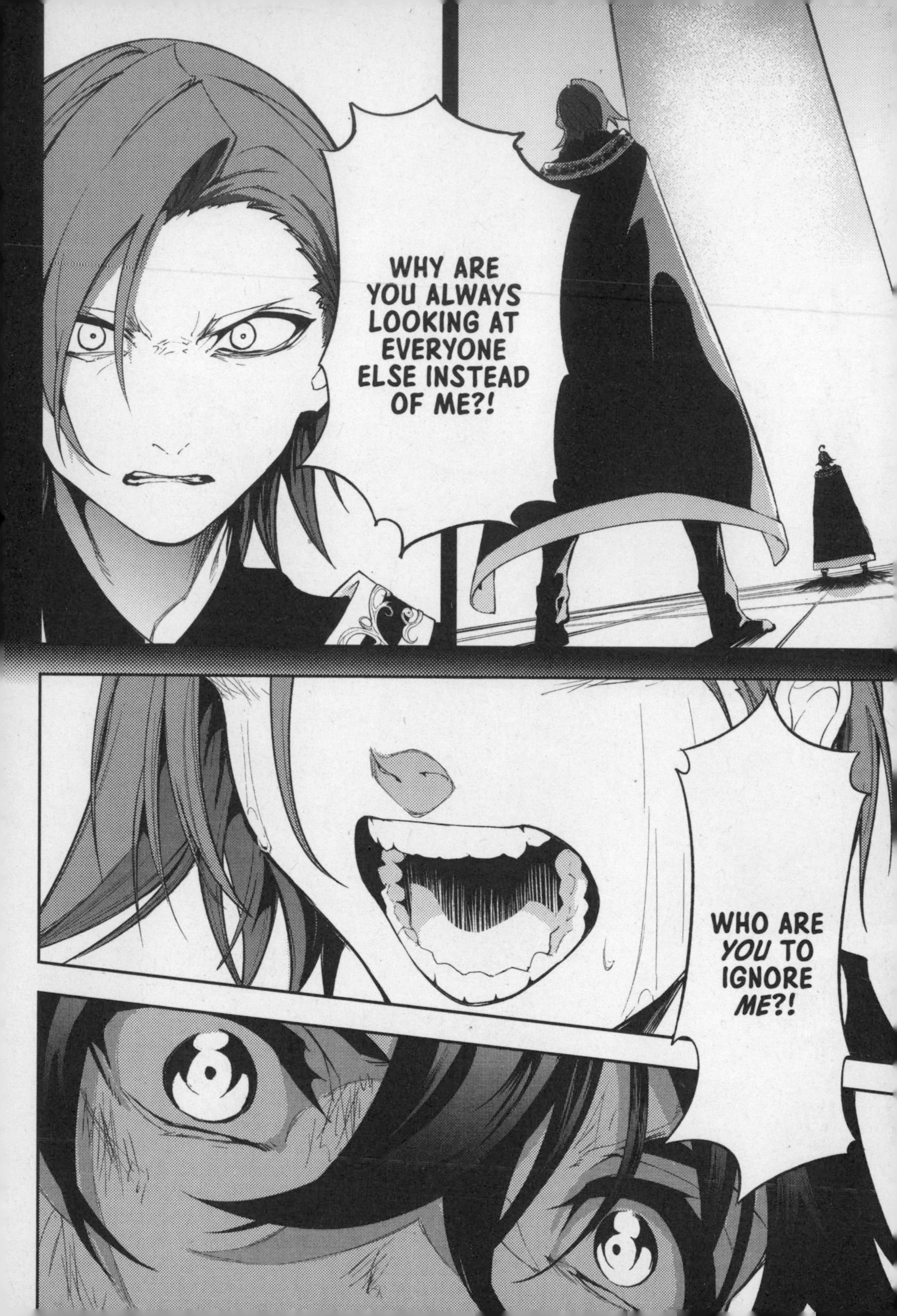
WHY ARE YOU ALWAYS LOOKING AT EVERYONE ELSE INSTEAD OF ME?!
WHO ARE *YOU* TO IGNORE *ME*?!

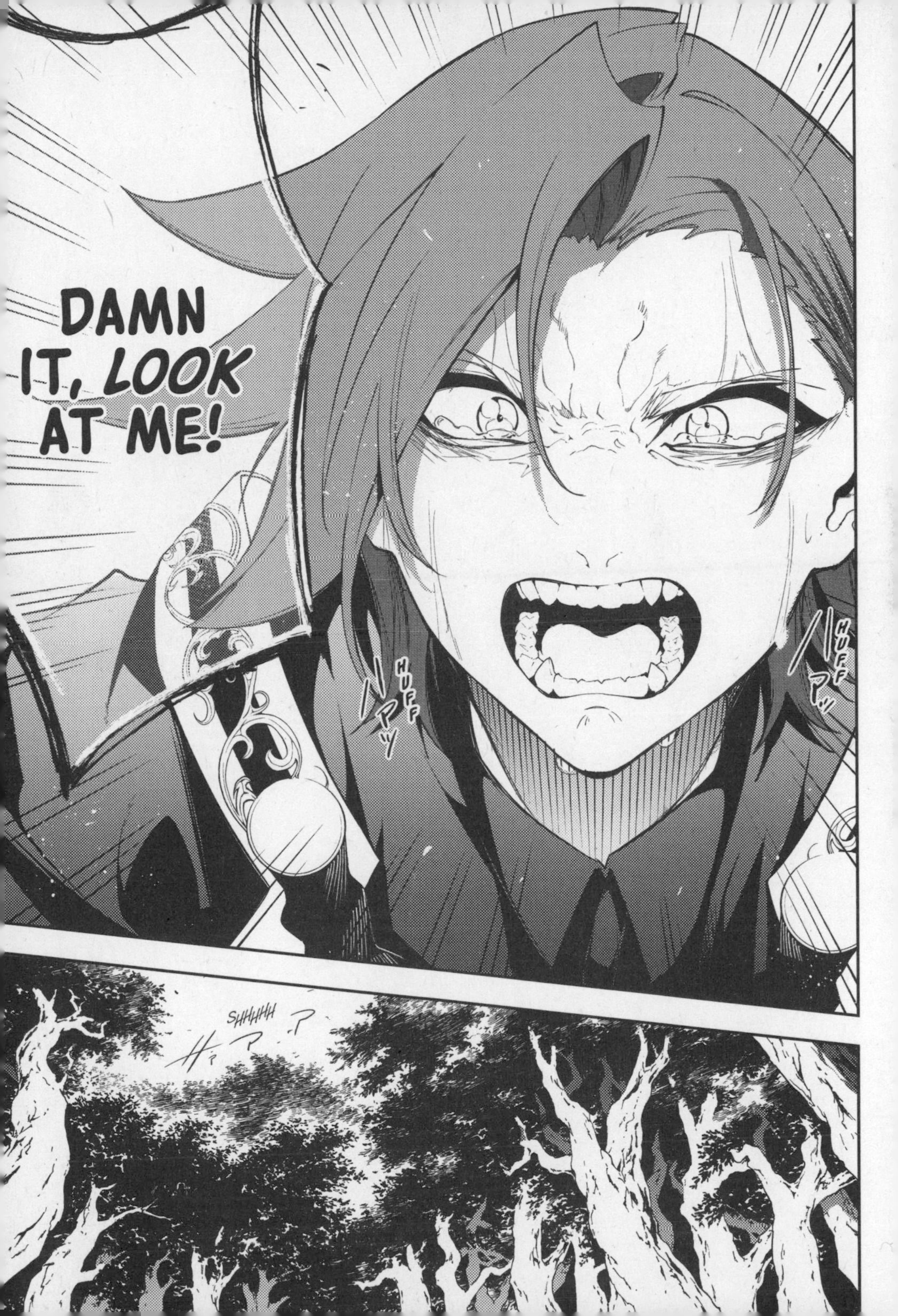
DAMN IT, *LOOK* AT ME!
HUFF
HUFF
SHHHHH

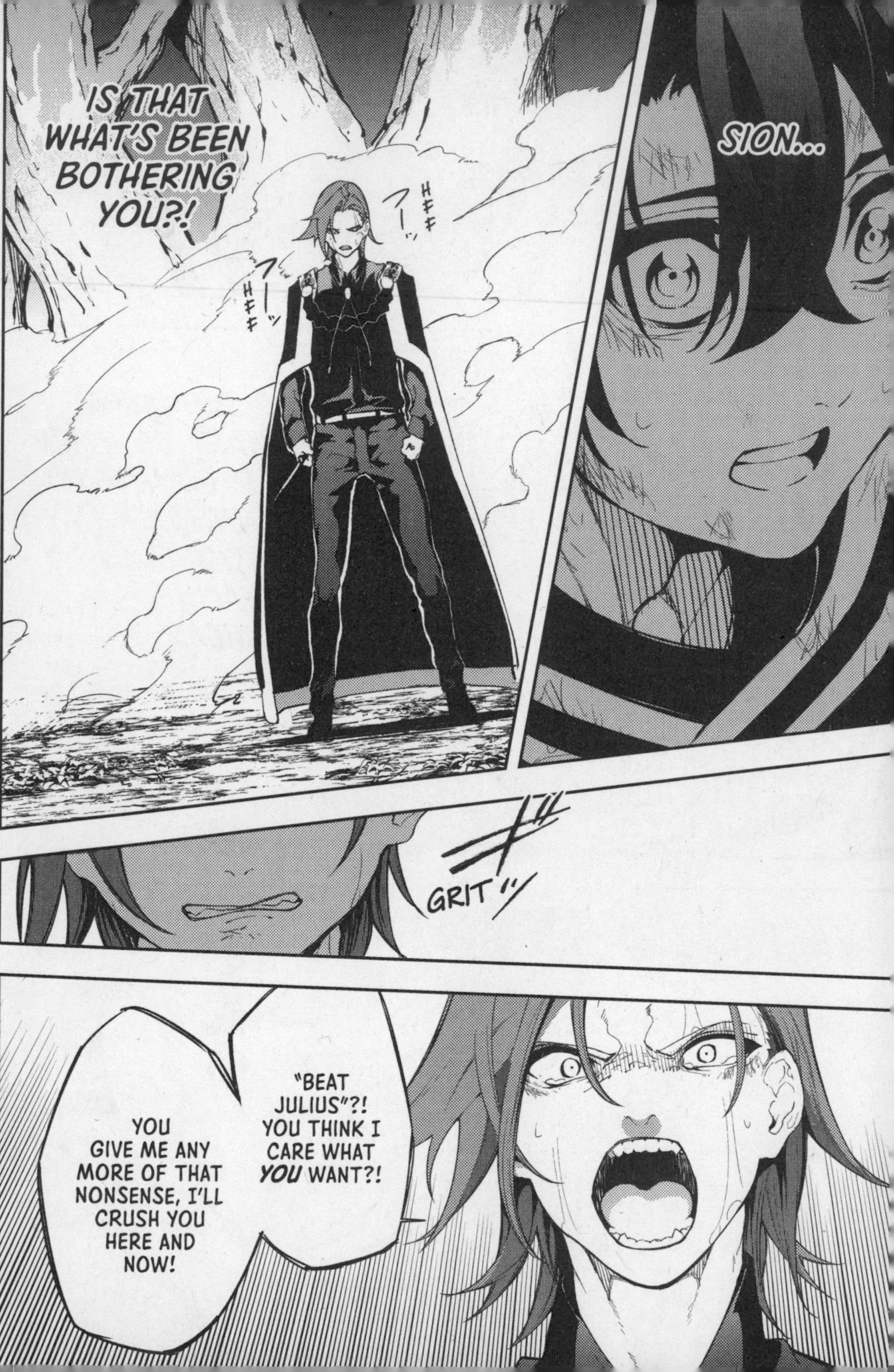
SION...
IS THAT WHAT'S BEEN BOTHERING YOU?!
HFF
HFF
GRIT
"BEAT JULIUS"?! YOU THINK I CARE WHAT *YOU* WANT?!
YOU GIVE ME ANY MORE OF THAT NONSENSE, I'LL CRUSH YOU HERE AND NOW!

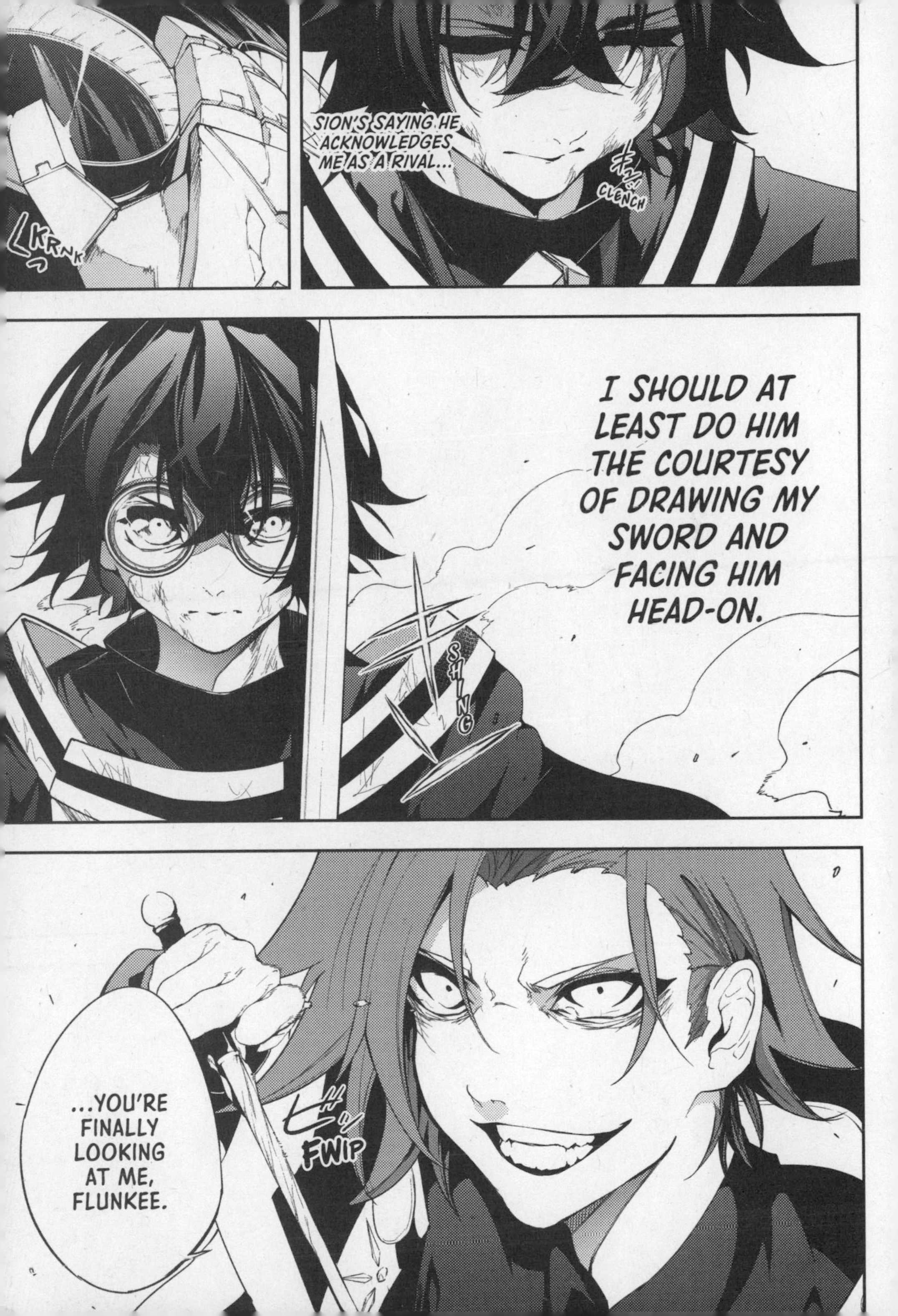
SION'S SAYING HE ACKNOWLEDGES ME AS A RIVAL...
CLENCH
KRNK
I SHOULD AT LEAST DO HIM THE COURTESY OF DRAWING MY SWORD AND FACING HIM HEAD-ON.
SHING
FWIP
...YOU'RE FINALLY LOOKING AT ME, FLUNKEE.

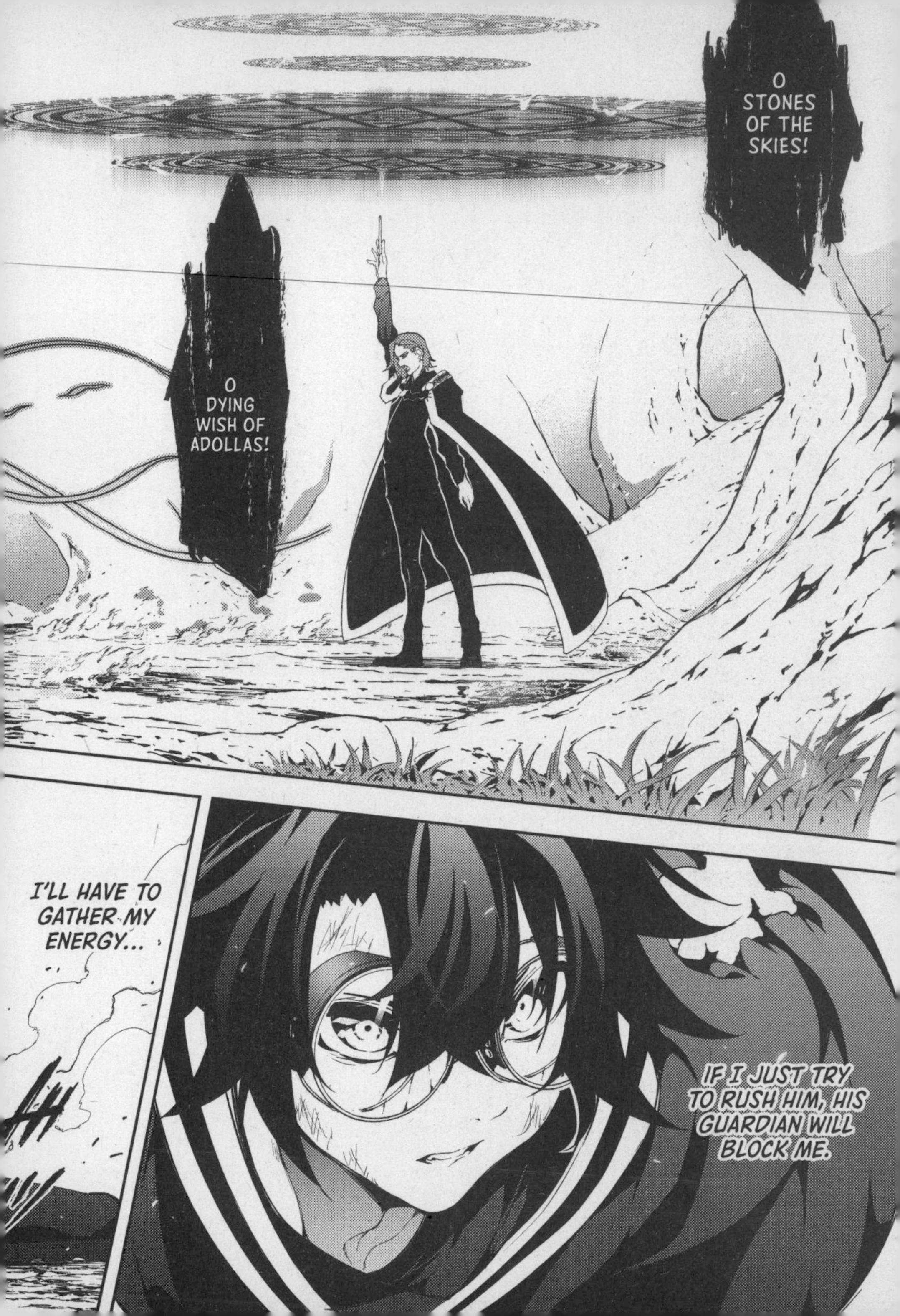
O STONES OF THE SKIES!
O DYING WISH OF ADOLLAS!
IF I JUST TRY TO RUSH HIM, HIS GUARDIAN WILL BLOCK ME.
I'LL HAVE TO GATHER MY ENERGY...

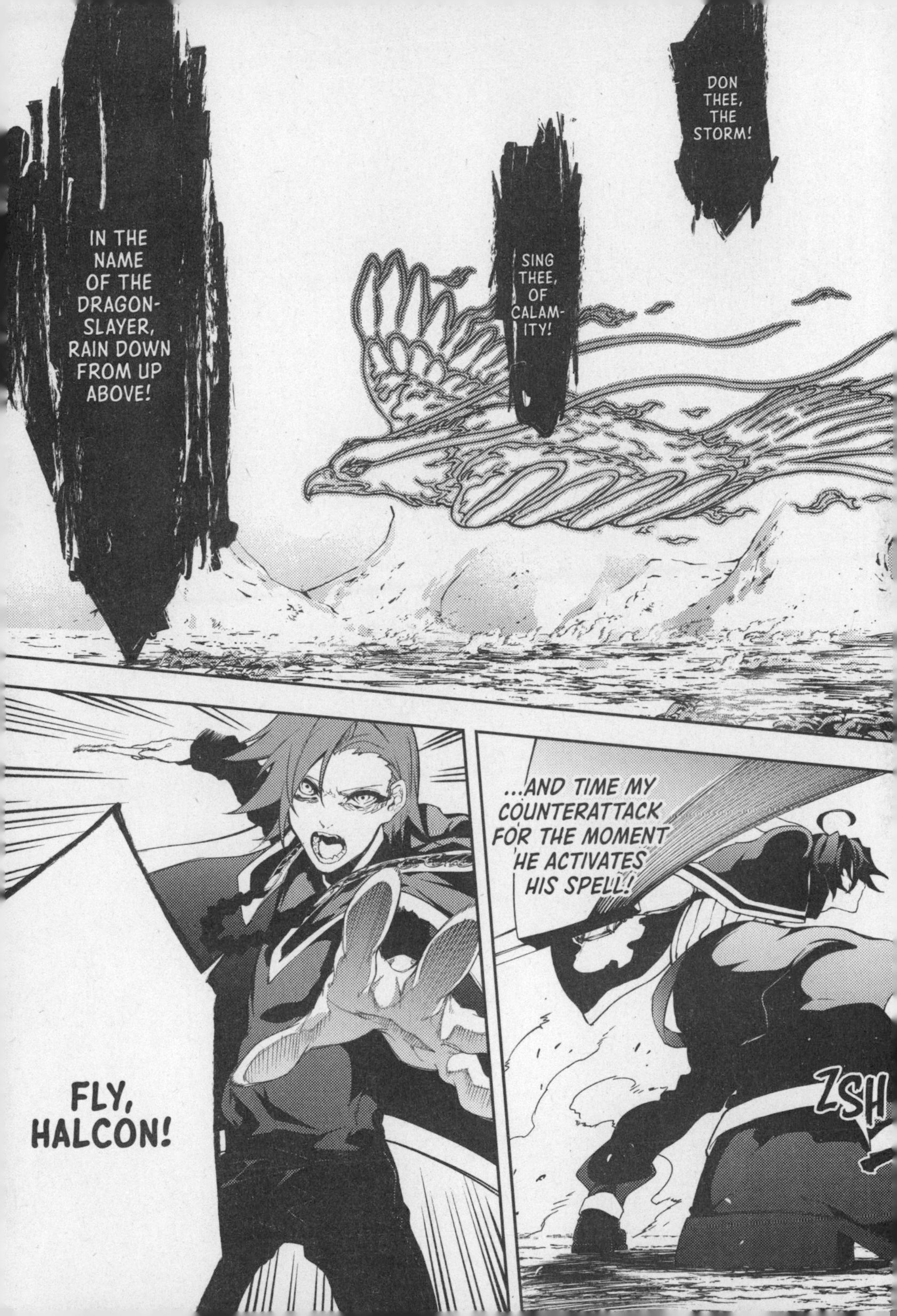
DON THEE, THE STORM!
SING THEE, OF CALAMITY!
IN THE NAME OF THE DRAGON-SLAYER, RAIN DOWN FROM UP ABOVE!
...AND TIME MY COUNTERATTACK FOR THE MOMENT HE ACTIVATES HIS SPELL!
ZSH
FLY, HALCON!

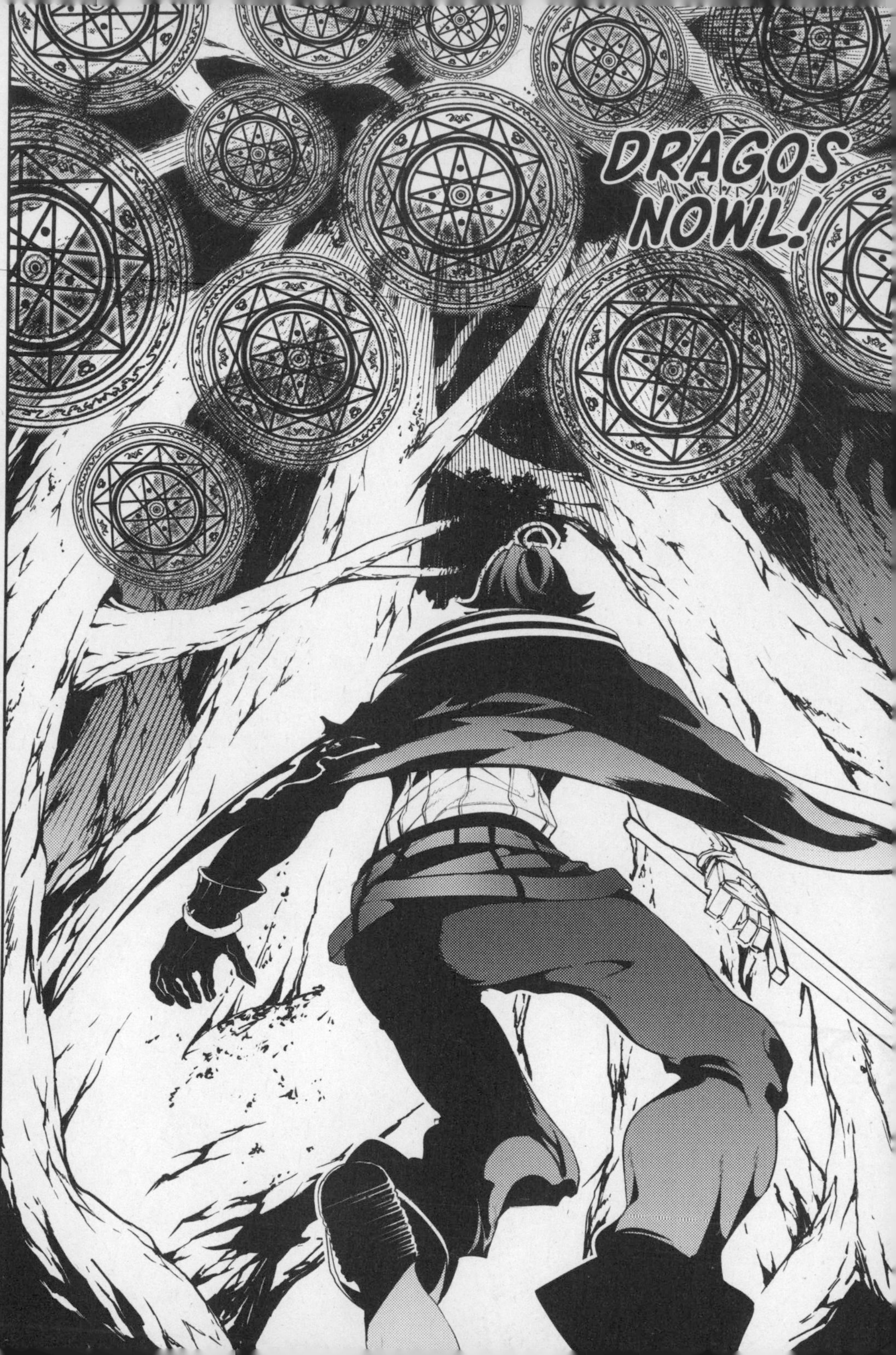
DRAGOS NOWL!

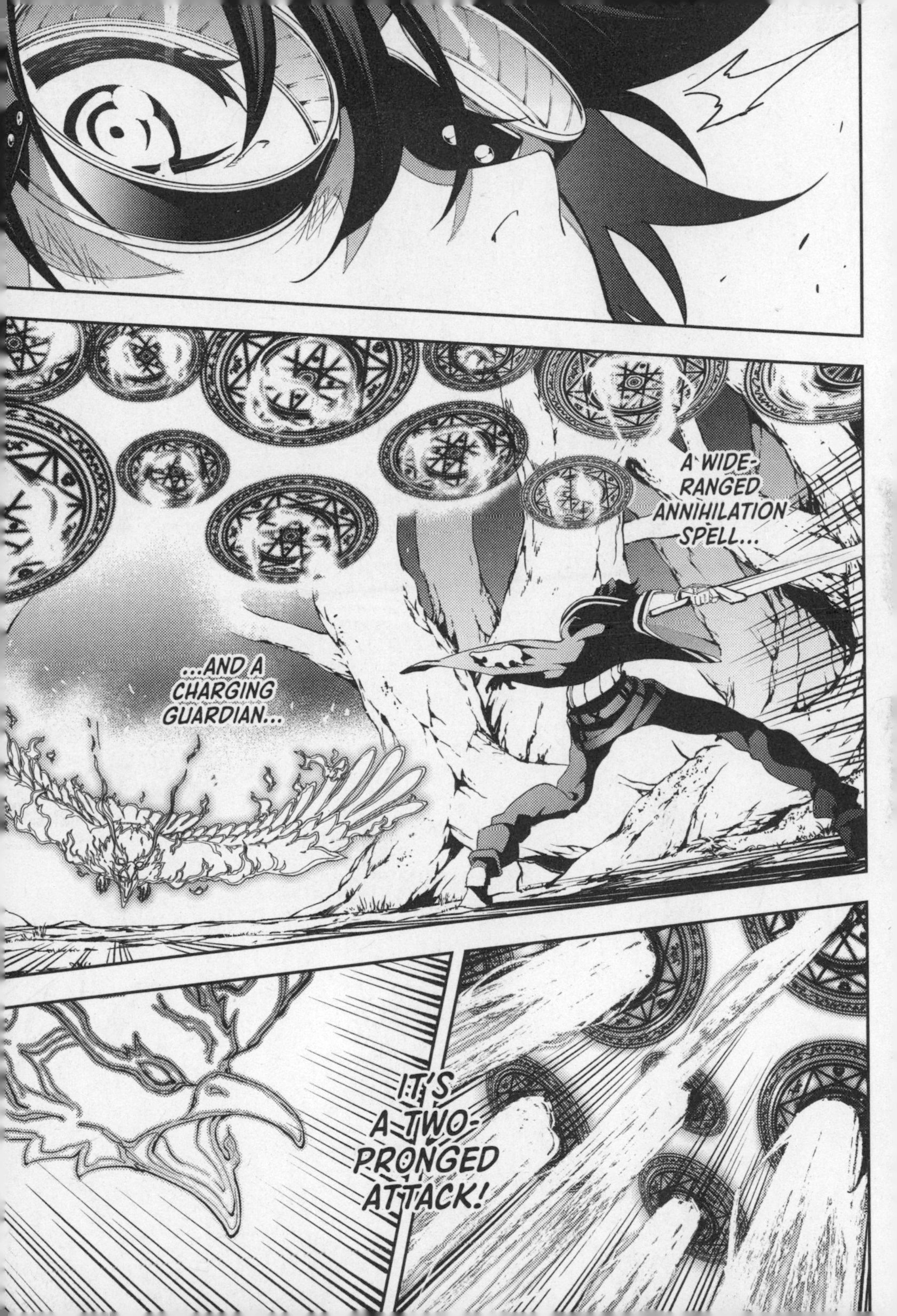
A WIDE-RANGED ANNIHILATION SPELL...
...AND A CHARGING GUARDIAN...
IT'S A TWO-PRONGED ATTACK!

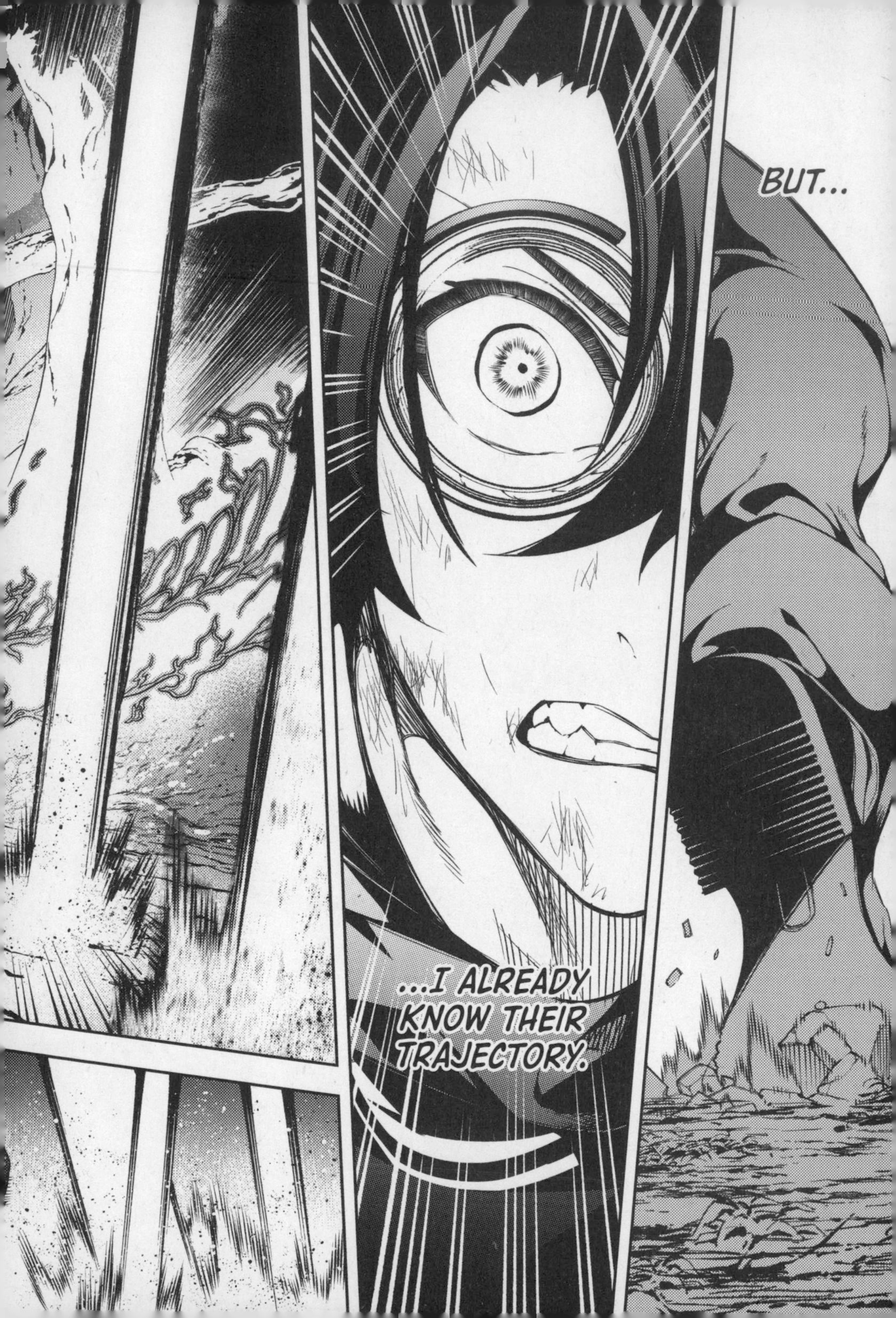
BUT...
...I ALREADY KNOW THEIR TRAJECTORY.

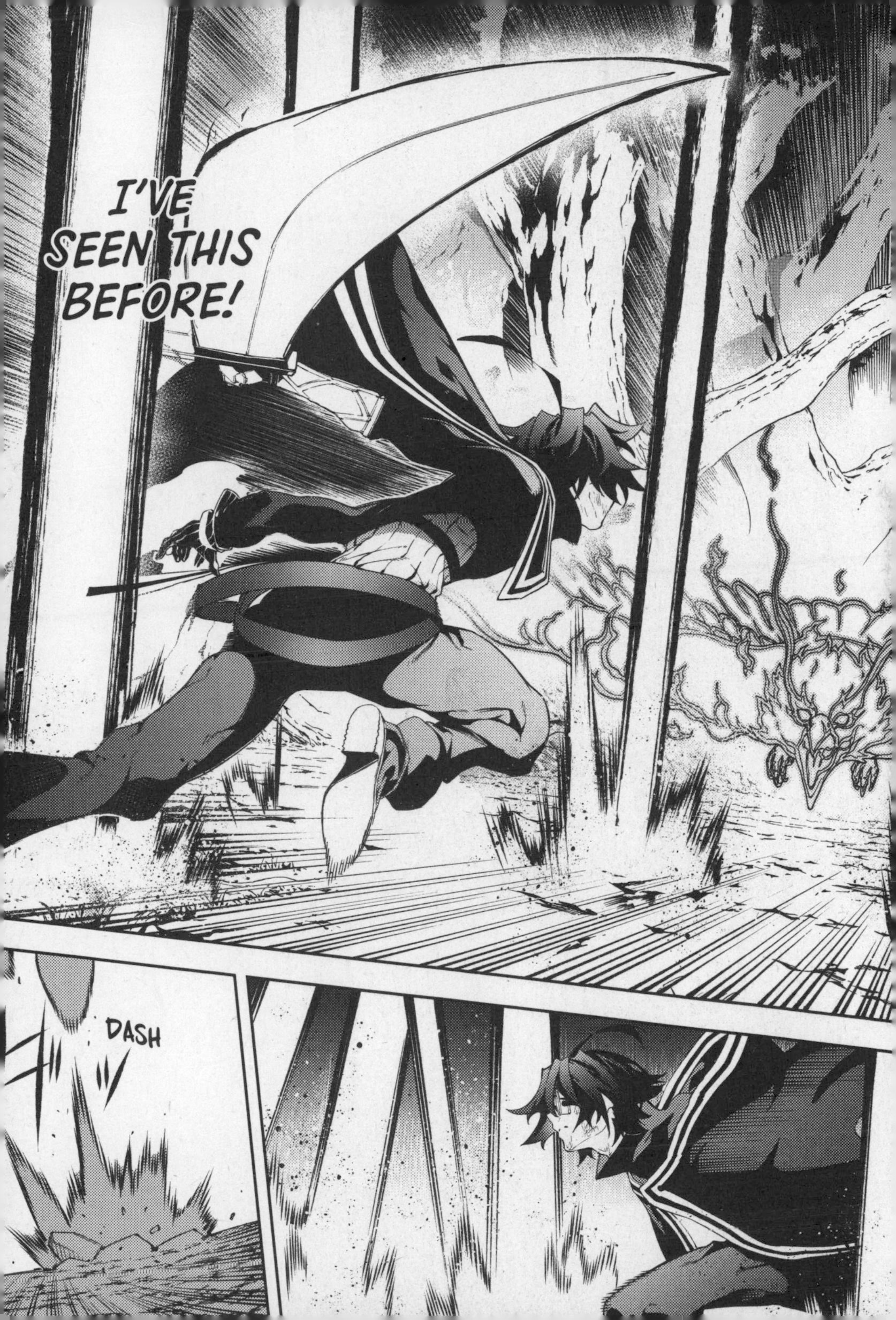
I'VE SEEN THIS BEFORE!
DASH

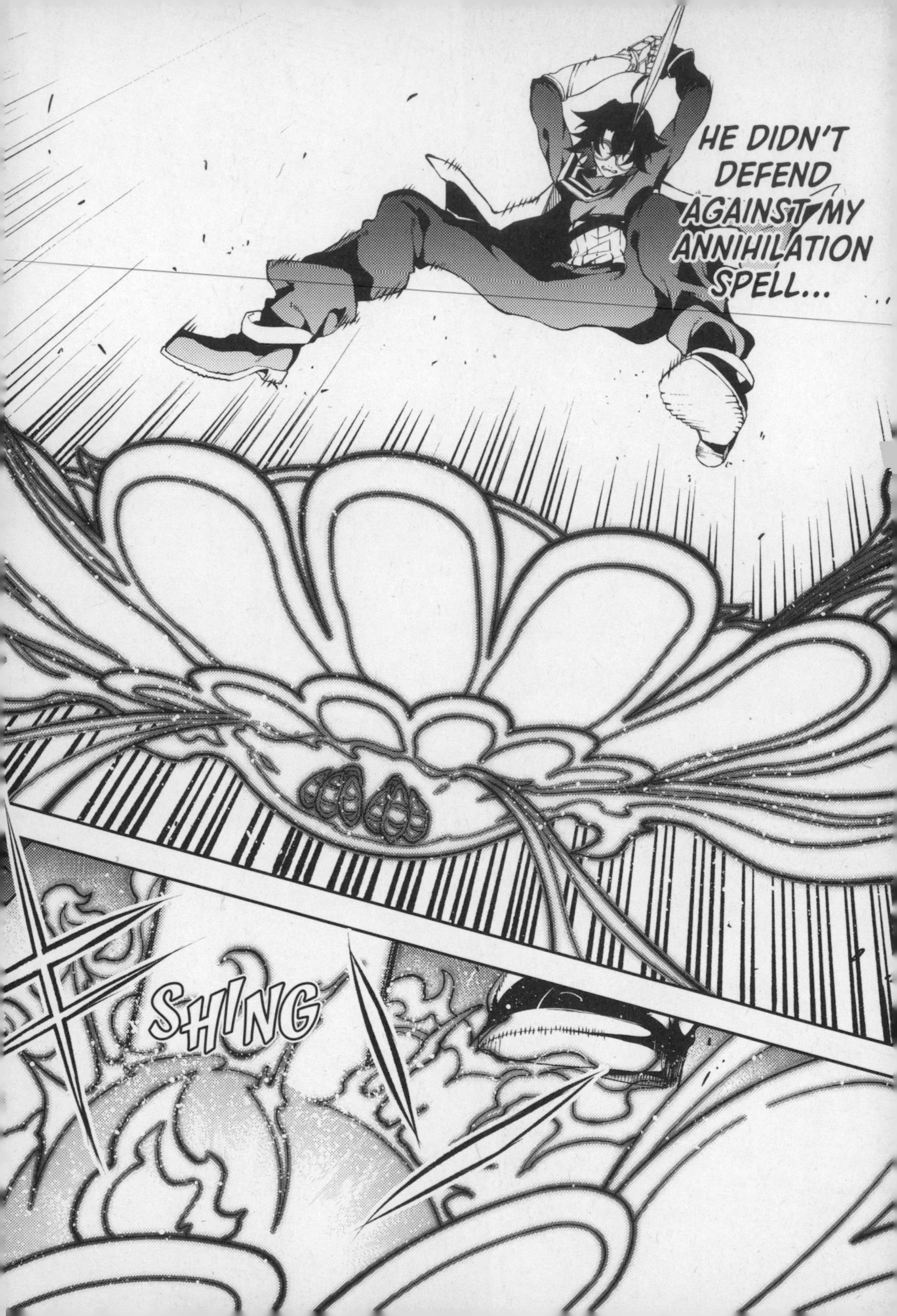
HE DIDN'T DEFEND AGAINST MY ANNIHILATION SPELL...
SHING

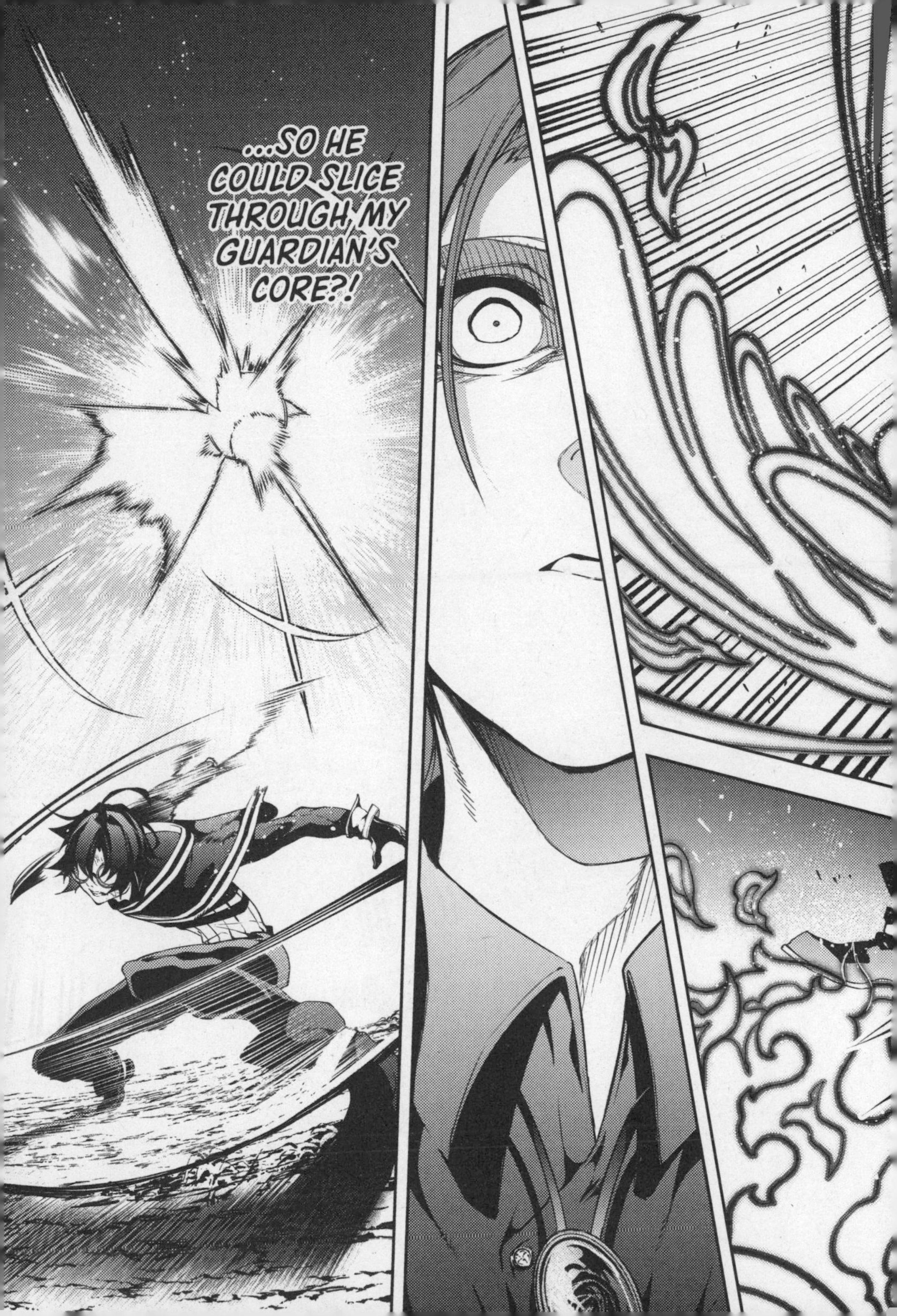
...SO HE COULD SLICE THROUGH MY GUARDIAN'S CORE?!

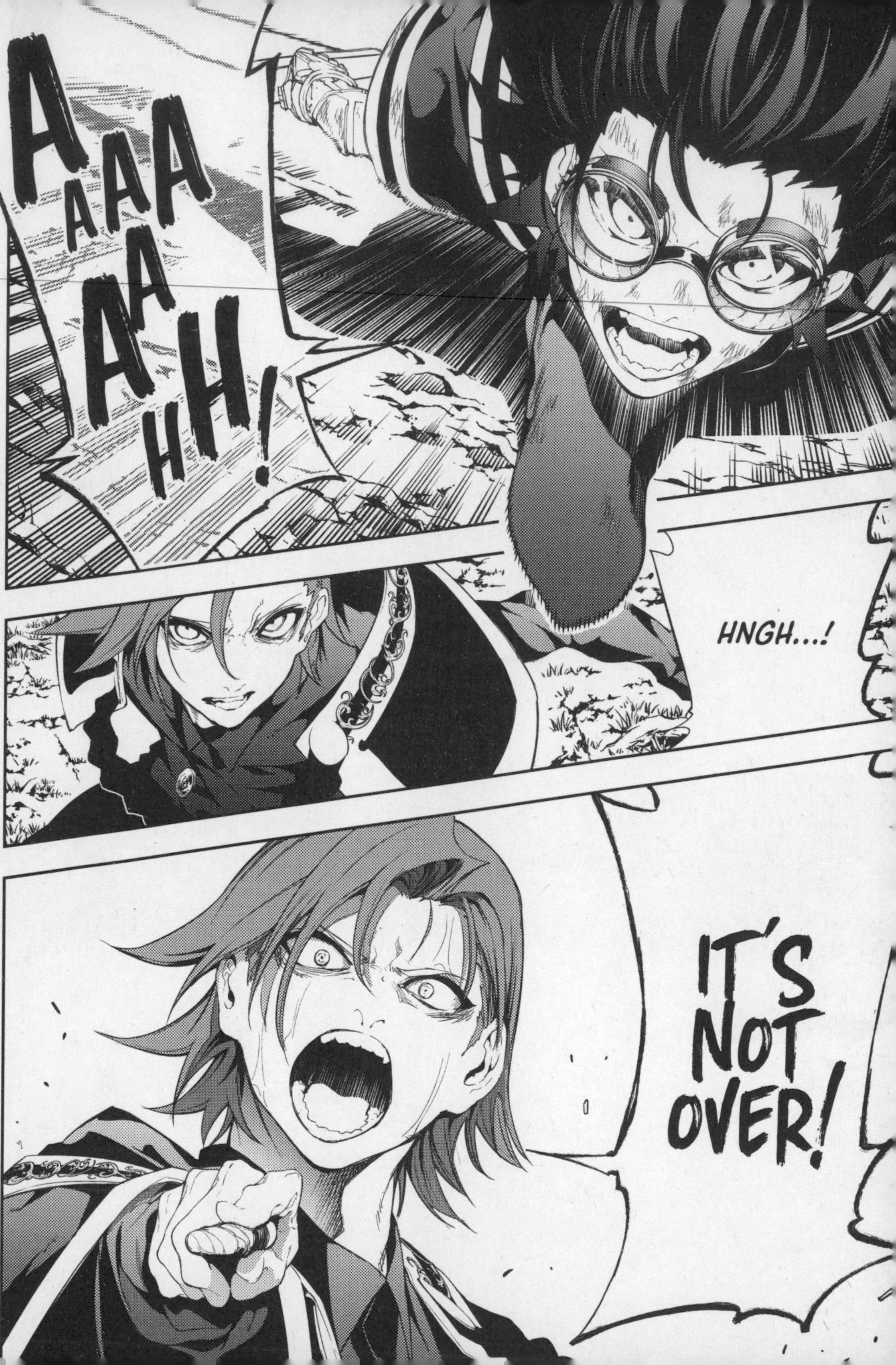
AAAAAAAHH!
HNGH...!
IT'S NOT OVER!

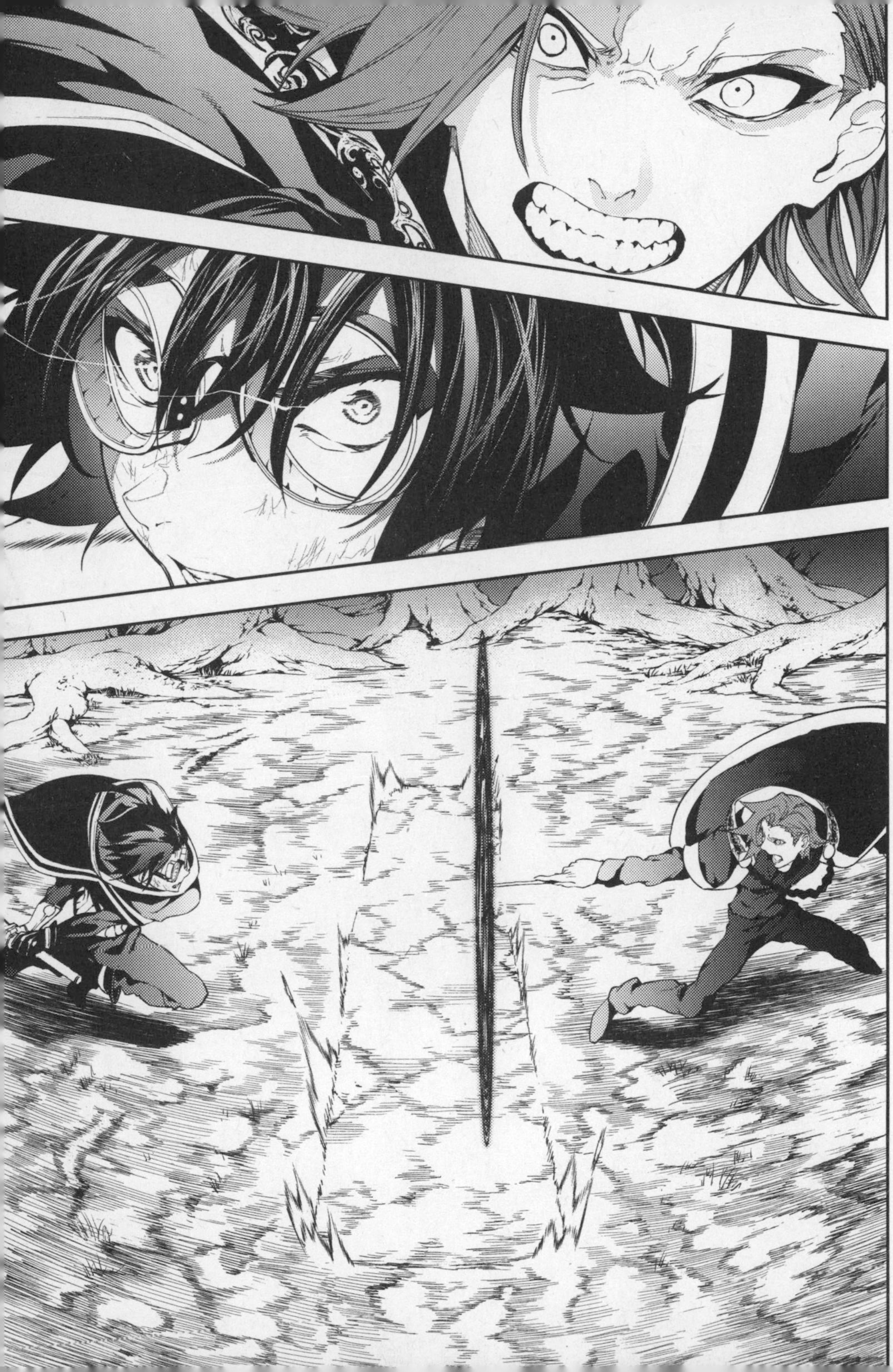

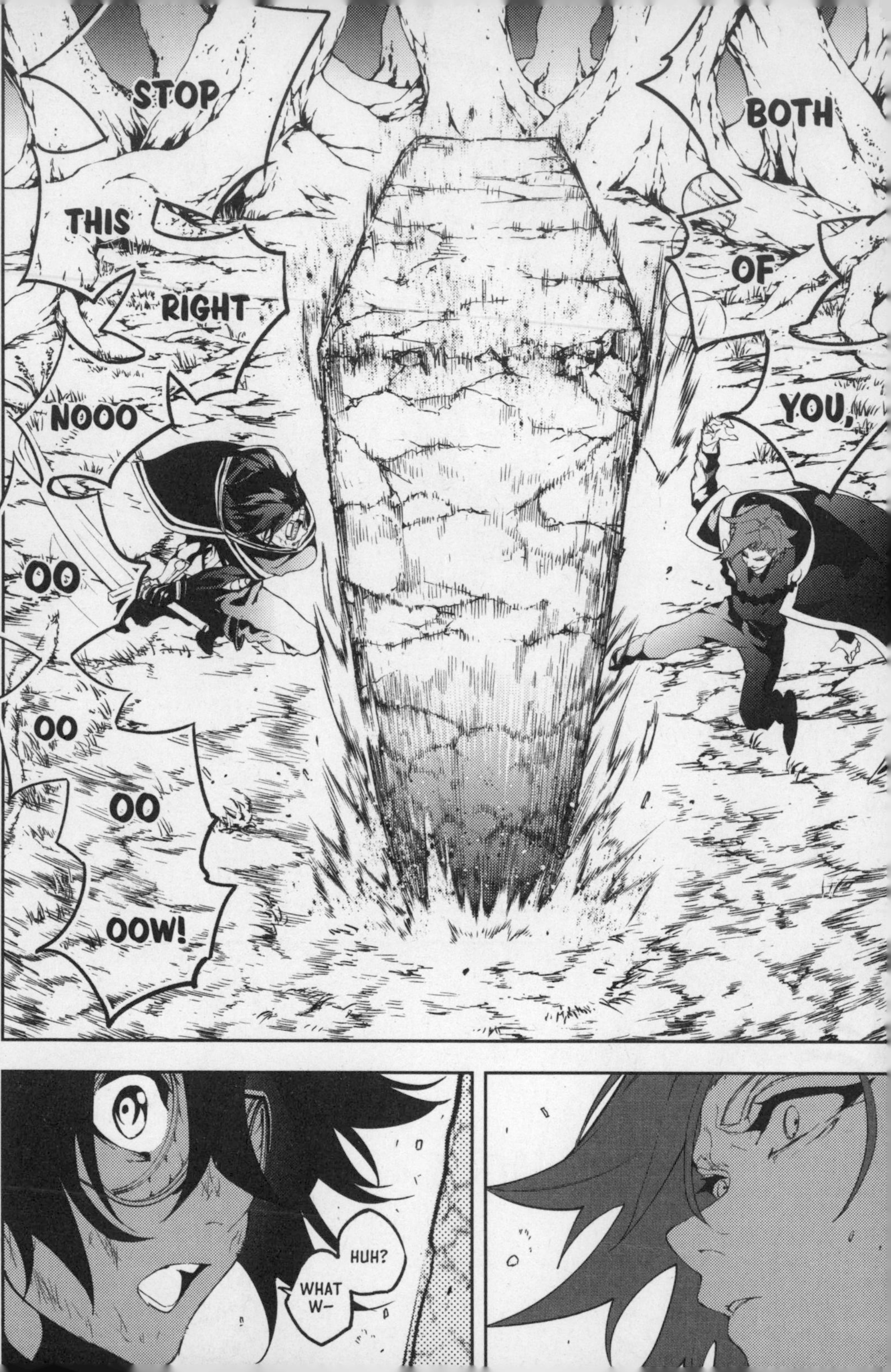

BOTH OF YOU,
STOP THIS RIGHT NOOOOOOOOOOOW!
HUH?
WHAT W–

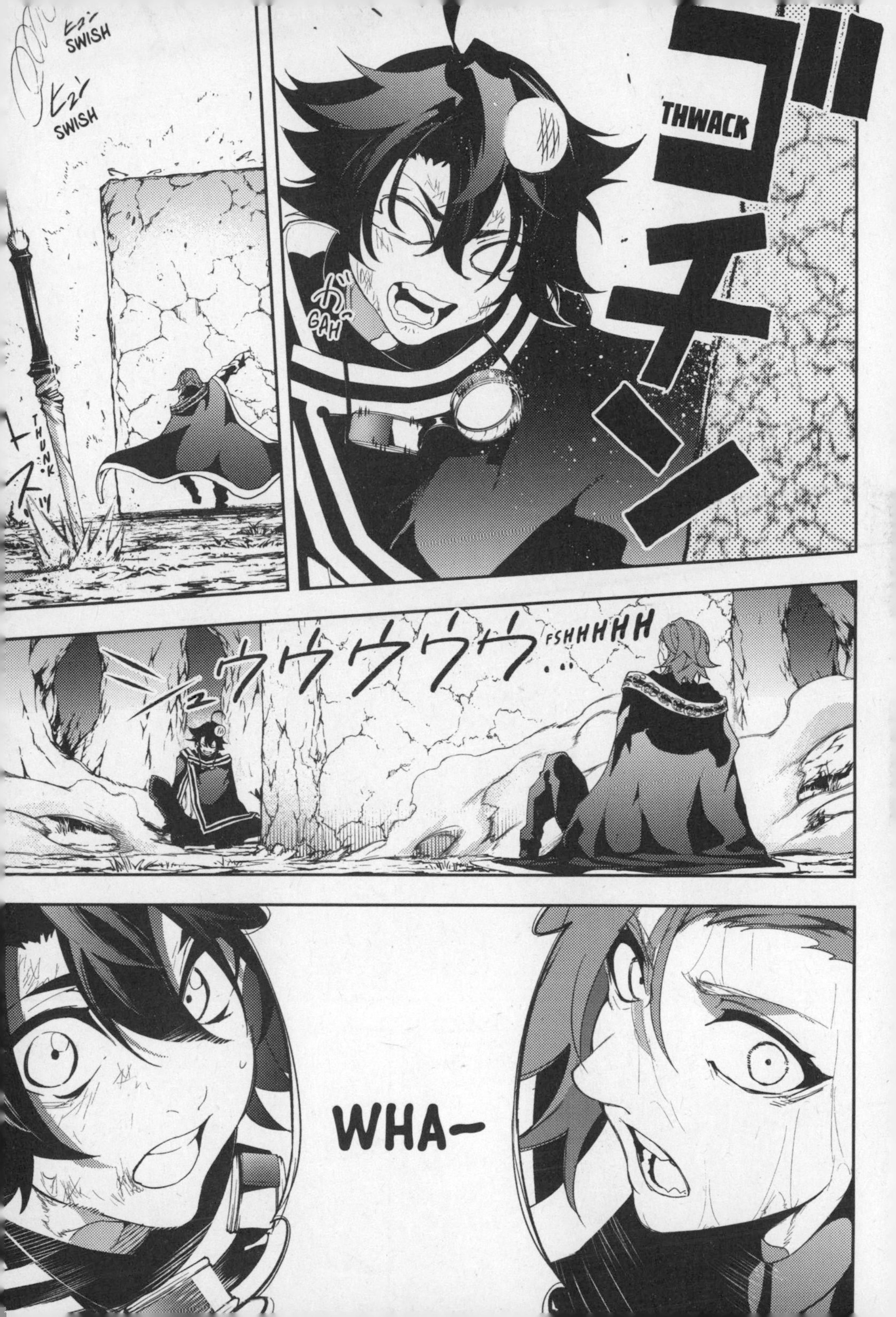

THWACK
GAH
SWISH
SWISH
THUNK
FSHHHHH
WHA-

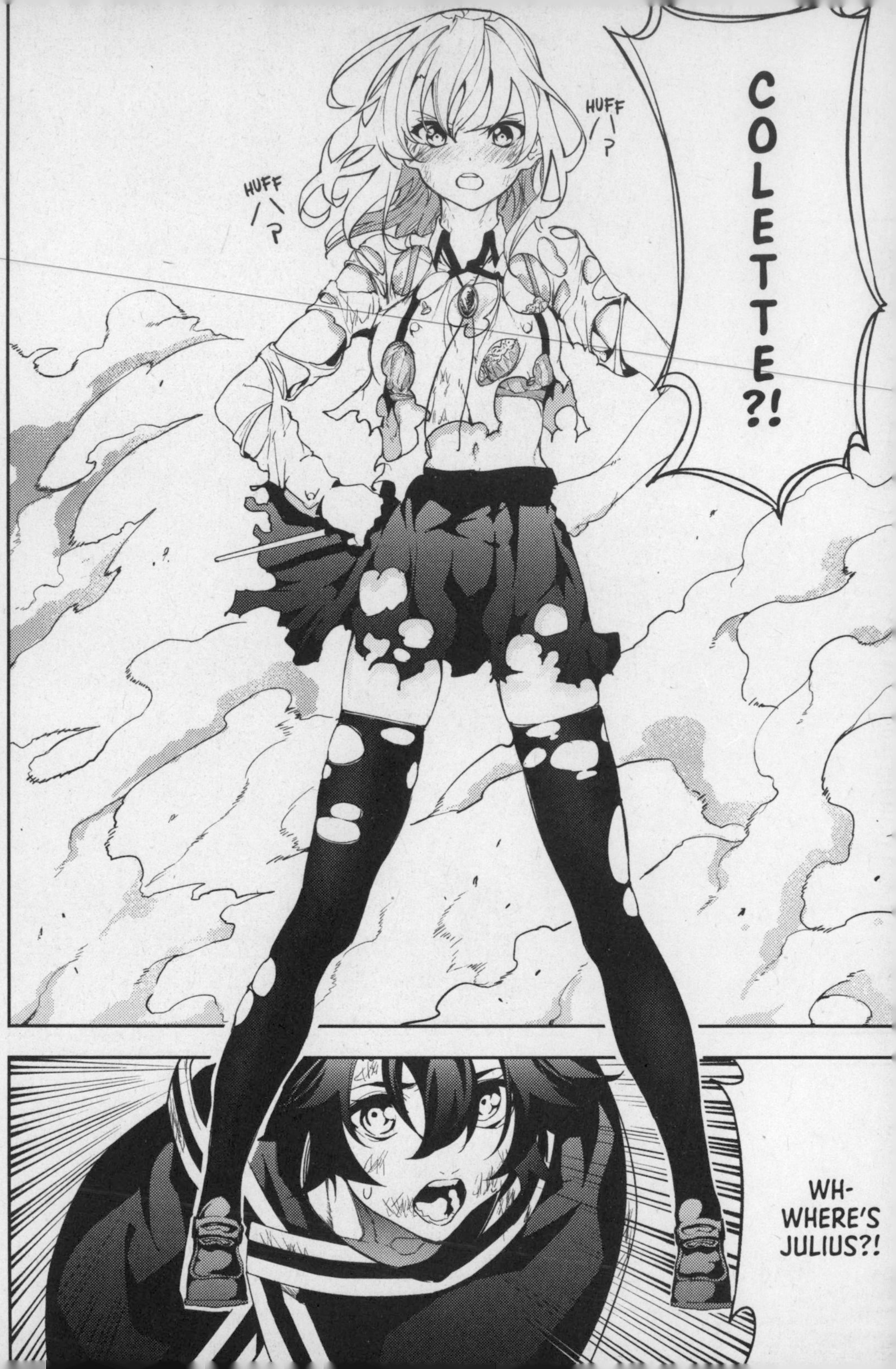
COLETTE?!
HUFF
HUFF
WH- WHERE'S JULIUS?!

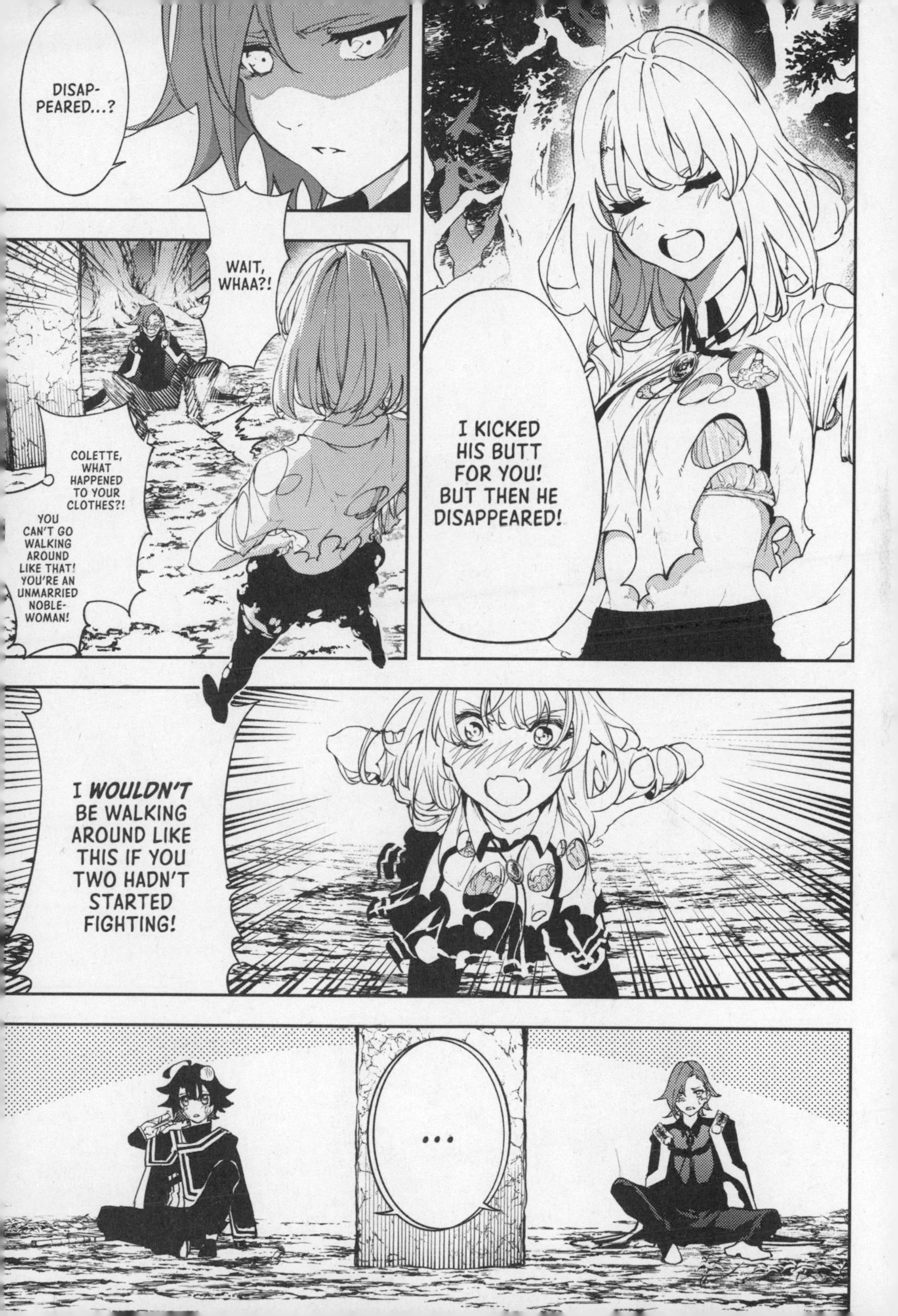
I KICKED HIS BUTT FOR YOU! BUT THEN HE DISAPPEARED!
DISAP-PEARED...?
WAIT, WHAA?!
COLETTE, WHAT HAPPENED TO YOUR CLOTHES?!
YOU CAN'T GO WALKING AROUND LIKE THAT! YOU'RE AN UNMARRIED NOBLE-WOMAN!
I *WOULDN'T* BE WALKING AROUND LIKE THIS IF YOU TWO HADN'T STARTED FIGHTING!
...

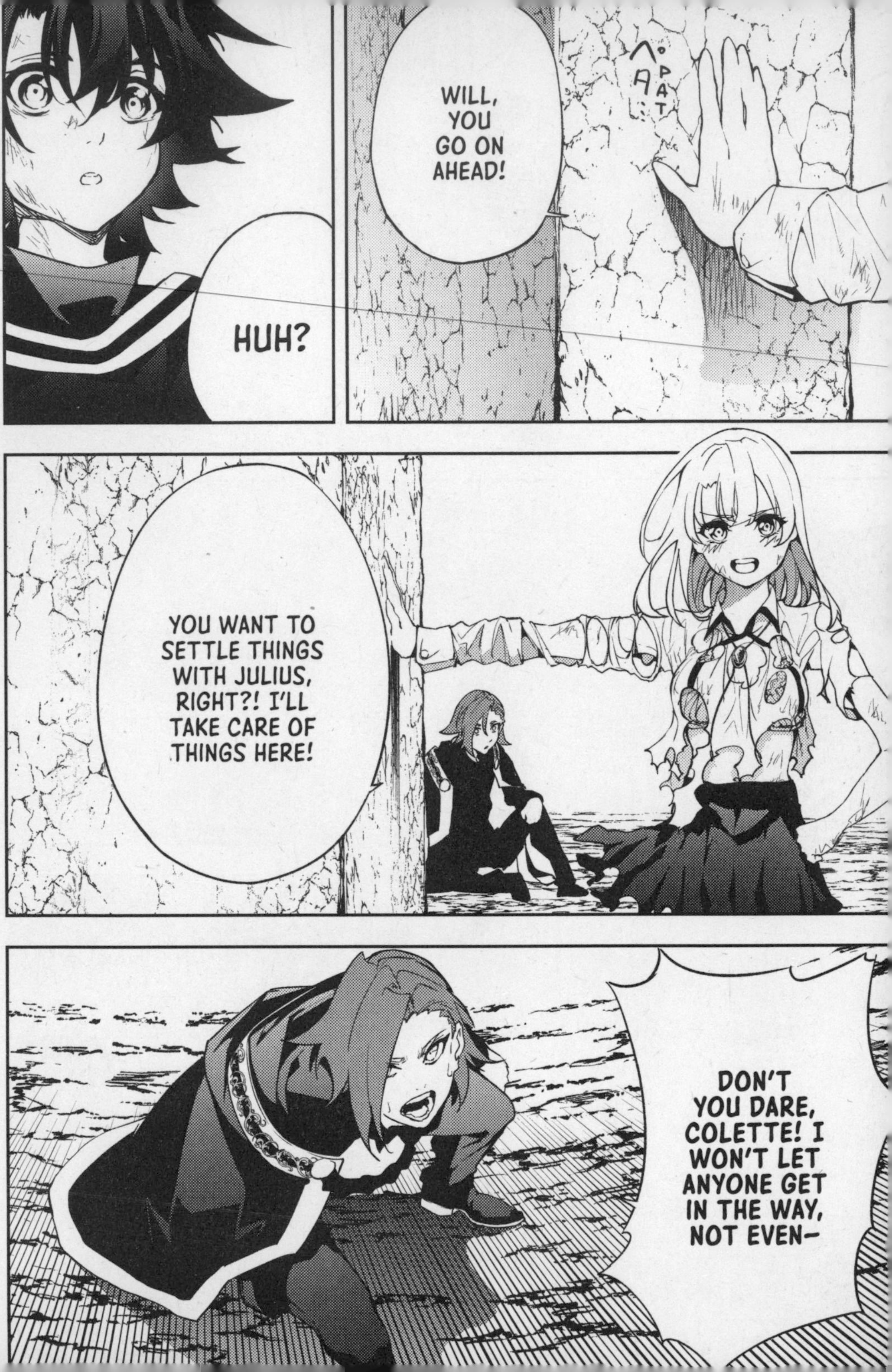
PAT
WILL, YOU GO ON AHEAD!
HUH?
YOU WANT TO SETTLE THINGS WITH JULIUS, RIGHT?! I'LL TAKE CARE OF THINGS HERE!
DON'T YOU DARE, COLETTE! I WON'T LET ANYONE GET IN THE WAY, NOT EVEN–

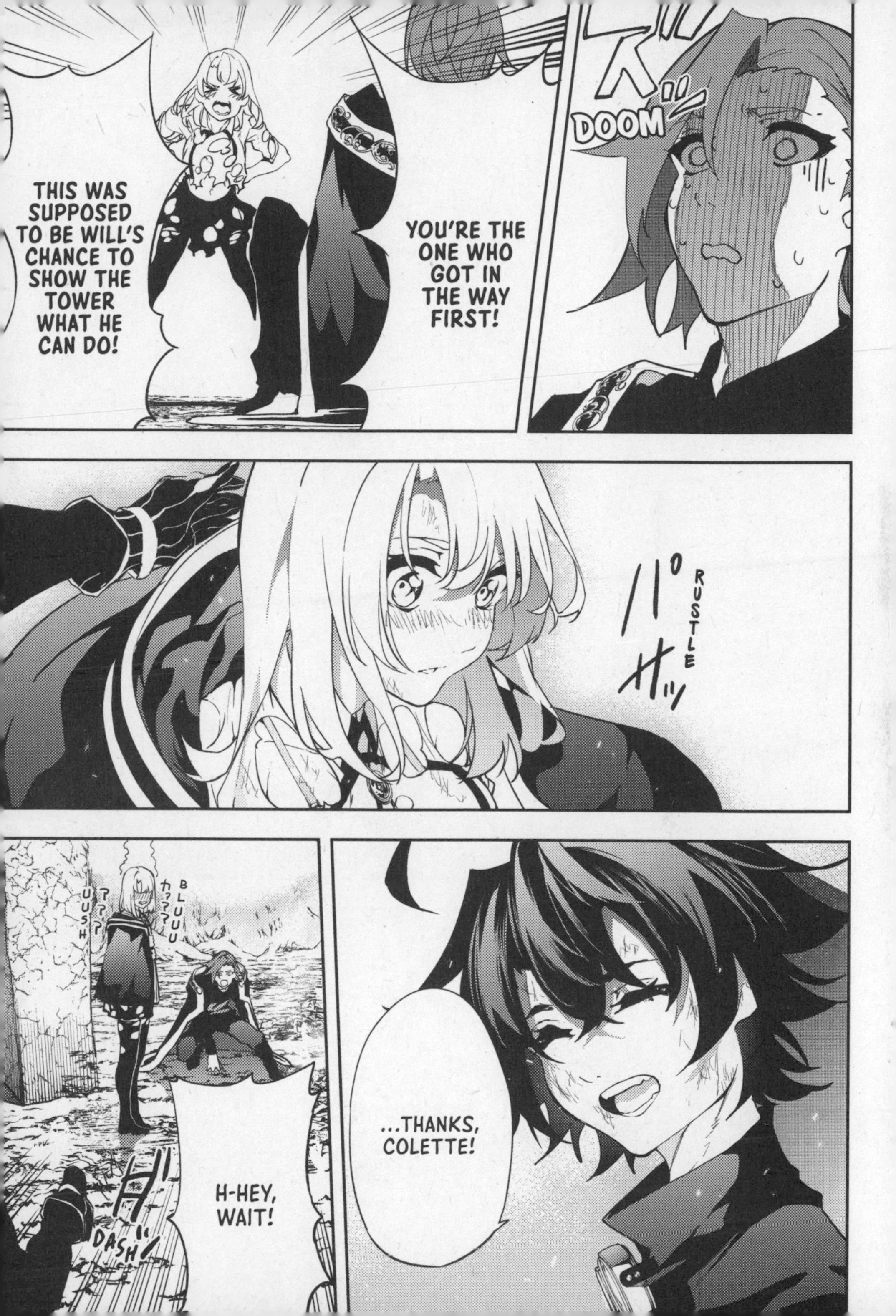
DOOM
YOU'RE THE ONE WHO GOT IN THE WAY FIRST!
THIS WAS SUPPOSED TO BE WILL'S CHANCE TO SHOW THE TOWER WHAT HE CAN DO!
RUSTLE
...THANKS, COLETTE!
BLUUU
UUSH
H-HEY, WAIT!
DASH

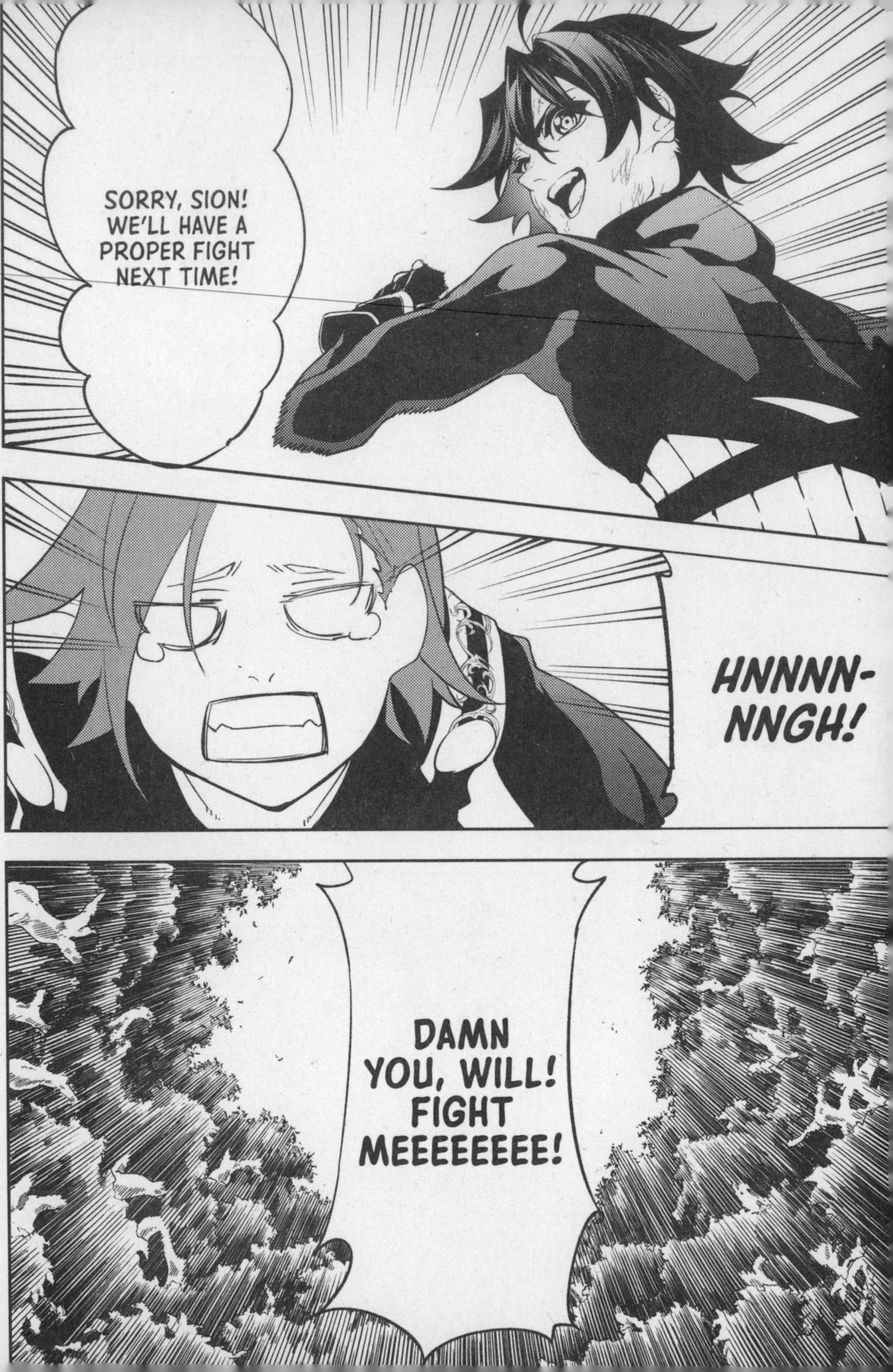
SORRY, SION! WE'LL HAVE A PROPER FIGHT NEXT TIME!
HNNNN-NNGH!
DAMN YOU, WILL! FIGHT MEEEEEEEE!

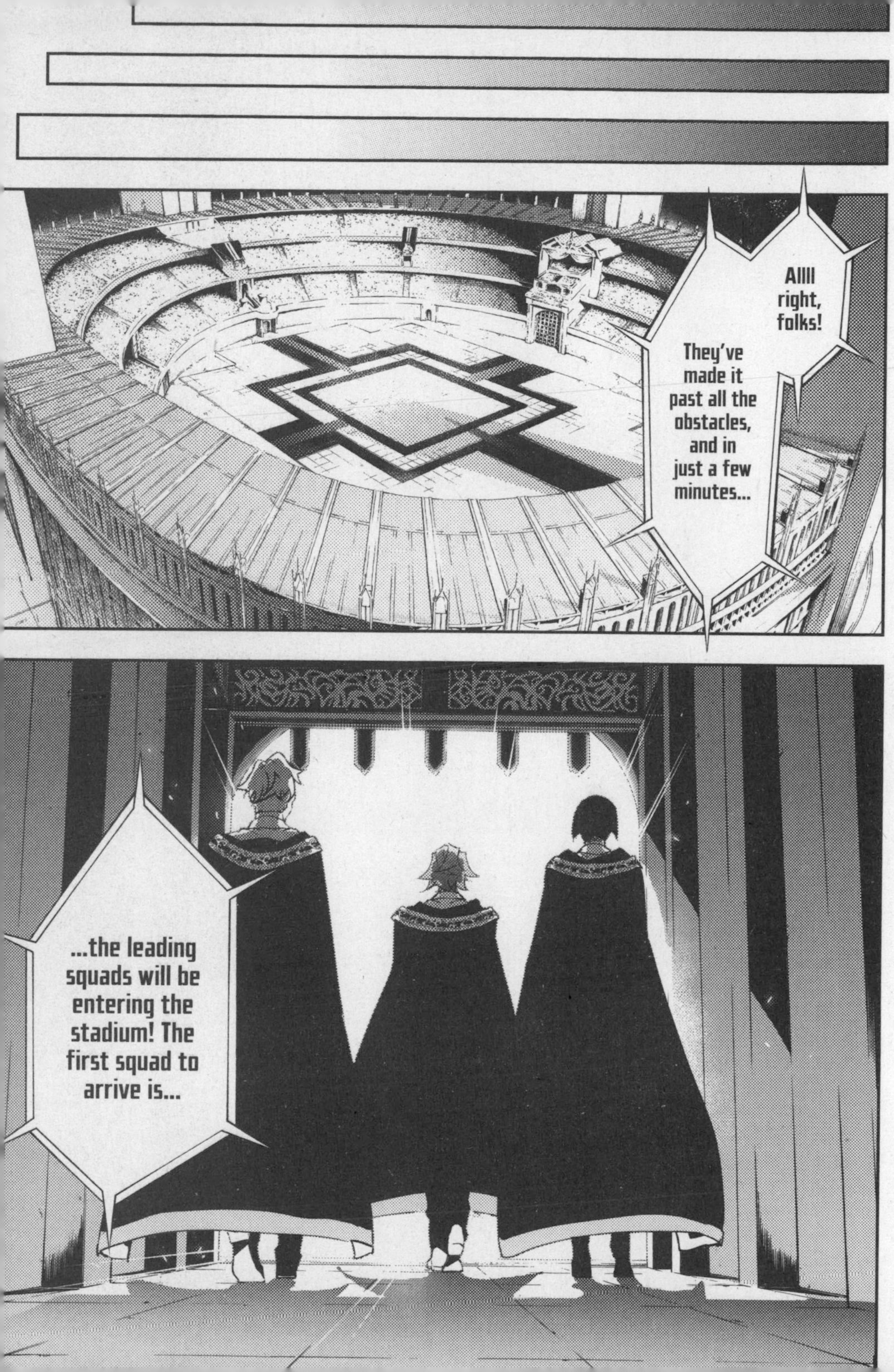
Allll right, folks!
They've made it past all the obstacles, and in just a few minutes...
...the leading squads will be entering the stadium! The first squad to arrive is...

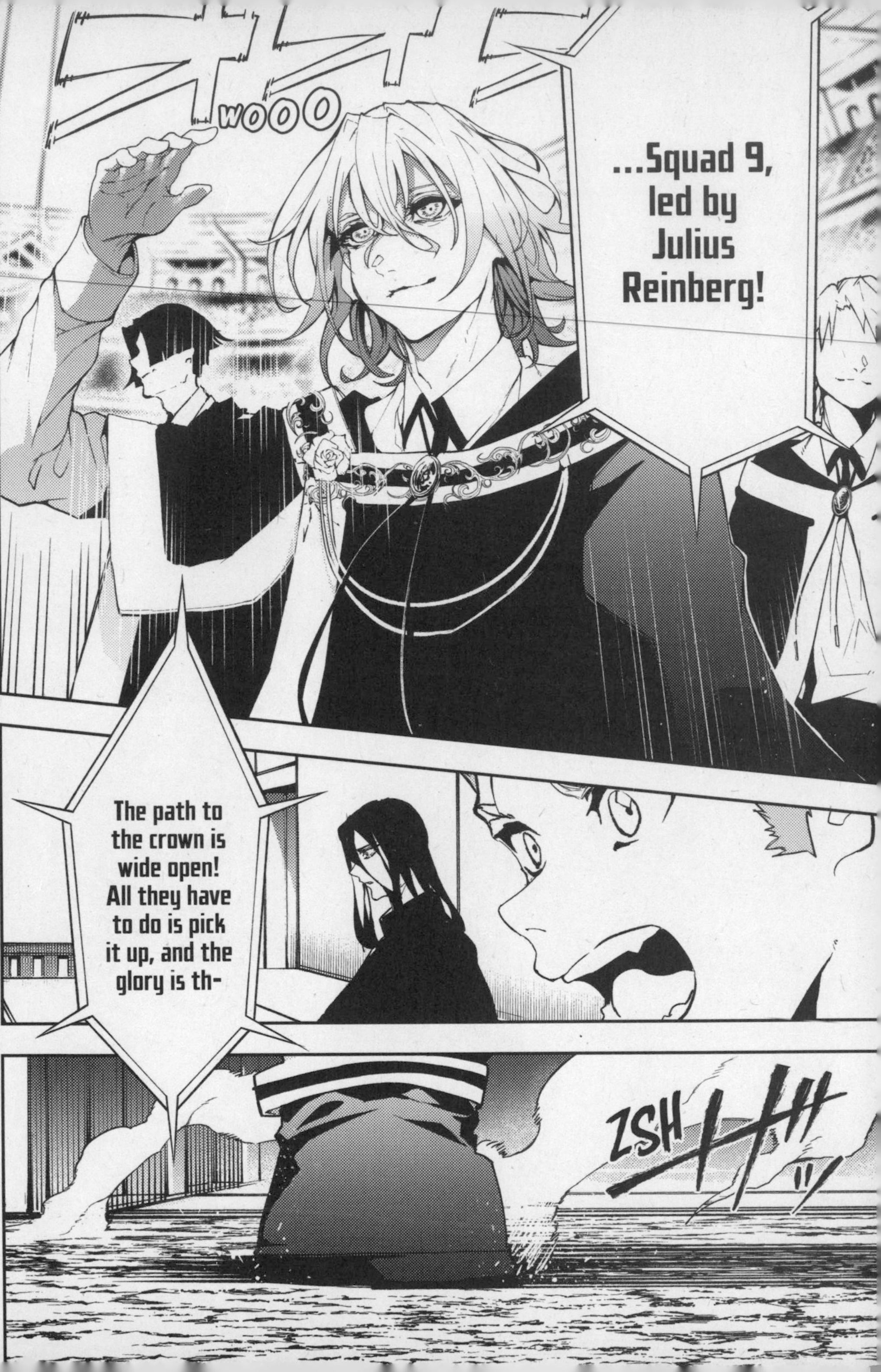

WOOO
...Squad 9, led by Julius Reinberg!
The path to the crown is wide open! All they have to do is pick it up, and the glory is th-
ZSH

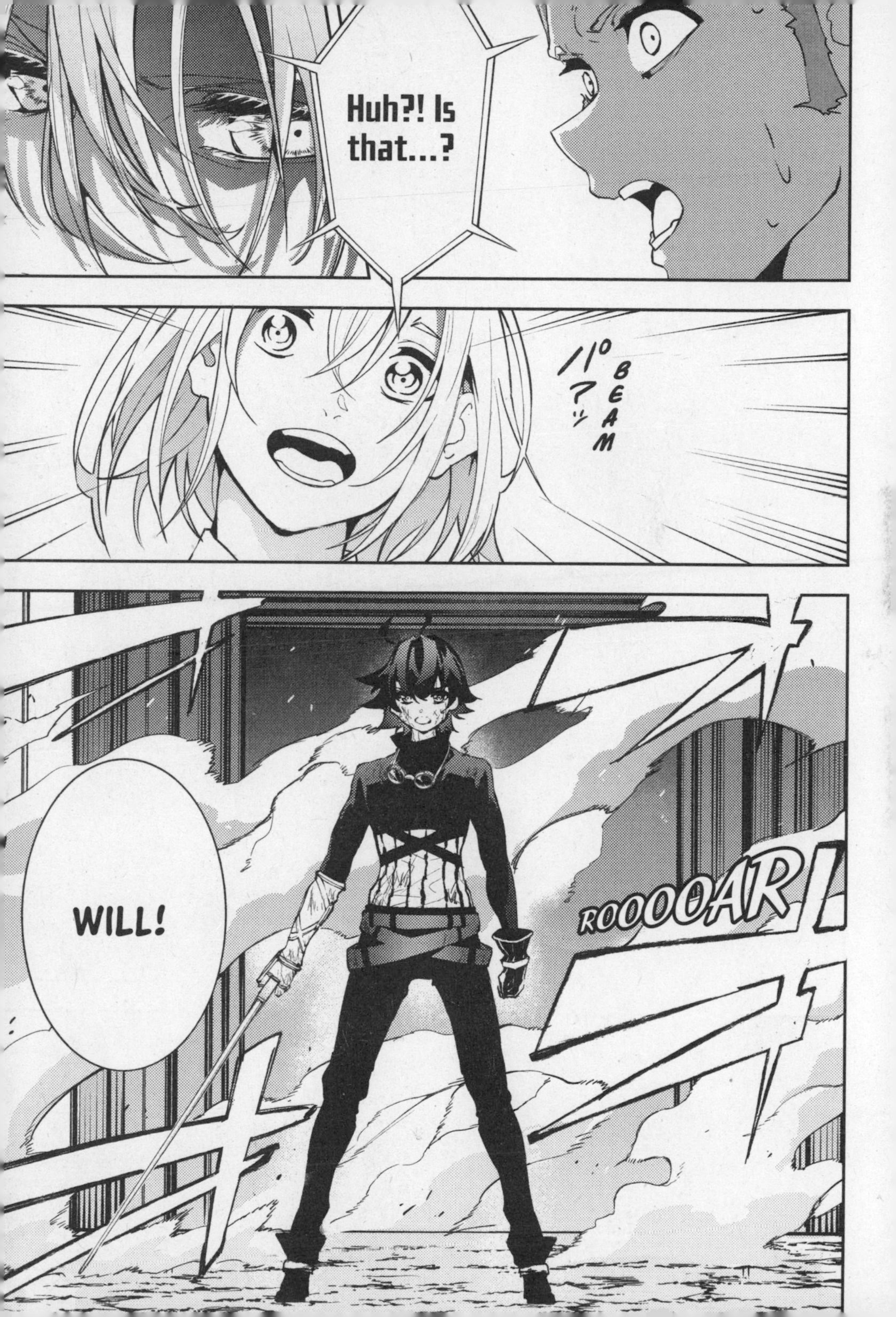
Huh?! Is that...?
パァッ
BEAM
ROOOOAR
WILL!

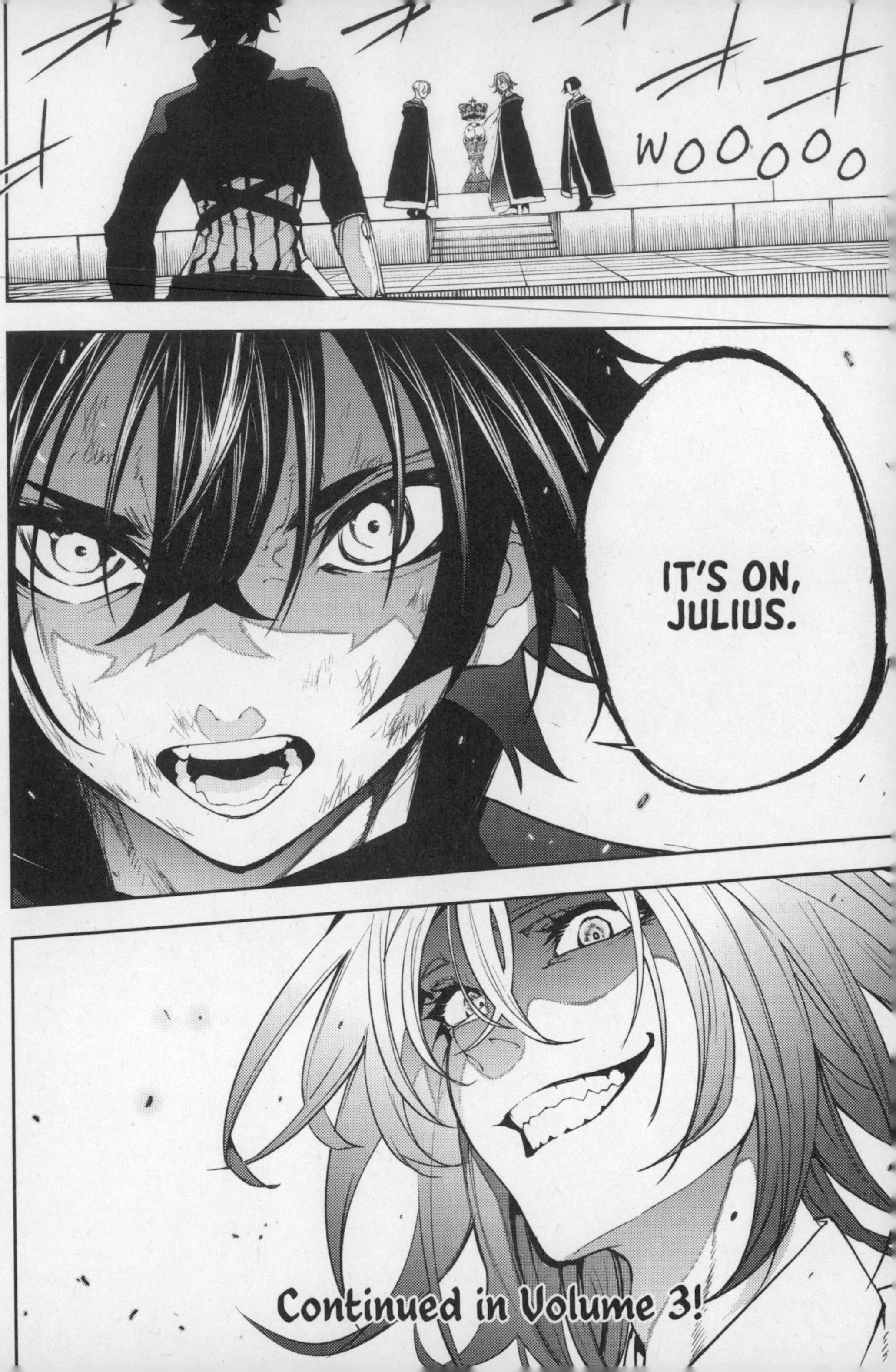
WOOOOO
IT'S ON, JULIUS.
Continued in Volume 3!

Wistoria: Wand and Sword

BONUS STORY

Perhaps It Was a Fleeting Reflection on a Silver Blade

by Katarina

Author Profile

Katarina's web novel *Shangri-La Frontier* began serialization on the website *Shousetsuka ni Narou* in 2017. The series attracted a massive readership, with over 400 million page views. Drawn by Ryosuke Fuji, the manga version has proved similarly popular during its current run in *Weekly Shonen Magazine*.

Once, there was a world closed off from the true sky by magic—a magic designed to repel the dreaded Celestial Host. In this world, there lived five great mages known as the Magia Vander. They were an indispensable part of the fabric of their society, and to become one was the wildest dream of anyone who ever picked up a wand.

One day, there came a boy who yearned to see the true sky. This boy had not been blessed with the gift of magic, and so he was cast aside. And yet, he refused to abandon his dream. Unable to conjure flames or summon thunder, he took up a sword in place of a wand. Armed with a burning passion and a blade swifter than lightning, the boy strove to reach the sky. Within his heart he carried a childhood promise, a vision of the sky, and hope for a reunion. His name was Will, and he was a wandless, sword-wielding warrior.

This is the story of one fleeting encounter—hardly more than a glint on his silver blade—on the boy's road to greatness.

"Kiki, are you okay?!"

A sea of flames engulfed the sixth floor of the dungeon. The heat was so intense, even the boy's ashes would have been reduced to nothing if not for the fire-rat cape draped over his shoulders. Shielding his familiar under the cape, he waited for the danger to pass.

"Baskervilles aren't supposed to travel in packs," he murmured. The fire-breathing demon hounds known as Baskervilles were a common enough sight on the sixth floor, but just now, he was looking out at four of them. Even worse, one of the hounds was several times larger than the others. If typically solitary monsters were travelling around in a pack, particularly one led by an abnormally large specimen, that could only mean one thing.

"A variant...!" Will exclaimed. Very rarely, a species would produce an individual with aberrant features. Had this variant been large from birth, or had something in its environment caused the change? There was no time to speculate now. *Those flames are too intense*, thought Will. Not only had the variant Baskerville gathered a pack around itself, its own abilities had somehow been enhanced beyond those of the average demon hound.

Though protected against the fire, unless Will could break out of this cocoon of flames, he would run out of air, and his insides would roast in the heat. *What do I do now?!* His fire-rat cape might have special properties, but it was still only a cape. He had stretched it out to its full length, using the entire area to cover and protect himself. Any attempt to go on the offensive would require exposing his body to the blaze. If even a fraction of his clothing caught fire, it wouldn't be long before he was wreathed in flames. Will's only choice now was death by suffocation or by fire. Hemmed in by an irregular pack of hounds, all he could do was wait out their attack. That was when it happened.

"Stay dead, you stupid dogs! I don't have time to waste on trash mobs like you!" It was a new voice, rising above the howls of the Baskervilles even as the flames slackened. Will seized the opportunity to scoop up his familiar and dash out from between the engulfing flames. He scowled at the singe marks on his clothes; still, that was preferable to being reduced to cinders. Brushing off his annoyance, Will spun around to face the hounds.

The stranger's voice came echoing off the walls again. "Here I am, minding my own business, when suddenly I'm getting blasted into some weirdo mystery dungeon. Seriously, what the hell? And Emul's not here, either! Damn it, I'm getting back alive, if it's the last thing I do!"

Will saw a shadow charge the Baskervilles as though in a blind rage. At first, Will thought a mage must have come to his rescue. But no… As he looked through the shimmering heat-haze, he saw the shadowy figure doing something that would have been totally out of character for any mage: getting up close and slashing at the enemy. The figure was fighting like a swordsman.

Suddenly, the stranger called out, "Hey, you!"

"Me?" Will replied uncertainly.

"If you can fight, then stand up and… hey! Ugh, outta the way! And back me up! Yo, don't bite my crotch!"

Just then, the stranger came fully into view. Will took in the half-naked body and the odd, bird-shaped head. His first thought was that it must be like an Evil Sentinel: a monster with a human form. Yet, it had clearly spoken to him in human speech. Will could only assume that despite the ridiculous appearance, this creature was, in fact, human.

"I'll help!" said Will.

"Phew, thanks!" said the stranger. "Ow! Damn it, this game's kinda laggy! Didn't anyone ever teach you guys some manners? How about a belly rub—with my daggers!"

This person (was it a person?) wasn't even wearing a layer of clothing, let alone armor; it was as though he actually *wanted* to show off the painful-looking scars crisscrossing his body. As the stranger bore down on the Baskervilles, Will couldn't help feeling that this was more akin to a fight between hungry wolves than between a human and monsters. As though sharing Will's sentiments, the outsized Baskerville variant howled a reprimand at its beaten pack before loping forward to face this new foe alone.

Squaring up against the Baskerville, the stranger said, "Time for the real boss battle, eh? Brace yourself, Goggles."

Will looked around perplexed for a moment. "Er... It's Will. My name is Will."

"I'm Sunraku. Thanks for joining my raiding party. We'll tag team him, Will. I'll take the front!"

A thunderous roar rang through the dungeon, intermingling with the roiling flames. Will and Sunraku readied themselves against the variant—Will with his longsword, and Sunraku with his two daggers. Between them, they were three blades and two warriors. Whatever fate had brought them together, in that moment they shared a common cause as they prepared to leap into ba—

"By the way, Will? Little problem here."

"What?"

"I've got this tentacle thing around me. What do I doaaaagh?!"

"That's probably a Cave Octo... Wait, what in the... Aaaahh!"

The world went black.

"...Huh?"

Back at Regarden Magical Academy, Will reeled in stunned confusion at Professor Workner's statement. Workner was explaining how he had watched Will defeat all four Baskervilles, including the one variant.

"I said from everything I saw, I'm absolutely certain that you fought the Baskervilles *alone*. There was no one else there. Honestly, how could you be so reckless?"

"That can't be right!" Will protested. "I mean, what about those smaller Baskervilles? Someone must have taken them out, right? Kiki, you saw who it was, didn't you?" Exasperated, he turned to Kiki for support, but his familiar only stared back at him as though he were spouting total nonsense—and not just because they didn't speak the same language.

Will *knew* someone else had been there; he and that primitive-looking warrior had definitely fought the variant Baskerville together. Yet, now he couldn't help but wonder if any of it had really happened. Could the variant Baskerville have made him hallucinate somehow? Looking at the trophies he had claimed from the four monsters, he could clearly make out marks where they had been severed with a blade—marks fundamentally different from those left by Will's Moria longsword. These could only have been made by dual blades, cutting in unison...

"The Watchful Ice Maiden: I Taught Him Everything He Knows"

Bonus Manga

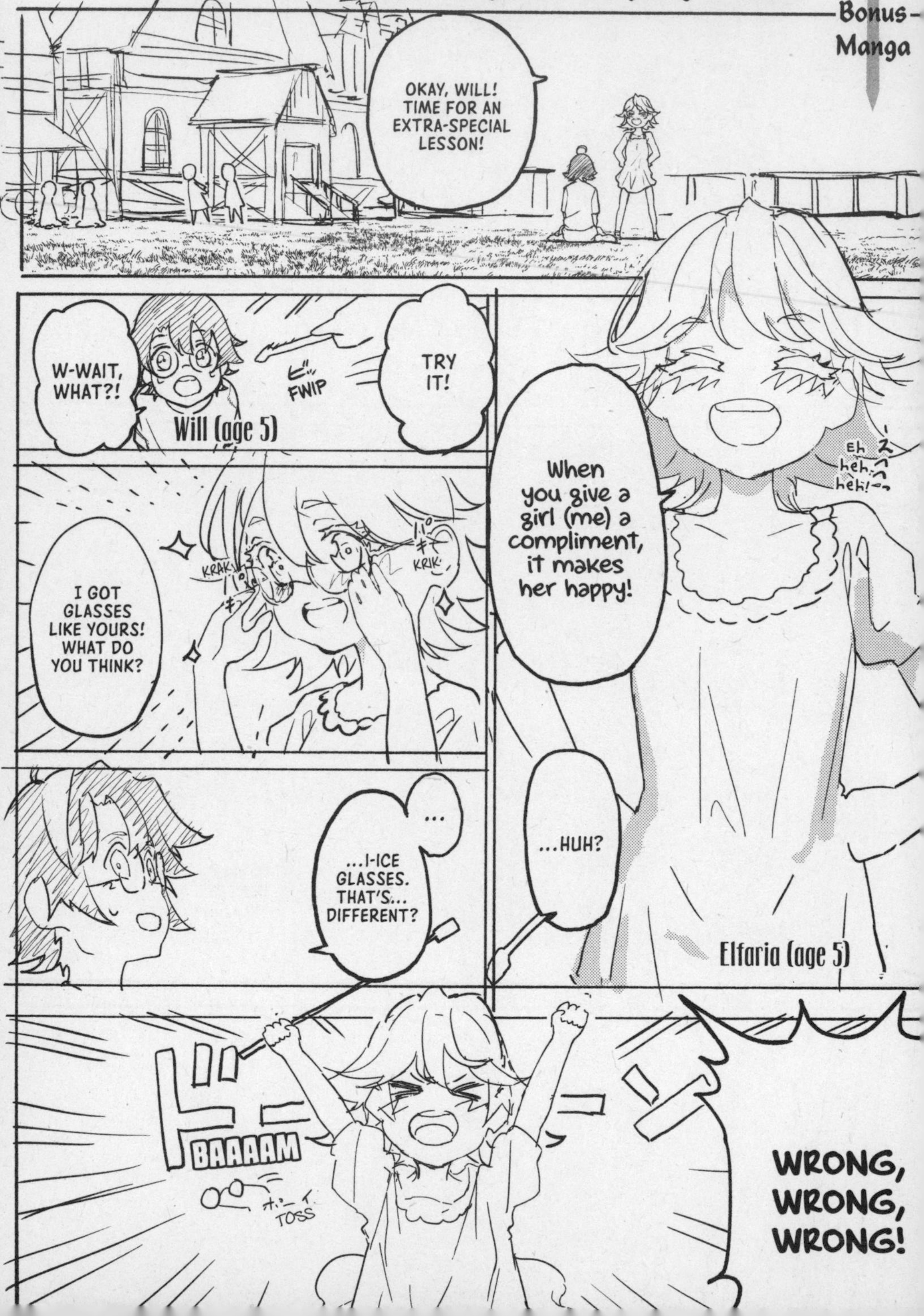
OKAY, WILL! TIME FOR AN EXTRA-SPECIAL LESSON!
When you give a girl (me) a compliment, it makes her happy!
Eh heh heh!
...HUH?
Elfaria (age 5)
TRY IT!
FWIP
W-WAIT, WHAT?!
Will (age 5)
KRIK
KRAK
I GOT GLASSES LIKE YOURS! WHAT DO YOU THINK?
...
...I-ICE GLASSES. THAT'S... DIFFERENT?
WRONG, WRONG, WRONG!
BAAAAM
TOSS

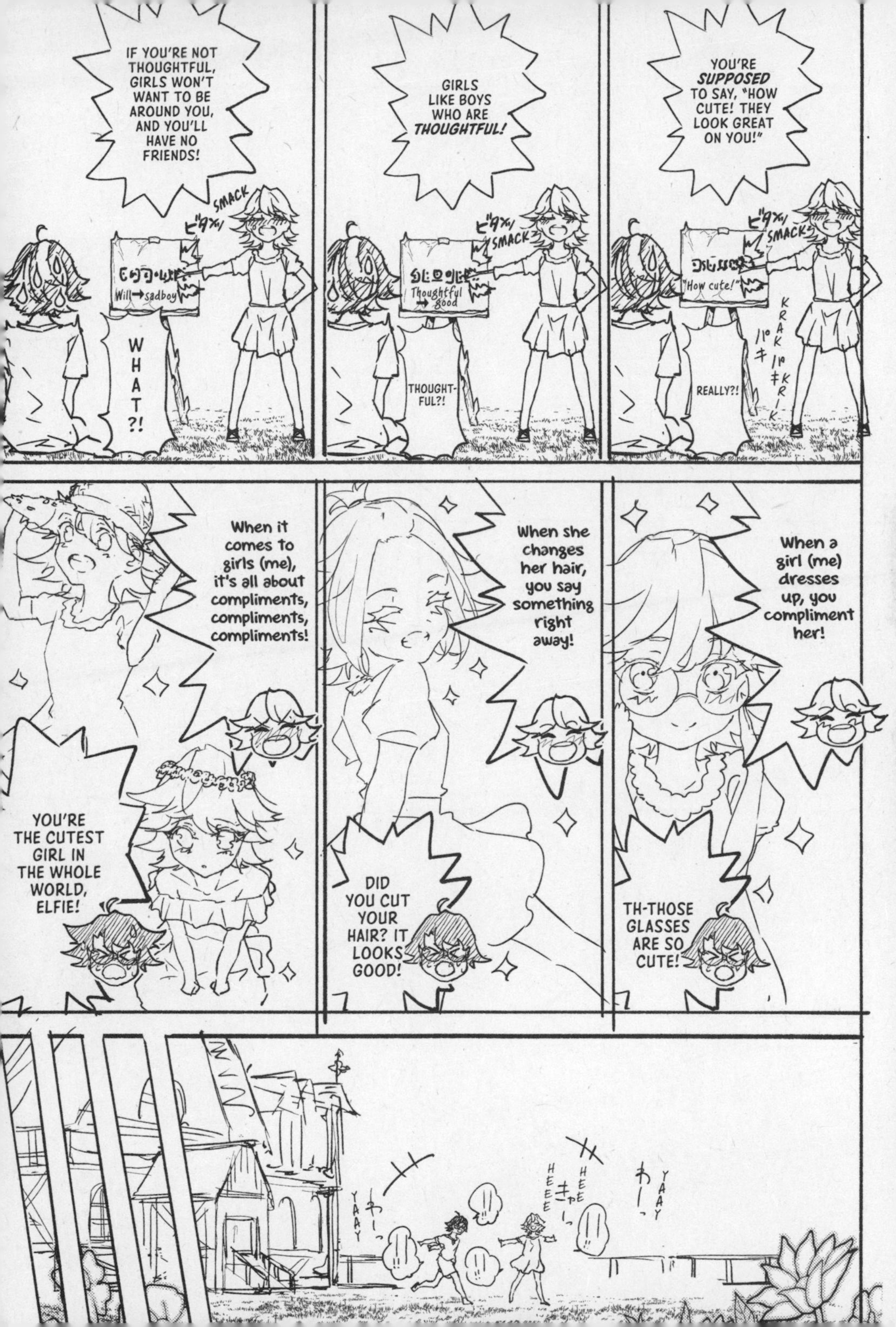
YOU'RE SUPPOSED TO SAY, "HOW CUTE! THEY LOOK GREAT ON YOU!"
ビタッ SMACK
"How cute!"
パキ KRAK
パキ KRIK
REALLY?!
GIRLS LIKE BOYS WHO ARE THOUGHTFUL!
ビタッ SMACK
Thoughtful → good
THOUGHT-FUL?!
IF YOU'RE NOT THOUGHTFUL, GIRLS WON'T WANT TO BE AROUND YOU, AND YOU'LL HAVE NO FRIENDS!
SMACK ビタッ
Will → sadboy
WHAT?!
When a girl (me) dresses up, you compliment her!
TH-THOSE GLASSES ARE SO CUTE!
When she changes her hair, you say something right away!
DID YOU CUT YOUR HAIR? IT LOOKS GOOD!
When it comes to girls (me), it's all about compliments, compliments, compliments!
YOU'RE THE CUTEST GIRL IN THE WHOLE WORLD, ELFIE!
わーっ YAAY
きゃー HEEE HEEE
やーっ YAAY

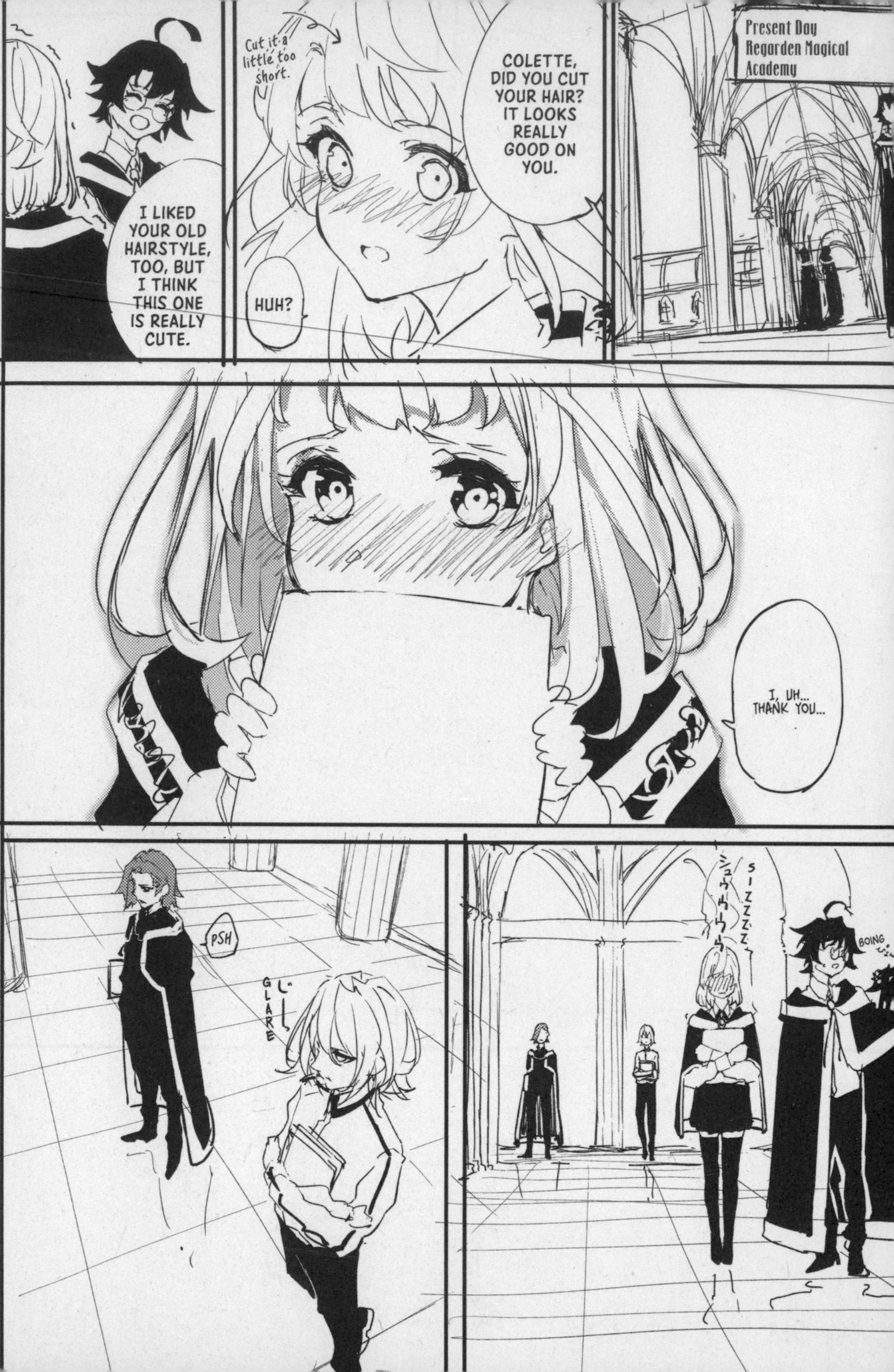
Present Day
Regarden Magical Academy
COLETTE, DID YOU CUT YOUR HAIR? IT LOOKS REALLY GOOD ON YOU.
Cut it a little too short.
HUH?
I LIKED YOUR OLD HAIRSTYLE, TOO, BUT I THINK THIS ONE IS REALLY CUTE.
I, UH... THANK YOU...
BOING
SIZZZZ
PSH
GLARE

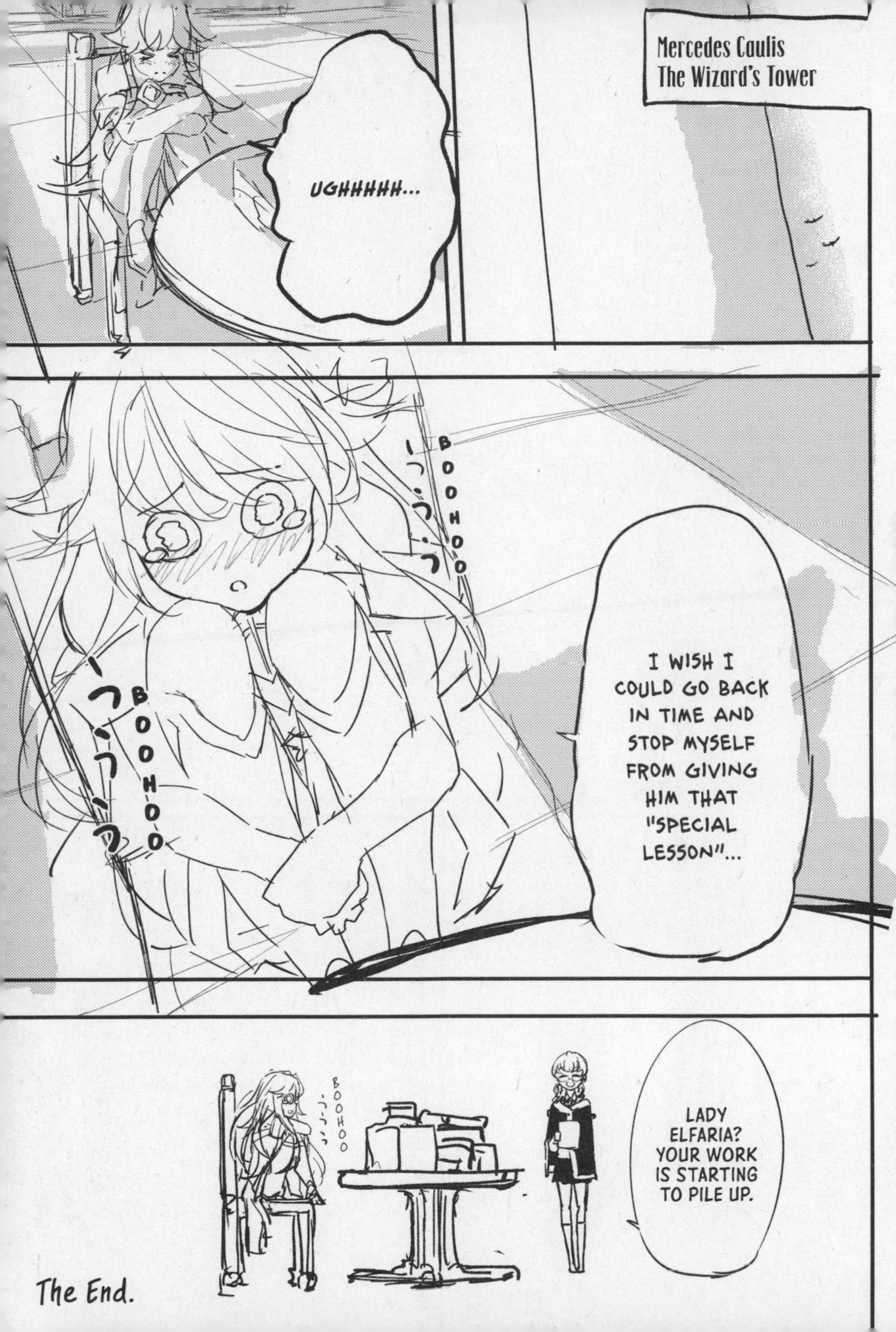
Mercedes Caulis
The Wizard's Tower
UGHHHHH...
I WISH I COULD GO BACK IN TIME AND STOP MYSELF FROM GIVING HIM THAT "SPECIAL LESSON"...
BOOHOO
BOOHOO
LADY ELFARIA? YOUR WORK IS STARTING TO PILE UP.
BOOHOO
The End.

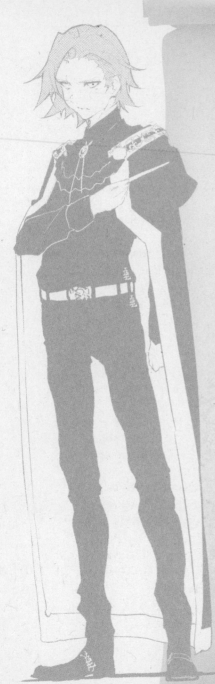

SION ULSTER

Race: Lyzance
Age: 16
Height: 5'7"

Birthday: 13th of Nullsmoon
(May 13th, in our world)

Likes: Marshmallows smothered in honey (hasn't told anyone)

Dislikes: No-talents who ignore him

First love: Colette Loire, five years ago

Lowest dungeon floor reached: 6th

Equipment: · Halcon wand
· Shirts and leather shoes from Les Aisles (luxury brand for nobles)

Specialty: · Low- and mid-level fire magic
· Iflamme Burdelyon (advanced spell)

Heir to House Ulster, a renowned line of fire mages. He has one younger sister. Following a certain incident during his first year at the academy, he became painfully aware of Will and came to see him as a rival.